MW01092050

Cambodian American Experiences

Histories, Communities, Cultures, and Identities
Revised Printing

Edited by
Jonathan H.X. Lee
San Francisco State Universtiy

Kendall Hunt
publishing company

Kendall Hunt
publishing company

www.kendallhunt.com
Send all inquiries to:
4050 Westmark Drive
Dubuque, IA 52004-1840

Copyright © 2010, by Kendall Hunt Publishing Company

Revised Printing 2015

ISBN 978-1-4652-6661-3

Printed in the United States of America

Dedication

*I dedicate this volume to the memory of
my big brother and mother.*

Contents

Section VII
Cambodian American Literature

Section VIII
Cambodian American Economic Integration

Section IX
Cambodian American Identity Formations

Section XII
Cambodian American Citizenship Post 9/11

Acknowledgments

This second edition could not have been produced without contributions by scholars dedicated to the development of scholarship on Cambodian Americans. Gratitude is extended to Frank Forcier, Acquisitions Editor, and Charmayne M. McMurray, Project Coordinator at Kendall Hunt Publishing Company, for work on this volume. Many thanks to Lorraine Dong, for her support in the development and design of the Cambodian American studies course—Asian American Studies 377. My teachers Vivian-Lee Nyitray and June O'Connor inspired this project in many ways, through their scholarship and mentorship. Gratitude is also extended to my colleagues and students in Asian American studies at San Francisco State University for providing feedback and suggestions for improving this revised second edition. Special thank you is due to Johnny Thach, whose body is on the cover of this volume. Deep appreciation is extended to Johnny Thach for modeling for the cover, and Andrew Ho, the photographer. Additionally, gratitude is extended to Maurita K. Quady for her thoughtful comments on several chapters in this volume. The following supporters must also be acknowledged: praCh Ly, Anida Yoeu Ali, R.J. Sin, and Sandra Sengdara Siharath for promoting Cambodian creativity and culture. Last, but not least, I wish to extend loving thanks to Mark S. Quady and Owen Edward Jinfa Quady-Lee for their support and patience that make this work possible.

Jonathan H. X. Lee
Berkeley, CA

Introduction

Jonathan H. X. Lee

Since the Cold War era, over 1.8 million Southeast Asian refugees from former French Indochina have entered the United States and re-established their lives, despite having survived war and displacement. Roughly 150,000 of them were from Cambodia. This volume examines the conditions that led these thousands of people to flee their homes in Cambodia. It critically and comparatively examines the ways Cambodian Americans—adult and child refugees and American-born children—have forged new lives, communities, and identities in the United States. It focuses on constraints and strategies—institutional, artistic, community, and cultural—deployed by Cambodian refugees and Cambodian Americans, to negotiate their marginal status in the United States, paying particular attention to the creative ways they maintain traditions, lifeways, institutions, and relationships, both locally and transnationally.

Growing up Asian in America, and for that matter, Cambodian in America, has its challenges. Many Asian American youth struggle with archetypical questions about self and identity: Who am I? Why am I here? This struggle is poignantly illustrated by Johnny Thach, whose body art is on this volume's cover. Mr. Thach self-identifies as a Cambodian American, but acknowledges that he is also part Vietnamese and Chinese. His body art documents his quest for self understanding. The body art on his arm shows himself as pieces of a puzzle coming together. The puzzle pieces are intermixed with the fruits and leaves of a mango tree, firmly planted in his ancestral homeland. At the center of his back, is an image of Angkor Wat—considered to be one of the greatest single architectural landmarks in human civilization. In Cambodia, tattooing is a form of spiritual art. In this cultural context, tattoos are considered magical, and believed to supply the carrier with power and the ability to influence good fortune. Mr. Thach's tattoos provide him an anchor, roots, and documentation of his quiet and private struggle to put together the pieces of his being, his multiple identities, and his quest to be Cambodian, Vietnamese, Chinese, and American. The images are sacred, and they confer onto him a value, a uniqueness, a sacred dimension, and an understanding of himself that brings him some solace and maybe momentary ease.

For many Cambodian Americans, first generation refugees, 1.5 and second generation Cambodian Americans, comfort and ease are often far from their lives. Seen—if they are seen at all—as perpetual victims, and as refugees, their social and economic struggles with gang activities and welfare dependency dominate the discourse about them, pointing out and blaming their recent history as the origins of their "plight." But they have survived, and even with scars, they thrive, and in so doing, have brought to America their wealth of culture, their wealth of community, and their tremendous strength that was gained through their struggle to survive.

This volume came about out of necessity—out of my need, as a teacher, to have a single source that covers the history and contemporary situation of Cambodian Americans. I wanted to focus on solutions, on the positive aspects of Cambodian American lives and communities, and their contributions to the American fabric and mosaic. This volume is for Cambodian Americans, and especially for Cambodian American students. Here, they will hopefully find information about their rich and diverse heritage; develop empathy for their parents' experiences and struggles, and more importantly, learn about themselves and find strength from their rich history, culture, and heritage. Lastly, it is my hope that Cambodian American youth and future college students realize their full potential, and their absolute right to be fully American—Cambodian and all.

Section 1

Cambodia

CHAPTER 1

An Outline History of Cambodia

Jonathan H. X. Lee

"To be Khmer is to be born in Cambodia, to be descended from ancestors who were born in Cambodia."

Christine M. Su, 2003

Once upon a time, the great ancestor of the Khmer people, Kaundinya, an Indian Brahman priest, dreamt that if he sailed to the shores of Tonlé Sap (Great Lake), he would find a myriad of riches. Kaundinya set sail with his magical bow and arrow. When he reached the Great Lake, Soma, a nagi-princess paddled out in a boat to greet him. Soma was the beautiful daughter of the Naga King. Kaundinya shot a magic arrow into her boat, which frightened her, at first. In due course, the two fell in love and married. Kaundinya gave her clothes to wear; as her dowry, her father sucked up the waters of his water-logged country therefore making the fertile land valuable and presented it to Kaundinya to rule over. This land would become Nokor Phnom, the first Kingdom of Cambodia. Kaundinya and Soma thus became the ancestral pair of the royal dynasty, from which all Khmer kings are descended.

Folktale of Kaundinya and Soma

This tale tells the origin of Kampuchea, or Cambodia, which resulted from the union between a Brahmin prince and a nagi-princess. It is the story of the genesis of the first kingdom, known as Funan. Gradually, it was used to explain the Hindu and Indian influence on Khmer civilization. The folktale of Khmer origin, "as a narrative of the people, gives expression to some of the elements of what it means to be Khmer," which is the figurative and literal connection to the ancestral couple (Su 2003: 59). There are various versions of the tale, but they all conform to the blending of two different entities: foreign and native, human and animal, culture and nature, and male and female. It is the assimilation and reconciliation of the two that informs what it means to be Khmer. This is a foundational theme in the history of Cambodia.

This chapter provides a historical sketch of Cambodia's two thousand year history, focusing on specific historical eras: the Kingdoms of Funan and Chenla; the Angkor Empire; the decline of the Angkor Empire; French era Cambodia; post-World War II independence; the Lon Nol era; and the Khmer Rouge regime. This history of Cambodia is the archetypical story of the rise and fall of a great empire. It is also a tale of a destabilizing encounter with modernity via European colonialism, and American ideological imperialism.

Contemporary Cambodia lies in the heart of Southeast Asia, bordered by Vietnam to the east and southeast, Laos to the northeast, and Thailand to the west and north. The cultural traditions of Cambodia predate those of Thailand, and unlike Vietnam, which was heavily influenced by China (111 BC—938 CE), the major influence on cultural and religious life in the Cambodian region was its greater subcontinental neighbor, India. At one time in Cambodia's history, from the 11th to 14th centuries, Cambodia was the dominant power in Southeast Asia, and ruled over much of what is now Vietnam, Laos, and Thailand.

Not much is known about prehistoric Cambodia, the period before the 9th century. There is evidence of human habitation in the northwest region: the remains of cave dwellers and their ceramic pots have been carbon dated to 4200 BCE. Showing resemblances to modern Cambodians, prehistoric human skulls and bones found in the northern region at Samrong Sen, date back to 1500 BCE. As far back as 1000 BCE, archaeological evidence shows that Cambodians lived in houses on stilts, as they continue to do today. Similar to the Cambodians of today, the prehistoric Cambodian diet relied heavily on fish; however they also domesticated pigs and water buffalo fairly early, and cultivated rice and root-crops using the technique of slash-and-burn. It is estimated that by the beginning of the Common Era, the inhabitants of Cambodia spoke languages related to modern Cambodian, or Khmer (Chandler 1983: 9). Various languages belonging to the Mon-Khmer language family are scattered throughout Southeast Asia. Vietnamese, although heavily influenced by Chinese, is a related language.

Indianization

As told by folktale of the origins of the Khmer people, India has been a source of major influence in all aspects of Cambodian civilization. Early Indianization most likely occurred through the trading settlements that were established around the 1st century CE. This Indianization process lasted for over one thousand years. Among the cultural forms Cambodia acquired from India, were a strict social hierarchy, a monarchic system, a system of codified law, a writing system, a system of poetic meter, a pantheon of deities, Buddhism, Hinduism, architecture, iconography, astronomy, and new aesthetics. This Indian influence on Cambodia was not imposed by force or direct colonization—Indian troops never invaded Cambodia. The process of Indianization, though long, was not totalizing. There were other major aspects of Indian culture and society that were never incorporated into Cambodian culture. For instance, the characteristic Indian caste system never became a part of Khmer society.

Indianization was all-encompassing: Its structure and worldview provided a unified social structure and national identity, until the Khmer Rouge attempted to eradicate the past and traditional culture (Welaratna 1993: 12). Unlike the Chinese influence in Vietnam, the Indian influence in Cambodia never developed into an identity crisis for the native population (Chandler 1983: 12).

Funan and Chenla

From the 3rd to 8th centuries, the Indianized kingdoms of Funan and Chenla covered present-day Cambodia and southwest Vietnam (Chhim 1989: 10). Though these were Indianized states, what is known of them comes from Chinese sources, because they kept intricate records. Thus the terms we know them by are the names given to them by these Chinese sources. During this period, Cambodia consisted of a collection of small states, each with their own elites who sometimes intermarried strategically, and sometimes warred against one another.

Funan was an important sea-port that transmitted Indian culture to the interior of Cambodia. The Funan period embraced the worship of the Hindu deities, Siva and Visnu, as well as Theravada Buddhism. The *lingam*, a phallic representation of Siva, was the focal point of many state rituals. Through Theravada Buddhism, the Buddhist concepts of *karma* and merit (*bon*) suffused the Cambodian concept of society. Being a person of lower social status and material wealth suggested that in a previous existence, one had lived a flawed life. Therefore, one's behavior in the here and now might affect one's future lot in life. To improve one's personal status and prospects for a better rebirth, one could accumulate merit by performing virtuous acts, such as subsidizing the construction of a Buddhist temple, or financing religious festivals. It is this principle that prefaced the building of the great temples of Angkor Wat.

Chenla, also a Chinese term, refers to the period after Funan's relevance as a port city declined, and before the rise of the Angkor Period. From the 6th to the 8th centuries, Cambodia was a collection of autocratic kings who ruled with absolute power (Chhim 1989: 10). During this period, Cambodia gradually became more politically cohesive. The wealth of this new kingdom was derived primarily from wet-rice agriculture, and the mobilization of physical labor for the construction of its infrastructure and great temples.

The Angkor Empire

From the 9th to the 15th centuries, Cambodia ascended into a period of political and cultural brilliance during the Angkor Empire, which was founded by King Jayavarman II in 802 CE. Jayavarman II (r. 802-850 CE) was the first of a long succession of god-kings, or *devarajas* to preside over the rise and fall of the Angkor Empire. Angkorian kings, known as *devarajas*, a Sanskrit term meaning "god-king," or "king of the gods," were understood to be the earthly incarnation of divinity, ruling the land and its people with absolute power. The god-kings were related to the cult of Siva—himself, a king of gods. For six hundred years, Cambodia was the mightiest kingdom in Southeast Asia. Visitors carrying tribute came from as far as present-day Burma, Malaysia, and Thailand.

A series of wars during the reign of Suryavarman II (r. 1113–1145 or 1150 CE), expanded the Khmer territory to encompass areas of northern Vietnam and the Irrawaddy River of Burma. During this time, Suryavarman II built Angkor Wat—considered to be the greatest single architectural work in Southeast Asia—which he dedicated to the god Visnu (Jacques and Lafond 2007). Suryavarman II also developed an extensive network of roads and large irrigation and reservoir systems. Suryavarman II was successful in defeating the neighboring Indianized Kingdom of Champa, by reducing it to a vassal state, and initiating what would become a long-term conflict between dynasties. So, in 1177, after thirty years of internal dynastic disputes, the Chams, at first an Indianized civilization that was now Muslim, struck back in a naval expedition up the Mekong and into the Tonlé Sap (Great Lake). The Chams took the City of Angkor by complete surprise, and killed its king.

Jayavarman VII (r. 1181-1218)—a devout follower of Mahayana Buddhism—then defeated the Chams in 1181, and was crowned the new leader. Under Jayavarman VII's reign, the Angkor Empire had reached its greatest territorial extent. He built Angkor Thom, the great capital city, as well as the famous temple of Bayon (Clark 2008). Although his countrymen benefited greatly from his extensive irrigation systems, and had accepted the full authority of his monarchy, scholars believe the vast public works he had commissioned, and his huge expansionist wars, required heavy taxes and forced slave labor. Thus, upon his death, the Angkor Empire entered a period of decline.

Decline of the Angkor Empire

During the 13th century, the former Angkor territory was divided by the establishment of independent Thai kingdoms. A Thai army captured Angkor in 1353. Angkor was looted a number of times, and the Thai army carried away thousands of Khmer artists and scholars. Continuous warfare between the Thai and the Khmer peoples culminated with the Thai capture and pillage of Angkor Thom in 1431. This resulted in the abandonment of Angkor as the capital, and its fall marked the end of a specific cultural cycle: One that had produced magnificent architecture with temples, monuments, sculptures, decorations, and inscriptions. By the 15th century, the Angkor Empire had declined politically and economically, and principalities that had formerly been vassals of Angkor, declared their independence (Welaratna: 13–14; Chhim: 12).

Scholars are not all in agreement about the actual factors that led to the decline of the great Angkorian Empire (Chandler: 55–81). Some posit that the decline was the result of a weakened economic system, further stressed by a sphere of influence that was too big to control. Others attribute it to damages to the canal and reservoir systems upon which Angkor had depended upon. Because of constant attacks from neighboring Thais and Chams, the canal and reservoir systems became irreparable. This problem was exacerbated by the then stagnant water, which caused an outbreak of malaria throughout Angkor. Still others claim that the construction of Angkor Wat and Angkor Tom caused an enormous strain on the population, because of taxes and exploitation of labor. The decline of Angkor's political influence on the peripheries of its empire was also a large contributor, as was the disunity among the members of its ruling families. Together, these conditions set the stage for the collapse of the Angkorian Empire. After the great City of Angkor was abandoned, the royal court moved to Longvek, near present-day Phnom

Penh. The new capital was surrounded by a defensive stone wall, as well as by Buddhist temples.

Just as Angkor was in decline, the Thais and Vietnamese were gaining strength and influence, gradually usurping much of the former territory of Cambodia. In 1594 the Cambodian capital of Longvek was captured by the Thais, which marked the first time a foreign power had seized control of the Cambodian state. During this period, perhaps because of the possibility for sea trade between China and Southeast Asia, the Chinese began to establish themselves in Phnom Penh. By the early 1600s, one seventh of the population in the city was ethnic Chinese, although they lived in separate quarters (Willmott 1967). The Vietnamese also gained control of a large portion of territory that had belonged to Cambodia. Legends and stories abound about Cambodians being mistreated by the Vietnamese, causing tension among the two ethnic groups that continue to this day. Sharing with Cambodia a belief in Buddhism, the Thais did not try to change Cambodian lifeways and cultures. On the other hand, the Vietnamese did attempt to disrupt the Cambodian structure and way of life, which the Cambodians resented.

In 1594, usurper Reamea Chung Prei ousted King Satha and took the throne. Two years later, a Spanish expedition arrived in Cambodia to assist King Satha fight the Thais, only to find that he was usurped by Chung Prei (Osborne 2000: 48). After killing Chung Prei, the Spaniards ransacked the Chinese quarter of Phnom Penh. There was then growing resentment toward the Spaniards among the court officials, which in 1599, resulted in the massacre of the Spanish garrison in Phnom Penh. Shortly afterward, with help from the Thais, Satha's brother, Barom Reachea IV ascended the throne. Between 1600 and the arrival of the French in 1863, Cambodia was ruled by a series of weak kings, who because of constant challenges from various members of the royal family, were often pressured to seek assistance from the Thais and Vietnamese. By the 1850s, plagued by Thai influence and control, King Norodom (r. 1860–1904) began secret negotiations with the French to eliminate Thai control. Thus, in 1863, the French signed a secret treaty with Norodom, offering him French protection in exchange for timber concessions and rights for mineral exploration. In 1864, the

French and the Thai agreed to co-sponsor Norodom's coronation. This marked the first time in Cambodia's history that a Cambodian king accepted his crown from a European power. It was Cambodia's need for protection that opened the door for the French to sweep in and gain control.

Today, the great kings and temples of the Angkor period continue to be viewed with great pride as symbols of past achievements and strengths. As such, the national flag of Cambodia, since independence from the French in 1953, features a picture of Angkor Wat.

French Era Cambodia

France, like other colonial powers, drained wealth, resources, and labor from its colonies and offered very little in return. France wanted to secure trade routes with China for its silk and tea, which is why they encouraged mountain tribal people, especially the Hmong of Laos, Vietnam, and southern China to grow opium poppies as their sole cash crop. The French then purchased all the opium that was produced. Because Cambodia's geography was not suitable for cultivating poppy, growing opium was not encouraged. France, like England, Portugal, and Holland, gained economic influence and power by trafficking opium into China, spreading addiction, and causing social and political decay. Besides opium for trade with China, France was also interested in the rubber, gems, teak, and spices that Indochina offered.

French rule in Indochina lasted almost one hundred years, until 1954. French control of Cambodia was an adjunct to its control and interest in Vietnam, having incorporated Cambodia into its protectorate in 1863. By 1884, all of Vietnam was under French control, and in 1893, Laos also became a protectorate of France. Laos and Cambodia were granted greater autonomy than Vietnam, because they had fewer natural resources.

Under French rule, the Cambodian god-king held only nominal power. In 1904, for political reasons, the French backed one line of the royal family, the Sisowath line, which pushed King Norodom's heirs aside. No more than forty years later, the French switched their support back to the Norodom line, again, for political reasons.

In 1941, 19-year-old Prince Norodom Sihanouk (b. 1922) was declared king, under the assumption that Sihanouk would be easy to manipulate and control because of his youth; however this was not the case (Chandler: 137–152).

Shortly after the young prince became king, Japan invaded and conquered Indochina, controlling the area from 1941 to 1945, through the end of World War II. Japan allowed Cambodia to be ruled by its young king, under the supervision of the Vichy French government. When Japan lost the war in 1945, it also lost control and domination of Indochina. But under the principle that Asia should be ruled by Asians, Japan urged Cambodia, Vietnam, and Laos to declare independence. France returned to its former rule, attempting to regain control of its territory in Indochina, albeit acting against a worldwide objection to colonialism. From 1945 to 1954, Sihanouk capitalized on the change in the political climate, and worked skillfully to apply pressure on the French through the worldwide disfavor, in an effort to gain independence for his Royal Kingdom of Cambodia (Kampuchea). Sihanouk became prime minister of Cambodia in 1952, appointing his own cabinet, and promising to gain independence within three years. In 1953, the French gave Sihanouk control over the Cambodian armed forces, the judiciary, and foreign affairs. However, France continued to control the Cambodian economy. On November 9th of that year, Sihanouk claimed independence from France.

It should be noted that even though Sihanouk played a key role in Cambodia's struggle for independence from France after World War II, the Viet Minh guerrilla forces who challenged France's colonial claim over Indochina, set the stage for his success. For decades, Viet Minh forces placed both economic and military strain on France's resources. On May 7, 1954, the Viet Minh won a decisive victory over the French, after a 57-day siege that resulted in the surrender of more than 10,000 starving French troops at Diem Bien Phu. This was a catastrophic defeat for France that shattered the remaining public support for the first French-Viet Minh Indochina war. Growing international pressure coupled with the cost of years of guerrilla warfare, forced France to give up its control and claim of

Indochina. In 1954, at the Geneva Conference, Cambodia was granted full independence—along with Laos and Vietnam.

Sihanouk and Independence

Concerned that his position and power as king would be weakened after the election, Sihanouk abdicated the crown in 1955, and declared his father, Norodom Suramarit, king in his stead. Sihanouk established the People's Socialist Community (the Sangkum Reastr Niyum), and won every parliamentary seat in the election of September 1955 through legal means. For the next fifteen years, Sihanouk would dominate politics in Cambodia, serving as prime minister until his father's death in 1960. Because no new king was named, Sihanouk became head-of-state.

In 1956, Sihanouk accepted United States' military aid. In the early 1960s, although he feared Vietnamese communists, he was deeply concerned about Thailand and South Vietnam, who were both allies of the United States. When the South Vietnamese President, Ngo Diem, was murdered in a coup backed by the Americans, Sihanouk was shaken. Thus, he claimed the United States' CIA was masterminding a plan to overthrow him. By 1963, Sihanouk rejected the United States' military and economic aid, and in 1965, he broke ties with Washington and sided with North Vietnam, the Viet Minh, and Communist China (Clymer 2004: 107-127). Sihanouk granted the North Vietnamese army use of Cambodian territory in their fight against South Vietnamese forces, and the United States.

As the Vietnam War escalated, Sihanouk was concerned that hostilities would spill over into Cambodia. So in June of 1969, he restored relations with Washington. However, his ability to balance relationships between the right and left, the United States, North Vietnam, and China, soon became precarious. Internally, support for his policies and his tolerance of the Viet Minh occupation of Cambodia's borders diminished. People from within his own government, the urban elite, and the military, began to voice their opposition. Working under the principal of "search and destroy," the United States' military secretly began to bomb the Cambodian countryside in March of 1969. The clandestine bombing targeted the Ho Chi Minh trail that ran through Laos and Cambodia. The bombing destroyed villages, created countless refugees, and also pushed Viet Minh forces deeper into Cambodia. General Lon Nol claimed that there were as many as 40,000 Viet Minh soldiers on Cambodian soil. The bombing killed thousands of civilians, and left hundreds of thousands homeless and refugees.

Because of the turmoil caused by U.S. military intervention, Cambodia's economy was stagnant by 1970; this, coupled with famine from an unsuccessful harvest, created unrest and discontent among the peasants. However, the majority of Cambodian peasants still considered Sihanouk a modern day god-king. By comparison to the tragic events to come under the Khmer Rouge, many Cambodians today consider Sihanouk's era to have been the "golden age" (Chandler: 190). Others blame his totalitarian rule as the cause of many of Cambodia's problems: immature political system, intolerance of pluralism, and lack of national debate. During Sihanouk's March 18, 1970 trip to France, General Lon Nol—albeit reluctantly, but with support from the United States—led a bloodless *coup d'état* that ousted Sihanouk (Becker 1986: 114). In April 1970, Lon Nol abolished the monarchy and established the Khmer Republic. Days later, Sihanouk established a government in exile, the National United Front of Kampuchea, seeking support from his old enemy, the Khmer Rouge. This move surprised many, because for years, Sihanouk had denounced and suppressed their activities, and had even derisively dubbed them "Khmer Rouge" (Red Khmer). Little did he know that he was laying the foundation for the Khmer Rouge victory that would come five years later.

Lon Nol Era

After the creation of the Khmer Republic, the newly formed republic had many problems that required immediate attention: bankruptcy, a collapsing economy, famine, internal corruption, a Communist-backed civil war, Vietnamese aggression, United States' retaliation, and an inability to control its own fate in its neighbor's escalating war. To make matters worse, many villagers and peasants did not support the new republic because their loyalty lay with the royal family and their ousted prince Sihanouk. The Khmer Republic maintained control for five terrible years, in large measure due to the economic and military aid from the United States and Thailand, who both feared a Communist takeover of the region.

From the beginning, the Lon Nol regime declared its neutrality in the region, while trying to maintain an anti-Communist campaign, which garnered support from the United States. Lacking support from the peasants, riots broke out in protest of his administration. In response, Lon Nol accused them of being inspired by the Viet Minh, legitimating his brutal suppression of them. Without foresight, Lon Nol was driving the peasants to join the Khmer Rouge, who, until that time, had only numbered a few hundred. Lon Nol also utilized the Cambodian fear of the Vietnamese by branding all Vietnamese within Cambodia members of the Viet Minh, demonstrating the Khmer Republic's hatred of the Vietnamese and Communists.

In June 1974, the United States withdrew its forces from Cambodia, reducing the Khmer Republic's control to only larger towns and cities, and only half the countryside. It was inconceivable that the Khmer Republic, backed by the United States, would lose to the Khmer Rouge, as it did the morning of April 17, 1975. Two weeks before the Fall of Saigon, roughly at the beginning of the Cambodian New Year, the Khmer Rouge entered Phnom Penh as victors, with wide popular support, and an increase in territorial control. Many of the Khmer Rouge cadres and soldiers were under the age of fifteen. That year would become Year Zero, ushering in a new phase of Cambodian history by eliminating its past cultures and traditions. Year Zero was a new start, a new beginning marking a complete revolution of what it means to be Khmer, revolutionizing Khmer life with the hopes of making Cambodia a self-sufficient nation.

Khmer Rouge

The Khmer Rouge regime, Democratic Kampuchea, lasted from April 1975 until January 1979. It would become one of the most radical and brutal periods in world history (Etcheson 2005: 4).

Under the leadership of a Paris-educated school teacher, Pol Pot (formerly Saloth Sar) and Chinese-Khmer Khieu Samphan (president of DK from 1976-1979) the Khmer Rouge attempted to transform Cambodian society into a Maoist peasant agrarian cooperative. Since 1903, the Khmer Rouge worked to gain peasant support—unsuccessfully. However, after Lon Nol ousted their prince, Sihanouk joined forces with the Khmer Rouge, eliciting support from the peasantry. Although Sihanouk hoped to use the Khmer Rouge to regain his power and kingdom, he became its pawn, instead giving the Khmer Rouge legitimacy and increasing peasant support.

Immediately after the Khmer Rouge swept into power, currency was abolished and postal services were suspended. Convincing people that the Americans were about to bomb the cities, the cities were abandoned, and the borders were closed. Urban dwellers, merchants, ethnic Chinese and ethnic Vietnamese Cambodians, along with other elites, were executed or sent to labor and re-education camps (Chandler 1999). Survivors report that during this period, people who wore glasses were executed because they represented intellectuals, beautiful Cambodian women were forced to marry malformed Khmer Rouge veterans, and there were no dogs in the countryside because hungry Cambodians ate them due to the shortage of food (Becker: 162). What followed was four years of starvation and slavery. The numbers of Cambodians who died under the Khmer Rouge remains a topic of debate: Vietnamese sources say three million, while others estimate 1–2 million deaths. Historians have called it the Cambodian Holocaust, a pogrom of ethnic cleansing and societal reform that still haunts many survivors and their descendants (Chandler 1999).

The Khmer Rouge state of Democratic Kampuchea was toppled on December 25, 1978, after Vietnamese forces entered Phnom Penh to address the Khmer Rouge murder of hundreds of ethnic Vietnamese along the Vietnam-Cambodia border region. This, however, did not mean freedom for the people of Cambodia; instead it set the stage for two decades of war in Cambodia. Cambodia was "liberated" from the Khmer Rouge's pogrom, but tens of thousands of Cambodians continued to endure Khmer Rouge terror. The

Khmer Rouge established military camps at the Thai border where they forced refugees into the camps and subjected them to systematic violations of their human rights. The Vietnamese finally withdrew from Cambodia in 1989, leaving their client regime, the People's Republic of Kampuchea, to fend for itself against the Khmer Rouge and their allies. For several decades, the Khmer Rouge haunted the Cambodian landscape and people through war crimes and crimes against humanity. Thus, since 1975, the stage was set for the massive global movement of Cambodian refugees, the remaking of Cambodia as a modern nation-state, and the making of Cambodian America.

References

Becker, Elizabeth. *When the War was Over: Cambodia and the Khmer Rouge Revolution.* New York: PublicAffairs, 1986. Print.

Chan, Sucheng. Survivors: *Cambodian Refugees in the United States.* Chicago: University of Illinois Press, 2004. Print.

Chandler, David. *A History of Cambodia.* Boulder: Westview Press, 1983. Print.

Chandler, David. *Voices from S-21: Terror and History in Pol Pot's Secret Prison.* Berkeley: University of California Press, 1999. Print.

Chhim, Sun-Him. *Introduction to Cambodian Culture.* San Diego: Multifunctional Resource Center, San Diego State University, 1989. Print.

Clark, Joyce, ed. *Bayon: New Perspectives.* Bangkok, Thailand: River Books, 2008. Print.

Clymer, Kenton J. *The United States and Cambodia, 1870-1969: from Curiosity to Confrontation.* New York: RoutledgeCurzon, 2004. Print.

Etcheson, Craig. *After the Killing Fields: Lessons from the Cambodian Genocide.* Lubbock: Texas Tech University Press, 2005. Print.

Hein, Jeremy. *From Vietnam, Laos, and Cambodia: A Refugee Experience in the United States.* New York: Twayne Publishers, 1995. Print.

Higham, Charles. *The Civilization of Angkor.* Berkeley: University of California Press, 2001. Print.

Jacques, Claude and Lafond, Philippe. *The Khmer Empire: Cities and Sanctuaries from Fifth to the Thirteenth Centuries.* Bangkok, Thailand: River Books, 2007. Print.

Osborne, Milton. *The Mekong: Turbulent Past, Uncertain Future.* St. Leonards, Australia: Allen & Unwin, 2000. Print.

Su, Christine M. "Tradition and Change: Khmer Identity and Democracy in the 20th Century and Beyond." Unpublished dissertation. University of Hawai'i, 2003. Print.

Welaratna, Usha. *Beyond the Killing Fields: Voices of Nine Cambodian Survivors in America.* Stanford: Stanford University Press, 1993. Print.

Willmott, William E. *The Chinese in Cambodia.* Vancouver, BC Canada: University of British Columbia, 1967. Print.

Section II

War, Pol Pot, and the
Khmer Rouge

CHAPTER 2

Bombings in Cambodia, 1971–1973

Jeremy Hein

Cambodia was drawn into the war as the Vietcong (VC)[1] and North Vietnamese Army (NVA) established base camps and supply routes along the Vietnam-Cambodia border. The United States believed these activities had great military significance, although subsequent investigation proved they were only a minor value (Karnow 1983). President Nixon proceeded to secretly attack the bases and routes by land and air, without congressional approval, for 13 months in 1969 and 1970. Prince Norodom Sihanouk had ruled Cambodia since independence from France (Sihanouk had been king since 1941, even though his title was merely titular until 1953) and kept the country neutral during most of the Vietnam War. In 1970, however, General Lon Nol took power in a coup widely believed to have been sponsored by the CIA, which wanted a pro-American government in Phnom Penh. The Lon Nol government quickly escalated military conflict with the NVA and the Communist guerrillas known as the

From *From Vietnam Laos & Cambodia: A Refugee Experience in the United States.* © 1995 Gale, a part of Cengage Learning, Inc. Reproduced by permission. www.cengage.com/permissions.

Khmer Rouge (Khmer is the term for the Cambodian people in their own language; *rouge* is French for "red"). The guerrillas were led by Pol Pot, the son of a low-level Cambodian civil servant. He had joined the French communist party while a university student in Paris and returned to Cambodia in 1953 with the goal of leading a peasant revolution like that in China.

The 1970 bombings of Communist sanctuaries in southern Cambodia displaced few civilians because the area was relatively unpopulated (Shawcross 1977). But between 1971 and 1973, when the United States flew sorties in support of the Cambodia army, the bombings hit populated areas. Although bomb tonnage declined from 63,646 in 1971 to 54,206 in 1972, the percentage from B-52s rose from 53 to 69 percent. When the Paris Peace Agreement ended U.S. participation in the Vietnam War in January 1973, the NVA violated article 20 calling for withdrawal of all foreign troops from Cambodia. The United States then concentrated on aerial warfare on Cambodia until August (Shawcross 1977: 266-67). In the first three months of 1973, 41,424 tons of bombs were dropped, 70 percent of B-52s (U.S. Senate 1973a: 24). In April and May 1973, B-52s dropped 71,000 tons of bombs (Shawcross 1977: 272). One off-course B-52 killed 125 civilians and wounded more than 250 in a government-held town (Shawcross 1977: 400).

The creation of a virtual free-fire zone in the eastern one-third of Cambodia dramatically increased the flow of refugees (U.S. Senate 1973a). Called "Freedom Deal," most air strikes in this area did not require the standard clearance process: a request by the Cambodia military, mediation by the U.S. embassy, examination by U.S. spotter planes, and final referral to U.S. air bases in Thailand. After much investigation Sydney Schanberg (a reporter for *The New York Times*) concluded that the intense bombing in 1973 was "an American operation that has been modeled to give the appearance that the Cambodians are playing a significant role in coordination and directing it" (U.S. Senate 1973a: 85). The U.S. Senate agreed that air strikes "are not cleared individually with the Cambodian General Staff, and the Embassy plays no coordinating role" (U.S. Senate 1973b: 50-51). A voluntary agency director returning from a fact-finding mission for the Senate Refugee Subcommittee reported the human results of the bombing: "Bombing is the most pervasive reason for refugee movement. Our interviews with refugees…largely confirm the findings of the General Accounting Office (GAO) interviewers in 1971. The GAO found that some 60 percent of the refugees interviewed cited bombardment as the principal reason for moving" (U.S. Senate 1973a: 7).

Given that the U.S. military considered war victims as an inevitable part of the campaign in Cambodia, the U.S. experience with refugees in South Vietnam and Laos would have suggested a major relief effort. But from the beginning of hostilities in 1970, the American government persistently ruled against such aid: "According to the U.S. Ambassador to Cambodia, it has been the policy of the United States to not become involved with the problem of civilian war victims in Cambodia" (U.S. Senate 1972a: 89). The rationale for this inaction was to keep a low profile in the country. Despite heavy bombing in 1970 and 1971, an AID official asserted that "during this period, it was the policy of our Government, reinforced by action of the Congress, to keep the U.S. involvement in Cambodia to an absolute minimum" (U.S. Senate 1973a: 32).

Cambodian officials also were reluctant to address the refugee problem. One relief worker voiced a protest against social-welfare policies in general, explaining that "the Government did not want to make beggars out of the people" (U.S. Senate 1972a: 90). Others cited the strength of the Cambodian family, the self-reliance of the Khmer people, and their distrust of the government as reasons that refugee relief was not a high priority. By 1973 only 10,000 refugees were receiving aid in government camps (U.S. Senate 1973a: 12). In what amounted to a debate over social-welfare philosophy, U.S. officials cited this figure as evidence that Cambodian refugees were able to provide for themselves (U.S. Senate 1973a). To assist Cambodian refugees, proponents had to start with the argument, first raised during the industrial revolution, that national governments had a responsibility for the welfare of their citizens.

By August 1972 the war had displaced 700,000 Cambodians, and nearly 60 percent were clustered in and around the capital of Phnom Penh (U.S. Senate 1973a: 64). That month Lon Nol finally requested assistance from the United States. An AID team then in

Cambodia to investigate the refugee problem modestly concluded, "The requirements of the refugees for assistance…are not being fully met by help currently being provided by the GKR [Cambodian government] and other donors. There is room for the USG [U.S. government] to augment such help…. USG assistance should be portrayed as a response to the GKR's August 10, 1972, formal appeal to the US" (U.S. Senate 1973a: 69). The report recommended, however, that the United States neither provide funds to the GKR directly nor to an outside voluntary agency. Either approach, it argued, would lead to an uncoordinated and inadequately supervised program or a further internationalization of the situation.

What was to be the only U.S. aid to Cambodian refugees came hesitantly. AID, the organization with the most experience in such relief efforts, argued that economic assistance was sufficient. On the topic of relief for Cambodian refugees one official stated: "In dealing with problems of housing and resettlement of people back in their own homes, bringing rice production back to peacetime levels…one finds that those are national problems and have to be dealt with not as refugee problem as such" (U.S. Senate 1973a: 43). Between July 1972 and July 1973 only $1.5 million was delivered to two voluntary agencies. By then there were more than 1 million refugees and an additional 500,000 dependents of Cambodian soldiers in flight (U.S. Senate 1973a: 4). In 1974 the United States finally provided another $1 million. These figures contrast with $517 million in military aid since the beginning of the war (Shawcross 1977: 319). In Cambodia the United States showed the most disregard for the plight of the war victims its military policies generated.

Conclusion

The U.S. government had a long history of managing the migration and resettlement of Vietnamese, Laotians, and Cambodians before the first Indochinese refugees arrived in the United States. Not only did U.S. Policy on refugees in Southeast Asia during the 1960s and early 1970s mirror the country's larger objectives in the region, but refugee migration itself was often a key tactic to further these objectives. Beginning with Operation Exodus in 1954, U.S. aid to refugees from North Vietnam established the organizations and ideologies used in later nation-building policies. The U.S. commitment to the refugees augmented arguments in favor of continued involvement in South Vietnam. In addition, these predominately Catholic refugees became actors significant beyond their numbers, particularly as supporters of South Vietnam's first president from 1954 to 1963. Following Operation Frequent Wind April 1975, President Gerald Ford used nearly $100 million in AID money for South Vietnam (now under Communist rule) to resettle this first wave of government officials and army officers, 40 percent of whom were catholic (Taft et al. 1980).

In the years between Operation Exodus and Operation Frequent Wind, the United States sponsored even more profound refugee migrations in Vietnam, Laos, and Cambodia. From 1965 to 1968 the American military gained control of relief operations for Vietnamese villagers displaced by the war. As civilian agencies increasingly left refugee aid to organizations engaged in counterinsurgency and pacification, the inevitable result was the forced migration of Vietnamese peasants to further military objectives. These objectives included depriving the Vietcong of a support population but also providing evidence that Vietnamese peasants were "voting with their feet" for the government in Saigon by migrating to areas it controlled.

In terms of the proportion of the population uprooted, American military policy in Laos and Cambodia led to even greater migration. Recruitment of the Hmong and other highland populations in Laos to serve as a "secret army" meant that the fate of entire ethnic group now depended on military victory. As Hmong troops were forced to withdraw against overwhelming North Vietnamese forces in 1969 and 1970, the retreat turned into a massive migration of extended families and communities. When the U.S. military attempted to stop the retreat through intensive bombing in the Plain of Jars, the result was an even greater flow as Laotian civilians became the target of indiscriminate attacks. A similar fate awaited many civilians in Cambodia between 1971 and 1973. A large portion of the country was opened to almost unrestricted bombing by the U.S. Air Force, with little or no regulation by the Cambodian government. The bombing created more than 1 million refugees in a population of 7 million, and the United States provided only the most limited aid to these refugees under the pretext of not intervening in Cambodian affairs.

The United States risked all during its military intervention in Southeast Asia, including the uprooting of civilian populations without their consent. Achievement of U.S. political objectives in Southeast Asia might have provided some justification for the destruction, since the new Communist regimes proved more brutal than their pro-American predecessors. But the collapse of allied governments in the spring of 1975 meant that the United States had failed in its mission despite making the populations of Vietnam, Laos, and Cambodia pay a heavy price in lives lost and ruined. As a result, the United States bore a special responsibility for Vietnamese, Laotian, and Cambodian refugees who fled to neighboring countries in the 1970s and 1980s.

Endnotes

1. Also known as Viet Minh.

References

Karnow, Stanley. *Vietnam: A History*. New York: Penguin Books, 1983. Print.

Shawcross, William. *Side-Show: Kissinger, Nixon and the Destruction of Cambodia*. New York: Pocket Books, 1977. Print.

Taft, Julia, David North, and David Ford. *Refugee Resettlement in the U.S.* Washington, D.C.: New Transcentury Foundation, 1980. Print.

CHAPTER 3

Who Was Pol Pot?

David P. Chandler

The man known to the world as Pol Pot started life with the name Saloth Sar. Pol Pot was his revolutionary name. When he announced his pseudonym in 1976, he followed precedents set by several Communist leaders, including Lenin, Stalin, Tito, and Ho Chi Minh. Their intentions, when in the underground, were to conceal their true identities from the police and in some cases their followers ("Stalin," for example, means "steel"; "Ho Chi Minh" means "the enlightened one"). Pol Pot, however, took a new name after he had come to power, concealing his former identity from the nation he was about to govern. The name he chose, although common enough among rural Cambodians (the Khmer), had no independent meaning.

In making this bizarre, self-effacing gesture, Saloth Sar/Pol Pot was behaving true to form. Beginning in the 1950s, he preferred working in secret to living in the open. When Pol Pot came to power in 1976, it took analysts more than a year to identify him with certainty as a former schoolteacher named Saloth Sar who had been the secretary of the Cambodian Communist party since 1963. Pol Pot admitted his original name offhandedly to an interviewer in 1979, several months after he had been driven from power.

Over the years this extraordinarily reclusive figure concealed, clouded, and falsified so many details about his life that it is not surprising that there is even some confusion about his date of birth. North Korean radio announced in 1977 (before Pol Pot had been identified as Saloth Sar) that he had been born in 1925. French colonial records prepared in Cambodia in the 1950s, however, state that he was born on May 25, 1928. The second date, which leaves less time unaccounted for, seemed more plausible than the earlier one to many writers but had been contradicted by Saloth Sar's siblings in recent interviews. Pol Pot himself insisted on the earlier date in his interviews with Nate Thayer in 1997. For these reasons, 1925 is now the preferred year of birth.[1]

Saloth Sar's parents were ethnic Khmer. He was born in the village of Prek Sbauv, less than two miles west of the provincial capital of Kompong Thom, some ninety miles north of Phnom Penh. His father, Pen Saloth, was a prosperous farmer with nine hectares of rice land, several draft cattle, and comfortable tile-roofed house. Saloth Sar's mother, Sok Nem, was widely respected in the district for her piety and good looks. Sar was the eighth of nine children, two of whom were girls. Five of the nine survived into the 1990s.[2]

Palace Connections

What set the family apart from others in the region were its connections with the Royal Palace in Phnom Penh. Saloth Sar's cousin Meak joined the royal ballet in the 1920s in the closing years of the reign of King Sisowath (r. 1904-1927). She soon became a consort of the king's eldest son, Prince Sisowath Monivong, and bore him a son, Kossarak, shortly before Monivong became king in 1927. She held the favored position of *khun preab me neang*—literally, "lady in charge of the women"—from which she controlled the women of the palace. The post was abolished after Monivong's death, but Meak continued to live near the Royal Palace and was attached to the *corps de ballet* as a senior teacher until the early 1970s.

Saloth Sar's family enjoyed other royal connections. In the late 1920s, Sar's older brother Loth Suong went to Phnom Penh to work at the palace as a clerk. Soon after, their sister Saloth Roeung (nicknamed Saroeun) joined the ballet and at some point in the 1930s became a consort of King Monivong. Suong worked in the palace as a clerk until 1975 and in the early 1940s married a dancer, Chea Samy. Saroeun, a favorite consort of the king, returned to Kompong Thom after Monivong's death in 1941 and eventually married a local policeman.[3]

In 1934 or 1935, when Saloth Sar was nine years old, he and his older brother Chhay were sent by their parents to live with Meak and Suong in Phnom Penh. Sar probably would have preferred the relatively carefree life of Prek Sbauv to the more demanding one of being raised by busy relatives in a strange city. Informal adoptions by prosperous relatives are a traditional feature in Cambodian life and therefore should not be taken as indicating estrangement between children and their natural parents. In fact, although Sar's brother and sister-in-law have insisted that Sar got along well with his parents, he is not known to have mentioned them in conversations with other people. This silence, however, may be related to a conscious effacement of personal information rather than animosity. There is no evidence that he had conflicts with his father of the sort that characterized the adolescent years of Stalin, Mao Zedong, and other prominent political figures. Indeed, his sister told an interviewer in 1997 that Saloth Sar had come back to Prek Sbauv for his father's funeral in the late 1950s and contributed to the cost of erecting a memorial *stupa*. In later life, Sar never mentioned his palace connections. Instead, he tended to emphasize his rural origins.

Soon after arriving in the capital, Saloth Sar spent several months as a novice at Vat Botum Vaddei, a Buddhist monastery near the palace that was favored by the royal family. At such a young age and recently separated from his parents, Sar must have been traumatized by the solemn discipline of the monastery, even though there would be other little boys with shaven heads wearing yellow robes with him. At the Vat Botum Vaddei he learned the rudiments of Buddhism and became literate in Khmer. Sar was also forced to be obedient. Ironically, for someone who embraced atheism and xenophobia so fervently in later life, this brief period was the only time in his formal education (which lasted until 1952) in which Khmer rather than French was the language of instruction.[4]

Loth Suong and Chea Samy, who looked after Saloth Sar in the 1940s, maintained that he was an even-tempered, polite, unremarkable child. As a primary student, Samy told the Australian journalist James Gerrand, Sar "had no difficulties with other students, no fights or quarrels." In examining his early years, I found no traumatic events and heard no anecdotes that foreshadow his years in power. People who met him as an adult found his self-effacing personality, perhaps a carryover from the image he projected as a child, hard to connect with his fearsome behavior in the 1970s. In Loth Suong's words, "The contemptible Pot [Khmer *a-Pot*] was a lovely child."[5]

Endnotes

1. See Ben Kiernan, *How Pol Pot Came to Power* (London, 1985; hereafter HPP), and other materials in Bibliographic Essays, pp. 243 ff., and Ben Kiernan, *The Pol Pot Regime* (New Haven, 1995).

2. I refer especially to Nate Thayer's October 1997 interview with Pol Pot himself, summarized by Thayer, "Day of Reckoning," Far Eastern Economic Review (*FEER*), October 30, 1997; the unpublished interviews with former Red Khmer cadre conducted since 1995 by David Ashley; and Stephen Heder's unpublished interviews with Ieng Sary and Mey Mann. I am grateful to Ashley and Heder for transcripts of their interviews and to Thayer for extensive conversations about his encounter with Pol Pot.

3. Before he fell from power in 1977, Pol Pot toyed with the idea of presiding over a biographical project that would, he hoped, secure his place in history. According to Nate Thayer (personal communication), he recruited a young Khmer Rouge cadre, Tep Kunnal, for the project and over several months Kunnal filled nine notebooks with data provided by his mentor. The notebooks, he told Thayer, were accidentally destroyed during the government assault on the Red Khmer base of Anlong Veng in 1998, shortly before Pol Pot died.

4. See David P. Chandler, *The Tragedy of Cambodian History: Politics, War, and Revolution Since 1994* (New Haven, Conn., 1991).

5. See Francois Ponchaud, "Social Change in the Vortex of Revolution," in Karl Jackson, ed., *Cambodia, 1975-1978: Rendezvous with Death* (Princeton, N.J., 1989); Soth Polin, "La diabolique douceur de Pol Pot," *Le Monde Diplomatique*, May 18, 1980l; and Roger Normand, "At the Khmer Rouge School: The Teachings of Chairman Pol Pot," *Nation*, September 3, 1990.

References

Chandler, David. *Brother Number One: A Political Biography of Pol Pot*. Boulder: Westview Press, 1999. Print.

CHAPTER 4

The Nature of the Khmer Rouge Revolution

Sucheng Chan

A single phrase, "the killing fields," taken from the title of a 1984 film has formed the world's controlling image of Cambodia. Although Cambodians themselves also use the term, more frequently they refer to this dark period in their history as *samay Pol Pot* (the Pol Pot time). Pol Pot, the *nom de guerre* of Saloth Sar, was also called "Brother Number One" to reflect his paramount status among the leaders of the Democratic Kampuchea (DK) regime that came into being on April 17, 1975.

Although Saloth Sar at first did not disclose that he was Pol Pot, that is the name by which he became known around the world. In retrospect, Cambodian refugees refer to his followers as "the Pol Pots" (Welaratna 1993). Khmer Rouge leaders liked to boast that their efforts were "without precedent." "What we are trying to do," declared Ieng Sary, "has never been done before in history" (Chandler 1991b: 240). Reflecting their French education, the leaders borrowed the concept of "year zero" from the French Revolution to indicate their desire to wipe their society's slate clean and start from scratch as they attempted to transform every aspect of Cambodian society.

It has been difficult for scholars to characterize the revolution that Pol Pot led. According to David Chandler, the Khmer Rouge never resolved "the contradiction between their revolution's being a genuine socialist one (and thus comparable to others) or uniquely Cambodian, without precedents or offsprings" (1991b: 245). Michael Vickery observes that the two major policies of the Khmer Rouge leadership were "poor-peasantism and anti-Vietnamese racism." He defines "peasant populism" as an "anti-intellectual ideology" based on "a belief in the sacredness of the soil and those who till it." Thus, the Khmer Rouge leaders were "petty-bourgeois radicals overcome by peasant romanticism" (1984: 264, 285, 287). Kate Grace Frieson, however, argues that the Khmer Rouge revolution was not a genuine peasant revolution. Relying on oral histories, she demonstrates that "the relationship between the peasantry and the Red Khmers...[was] one of mutual mistrust, misunderstanding, and inequality." Moreover, peasants perceived that "[d]eference to whatever side in the war had local power at a given time was... their best defense." She concludes that "the Red Khmer movement did not represent the needs of the peasants as they themselves defined them" (1992: iii, 249, 255).

As for whether the Khmer Rouge followed any other country's model, Karl Jackson points out that "[a]lthough it is useful to search for the intellectual antecedents of the Khmer Rouge... the ferocity and the literalism with which they pursued these formal ideologies cannot be explained merely by reference to abstract formal ideologies...The proclivity toward violence, the fear of contamination by outsiders, the moral self-righteousness, and the literal and doctrinaire way of pursuing goals are what separate the Khmer Rouge from comparable revolutionary phenomena" (1989c: 7). In Jackson's opinion, the Khmer Rouge belonged to a "sectarian movement" guided by a "dichotomous" worldview in which the world is divided into two, "believers, who are good, and nonbelievers, who are evil" (8). Khatharya Um aptly characterizes the Khmer Rouge as a "brotherhood of the pure" (Um 1990 and in press). Fearing pollution or contamination, they savagely went about eradicating all those whom they deemed impure.

In the most detailed study of the Khmer Rouge to date, Ben Kiernan argues that the revolution they led made extensive use of what we would today call "ethnic cleansing," a term not popularized until the civil war in the former Yugoslavia two decades later: "Khmer Rouge conceptions of race overshadowed those of class.... Race also overshadowed organizational imperatives. Non-Khmer Cambodians with extensive revolutionary experience and CPK seniority were removed from the leadership and usually murdered.... This was neither a Communist proletarian revolution that privileged the working class nor a peasant revolution that favored all farmers.... Membership in the single approved race [Khmer] was a condition, though not a sufficient one, of official approval" (1996: 26).

Unlike historians and political scientists, who tend to focus on the Khmer Rouge leadership and its ideology, anthropologist Alexander Laban Hinton analyzes how the Khmer Rouge drew on "preexisting cultural models that were emotionally salient to the perpetuators" to motivate them to kill (1997: 226; 1996; 1998a; 1998b). These include Khmer conceptions of honor, revenge, paranoia, patronage, and obedience—concepts deeply embedded in the hierarchical Khmer social structure. According to Hinton, Khmer Rouge soldiers and cadres followed orders because Cambodians are socialized to obey their elders and patrons. Cambodians generally carry out the wishes of their superiors in order not to lose face (*mukh*)—which depends greatly on the evaluation of others—and to avoid potential punishment. In Democratic Kampuchea, those who actually did the dirty work of killing felt no contrition because they could "deflect responsibility" from themselves as the "orders came from Angkar" ("angkar" meaning "organization" and referring to the upper echelon of the Khmer Rouge). Those who actually committed the acts of violence, that is, did not do so of their own volition. Moreover, the Khmer concept of *kum* (*kum* or *kam* is the Khmer transliteration of the Indian word *karma*) helped justify a phenomenon that Hinton calls "disproportionate revenge"—revenge that is "much more damaging than the original injury"—because the youthful soldiers and cadres were told that the *kbat* (traitors) were "people who had been responsible for traditional class inequalities and the wartime death of numerous comrades" (1996: 823-28; Hinton 1998a). Hinton argues that the ethic of gentleness, so observable among Cambodians, has always coexisted with an ethic of violence. What the Khmer Rouge did was legitimize the latter and render the "economic and ecological conditions that had previously necessitated cooperation... irrelevant" (1996: 823).

To those analyses I would add two others. First, although there were some parallels between the revolutionary conditions in China and Cambodia, based on the extensive research I have done on Maoist revolutionary tactics and strategy I would argue that Mao Zedong and Pol Pot differed in one fundamental way. Mao emphasized the importance of analyzing "concrete conditions" and devising political and military strategies to address them as they evolved stage by stage. Pol Pot, in contrast, attempted to leap-frog over other socialist revolutions and transform Cambodia overnight into the most advanced communist society in the world. Second, Khmer Rouge leaders were not "mad men" in the sense of being irrational. On the contrary, they had a clearly articulated scheme that they carried out methodically in the coldest, most calculating way. They acted as they did because they were idealists in two senses of that word. They had a utopian vision of what they considered to be the perfect society, and they thought about the world not in terms of human strength and frailties but in abstract categories. That is why they could go about implementing their policies with no regard for the human costs of their actions.

References

Chandler, David P. *The Land and People of Cambodia*. New York: Harper-Collins, 1991a. Print.

_____. *The Tragedy of Cambodian History: Politics, War, and Revolution since 1945*. Boulder: Westview Press, 1991b. Print.

Frieson, Kate Grace. "The Political Nature of Democratic Kampuchea." In *Pacific Affairs* 61:3 (1988): 405-27. Print.

Hinton, Alexander L. "Agents of Death: Examining the Cambodian Genocide in Terms of Psychosocial Dissonance." In *American Anthropologist* 98:4 (1996): 818-31. Print.

_____. "Cambodia's Shadow: An Examination of the Cultural Origins of Genocide." Unpublished dissertation, Emory University, 1997. Print.

_____. "A Head for an Eye: Revenge in the Cambodian Genocide." In *American Ethnologist* 25:3 (1998a): 352-77. Print.

_____. "Why Did You Kill?" The Cambodian Genocide and the Dark Side of Face and Honor." In *Journal of Asian Studies* 57:1 (1998b): 93-122. Print.

Jackson, Karl D. "Introduction: The Khmer Rouge in Context." In *Cambodia 1975-78: Rendevous with Death*, edited by Karl D. Jackson. Princeton: Princeton University Press, 1989. Print.

Um, Khatharya. *Born of the Ashes: World Revolution and Exile-the Cambodian Experience.* Berkeley: University of California Press. In press.

Vickery, Michael. *Cambodia, 1975-1982.* Boston: South End Press, 1984. Print.

Welaratha, Usha. *Beyond the Killing Fields: Voices of Nine Cambodian Survivors in America.* Stanford: Stanford University Press, 1993. Print.

CHAPTER 5

Discovering S-21

David P. Chandler

On 7 January 1979, a bright, breezy day in Cambodia's cool season, heavily armed Vietnamese forces, accompanied by lightly armed Cambodian allies, reached the outskirts of Phnom Penh after a blitzkrieg campaign that had begun on Christmas Day. For over a year, Vietnam had been at war with the Maoist-inspired regime of Democratic Kampuchea (DK), known in the West as the Khmer Rouge. Their invading force of over one hundred thousand troops, including armored units, was reinforced by a sustained aerial bombardment.[1]

The rapidity of the Vietnamese success took their commanders by surprise. After barely two weeks of fighting, Cambodia cracked open like an egg. The leaders of DK, most of their army, and tens of thousands of their followers fled or were herded out of the city. The invaders were welcomed by nearly everyone who stayed behind. These were people terrorized and exhausted by nearly four years of

Voices from S-21: Terror and History in Pol Pot's Secret Prison (Paper) by Chandler, David. Copyright 1999 by University of California Press Books. Reproduced with permission of University of California Press Books in the format Textbook

undernourishment, back-breaking labor, and widespread executions. A similar welcome, tragically misplaced, had greeted the Khmer Rouge themselves when they had occupied Phnom Penh in April 1975 and ordered its population into the countryside to become agricultural workers. In both cases, people were longing desperately for peace.[2]

By late afternoon the Vietnamese forces had occupied the city. Aside from a few hundred prisoners of war and other people—including some of the workers at S-21—who were in hiding, waiting to escape, Phnom Penh was empty.[3]

After the Khmer Rouge had emptied the city in 1975, Phnom Penh had remained the country's capital, but it never regained its status as an urban center. The bureaucrats, soldiers, and factory workers quartered there probably never numbered more than fifty thousand. During the DK era, the country had no stores, markets, schools, temples, or public facilities, except for a warehouse in the capital serving the diplomatic community. In Phnom Penh, barbed-wire fences enclosed factories, workshops, barracks, and government offices. Street signs were painted over, and barbed-wire entanglements blocked many streets to traffic. Banana trees were planted in vacant lots. Automobiles abandoned in 1975 were rusted in piles along with refrigerators, washing machines, television sets, and typewriters. Scraps of paper in the gutters included pre-Revolutionary currency, worthless under the Khmer Rouge. On 7 January 1979, no people or animals could be seen. As in 1975, the central government, such it was, had disappeared. Once again, Cambodians were being made to start at zero.[4]

The effect of the desolation on the newcomers was phantasmagoric. Chey Saphon, for example, was a forty-seven-year-old Cambodian Communist who had fought against the French in the 1950s. He had lived in Vietnam since 1955 and had been trained as a journalist. On 7 January he was thrilled to be returning home with the Vietnamese troops. He was so unnerved by what he saw, however, that years later he recalled that he "spent the whole afternoon in tears."[5]

Over the next few days Vietnamese troops fanned out across Phnom Penh. On 8 January, in the southern sector of Tuol Svay

Prey, two Vietnamese photojournalists who had accompanied the invasion were drawn toward a particular compound by the smell of decomposing bodies.[6] The silent, malodorous site was surrounded by a corrugated tin fence topped with coils of barbed wire. Over the gate was a red placard inscribed in yellow with a Khmer slogan: "Fortify the spirit of the revolution! Be on your guard against the strategy and tactics of the enemy so as to defend the country, the people and the Party." The place carried no other identification.[7]

Pushing inside, the two photographers found themselves on the grounds of what appeared once to have been a high school. The spacious, dilapidated compound measured roughly four hundred meters from east to west and six hundred meters from north to south. It consisted of four whitewashed concrete buildings, each three stories high, with balcony corridors running along each upper story. A fifth, single-story wooden building, facing west, split the compound into two identical grassy spaces. To the rear of each of these, one of the taller buildings faced east, toward the entrance. Similar buildings marked off the northern and southern boundaries of the compound.[8] The purpose of the compound was unclear to the two men, although the single-story building, littered with papers and office equipment, had obviously been used for some sort of administration.

In rooms on the ground floor of the southernmost building, the two Vietnamese came across the corpses of several recently murdered men. Some of the bodies were chained to iron beds. The prisoners' throats had been cut. The blood on the floors was still wet. Altogether the bodies of fourteen people were discovered in the compound, apparently killed only a couple of days before.[9]

In large classrooms on the upper floors of the western buildings, the patrol found heaps of shackles, handcuffs, whips, and lengths of chain. Other rooms on the upper floors had been divided by clumsily bricked partitions into small cells where each prisoner's foot had been manacled, as William Shawcross later wrote, "to a shackle large enough to take ship's anchor." Ammunition boxes in some of the cells contained human feces.[10] On the third were slightly larger, more elaborately constructed cells with wooden walls and doors.

The two intruders took photographs of all the rooms in the facility, adding photos of the corpses. They then "informed the Vietnamese authorities" of what they had found. That evening the corpses were burnt "as a sanitary measure." Some of the photographs taken at that time now hang in the rooms where the bodies were found.

Over the next few days the Vietnamese and their Cambodian assistants discovered in nearby houses thousands of documents in Khmer, thousands of mug-shot photographs and undeveloped negatives, hundreds of cadre notebooks, and stacks of DK publications. In a workshop near the front gate they found several recently completed oversized concrete busts of the DK prime minister, Pol Pot, a concrete mold for the statues, and some portraits of him, apparently from photographs.

The Vietnamese had stumbled into a vicious and important Khmer Rouge facility. Documents found at the site soon revealed that it had been designated in the DK era by the code name S-21. The "S," it seemed, stood for *sala*, or "hall", while "21" was the code number assigned to *santebal*, a Khmer compound term that combined the words *santisuk* (security) and *nokorbal* (police). "S-21," and *santebal*, were names for DK's security police, or special branch.[11]

Over the next few weeks the history of the site was pieced together. In the early 1960s, when Cambodia had been ruled by Prince Norodom Sihanouk, it had been a high school. It was named after Ponhea Yat, a semilegendary Cambodian king associated with the foundation of Phom Penh.[12] After Sihanouk was overthrown in 1970—the event that sparked Cambodia's civil war—the school had taken the name of the surrounding district, Tuol Svay Prey (hillock of the wild mango). An adjoining primary school was called Tuol Sleng (hillock of the sleng tree). This name was used to designate the entire compound after it became the Museum of Genocidal Crimes in 1980, perhaps because the sleng tree bears poisonous fruit.[13]

The code name S-21 began to appear on Khmer Rouge documents in September 1975. For the next nine months, until the facility came into operation in May or June 1976, the security service's work was spread among several units in Phnom Penh, the southern suburb of Ta Khmau, and in Sector 25, north of the capital.[14] By the end of 1975, according to a former guard, Kok Sros, interviewed in 1997, *santebal* coalesced under the command of Kang Keck Ieu (alias Duch), a former school teacher who had been in charge of security in the so-called special zone north of the capital during the civil war. Duch became the director of Tuol Sleng facility in June 1976. He remained in command until the day the Vietnamese arrived.[15]

Sensing the historical importance and the propaganda value of their discovery, the Vietnamese closed off the site, cleaned it up, and began, with Cambodian help, to examine its voluminous archive. On 25 January 1979, a group of journalists from socialist countries was invited to Cambodia by the Vietnamese to report on and celebrate installation of the new Cambodian government, known as the People's Republic of Kampuchea (PRK). The journalists were the first official visitors to see Tuol Sleng. Chey Saphon accompanied them to the site. One of the journalists, the Cuban Miguel Rivero, wrote later that "there were still traces of blood on the floor. The smell was even more penetrating. There were thousands of green flies circling the room." Rivero added that he saw documents "written in Sanskrit" and "several" copies of Mao Zedong's *Little Red Book* at the "Dantesque" site.[16]

Soon afterwards, in February or March 1979 (his own memory is uncertain), Mai Lam, a Vietnamese colonel who was fluent in Khmer and had extensive experience in legal studies and museology, arrived in Phnom Penh. He was given the task of organizing the documents found at S-21 into an archive and transforming the facility into what David Hawk has called "a museum of the Cambodian nightmare."[17] The first aspect of Mai Lam's work was more urgent than the second. It was hoped that documents found at the prison could be introduced as evidence in the trials of Pol Pot and Ieng Sary, DK's minister of foreign affairs, on charges of genocide. These took place in Phnom Penh in August 1979. Although valuable information about S-21 was produced at the trials, none of the documents in the archive provided the smoking gun that the Vietnamese and People's Republic of Kampuchea (PRK) officials probably hoped to find. No document linking either Pol Pot or Ieng Sary directly with orders to eliminate people at S-21 has ever been discovered, although the lines of authority linking S-21 with the Party Center (*mochhim pak*) have been established beyond doubt.

Because of his penchant for history, his experience with museums (he had organized the Museum of American War Crimes in Ho Chi Minh City), and the criminality of what had happened at S-21, Mai Lam approached his work with enthusiasm and pride. His genuine, somewhat patronizing fondness for Cambodia and its people, based on his experiences in Cambodia in the first Indochina war, also inspired him. "In order to understand the crimes of Pol Pot—Ieng Sary," he told interviewers in 1994, "first you should understand Cambodians, both the people and the country."[18]

In turning S-21 into a museum of genocide, Mai Lam wanted to arrange Cambodia's recent past to fit the requirements of the PRK and its Vietnamese mentors as well as the long-term needs, as he saw them, of the Cambodian people. Because numbers of the "Pol Pot—Ieng Sary genocidal clique," as the Vietnamese labeled them, had been Cambodians themselves, the message that Mai Lam was trying to deliver was different from the one that he had hoped to convey in the Museum of American War Crimes, but it was just as harsh. The history that he constructed in the exhibits at S-21 denied the leaders of the Communist Party of Kampuchea (CPK) any socialist credentials and encouraged viewers to make connections between the DK regime and Tuol Sleng on the one hand, and Nazi Germany and what Serge Thion has called the "sinister charisma" of Auschwitz on the other. The comparisons were fitting insofar as S-21, like the Nazi death camps, was a secret facility where all the inmates were condemned to death, but any more explicit links between Nazism and DK, although seductive, were inexact.[19]

A Cambodian survivor of S-21, Ung Pech, became the director of the museum when it opened in 1980. He held the position for several years and traveled with Mai Lam to France, the USSR, and Eastern Europe in the early 1980s to visit museums and exhibits memorializing the Holocaust. Although Mai Lam remained in Cambodia until 1988, working at Tuol Sleng much of the time, he concealed his "specialist-consultant" role from outsiders, creating the impression that the initiatives for the museum and its design had come from the Cambodian victims rather than from the Vietnamese—an impression that he was eager to correct in his interviews in the 1990s.[20]

Over the next few months, people working at the prison constructed a rough history of the facility, drawing on entry and execution records, memoranda by prison officials, and the memories of survivors. Between April 1975 and the first week of 1979, they discovered, at least fourteen thousand men, women, and children had been held by S-21. Because the entry records for several months of 1978 were incomplete, the true number of prisoners was undoubtedly higher. Of the documented prisoners, all but a dozen specially exempted ones, including Ung Pech, had been put to death. Since 1979, seven of these survivors have come forward. Their memories, corroborated by those of former workers at the prison, have been invaluable for this study.[21]

The records from S-21 also showed that most of the lower-ranking prisoners had been held for a few days or weeks, whereas more important ones, and lesser figures suspected of grave offenses, had been incarcerated for several months. Thousands of the prisoners, regardless of their importance, had undergone interrogation, prepared "answers" (*chomlaoy*) or confessions admitting counterrevolutionary crimes, and submitted lists of their associates, titled "strings" or "networks of traitors" (*khase kbot*), that sometimes ran to several hundred pages. Roughly 4,300 of them have so far come to light, including those of nearly all the important DK figures known to have been purged.[22]

Confession texts, survivors' memories, and the grisly instruments discovered at the site made it clear that torture was widely inflicted at S-21. Tortured or threatened with torture, few prisoners maintained their innocence for long. Considered guilty from the moment they arrived—the traditional Cambodian phrase for prisoner, *neak thos*, translates literally as "guilty person"—thousands of these men and women were expected to confess their guilt in writing before they were taken off to be killed. This bizarre procedure drew some of its inspiration from the notion of revolutionary justice enshrined in the Reign of Terror in eighteenth-century France and enacted in the Moscow show trials in the 1930s and also from the land reform and "reeducation" campaign in China in the 1940s and in Vietnam a decade later. In spite or perhaps because of these manifold influences, no precise or overriding foreign model for S-21 can be identified. Moreover, the severity of practices at S-21 and the literalness with which interrogators went about their business also reflected pre-Revolutionary Cambodian punitive traditions, by which prisoners were never considered innocent and crimes of *lèse-majesté* were mercilessly punished.

Although DK's economic and social policies do not fit into a fascist framework, the resemblances between S-21 and Nazi death camps are striking. Works discussing the Holocaust provide insights into the psychology of tortures, administrators, and victims at the prison, as do more recent works that deal with torturers in the "dirty war" in Argentina in the 1970s and early 1980s. The list of materials that I have found useful for comparative purposes could easily be extended.[23]

The most striking difference between the German and Cambodian cases lies in the extent of the documentation produced at S-21. Prisoners both under the Nazis and in DK were removed from any semblance of legal protection; but whereas those in the Nazi death camps were simply exploited for physical labor while awaiting execution, those in S-21 were treated almost as if they were subject to a judicial system and their confessions were to provide evidence for a court of law. In this respect they resemble the alleged counterrevolutionaries who went on "trial" in the Soviet Union in large numbers in the 1930s. In Nazi Germany, political prisoners were kept in separate camps from those targeted for execution and were somewhat better treated. At S-21, all were charged with political offenses, and all were to be killed.

Like the Nazi extermination camps and the Argentine torture facilities, S-21 was a secret facility, and the need for secrecy influenced much of what happened inside its walls. The prison's existence was known only to those who worked or were imprisoned there and to a handful of high-ranking cadres, known as the Party Center, who reviewed the documents emerging from S-21 and selected the individuals and the military and other units to be purged. Interrogators, clerks, photographers, guards, and cooks at the prison were forbidden to mingle with workers elsewhere, and the compound soon earned an eerie reputation. A factory worker in a nearby compound, interviewed in 1989, referred to S-21 as "the place where people went in but never came out."[24] The factory workers were uncertain about what went on inside its walls but were ready to think the worst. Party leaders never referred to S-21 by name. In 1997, when questioned by the journalist Nate Thayer, Pol Pot denied any knowledge of "Tuol Sleng," hinting that the museum and its archive were Vietnamese concoctions. "I was at the top," he said:

> I made only big decisions on big issues. I want to tell you— Tuol Sleng was a Vietnamese exhibition. A journalist wrote that. People talk about Tuol Sleng, Tuol Sleng, Tuol Sleng.... When I first heard about Tuol Sleng it was on the Voice of America. I listened twice.[25]

Guided tours of S-21 were first organized in March 1979, but for over a year, as the museum took shape, only foreigners were admitted because, as a PRK Ministry of Culture, Information, and Propaganda document from 1980 asserted, the site was intended primarily "to show...international guests the cruel torture committed by the traitors to the Khmer people." In the meantime, Mai Lam and his associates were slowly transforming the site into a museum. In July 1980 the ban on Cambodian visitors was lifted, and tens of thousands visited S-21, many of them seeking information about relatives who had disappeared. They consulted hundreds of enlarged mug shots of prisoners on view on the ground floor of the prison, which formed a major component of the museum display. As Judy Ledgerwood has written, many of the visitors were also "searching for meaning, for some explanation of what had happened. A visit would not have been an easy task; people who went through the museum in the first year said that the stench of the place was overwhelming."[26] Some thirty-two thousand people visited the museum in the first week it was open to the public. By October 1980, over three hundred thousand Cambodians and eleven thousand foreigners had passed through the facility.[27]

Endnotes

1. See Bui Tin, *Following Ho Chi Minh*, 117ff., an eyewitness account. For background to the conflict, see Elliott, ed., *The Third Indochina Conflict*. For a contemporary overview of the campaign, see Chanda, "Cambodia: Fifteen Days."

2. The best general accounts of the Khmer Rouge period are probably three of the earliest: Becker, *When the War Was Over*; Etcheson, *The Rise and Demise of Democratic Kampuchea*; and Ponchaud, *Cambodia Year Zero*. Subsequent studies include Burgler, *The Eyes of the Pineapple*, and Kiernan, *The Pol Pot Regime*. Two collections of essays dealing with the period are Chandler and Kiernan, eds., *Revolution and Its Aftermath*, and Jackson, ed., *Cambodia 1975-1978*.

3. Author's interviews with Nhem En and with Kok Sros. These S-21 workers spent 7 January 1979 in hiding before walking out of the city the next day.

4. On the appearance of Phnom Penh in the DK era, see Becker, *When the War Was Over*, 420 ff. Becker visited the city in December 1978. See also Pilger, *Heroes*, 380 ff. Pilger came to Phnom Penh in the summer of 1979 and apparently first saw S-21 a year later. When I was there in August 1981 prerevolutionary banknotes could still be picked up off the streets. The notion of "year zero," drawn from the French Revolution, was never explicitly adopted by the Khmer Rouge, who followed the Christian calendar throughout their time in power.

5. Author's interview with Chey Saphon, October 1997.

6. Chanda, "The Cambodian Holocaust," includes a photograph of a "sinister school building" and one of the pictures taken of corpses discovered there "by the invading Vietnamese forces on 8 January 1979." On the smell, see Rivero, *Infierno*, 24. For a useful history of the site, see Ledgerwood, "The Cambodian Tuol Sleng Museum."

7. The placard is shown in the 1981 East German documentary film *Die Angkar*. I am grateful to Peter Maguire for providing me with a copy of the book containing the storyboards for the film and a transcript of his 1995 interview with the filmmaker, the late Gerhard Schuemann. Maguire arranged for a showing of the film at Bard College in October 1998, which I attend. Many of the still photographs used in the film, which were found at Tuol Sleng in 1979 and 1980, have apparently disappeared.

8. These details come from People's Republic of Kampuchea, People's Revolutionary Tribunal, *The Extermination Camp of Tuol Sleng*. The original,

French-language text was prepared by Ung Pech, an S-21 survivor and the first director of the Tuol Sleng Museum of Genocidal Crimes.

9. Douglas Niven's interview with Ho van Thay. Kok Sros, a former guard at S-21, recalled that "about twenty" prisoners were murdered at S-21 just before the Vietnamese invasion (author's interview). From other sources we know that by 1978 the southernmost building had become a "special prison" (*kuk pises*) where high-ranking prisoners were confined. Several confessions were transcribed on 6 January 1979, either just before or shortly after the last prisoners were killed.

10. Shawcross, *The Quality of Mercy*. Shawcross first visited the prison in 1980. On feces, see Rivero, *Infierno*, 24.

11. Some writers have assumed that "S" stood for *santebal*, but the prefix recurs in reference to other DK entrities: S-71, the Party School, and S-8, the Party's logistical heardquaters. See Hawk, "The Tuol Sleng Extermination Center," in which "21" is fancifully explained by Ung Pech as representing the "Second Bureau" (intelligence) reporting to "Number One" (Pol Pot). The fact that Vietnamese prisoners of war were held and interrogated at S-21 in 1978 suggests that it was not only a counterintelligence operation aimed at internal enemies but also a military prison.

12. On Ponhea Yat, see Vickery, *Cambodia after Angkor*, 492 ff. Serge Thion, who has written widely about Cambodia, taught at the Ponhea Yat *lycée* in 1966 and 1967.

13. Chhang Youk, "The Poisonous Hill."

14. People's Republic of Kampuchea, *The Extermination Camp of Tuol Sleng*, lists these *santebal* sties as "the camp of Ta Khmau, formerly a psychiatric hospital, the former National Police headquarters south of the new market, the former Lycée Descartes, Wat Phnom in the former Navy Officer's building, the former Lycée Sangkum and the camp of Prey Sar west of Phnom Penh in Kandal province." Corroboration that *santebal* operated at these locations occurs in several S-21 confession texts and in Douglas Niven's interview with Nhem En, a photographer for *santebal*.

15. See Document N0001223, "Summary of 3 May 1976," a memorandum from Pheap of Regiment 588 to "Brother 89" (Son Sen, the DK minister of defense, in charge of military and security affairs) in the DC-Cam archive, Phnom Penh. The memorandum reports that "at the Tuol Svay Prey School a 20-man party cleaned up two levels of the facility, removed 250 tables, and cut 20 square meters of grass." When S-21 received its first prisoners is not known. On its closing days, see interviews with Kok Sros, Nhem En, and Him Huy. In late 1978 some of

the functions of S-21 may have been transferred to Division 502, reflecting suspicions inside the Party Center directed at Son Sen (Steve Heder, personal communication).

16. Rivero, *Infierno*, 25. For another journalist's report from 1979, see Mate, *Genocide in Cambodia*. Rivero's final observation may have reflected wishful thinking, for no Cambodian edition of the *Little Red Book* was ever published. According to Kiernan, *The Pol Pot Regime*, 465, S-21 was introduced to nonsocialist readers by Wilfred Burchett in the *Guardian* (London), 11 May 1979.

17. Hawk, "Cambodia: A Report from Phnom Penh," *New Republic*, 15 November 1981. Mai Lam, now in his seventies, was interviewed on two occasions in Vietnam by Sara Colm and once by Peter Maguire and Chris Riley. I am grateful to them for providing transcripts of their interviews.

18. Maguire and Riley, interview with Mai Lam. Talking with Sara Colm, Mai Lam suggested that certain Cambodian cultural elements kept Cambodians from understanding what had happened to them under DK. "The Cambodian people's nature is that they want to stay in a quiet, peaceful atmosphere—Buddhist temple, rice farm, village," he said. "They are very nostalgic about the quiet times they had." Mai Lam's attitude toward the Khmer fits into what Christopher Goscha has called the "evangelistic" tendency in Vietnamese relations with Cambodia and Laos (personal communication).

19. Serge Thion, "Genocide as a Political Commodity," in Kiernan, ed., *Genocide and Democracy in Cambodia*, 184.

20. Mai Lam's interviews with Colm, Maguire, and Riley, and Ung Pech's interview with David Hawk. See also Heder interviews, 10-11 and 14 ff., with Ong Thong Hoeung, a Cambodian intellectual who worked in the S-21 archive between June and November 1979. Hoeung told Heder that "ten other Vietnamese" worked with Mai Lam at S-21 at that time. See also On Thong Hoeung, "Le 30 novembre j'ai quitté Phnom Penh precipitamment," in Scalabrino, ed., *Affaires cambodgiennes*, 121-28.

21. See in particular Vann Nath, *Prison Portrait*. I am grateful to Sara Colm for introducing me to Vann Nath in 1995. Another survivor, Ten Chan, was also interviewed on several occasions, as was the late Ung Pech. See also Lionel Vairon's interview with Pha Thachan, who became a typist at S-21, and DC-Cam document D-17, 4 December 1985, an interview with Ruy Nikon, who worked as a carpenter at S-21 from 1976 until the Vietnamese invasion.

22. It is impossible to determine what percentage of the total number of confession texts has survived. If every prisoner produced a confession,

then as many as ten thousand texts must have disappeared, which seems unlikely. While as many as half this number of confessions may well have disappeared, it seems more probable that several thousand of the prisoners at S-21 never prepared confessions. Two key confessions that apparently have disappeared are those of Chau Seng, a leftist intellectual who served as information minister under Sihanouk, and Chea San, DK's ambassador to the USSR and Romania, whose Tuol Sleng mug shot from February 1978 appears in *Die Angkar*.

23. The Holocaust-oriented texts that have most inspired me are Améry, *At the Mind's Limits*; Bauman, *The Holocaust and Modernity*; Browning, *Ordinary Men*; Levi, *The Drowned and the Saved*; Sereny, *Into the Darkness*; Sofsky, *The Order of Terror*; and Todorov, *Facing the Extreme*. The books by Sereny and Feitlowitz contain extended interviews with perpetrators. Studies on the massacres in Indonesia in 1965-1966 and on state-sponsored violence in the Cultural Revolution in China have also been useful, and my discussion of S-21 from a comparative standpoint benefits from comments by students at the University of Wisconsin in 1998 who attended my seminar on twentieth-century political killing.

24. Author's interview with Taing Kim Men. See also the confession of Seat Chhe (alias Tum), CMR 138.11, in which he writes to the prison director, Duch: "I understand that as for entering S-21, there is only one entry. As for leaving, that never happens." CMR 179.16, Tot Ry, expresses a similar idea.

25. Thayer, "Day of Reckoning." Pol Pot would have known Tuol Sleng by its code name S-21. See Christine Chameau's interview with Ieng Sary, "Rehabilitation Completed," in which Sary said, "I said I never heard of Tuol Sleng....We were always talking in code names and security was S-21." Asked who gave orders for S-21, Sary replied, "For political things like that, Khieu Samphan." There is no corroboration in the archive for this assertion.

26. Ledgerwood, "The Cambodian Tuol Sleng Museum," 90. Cambodians are still looking. See Seth Mydans, "Twenty Years On."

27. Ledgerwood, "The Cambodian Tuol Sleng Museum," 88, quoting the Ministry of Culture report. Ledgerwood adds that "the museum was open to the public every Sunday…[while] organized visits by foreign and local groups took place on weekdays."

Reference

Chandler, David P. *Voices from S-21: Terror and History in Pol Pot's Secret Prison.* Berkeley: University of California Press, 1999. Print.

Section III

Development
of Cambodian
American Communities

CHAPTER 6

1970s:
Escape from War and the
Creation of Refugees

Dori Cahn and Jay Stansell

As Southeast Asia was imploding during the 1970s, hundreds of thousands of Cambodians, Vietnamese, and Laotians were escaping their countries' borders by any means possible. Walking through fields of land mines, floating on anything resembling a boat, refugees flowed into other parts of Southeast Asia. Refugee camps mushroomed along the Thai borders, while some refugees made their way to Malaysia and Indonesia.

In Cambodia, the demise of the national government in 1975 was followed by four years of unimaginable terror under the Khmer Rouge. Millions of people were displaced, particularly from urban areas, and forced to live in "collective" rural camps where the displaced experienced the day-to-day possibility of arbitrary brutal death, torture, or starvation. Survivors have attempted to detail the depth of brutality and terror that defined life under the rule of the Khmer Rouge (see especially Him 2000; and Ung 2000; for descriptions of children living in Cambodia during these years; see also Ngor 1987; Pran 1997). Dr. Haing Ngor dedicates his 1987 memoir to the memories of his parents and wife, who "died in the most miserable, uncivilized, and inhuman ways under the Khmer communist regime." Another survivor describes his childhood experiences:

> I saw my mother's tears glistening in the dim light of dying bonfire. A farm labor overseer had just ordered fifteen children to kick me. I was seven. Each child was to kick me five times, and my mother could do nothing to stop it.... My mother's tears. Endless labor without pay. Hunger. Beatings. Executions. These are the memories I have of my childhood in Cambodia during the holocaust of the Khmer Rouge (Darith Keo, in Pran, 1997).

The most horrifying aspect to survivors is the fact that other Cambodians were the perpetrators of the atrocities—unlike the holocaust visited upon Jews by the Nazis during World War II or the "ethnic cleansing" in Bosnia or the tribal rivalries between Hutus and Tutsis in Rwanda in the 1990s. In fact, the term "autogenocide" was coined specifically to refer to the situation of Cambodia under the Khmer Rouge, where atrocities were committed by members of a single social and ethnic group on its own members (Chung 2000).

By the time the Vietnamese army invaded Cambodia and took over its governing powers in 1979 (a point in time referred to by survivors as the "liberation"), as much as one quarter of the population had died by starvation, illness, or execution as a result of the Khmer Rouge policies and political purges. Thousands of those remaining fled the country in the days and months following the Vietnamese takeover. Most of these came from the northwestern part of the country. Closest to the border of Thailand, where escape by foot was possible.

In Thai refugee camps, those who fled Cambodia were generally safer than in their home, but they were still subject to atrocities. In one well-documented incident, Thai soldiers forced close to 45,000 Cambodian refugees down a steep cliff face, back across the border into the Khmer Rouge minefields that they had all managed to avoid on their escape to Thailand (Kamm 1998). Other refugees speak of harassment, extortion, exploitation, and assault by Thai soldiers (Him 2000; Kamm 1998).

As thousands of people jammed camps that Thailand grudgingly allowed within its borders, the international community, and in particular the United States, recognized the need for an organized process that would allow refugees to escape while preventing Thailand from being overwhelmed. The policies applied to Southeast Asian refugees were the product of decades of public policy debate in the United States regarding the treatment of those fleeing war and terror throughout the world.

The United States' experience with massive numbers of war refugees prior to the end of World War II was fairly limited. Even during the war, when many Jews were desperate to flee the pogroms and Nazi roundups throughout Eastern Europe, the United States refused to increase its immigration quotas to accept these refugees (Simon Wiesenthal Center 1997). After the end of the war, "[m]uch of the impetus for new American and international efforts…derived from the recognition that pre-war efforts, especially on behalf of Jewish refugees, were shamefully inadequate" (Aleinikoff et al. 1998).

Following World War II, the international community established two important international treaties, the Convention Relating to the Status of Refugees, in 1951, and, in the face of the worsening situation in Southeast Asia, the Protocol Relating to the Status of Refugees in 1967 (Goodwin-Gill 1996). Initially, post-World War II refugee policies in the United States allowed entrance of refugees as parolees with no permanent status, but it quickly became apparent that this approach was inadequate, as "refugee problems" did not dissipate in the years following the war. In 1965, the United States institutionalized refugee admissions as one of the several categories of noncitizens to allow into the United States on a fluctuating and numerical basis. But this approach too proved inadequate, particularly in the face of the exodus of refugees from Southeast Asia in the 1970s. Congress then passed the Refugee Act of 1980, establishing the legal framework that is largely still in place today (Aleinikoff et al. 1998).

The 1980 act repealed the congressionally controlled numerical limits of the refugee laws of 1965 and replaced them with a provision for the president to establish yearly ceilings on refugee admissions. The act defined a refugee as a person who fears return to his or her home country because of a well-founded fear of persecution on account of race, religion, nationality, membership in a particular social group, or political opinion. Under the act, 50,000 Southeast Asian refugees a year were allowed into the United States during the first few years, a ceiling that could be raised by the president. In the first year alone, President Carter agreed to accept 166,700 Southeast Asians for resettlement in the United States (Smith-Hefner 1999).

The increase of admissions from Cambodia was particularly dramatic. From 1952 until 1974, there were a recorded 390 non-refugee immigrant arrivals in the United States from Cambodia. In the 5 years between 1975, the year of the Khmer Rouge takeover, and the passage of the 1980 Refugee Act, about 13,000 Cambodian refugees were admitted to the United States. In the first year alone after the act's passage, refugee arrivals grew to 16,000, followed by a peak of more than 38,000 the following year. Overall, between 1975 and 1999, there were a total of 145,149 Cambodian refugees who arrived in the United States, with an additional 42,000 nonrefugee arrivals recorded in the same period (Southeast Asia Resource Action Center [SEARAC] 2002b; Smith-Hefner 1999). The 2000 census counts a total of 206,000 people claiming single or combined Cambodia ethnicity.

The earlier refugees from Southeast Asia that came before the Refugee Act of 1980 was implemented were generally urban and well educated. The Cambodians who came in this period mainly had worked for the U.S. government or had otherwise been involved in the war effort. The later, larger wave, between 1980 and 1987, when the bulk of Cambodians arrived, tended to be rural and less educated, in part because the purges conducted by the Khmer Rouge were targeted at the educated, professional, and urban residents (Smith-Hefner 1999).

Initially, U.S. domestic resettlement policies were intended to disperse refugees throughout the country so that no one community would be overburdened. Often these placements were based purely on wherever sponsors were available. However, the refugees would frequently move on from their initial placements to join family members or friends, or to move from uncomfortable climates (Smith-Hefner 1999). Government policy was later changed to concentrate resettlement in locations where housing and jobs were available and where services could be distributed more centrally. These locations were all medium to large urban environments (Fadiman 1997). The Cambodians faced a process of resettlement and establishing new communities that were different from the Vietnamese communities in the United States, many of which were established by better educated and more prosperous refugees fleeing before the end of the war in 1975; these communities were able to absorb the later wave of rural and less skilled refugees into their midst (Elliot 1999; Nguyen 1994; Office of the Surgeon General 1999).

Federal funding was provided to assist refugees upon their arrival in the United States. Refugees were given language classes, job training, and housing and employment assistance. Many then found their way into minimum wage jobs. However, there was generally little to no follow-up. In fact, although the Refugee Act of 1980 authorized reimbursement to states for assistance, the number of months allowed was continually cut in subsequent years (Jung 1993). Moreover, the length of assistance varied from state to state, with as little as 4 months in states such as New York. Assistance networks were severely strained by the huge influx of refugees throughout the 1980s while sources of funding were decreasing (Bass 1996).

References

Aleinikoff, Alexander, David Martin, and Hiroshi Motomora. *Immigration and citizenship process and policy.* St. Paul: West Group, 1998. Print.

Bass, Thomas. *Vietnamerica: The war comes home.* New York: Soho Press, 1996. Print.

Chung, Margaret. Intergenerational effects of the genocidal disaster among Cambodian youth. National Association of Social Workers New Your City Chapter, Disaster Trauma Working Group. Web; November 1, 2002.

Elliot, Duong Van Mai. *The sacred willow: Four generations in the life of a Vietnamese family.* New York: Oxford University Press, 1999. Print.

Fadiman, Anne. *The spirit catches you and you fall down: A Hmong child, here American doctors, and the collision of two cultures.* New York: Farrar, Straus, and Giroux, 1997. Print.

Goodwin-Gill, Guy. *The refugee in international law.* New York: Oxford University Press, 1996. Print.

Him, Chanrithy. *When broken glass floats: Growing up under the Khmer Rouge.* New York: W. W. Norton, 2000. Print.

Jung, Helene. "Roles swaps hurt refugee families: Newcomers' children adapting to U.S. faster than their parents." In *Seattle Times* (November 7, 1993). Print.

Kamm, Henry. *Cambodia: Report from a stricken land.* New York: Arcade Publishing, 1998. Print.

Ngor, Haing. *A Cambodian odyssey.* New York: Macmillan Publishing Company, 1987. Print.

Nguyen, Qui Duc. *Where the ashes are: The odyssey of a Vietnamese family.* Reading: Addison Wesley, 1994. Print.

Pran, Dith, ed. *Children of Cambodia's Killing Fields: Memoirs by survivors.* New Haven: Yale University Press, 1997. Print.

Smith-Hefner, Nancy. *Khmer American: Identity and moral education in a diasporic community.* Berkeley: University of California Press, 1999. Print.

Ung, Luong. *First they killed my father: A daughter of Cambodia remembers.* New York: HarperCollins, 2000. Print.

CHAPTER 7

How Long Beach Became the "Cambodian Capital in America"

Sucheng Chan

By the late 1970s, one identifiably Cambodian enclave had emerged in the United States. It is located in the city Long Beach, the second-largest city in Los Angeles County and the fifth-largest city in California. During the early years of Long Beach's existence, it attracted many retirees from the Midwest as well as tourists in search of sun, sand, and sea. An oil boom enriched its economy during the 1920s and 1930s, and a U.S. Navy shipyard and the aerospace industry provided jobs for residents from the 1940s to the early 1980s. Long Beach harbor and San Pedro harbor in the southern part of Los Angeles County together handle the third largest volume of container cargoes in the world today. But the city experienced hard times during the 1980s and 1990s as a result of downsizing in the defense industries, closure of the naval shipyard, and severe downturn in the southern California real estate market.

From *Survivors: Cambodian Refugees in the United States.* Copyright © 2004 by Board of Trustees of the University of Illinois. Used with permission of the University of Illinois Press.

Long Beach became the largest Cambodian community in America by chance. During the late 1950s and 1960s, Long Beach State University—now California State University, Long Beach—hosted more than a hundred college students from Cambodia, who came to study engineering and agriculture. In 1958 these students formed the Cambodian Students Association of America. Most returned to Cambodia after they graduated, but as political instability increased during the late 1960s and early 1970s several dozen came back to the United States, some to the Long Beach area.

When they and a handful of Cambodian military officers who were in southern California for training heard that a thousand or more from their country had arrived in Camp Pendleton in April and May 1975, they went to visit the camp. They brought Cambodian food to welcome their compatriots, and those who had the means to do so offered to serve as sponsors. Several Long Beach State University professors who had taught Cambodian students in the past also volunteered as sponsors. Him S. Chhim, executive director of the Cambodian Association of America, which evolved from the Cambodian Students Association in November 1975, estimates that somewhere between one and two thousand Cambodian refugees were resettled in Long Beach as a result of the students' initiative (Chim interview 1996 in Chan, ed. 2003a: 47-48).

In those days, central Long Beach was a depressed area, as a former Lon Nol government official told anthropologist Usha Welaratna: "Back then, Long Beach looked like a vacant lot. It was occupied mainly by retired people...if you walked down Anaheim Street, in a ten-unit apartment building only two or three would be occupied...back then the population was made up of about 30 percent White and 30 percent Black, with the rest being Hispanic, Thai, Japanese, Korean, and Filipino, and just about three Cambodian families" (Welaratna 1998: 56).

Scott Shaw, who studied the Long Beach Cambodian community in the late 1980s, notes, however, that seven Cambodian families resided in Long Beach before the refugees arrived in 1975. By 1980 the local Cambodian population had grown to approximately seven thousand. Some were refugees resettled directly in Long Beach from 1975 to 1979; others arrived as secondary migrants—that is, people who had initially been placed in other states but moved to the new location on their own initiative (Shaw 1989). The secondary migrants were attracted to what may be called the "cultural comfort zone" offered by Long Beach.

By the mid-1980s Long Beach had at least thirty-five thousand—in some estimates, fifty thousand—Cambodians. It is the largest Cambodian community outside of Cambodia. The 2000 census counted only 17,396 Cambodians in Long Beach City, but that is very likely a gross undercount. Cambodian community leaders, voluntary agency staff members, and local and state officials who deal with Indochinese refugees have all said that official census numbers are too low because Cambodians do not speak English well and are wary of government officials and the forms they ask people to fill out. Him S. Chhim maintains that the Cambodian population in Long Beach "stabilized" during the mid-1990s, with few people leaving or coming in (Chhim interview root in 2001 Chan, ed. 2003a: 46).

About 70 percent of Long Beach's Cambodian residents have lived in the central area of town since the early 1980s—the so-called inner city bounded roughly by the Pacific Coast Highway to the east, Seventh Street to the west, Long Beach Boulevard to the north, and Redondo Avenue to the south (Shaw 1989: 16). Most are renters, and before welfare reform was introduced in 1996 they depended almost entirely on public assistance for survival. About 15 percent of the better-off Cambodians live in a suburban neighborhood of single-family houses in the northwestern part of the city— areas where about half the residents are European Americans. Another 15 percent live in multistory apartment buildings in a light-industrial area of the city's northeastern section (Tan 1999: 161). These apartment-dwellers consist of both welfare recipients and the working poor.

The heart of the Cambodian community is Anaheim Street or the "Anaheim Corridor," commonly called "Little Phnom Penh." It contains several hundred Cambodian-owned businesses, including restaurants, take-out food stands, bakeries, grocery stores, clothing stores, jewelry stores, souvenir shops, automobile repair shops, and video rental stores. There are also many pawn shops because

Cambodians who gamble often pawn jewelry, watches, and other valuables. Many of these stores are owned by Cambodians of Chinese ancestry (Chhim interview 1996 in Chan, ed. 2003a: 57). Various professional services are also found there, including pharmacies, medical clinics, beauty parlors and barber shops, and dressmakers (Tan 1999: 161-62). Few storeowners, who are among the better-off Cambodians, live in the inner city itself, but they go there every day to run their businesses.

Buildings in the area are very run-down, and streets are narrow and dirty. The bustling atmosphere is nevertheless attractive to Cambodians who live elsewhere. As a male teenager interviewed by anthropologist Usha Welaratus commented:

> I lived with my aunt in Riverside, where it was very quiet. All I did was go to school, come back home, and stay home...we hardly did anything.... Then my other aunt came to Long Beach. I visited her one time, and I found that in Long Beach, there were people on the streets, they had Cambodian parties, they had everything! So I thought, Wow, I am going to move here...I was in eighth grade, and all the teachers liked me. But I was the only Cambodian student at my school...I didn't understand English. I found the work real hard, and decided to move to Long Beach. (1998: 74-75)

Cambodians in Long Beach share the inner city with other Asian immigrants and their American-born progeny, African Americans, and Mexican Americans and other Spanish-speakers. Latino Americans compose approximately one-fifth of the city's half-million residents, Asian Americans another fifth, African Americans about a tenth, and European Americans about half. Roughly half the Asian Americans are Cambodians, some 15 percent are Vietnamese, and about 8 percent are Filipinos. Smaller numbers of Koreans, Japanese, Chinese, Lao, Hmong, Thai, Pacific Islanders (mostly Samoans), and Native Americans also live in the area (Chittapalo interview 1996 in Chan, ed. 2003a: 96-97; Welaratna 1998: 3). Such ethnic diversity notwithstanding, the state of California recognized the significance of Long Beach as the capital of Cambodian

America and erected a freeway exit sign, "Little Phnom Penh," in 2001 to alert drivers to its whereabouts (Wride 2001).

The Cambodian population in Long Beach reached a plateau in the late 1980s and then began to decline after an earthquake struck the greater Los Angeles area in October 1987. Frightened by that event, approximately five hundred families, numbering some two thousand persons, moved to the Central Valley of California, the southern half of which is called the San Joaquin Valley and the northern half the Sacramento Valley. They settled in cities such as Fresno, Stockton, Sacramento, Merced, and Modesto (Shaw 1989: 18). As Sam Chittapalo, a former Cambodian police officer in Long Beach, put it, the quake was "not only something to fear on its own, but a powerful reminder of their loss of country and loved ones" (Arax 1988). Ernest Velasquez, assistant director of social services in Fresno County at the time, told a reporter that 350 Cambodians signed up for the welfare rolls in his county in the months following the quake (Arax 1988).

According to the 2000 census, the Central Valley, stretching from Redding in the north to Bakersfield in the south, contains 18,695 Cambodians. As defined by the census bureau, the Central Valley includes Redding, Chico, Yuba City, Sacramento-Yolo, Stockton-Lodi, Modesto, Merced, Fresno, Visalia-Tulare-Porterville, and Bakersfield metropolitan statistical areas (MSAs). The greater Stockton area has by far the largest concentration, with 9,313 enumerated in the 2000 census (Pfeifer 2002).

Two other regions in California also developed sizable Cambodian communities—the San Francisco Bay area and the greater San Diego area. The San Francisco-Oakland-San Jose metropolitan statistical area reported a Cambodian population of 10,552 in the 2000 census, and the San Diego MSA counted 4,314 (Pfeifer 2002). The 2000 census indicates that 70,232 persons of Cambodian ancestry now live in the state of California, a slight increase from the 68,190 counted in the 1990 census, but their distribution pattern remained the same in the ten-year interval.

Unfortunately, the areas in which Cambodians moved are not free of danger. On January 17, 1989, an unemployed welder named Patrick Purdy found his way onto the playground of Cleveland

Elementary School in Stockton. He fired more than one hundred rounds indiscriminately at the children playing there during recess, killing five of them and wounding twenty-nine others as well as a teacher before taking his own life. Four of the children who died were Cambodians; the fifth was Vietnamese. A mother of one of the dead children had thought the United States would be "a place of peace and freedom" and was distraught when that was not the case. Chun Keut, the father of another victim, collapsed after hearing of his eight-year-old daughter's death and died of an apparent heart attack. "I think his heart broke" explained a relative (Sahagun and Stein 1989).

The event revived the Cambodians' trauma and kindled new anxieties. It also, ultimately, transformed the entire city of Stockton. Social service agencies began paying more attention to the refugees in their midst, comforting the bereaved and helping the needy population in myriad other ways. Perhaps what helped the most was that a respected Cambodian monk who had come to the United States in 1979, Dharmawara Mahathera, went to the schoolyard to chant prayers and sprinkle holy water on the ground where the children had been struck down. "We are going to take away the evil action of an evil man," he said. "We are going to send the good spirit of those who lost their lives and purify this school so the children can come to study again" (Groin 1989).

Then, on October 17, 1989, an earthquake struck the San Francisco Bay area where some four thousand Cambodians lived, most of them in the Tenderloin area. The commotion and chaos that followed the quake made the terrified Cambodians feel like they were "back in the war" said Sophat Pak. When the earth trembled, the English-speaking Pak ran out of his apartment and spent hours translating the news blaring from his car radio to frightened non-English-speaking neighbors who gathered around him. "I call it my second escape," he said in obvious reference to his escape from Cambodia. As Holbrooke Teter, a psychologist working with Cambodians in San Francisco at the time, observed, "Cambodians were so traumatized under Pol Pot that it's as though they have a well of emotional dislocation that any new trauma, like the earthquake, taps into and re-evokes the original tragedy." A Cambodian social worker,

Sam Ath, also described the connection: "Many of them said they didn't trust Pol Pot and now they don't trust the earth" ("Cambodians Flee New Terror" 1989).

The warfare that erupted between Cambodian and Latino gangs during the late 1980s also drove some Cambodians away from Long Beach. As the frequency and intensity of violence increased—people who desired to live in safer environments began to look for homes elsewhere (Rim interview 1995 in Chan, ed. 2003a: 158; Tauch interviews 1996 and 2001, in Chan, ed. 2003a: 212, 207). As another of Welaratna's respondents revealed, "We came to this country in 1981 and our family went to Chicago. But we could not stand the cold, so we came to California. We moved to a small town first, but life was so hard there...we decided to move to Long Beach,... [but] before I moved...I didn't know that this was a scary place...there's shooting at night, drugs sold, extortion...and gangs. So now I am doing two jobs and my wife also works, because we want to get out" (Welaratna 1998:190).

Even as the pace of out-migration quickened, a new kind of secondary in-migration began in the early 1990s, when Cambodians from other countries began to arrive. The influx has helped prevent the number of Cambodians in Long Beach from declining too much. Sam Chittapalo explained why Cambodians from other countries have found their way to Long Beach:

> Cambodians from Paris, from Australia, from Canada, from all over the world they come to Long Beach. Even from Cambodia they now come to Long Beach. Cambodians from Japan come in Long Beach, too.... We had one Cambodian [Sichan Siv] working in the White House with the Bush administration... he's referred to all over the country, even in Japan, even in France, even in Australia. Cambodian people are starting to see if a guy has ability, he has a chance to work in the White House. Why shouldn't I come here, bring my daughter, my kid, my son, to study here? (Chittapalo interview 1996 in Chan, ed. 2003a: 97)

Many new international secondary migrants bring money to invest. They open businesses and hire local Cambodians as workers.

They compose an emerging transnational Cambodian bourgeoisie—a mobile population whose members maintain connections with fellow Cambodians in several countries and go wherever they think the best opportunities for upward socioeconomic mobility may be found. Given their desire to make money and gain social prestige, such people can be easily influenced by stories of successful individuals such as Sichan Siv, a resident of the East coast.

That a Cambodian on the opposite side of the country helped draw Cambodian entrepreneurs to Long Beach is not as amazing as it sounds, for educated Cambodians around the world tap into transnational information networks that enable them to keep up with what is going on among compatriots in the various countries where Cambodians live.

Siv, a college graduate, was working for CARE in Phnom Penh in 1975. The U.S. embassy staff had offered to evacuate him because Khmer Rouge victory seemed imminent, but he missed the last American helicopter out of Phnom Penh on April 12 by thirty minutes (DeLoughery 1989: A22). As a consequence, he and his family lived through the Khmer Rouge horrors. Because it was impossible for the entire family, which included young children, to escape together, the family urged Sichan to flee by himself. He did so but was arrested when he reached the Thai border. By then the border had closed, and the Thai authorities considered him an illegal entrant. Luckily, Japanese friends learned of his arrival and contacted CARE, which arranged for him to be resettled in the United States four months later.

The voluntary agency handling Siv's case sent him to a small town in Connecticut, where he picked apples to support himself and declined loans from his sponsor. "Once you've been a slave, then find yourself free you want very much to earn your own living," he explained to journalist Sheldon Kelly (Kelly 1991: 141). He subsequently worked as a janitor, cab driver, and bank teller, all the while sending letters to various colleges to seek admission with financial aid. His persistence bore fruit when Columbia University's School of International Relations and Public Affairs admitted him and gave him a full scholarship. He earned an M.A. degree there in 1981 and became a naturalized U.S. citizen in 1982.

By then, large numbers of Cambodian refugees were arriving, so Siv went to work at an Episcopalian Church that was helping resettle them. He married an American woman in 1983. In the mid-1980s he worked for the Coalition Government of Democratic Kampuchea delegation that held Cambodia's seat at the United Nations but eventually became disillusioned with that group and quit his job in 1987. He did volunteer work in George H. W. Bush's presidential campaign in 1988, during which he caught the eye of Republican Party stalwarts. The Bush White House tapped Siv in February 1989 to serve as a deputy assistant to the president for public liaison. He thus became, at forty-one, the first Asian American to be appointed as a ranking presidential aide (Kelly 1991: 138-42). It is not surprising that his Horatio Alger story inspired ambitious Cambodians in other countries to immigrate to the United States.

Except for those who resettled in Long Beach, the first wave of Cambodian arrivals were scattered across the country. The most important factor determining their settlement pattern was the federal government's dispersal policy to place no more than three thousand Southeast Asian refugees in any one locality in order to minimize their impact upon the budget, social services, and school system in each community. The location of the various regional offices of voluntary agencies was a second factor that influenced where refugees were sent. Although many early sponsors were individuals, families, or Catholic parishes and Protestant congregations, as time passed and problems surfaced between the refugees and their sponsors, agencies increasingly took on the sponsorship role themselves. Thus, later arrivals tended to congregate in the cities where voluntary agencies had branch offices.

References

Arax, Mark. "Cambodians in L.A. Area Flee, Fearing Quake." In *Los Angeles Times*, May 20, 1988. Print.

DeLoughery, Thomas. "Former Prisoner of Khmer Rouge Now Provides Higher Education." In *Chronical of Higher Education* 36:1 (1989): A21-22. Print.

Kelly, Sheldon. "The Rebirth of Sichan Siv." In *Reader's Digest* 138:826 (1991): 138-42. Print.

Pfeifer, Mark. "Census shows growth and changing distribution of the Cambodian Population in the United States." "Hmong Studies Internet Research Center." Web; Sept. 15, 2002.

Sahagun, Louis and Mark Stein. "Cambodian Relives Pain of Killing Fields." In *Los Angeles Times* Jan. 19, 1989. Print.

Shaw, Scott. *Cambodian Refugees in Long Beach, California: The definitive study*. Hermosa Beach: Buddha Rose Publication, 1989. Print.

Tan, Terpsichore. "Cambodian Youth in Long Beach, California: Parenting and other sociocultural influences on educational achievement." Unpublished dissertation, University of Hawai'i, 1999. Print.

Welaratha, Usha. *Beyond the Killing Fields: Voices of Nine Cambodian Survivors in America*. Stanford: Stanford University Press, 1993. Print.

Wride, Nancy. "Cambodian Community Makes Banner Statement." In *Los Angeles Times*, July 15, 2001. Print.

CHAPTER *8*

Cambodian American
Secondary Migration and
Community Growth

Susan Needham and Karen Quintiliani

Introduction

Between 1975 and 1985, Cambodians seeking refuge from war, disease, and starvation, scattered throughout the world, establishing a network of communities in France, Canada, Australia, and the United States. Where possible, they recreated cultural practices through the establishment of institutions, businesses, religious practices, and classes in literacy and dance. Among all these communities, none is as well known as the community of Long Beach, California. Home to the largest population of Cambodians outside Cambodia, Long Beach has become the symbolic and actual center of the worldwide Cambodian diaspora. In the 1980s, the community played a critical role in the maintenance of Khmer (Cambodian) culture.[1] It has since become an important economic and political center with complex familial and cultural linkages throughout the diaspora.

The most frequently asked question about this community is "Why Long Beach?" In other words, how did it come to be the largest community outside of Cambodia? The stock answer is the weather, which Cambodians will tell you "is just like Cambodia, only not as hot or humid." Most people are content with this answer, but Lowell, Massachusetts, home to the second largest concentration of Cambodians outside Cambodia has long, cold winters, so there must be more to this story. A number of scholars, reporters and community members have proposed additional reasons for the growth of Long Beach, among them are the presence of Cambodian students at California State University, Long Beach who sponsored new arrivals (Roberts 1988), a large Asian population in the Los Angeles area contributing to a familiar and comfortable "ambience" in Southern California (Coleman 1987: 365), a port through which Asian foods and goods come cheaply and in large quantities, and "generous welfare payments" (Chan 2004: 97). In this article, we examine these claims and suggest that the growth of the community has been result of several factors. The main catalyst has been the vision and desire of Cambodians themselves to recreate social and cultural institutions.

Secondary Migration and Community Growth

To promote the integration of Cambodians and other Southeast Asian refugees, U.S. federal resettlement policy allocated monies for a "Cluster Project" to prevent one city or state from taking on the burden of receiving too many refugees. The idea was to create small "clusters" of refugees and fund Mutual Assistance Associations (MAAs) in Cluster Project cities throughout the United States. These ethnically directed Mutual Assistance Associations (MAAs) were identified by the framers of resettlement policy as the best means through which local needs could be assessed and resources allocated (Gold, 1992). MAAs hold a unique position between the larger society and the community they serve. Generally organized by the most educated members of a community, they identify and attempt to meet the needs of an array of constituents, while at the same time representing the interests of the federal agencies funding their programs (Breton, 1987). The two Long Beach MAAs, Cambodian Association of American (CAA) and United Cambodian Community (UCC), were viewed by Office of Refugee Resettlement (ORR) as national models for developing job training, mental health, and other social adjustment programs. These programs also attracted Cambodians in other parts of the U.S. to Long Beach.

Through a process known as secondary migration (Mortland and Ledgerwood 1987), thousands of Cambodians moved from their initial place of resettlement to regional centers throughout the United States, like Lowell, Massachusetts; Seattle, Washington; and Long Beach. Mortland and Ledgerwood (1987) have argued that secondary migration was part of the survival strategies Southeast Asian refugees brought with them and was motivated in part by the desire to join with family members and to reconstruct familiar cultural networks of support. By 1987, when Mortland and Ledgerwood wrote about the phenomenon, nearly half of all Cambodian refugees resettled in the United States since 1975 had moved at least once to another part of the country (Mortland and Ledgerwood 1987).

Cambodians came to Southern California for the mild weather which among other things, allowed them to grow familiar fruits, vegetables, and herbs year round. Los Angeles County was attractive because of the presence of an established Asian population and the local ports, which provided jobs and an abundance of Asian foods, goods, and services at lower prices than in other parts of the country. Additionally, easy access to the ocean and fishing provided a cheap source of food. Factors stimulating secondary migration to Long Beach specifically included the high concentration of Cambodia elite who were now in a position to construct essential Cambodian cultural institutions, such as a Buddhist temple, and provide jobs and housing to both extended family and those they sponsored. Cambodians were not accustomed to going to government agencies or strangers for aid and in fact worried over the obligations such activities would entail. Instead, Cambodians depended on family for emotional, physical, and economic support. Cambodians feel a strong moral obligation to offer assistance and protection to family which included the families of those related through marriage (Ebihara 1968).

Many opened small businesses, in particular the highly successful and well known doughnut shops, and called relatives in other parts of the country to come to work. Many bought apartments and homes which they rented to more than one family, thus making housing more affordable. As the elites engaged in these activities, they were also creating social connections with the larger American society which strengthened the community and benefited the newcomers.

Throughout the 1980s businesses catering to Cambodians, such as groceries, tailors, jewelers, and gift stores opened. Other businesses specifically serving Cambodians included video stores, real estate, insurance, pharmacies, a medical clinic and acupuncturist. At the same time, Cambodian entrepreneurs expanded into a broader service market which included auto repair, a few sandwich and yogurt shops, and doughnut shops. In 1982 the Khemara Buddhikaram (Khmer Buddhist Temple), which currently is located in west Long Beach on Willow Street, was founded in a home in nearby Lakewood (Haldane 1987). As many as eight more temples have been established in Long Beach since then, each serving a specific sub-group, such as the Lao-Khmer. The first Cambodian newspaper, *Nokor Thom*, began publication in 1984. In addition to reporting news from Cambodia and running serialized stories translated into Khmer from French and English, it also published drawings and cartoons, poetry, and personal ads from people looking for missing family and friends. Since then, at least four other newspapers have been started along with two magazines and a television and radio station.

Preservation and transmission of Khmer culture became a high priority among the members of the early community and was intensified as the population grew. The ruin of their country and deaths of so many people at the hands of the Khmer Rouge, followed by the Vietnamese invasion and occupation of Cambodia in late 1978, left most Cambodians convinced their beloved country had been lost and their culture destroyed (Coleman 1987). Classes for children and young adults in Khmer literacy and classical dance were formed. Over the years Khmer literacy classes have been offered by the two

Mutual Assistance Associations (MAAs), the Buddhist temples, and parents who taught their children at home. The first classical dance class began in 1983.

The two MAAs in Long Beach were the Cambodian Association of America (CAA) and United Cambodian Community (UCC). These institutions were instrumental in sponsoring and supporting cultural events in the community, bringing people together to participate in traditional celebrations, such as *chol chenam thmey* (Cambodian New Year held in mid-April), as well as landmark events for the community, such as the opening of a vocational training center. Their support of Cambodian fine arts was extensive. The Arts of Apsara Gallery on the first floor of the United Cambodian Community center contained Khmer paintings, sculpture, weavings, and batik from local artisans. The United Cambodian Community also supported a master musician, who conducted a children's musical troupe. After school programs in dance, music, art, and literacy provided children with an atmosphere of companionship and learning where they could escape the dangers on the streets, make friends, and share their experience as Cambodians in America.

Cambodians worked hard to adjust to life in America; to fit in and get jobs, but they faced many challenges. The number of Cambodians coming into Long Beach strained the public schools, health care facilities, and police services. Very few people in the City had any prior knowledge of Cambodia or Cambodian culture and no public institutions were fully prepared to deal with their needs. Very few Cambodians spoke English and no one in the Long Beach City government spoke Khmer. The number of Cambodians needing vocational and language training exceeded available programs. Such courses offered through Long Beach Community College were severely impacted. In the fall of 1981, for example, 275 Cambodians signed up for a vocational class that had only 30 available seats and over 850 applied for English classes (Trounson 1981). Another obstacle to getting the training they needed was the violence Cambodians experienced in Long Beach. The area surrounding Long Beach Community College at the time was unsafe. Some Cambodians were threatened and physically attacked by members of other ethnic groups as they walked to the campus and as a result many dropped out. Finally, among those who managed to get into classes and continue school, many reported they found learning difficult. People described feeling that they couldn't think or remember new information like they used to. As one man said, "My head is too full and confused. I don't have room for any more." Many people were overwhelmed by lingering symptoms of the trauma they had experienced, including sleeplessness, nightmares, panic, and headaches that many said caused them to drop out. The memories and physical pain from the "Pol Pot Time" was intensified by the violence and crime they faced in Long Beach, which increased personal fear and uncertainty. Such a situation is not conducive to problem solving, improving job skills, or overcoming language barriers and cultural conflicts.

The effect of the Cluster Project, which was meant to disperse refugees throughout the United States to prevent the development of ethnic communities, was beginning to be felt in Long Beach. Federal refugee funds meant to assist Cambodians in their adjustment to American society did not necessarily follow them when they moved from other parts of the United States to Long Beach. In fact, because of limits on federal reimbursements, federal monies for education, health, and social services were being cut, severely affecting the ability of the school district, the library system, the county health department, and Cambodian organizations to provide for the multiple needs of those arriving in the 1980s. Because of the great need and lack of funds, students in English as a second language classes were being pushed through as quickly as possible to make room for other refugees needing the same services.

Refugees arriving in the 1980s quickly learned that welfare benefits were not enough to survive in California. Unable to support themselves or their families on welfare benefits alone or find jobs with adequate wages, people turned to work in the informal economy. These jobs included supplying baked goods for local Cambodian restaurants, renting wedding goods and apparel, and wedding videography (Bunte and Joseph 1992:13).

Because it required few skills and could be done in the home, the most common cash job Cambodians sought was sewing or piecework. Women with school-age children engaged in piecework so they could raise children and still earn an income. In some cases, married couples and whole families engaged in sewing activities. A 45-year-old Cambodian woman's description of her experience with this kind of work makes evident how economic hardship and emotional stress weighed on the lives of refugees coming to the United States:

> I do everything at the same time. When my kids are home, I stop and start cooking for them. When I sew, I still try to watch them and tell them what to do. Sometimes when they are asleep, I sew till midnight. When I'm tired and I sit too long at the sewing machine, my blood pressure goes up and I have dizzy spells. I don't think I'll live a long life.

Although federal refugee grant monies were diminishing, the growing population of refugees with specialized needs gave Long Beach a competitive edge when applying for federal, state, and county grants. The MAAs, school district, library system, and health department successfully competed for grant money, bringing millions of dollars into the community, benefiting not only Cambodians, but also the greater City of Long Beach. Social services not only created jobs for Cambodians seeking entry into the middle class, but also helped to establish a topnotch health and social service network of city employees of various ethnic backgrounds. Although funds were earmarked for Cambodians, many services (even those offered through the Cambodian-run MAAs) were available to anyone in need. The increased funding brought into Long Beach because of the Cambodian presence helped many more Long Beach residents receive job training and job placement services.

The Community Continues to Change

All through the 1990s, political events in the homeland and locally challenged the Long Beach Cambodian community. Many community leaders went back to Cambodia to participate in the country's first election process in the early 1990s. The exodus of key leaders combined with a faltering social service network made the future uncertain for a community grappling with poverty. However, as the community marked its twenty-fifth anniversary in 2000, Cambodian business owners and a new generation of Cambodians who have grown up in the United States were stepping forward as leaders in the community. Despite generational differences and cultural expectations about deference to elders, older and younger community members are working together to form a shared vision of the Cambodian community in Long Beach. Groups, such as the Cambodian Coordinating Council and Cambodia Town, Inc. have worked together on political and humanitarian fund raising and have sponsored major community events, such as the annual Cambodian New Year celebration and the first ever, Cambodian New Year Parade, held in 2005. In a relatively short period of time they have turned around negative images from the past, bridged the generational gap, and developed a formidable political presence in the City.

The reopening of Cambodia has also brought benefits to both the community and City of Long Beach. As early as 1993, Long Beach and Phnom Penh, the capital of Cambodia, became Sister Cities. Economic and cultural exchange has grown as communication and travel have become less expensive and easier. A growing number of people, including leaders who left in the early 1990s, travel back and forth between the two countries frequently. Some have established homes in both countries, and live and work part time in both. Together with city officials and local universities (including CSU, Long Beach and CSU, Dominguez Hills) Cambodians have helped forge cooperative economic, educational, and cultural exchange.

Cambodians throughout the world know about Long Beach and many now come from other parts of the world to visit as tourists, or to live and work here. The population between 1990 and 2000 has stabilized with new immigration from Cambodia limited to family-sponsorship and reunification. As has been explained, it is not possible to say exactly how many Cambodians live within Long Beach, but most of the 43,887 Cambodians living in Los Angeles County and many of those in Orange County participate in and contribute to its sense of place.

Younger Cambodians growing up in other parts of the country now come to Long Beach to find their culture and learn about themselves; often attending local universities or working in the area.

Some have been to Cambodia, but found the social and economic expectations placed on them as Cambodians from America too great, or they found Cambodian society too foreign. Long Beach is more familiar; bi-cultural like themselves—it is a Cambodian community offering Cambodian culture in an American context. As a 26-year-old Cambodian transplant from New York notes, Long Beach is about having a place of one's own:

> I think, as a Cambodian American in Long Beach, it's home. We would like to think this is home. This is the largest. This is something you can be proud of. You want to be proud of Long Beach, of all the things we do. We have a city, where there are a lot of Cambodians. It's just something about your identity; Long Beach represents that. It's not the richest community, but it's a working class community. We get through even though we have been through so much. You don't want to take too much pride in it, because you know there's a lot of work to be done, but when you have something like Long Beach, whether you're in New York or Boston, you want to feel proud about Long Beach because you want that big community to reflect you too.

This commitment and sense of belonging expressed by the next generation may be the determining factor in whether the community will thrive into the future

Conclusion

Cambodians in Long Beach have created a unique place for rebuilding lives and cultural institutions, and revitalized a formerly depressed area of Long Beach. In a short period of time, a relatively small group of students, professionals, and evacuees built the foundation for a comprehensive infrastructure to meet the needs of a growing refugee population. Despite policies aimed at keeping Cambodians from forming a large ethnic community, Long Beach became the place of choice for thousands throughout the 1980s and 1990s. The city's geographic location and weather as well as the close proximity to the ocean and the port certainly contributed to the attractiveness of Long Beach to Cambodians. However, the concentration of elites and their successful model refugee programs and their re-creation of cultural institutions along with the responsiveness of local and state government agencies in hiring Cambodians to provide social services were major contributing factors to this community's growth. This combined with the desire of Cambodian refugees arriving after 1980 to reunite and recreate a kin system of support, made Long Beach the largest Cambodian community outside of Cambodia.

Endnotes

1. Khmer (pronounced *khmae*—the final 'r' is silent) is the term used to identify the dominant ethnic group living in the country of Cambodia. Cambodians use the term Khmer to refer to themselves (*menuh khmer*), their language (*piasaa khmer*) and their homeland (*srok khmer*). *Cambodia* is an Anglicized version of the formal Khmer term used to identify the country: *Kampuchea*. Cambodians in Long Beach use *Cambodia* and *Cambodian* when speaking to anyone outside the Cambodian community and use *Khmer* when speaking among themselves. Since many Cambodians in Long Beach may also be of Chinese, Thai, Lao, or Vietnamese heritage as well as Khmer, we refer to all nationals from Cambodia as Cambodian. Unless otherwise noted, we use Khmer to refer to the culture and language.

References

Bunte, Pamela an Rebecca Joseph. *The Cambodian community of Long Beach: An ethnographic analysis of factors leading to census undercount* (Center for Survey Methods Research, Bureau of the Census). Final report for Joint Statistical Agreement 89-31: Washington D.C., March 1992. Print.

Chan, Sucheng. *Survivors: Cambodian refugees in the United States*. Chicago: University of Illinois Press, 2004. Print.

Coleman, C. "Cambodians in the United States." In *The Cambodian Agony*, edited by David Ablin and Marlow Hood. Armonk: M.E. Sharpe, 1987. Print.

Ebihara, May M. "Svay: A Khmer village in Cambodia." Unpublished dissertation, Columbia University, New York, 1968.

Haldane, David. "Khmer backbone: Cambodian Buddhism thrives inside unobtrusive temple." In *Los Angeles Times*, pp. 1. (1987. Print. August 23). Print.

Mortland, Carol, and Judy Ledgerwood. "Secondary migration among Southeast Asian refugees in the United States." In *Urban Anthropology*, 16 (1987): 291-326. Print.

Roberts, Jason. "Cambodia, CA: Caught in a cultural tug-of-war." In *University Magazine*, 10:1 (1988): 7-9. Print.

Trounson, Rebecca. "8, 000 Refugees make Long Beach Cambodia capitol for U.S." In *Los Angeles Times*, H1. (1981, December 27). Print.

Section IV

Cambodian American
Personal Adjustments
and Societal Integration

CHAPTER 9

Cambodian Resettlement
in America

Carol A. Mortland

Movement to the United States

Before 1975, the few Cambodians living in the United States were
predominantly students and government or military personnel,
numbering less than several hundred (Coleman 1987). As the Amer-
ican-backed government of the Khmer Republic lost control and the
Khmer Rouge assumed power in Cambodia in 1975, thousands able
to do so fled Cambodia. Over the next decades, influenced by political and humanitarian considerations and international pressure, the
United States accepted a number of Cambodians as refugees[1] for
resettlement in America.

The **first wave** of refugees arrived between 1975 and 1977, and
consisted of approximately 6,000 men, women, and children.[2] The
majority of these were educated, middle class people from Cambodia's cities, and most had been connected to American businesses
and war efforts in Southeast Asia through the early 1970s. An additional 1,300 Cambodians arrived in 1978.

A **second wave** of Cambodian refugees arrived in the United States in 1979, when increased international concern over the refugee situation in Southeast Asia prompted the United States to increase admission quotas and ease selection criteria. This allowed entry to another 10,000 Cambodians who had fled Cambodia before the Khmer Rouge takeover but had lacked sufficient ties to America (Ebihara 1985). Unlike the first wave, this second wave consisted primarily of rural farmers, fishermen, and artisans. Because they lacked familiarity with urban life and had little education or English language experience, second wave Cambodians had more difficulty settling into urban life in America, finding employment and housing, or comprehending American school and social service networks.

The largest and most sustained migration of Cambodians to America was the **third wave** of refugees. Almost three times as many Cambodians arrived in 1980 as in 1979, and the numbers continued to expand through 1985. Although figures began to recede in 1986, the total number of Cambodian refugees accepted by the United States between 1980 and 1986 totaled 122,228 (Niedzwiecki and Duong 2004).

As selection criteria for Cambodians entering the country stiffened considerably, a **fourth wave** of Cambodian refugees consisted of rapidly falling numbers (Robinson and Wallenstein 1988). Between 1987 and 1993, 9,579 Cambodian refugees were resettled in the United States (Niedzwiecki and Duong 2004). The fourth wave consisted primarily of family members coming to join relatives, and many came as immigrants[3] rather than as refugees. In addition to the 9,579 refugees admitted, the United States also accepted close to 1,000 Cambodian immigrants from 1980 through 1985, then jumped to 9,103 immigrant acceptances in 1986. From 1987 through 1993, 27,867 more Cambodian immigrants were accepted for resettlement (Niedzwiecki and Duong 2004).

This immigrant wave continued over the next two decades. As immigrants, these family reunification cases became the responsibility of their families, while social services to all refugees declined dramatically. From 1994 through 2001, 12,146 immigrants and a mere 65 refugees were resettled from Cambodia (Niedzwiecki and Duong

2004). Between 1999 and 2008, 68 Cambodians were accepted as refugees and fewer than 400 were granted asylum (U.S. Department of Homeland Security 2010).[4]

In general, the first wave of resettled Cambodians were educated, urbanized, and middle class. The second wave, in contrast, were rural, less educated, and unfamiliar with urban or western concepts, amenities, and lifestyles. Due to circumstances they never anticipated, both the first and second waves of Cambodian refugees to the United States struggled with the consequences of living among strangers in an unfamiliar land facing uncertain futures. Despite their travails, however, most first and second wave refugees had not endured the terrors of the Khmer Rouge regime.

The third wave of refugees resembled the second wave in being primarily rural and with fewer resources of education, occupational skills, and urban contacts with which to meet the challenges of resettlement. In addition, they had endured nearly four years of Democratic Kampuchea rule, so terrible that most fled their homeland at the earliest opportunity. Their trauma was increased by lack of knowledge about what would happen to them, with their survival dependent on strangers.

Like the third wave, the fourth wave endured the Khmer Rouge, but had the advantage of overseas relatives and resources to help them re-establish families and lives in the homeland. In addition, they had the potential to rejoin their family members, which has made their eventual resettlement more bearable for many.

In addition to the traumatic loss of one's homeland, occupation, and daily life and relationships, and the difficulties of resettlement, discrimination, and hardship in a new country, refugees also faced other singular experiences. For most in the third wave, becoming a refugee involved flight from Cambodia, a life-threatening experience that remained a searing memory for most, one whose description, along with their experiences under the Khmer Rouge, took up a major portion of their subsequent personal narratives.

The additional experience of living in refugee camps influenced the lives of each wave of Cambodian refugees (The Committee for Co-ordination of Services to Displaced Persons in Thailand 1982). The first refugee wave were brought fairly rapidly to the United

States, and the vast majority spent at most some months in refugee camps knowing they were going to be resettled in the United States. The second and third waves, on the other hand, often experienced many months, even years, in refugee camps in Thailand before being accepted for resettlement. For much of that time, they had no idea where, or even if, they would be accepted for resettlement.

Resettlement American Style

While Americans envision the United States as a refuge for immigrants and a country built by immigrants who have contributed the best of themselves and their cultures, ambivalence and hostility toward specific groups of immigrants has been common throughout American history (Reimers 1998). Cambodians, whose existence was unknown to most Americans prior to their appearance in local neighborhoods, also experienced varied American reactions to their arrival. Their initial resettlement was strongly resisted and only overcome after extensive lobbying of Congress by the Citizens' Commission on Indochinese Refugees in 1978. Cambodians were then finally added to the list of Indochinese eligible for admissions under presidential parole authority (Loescher and Scanlan 1986).

Americans who greeted refugee newcomers with disdain, dislike, and discrimination viewed them as competitors for scarce resources, representatives of yet another poor, dark-skinned group of intruders—unfamiliar and thus suspicious. American hostility toward new arrivals was often accompanied by verbal or physical attacks on them or their possessions. Less threatening to specific individuals but damaging to their resettlement success were efforts to restrict them to certain neighborhoods, deny or reduce funding for services to assist them in resettlement efforts, and the encouragement of discriminatory housing, education, and employment opportunities and options.

In contrast, hundreds of thousands of Americans welcomed Cambodian refugees with open hands, and went to extraordinary degrees to help them in their resettlement. Individuals, churches, and a myriad array of small and large private and public organizations reacted to the arrival of Cambodians with compassion, resources, and services.

While differing in their reactions to Cambodians and their needs, both American disdainers and welcomers had similar conceptions of these newcomers. Many Americans saw Cambodians as lacking essential characteristics for success in America: English language, relevant job skills, good health, knowledge of urban and westernized life, and an awareness of American values. Even most Americans who welcomed Cambodians with compassion and assistance saw them as dark-skinned, foreign, poor, damaged, and psychologically ruined victims who needed to be taught how to live in America.

For centuries, the United States has treated immigrants as people whose difference is less an advantage than a handicap to their integration into American society. The American reception of Cambodians has mirrored that given to immigrants and others, such as Native Americans and African Americans, before. The 20th century effort to change Cambodians and other refugees into Americans, or as close as possible, reflected ideas expressed toward immigrants in the Americanization movement of the late 1880s and early 1900s, almost a century earlier.

Such efforts were based on American assumptions of superiority. A good educational background, economic success, speaking proper English, and displaying appropriate manners and behavior were seen primarily as the provenance of Americans of European descent, and that became the yardstick for measuring how much a foreign person needed to change, and how much he or she was changing. Most American immigrant education programs in both the 19th and the 20th centuries were designed to teach immigrants to abandon their supposedly inferior traditions, seen to encompass notions of hierarchy and privilege, laziness, lack of self-reliance, and dependency. Instead, immigrants were taught in orientation, English, and training classes that success came from holding attitudes, values, and behaviors thought to be uniquely American, such as hard work, self-sufficiency, and individuality. Practicing these traits would lead them to be free, democratic, and rational and thus better able to assimilate to American life (Tollefson 1989).

Although resettlement in the United States brought Cambodians escape from the powerlessness they had experienced in Khmer Rouge-ruled Cambodia and in the refugee camps, most moved into yet another structured setting controlled by other people's perceptions of them and goals for them. Despite Americans' expressed desire for refugees to become self-sufficient, successful, and democratically-minded, their lives were tightly controlled in refugee and border camps, and considerable control continued in the United States. Even before the arrival of Cambodian refugees to the United States, Americans began the attempt to transform them into American citizens. By 1980, processing centers had been established in Thailand, Indonesia, and The Philippines to provide up to six months of orientation, English language, and vocational training to refugees before sending them on to the United States (Mortland 1987).[5]

In addition to entering a strange world controlled in ways that worked against refugees developing skills and self-sufficiency, Americans disregarded Cambodians' central concerns. Americans were unaware of key social distinctions within Khmer society, and distinctions they themselves considered important were ignored. These included factors such as social and economic class, level of education, and residence that existed when they were in Cambodia. Villagers were lumped with Phnom Penh elite, farmers with bureaucrats, soldiers with schoolteachers. They were now recognized as "Southeast Asians," "Cambodians," and "refugees" by those around them. They were part of a larger Southeast Asian population, including Vietnamese, Lao, and a number of highland groups, such as the Hmong. Cambodian refugees and immigrants totaled a little under 200,000 of the million and a half refugees resettled between 1975 and 2002 (Niedzwiecki and Duong 2004).

Many refugee programs and Americans treated these refugees as a homogeneous group, with similar experiences and expectations. The Khmer were categorized with people whose language they did not understand, often surrounded by those they had always thought of as traditional enemies. In addition, social services often encompassed refugee and immigrant clients from elsewhere in the world. This caused confusion and hardship for both Americans and refugees but led also to unique personal and working contacts for some Cambodians, as their world was enlarged to include both Americans and other newcomers.

When Americans *did* recognize Cambodians as a distinct group, they noted that Cambodians had less knowledge than other immigrant, even Southeast Asian refugee groups. Virtually every popular and scholarly article on Cambodians emphasized their problems, underscoring first the enormity of the horrors they had experienced during the Khmer Rouge years, the changes they endured after resettlement, and the scars they bore from anguish, malnutrition, overwork, terror, and loss. Since Americans saw Cambodian arrivals as wounded in body and mind, and lacking language, work skills, or appropriate attitudes, they set about helping Cambodians gain this knowledge through individual assistance and instruction, using existing language, orientation, and job skills classes, and creating courses designed for refugees.

Most Cambodian families came to America with a suitcase or box of belongings and nothing else—no money and few contacts. They needed food, housing, clothing, and health care, and most of these resources were supplied by Americans. American sponsors and volunteers devoted literally millions of unpaid hours assisting Cambodians in a myriad of tasks. The American government, through resettlement and social service agencies, spent hundreds of millions of dollars on the resettlement of Cambodians, attempting to teach them not only English and employment skills but American values and behavior.

One primary concern of the American refugee program was that refugees become economically self-sufficient as quickly as possible after arrival (Refugee Act of 1980). The Office of Refugee Resettlement (1994) concluded that English language ability and job skills appropriate to the American workplace were the pre-eminent factors influencing Cambodians' employability. In addition, the level of education received in Cambodia, familiarity with Western culture, an urban background, literacy, and youth were thought to contribute to employability in America. In an effort to create self-sufficient Cambodians as quickly as possible, some states (California, New York, Washington) chose to spend resources on providing economic support while refugees attended English language, cultural orientation, and vocational training classes.

The quality and duration of programs and eligibility requirements for students varied greatly across the country. In some locales, Cambodians were encouraged to study for as long as two years at government expense, then to continue their education at already-established institutions. Only after extensive training were they expected to seek full-time employment (Bach 1988). In other states (Texas, Louisiana), Cambodians were required to obtain employment as quickly as possible, studying English in their free hours. Sponsor expectations and connections, local job opportunities, and the national economic situation at the time of arrival also affected the rate and type of employment accessed by Cambodians. As the 1980s passed and the number of Cambodian arrivals increased, refugee resettlement programs shifted toward early employment above all else.

In the 1990s, the federal government and resettlement programs continued this emphasis on early employment for refugee and immigrant arrivals (Office of Refugee Resettlement 1994). Federally-funded English language courses, vocational training, and employment skills classes were drastically reduced, and those that remained were usually local creations, often maintained by volunteers. Younger Cambodians learned English in the public schools, speaking without accent and often at the expense of Cambodian language acquisition. Cambodians whose employment depended on English and improving language skills continued their efforts to learn English, while many of those employed in jobs where English was less necessary (working under a fellow Cambodian boss, in an ethnic store, or picking mushrooms or fruit) often abandoned efforts to learn the new language. Some Cambodians concentrated on gaining additional education or settled into professional jobs, while most worked at entry-level and manual jobs.

Another major concern of the American government and the refugee program was refugee impact on local communities, resources, and services. Aware of hostility toward Cambodian newcomers, policy-makers and resettlement agencies were concerned with lessening the impact of Cambodians and other refugees on

Americans (Refugee Act of 1980). In addition to efforts to promote Cambodian assimilation into American communities through language, vocational, and cultural orientation courses, efforts were made to place Khmer in areas where they would "blend" into surrounding communities. Khmer were thus "scattered" throughout the United States and initially placed with American sponsors because of the scarcity of Cambodians living in America (Mortland and Ledgerwood 1987). Policy-makers tried to prevent Cambodians from settling into ethnic enclaves, hoping thus to reduce refugee visibility, increase their economic prospects, and decrease refugee costs to American taxpayers.

Cambodians, however, did not remain dispersed, and many began a secondary migration to be with one another, for better jobs, compatible weather, or to escape unpleasant neighbors. The immediate result of their movement was the rapid creation of Cambodian enclaves in several cities (Mortland and Ledgerwood 1987). As Cambodians increasingly sponsored their relatives and fellow Cambodians, Cambodian communities continued to concentrate in particular areas, such as Long Beach, Seattle, and Philadelphia.

Policy-makers responded by clustering Khmer arrivals in twelve cities: Atlanta, Boston, Chicago, Cincinnati, Columbus, Dallas, Houston, Jacksonville, New York City, Phoenix, Richmond, and Rochester (Refugee Resource Center 1982). The program had mixed results (Bruno 1984). Some Cambodians received insufficient assistance, while others were unhappy to be deliberately placed far from family members or friends, or felt coerced into particular options by program requirements and staff. In response, many moved to new locations despite pressure not to do so.

By the early 1990s, refugee resettlement policy-makers and service providers became increasingly aware that Cambodians were continuing to migrate to join one another and to seek better employment and opportunities. The Office of Refugee Resettlement in the Department of Health and Human Services funded the research and publication of a report entitled "Profiles of Some Good Places for Cambodians to live in the United States" (North and Nim Sok 1989). The report describes 22 communities, where there were available jobs, generally self-sufficient Cambodian residents, a moderate-sized Khmer community, and minimum crime problems. The presence of a Cambodian enclave with uniquely Khmer services, such as Buddhist temples, self-help organizations, and cultural and language preservation groups, was one of the attractions of these "good places for Cambodians to live." Included were Mobile Bay, Phoenix, Denver, Des Moines, and Portland. Although American officials saw some value in ethnic community resources, they continued to worry about Cambodian "impact."

Americans continued to worry about the health of Cambodians. The physical and mental consequences of the Khmer Rouge years were enormous, especially for first-generation immigrants, and included premature death, illness, and depression (Kulig 1991, Kinzie 1987, Eisenbruch 1991). Cambodians came to America with serious medical conditions, such as tuberculosis, complications from malnutrition, and injury. Older women, especially, exhibited multiple problems, such as headaches, dizziness, confusion, even blindness. In the 21st century, Cambodians are suffering premature death from a variety of complaints stemming from the Khmer Rouge years and the stresses of resettlement.

As the years have passed and decreasing numbers of Cambodians have come to the United States, government funding has declined dramatically and programs designed specifically for refugees have disappeared. The recession of 2008 put a further dent in services available for Cambodians and, by 2010, few resources and services exist specifically for Cambodians. Cambodians have been left increasingly to their own devices for survival and educational, occupational, and financial advancement, or seek assistance as members of the largest community. Thus, they receive educational support, occupational training, health care, or public assistance as Americans or legal residents, not as Cambodian refugees.

Resettlement Cambodian Style

Cambodians viewed resettlement differently than did Americans, not surprising in view of the losses, challenges, and difficulties it presented them (Nguyen-Hong-Nhiem and Halpern 1989, Welaratna 1993). Cambodians did not see themselves as part of migration waves.

Rather, they saw themselves as having come when they were adults or children, and contrasted Cambodians who had experienced the Khmer Rouge terrors from those who had not. They distinguished those who arrived in the United States in 1975 from those who had escaped Cambodia and spent time in refugee camps, and both groups from those who arrived in the following decades to join relatives.

Just as Americans viewed Cambodian refugees with ambiguity, so Cambodians had conflicting views of Americans. Cambodians varied in the degree of gratitude, regard, resentment, and anger they held toward Americans. Most Cambodians were grateful for the assistance Americans gave them, especially when Americans gave them what Cambodians themselves thought they needed. While Cambodian resettlement concerns have not always coincided with Americans' concerns for them, Cambodians frequently commented on the enormous efforts American organizations and individuals have made on their behalf. Even decades later, Cambodians talked of their gratitude to American sponsors, teachers, and neighbors who had assisted them through the years.

But as the years passed and their awareness of American attitudes of superiority and condescension grew, Cambodians became increasingly resentful of American ideas and behavior, particularly as it pertained to Cambodians. In contrast to Americans who saw Cambodians as needy victims requiring considerable assistance to learn how to live in America, most Cambodian refugees did not think they needed transformation at the hands of Americans, at least not to the extent Americans thought they required. Some Americans agreed with them, and questioned the transformation efforts that began in the refugee camps and processing centers that were thought to be valuable in helping refugees in their resettlement (Tollefson 1989, Mortland 1987).

Resettlement in the United States meant for many Cambodians the end of powerlessness, the beginning of a life with economic promise and hope. They were freed of the horrors that had occurred in their homeland and the years they had been trapped in refugee camps. Cambodians' flight and refugee camp stories reveal a sense of the powerlessness they felt in the camps. Cambodians remember their flight from Cambodia as a specific, separating event. A dangerous, harrowing, and frightening event, yes, but Cambodians remember themselves as active and capable during their flight. They were sick, tired, and afraid, but they made decisions, were at least somewhat in control of their destiny, and were daring, even heroic. Refugee camp stories, in contrast, are condensed; Years are described in a sentence or two. Camp life is remembered as a blur, a lengthy span of relative nonevents. Life in the camps—its beginning, endurance, and ending—was controlled by others, and the passivity of the Khmer made them anything but heroic in their own eyes. To remember that time is to recall their powerlessness.

After resettlement, although acutely aware of how much they had to learn in order to survive in America, most Cambodians were willing and anxious to take control over their lives. While Americans viewed resettlement as assimilation to American behavior and ideas and judged it in terms of success and failure, Cambodians saw resettlement as survival. For most Khmer, resettlement in America was initially a dream come true. For most, over time, the dream changed as awareness of the permanency of their losses and the strangeness of America gradually settled over them. The ability to support themselves in America brought satisfaction, as it had before in Cambodia, yet their inability to regain what they had lost has brought them great sadness. All were occupied with the daily necessities of living with strangeness.

Much of what Americans want to change about Cambodians is what Cambodians value most. Even when Cambodians themselves want the change, they often want it differently than do Americans. Language is a case in point. Most Cambodians knew they had learn English, and they made valiant efforts to do so despite the competing obligations of work and school, the unfamiliarity of many with being students, and the difficulty of learning a language so different from their own. Cambodians also wanted to retain their own language, and to have their children learn it. Cambodians were concerned that their children would not learn their own language, especially how to read and write. Some of their earliest efforts went to setting up language classes, and a major disappointment has been that most children of Cambodian-speaking parents can understand some Cambodian, but are hesitant to speak it. Few know how to read and write Cambodian, and most parents have become reconciled to the fact that their children are not interested in retaining their parents' native tongue.

The greatest concern of resettled Cambodians was to find a way to survive in America. Cambodians were active participants in utilizing all the resources of their environment, just as villagers in rural Cambodia had long drawn their income from a mix of farming and fishing, and townspeople supplemented their income with part-time businesses or jobs. Realizing that employment was the swiftest and most respectable way in America to obtain resources, Cambodians sought employment at the highest levels of income and prestige available to them. Many studied at night to enhance their language and job skills. Since many Khmer were limited to entry-level positions by rudimentary English and few job skills suitable for the American workplace, Cambodians increased their household income by pooling resources, working several jobs, having multiple job holders in the household, and using family members' eligibility for social services when appropriate.

Many Cambodians sought human service employment in the United States, such as nursing (Welaratna 1993), and others able to go to school trained in areas they felt were most likely to result in jobs, such as business, computer-related technologies, and electronics. The dream of many was to begin their own business, and some have done so, purchasing donut shops (Mydans 1995), laundries, grocery stores, and restaurants. Over time, like immigrants before them, increasing numbers of resettled Cambodians obtained employment and became economically self-sufficient (Office of Refugee Resettlement 1994). Childcare, cooking, and household chores were usually performed by the family member least able to become employed, usually because of age, physical or mental difficulties, or lack of English language and relevant job skills.

Many educated and urbanized resettled Cambodians experienced a decline in socioeconomic status after resettlement, and most never regained the status and wealth they enjoyed in Cambodia. In contrast, American jobs have brought knowledge, possessions, and independence to former peasants that would have been inconceivable for them in Cambodia. Women, too, have benefited from expanded opportunities in education and employment, sometimes becoming more successful than their menfolk in obtaining employment (Ui 1991). The relative advancement of family members has had a great deal to do with their ability to quickly acquire English language and vocational skills. Cambodian women were more eager to seize these opportunities than men were to see them do so, for such employment had a tendency to shift the traditional balance of power away from men. Because of the high percentage of widows, thus female-headed households, among resettled Cambodians, employment was often a necessity rather than an option.

In addition to employment, Cambodians utilized American services, both as provided and instructed by Americans and in ways unique to refugee and immigrant communities. Rasbridge and Marcucci (1992) described unique techniques Cambodians in Dallas used to access public resources. Cambodians took advantage of other resources wherever available, often advising startled American neighbors on the best places to find little-known sales, overstocks, giveaways, and good fishing spots. Some utilized public services in unorthodox ways, usually by receiving benefits for which they were not eligible or working for cash (so that neither employer or employees had to pay taxes), always with an eye to maximizing resources and future opportunities. Some Khmer justified their actions by saying they were just doing what Americans do. Others suggested that what they were doing seemed less criminal than what Americans were doing: drugs, crime, and theft. Some claimed that Americans owed them because of the tragedies they had endured and because of America's previous involvement in Cambodia.

Another major concern of Cambodians was the re-establishment of traditional social relationships among themselves. From their initial arrival, they expended considerable effort on this. They used the resources they obtained in America, such as money, jobs, and technology, to retain and re-establish contact with other Cambodians (Hopkins 1992). They used cars, telephones, and electronic devices to communicate with family and friends within their own town, and DVDs, cassettes and videotapes to correspond with relatives throughout the United States, in Cambodia, and in other resettlement countries.

Cambodians attempted to contact, then often joined relatives, fellow villagers, and friends, both from Cambodia and the refugee camps, as soon as possible after arrival in the United States. Seeing secondary migration as a solution rather than a problem, as Americans saw it, Cambodians often moved from their initial placement site in the United States to rejoin extended family members. They sought to re-assemble their families, often out of the fragments left by Khmer Rouge atrocities and resettlement procedures that separated nuclear from extended families. By living near one another in tenements or apartment complexes, or driving several hours on weekends to join countrymen, Cambodians were able to share information and resources.

Cambodians occasionally moved in large groups. Smith (1989) tells of a migration of 400 Khmer who moved from Chicago to Michigan, giving as their reason for doing so Michigan's lower crime rate and more rural aspect. Their fishing and gardening activities in Madison, combined with specific economic strategies and cultural practices, allowed the Khmer to reproduce many aspects of traditional Cambodian life. Numerous other migrations occurred, for example, as Cambodian Cham Muslims left initial placement sites to settle together in Olympia and Seattle in the early 1980s (Killen and Silk. 2004), or when Cambodians left California after the 1989 San Francisco Bay area earthquake, fearing another frightening event.

Cambodians have joined other Cambodians not only in a geographical sense but in a community sense. Across the country and over time, many Cambodian adults have effectively retired into their ethnic communities, restricting their contacts primarily to other Cambodians and having little to do with the larger surrounding community. Although such residence patterns result in considerable conflict with other Cambodians, strife among one's own people is preferable for many Khmer than being alone among strangers. Avoiding such conflict, however, is one reason some Cambodians move away from other Cambodians, separating themselves by residence while often continuing to observe Cambodian traditions of language, food, culture, entertainment, and religion.

Cambodians also utilized a strategy of restoring traditional Khmer behavior and order among themselves. Even before the Khmer Rouge period, Cambodians had suffered a tremendous loss of order, and even more so during it and following their escape to Thailand. Their sense of lost order continued after resettlement, replaced by American concepts of what is proper and right. While Americans attempted to convert Cambodians to an American sense of order, Cambodians eagerly attempted to re-create proper Cambodian etiquette based on traditional Khmer hierarchical relationships. Sharp distinctions in class and behavior have continued throughout Cambodian history, and remain evident among Cambodians in America. Cambodians emphasize that inferiors must obey superiors: thus, children must obey their parents; wives, their husbands; youth, their elders; and students, their teachers. Cambodians have struggled especially to keep their women virtuous and their daughters pure, even to the extent of marrying them at even younger ages than in Cambodia (Ledgerwood 1990a). What Chandler (1982) says of the 19th century is true for the 20th: When Cambodians live in their proper places, they experience more balance, safety, and Cambodian identity than when they do not.

The tendency of the Khmer people toward extravagant deference to superiors is backed by a religious tradition that relates position to meritorious behavior, with individuals deserving their place in life. Deference to superiors has also come from a social structure that overwhelmingly favors those at the top with wealth and strength. Ordinary Cambodians have little choice but to defer. In Cambodia, this tendency has contributed to what Chandler (1991) has called "Cambodia's tragedy." The best most Cambodians could do was to align themselves with a patron of higher social and economic standing, seeking patron protection in exchange for client loyalty and labor.

Cambodians also re-established patron-client ties in America (Mortland and Ledgerwood 1988). For resettled Cambodians, a patron could be one of the best hedges against a repeat of past experiences. Thus, in traditional Khmer fashion, they cultivated patrons from among more powerful and resourceful Cambodians and Americans. These patrons provided resources, services, and information desired by Cambodians in exchange for loyalty and service. Cambodian patrons gained additional access to resources by acquiring official recognition as leaders of their community, forming organizations to receive additional benefits that were then funneled to both patrons and followers (Mortland 1993). The federal government continued to fund these Cambodian self-help organizations for some years (Office of Refugee Resettlement 1994) as they engaged in a number of different activities. Cambodian self-help groups have provided social services such as counseling, substance abuse treatment, job placement, and vocational training; and cultural preservation, including teaching the Khmer language, forming dance troops or orchestras, and encouraging traditional crafts.

Traditional Khmer concepts of leaders' rights, followers' obligations, and patronage continue to shape the attitudes and activity of many Cambodians in the United States, although many are establishing American ideas of equality and independence as goals of their family. Some have escaped their traditional ties to patrons in order to control their own and their children's lives in the light of new options and constrains existing in America. Many sought social mobility through education and occupation, and escape from the control of local or religious leaders. As time has passed, an increasing number of Cambodians, especially the younger generation, have escaped or never experienced the control of traditional patrons.

After resettlement, Cambodians said often that if they lost their culture, they would lose their identity as Cambodians (Ngor Haing 1987, Ebihara, Mortland, and Ledgerwood 1994), and they exhibited vital interest in preserving their culture for themselves and their children. They were passionate in their efforts to re-establish their religion, considering the practice of Khmer Buddhism vital to the preservation of their culture. As Cambodians frequently said, "To be Khmer is to be Buddhist." Almost immediately after arrival in the United States, the Khmer sought ways to observe religious rituals, one of their first desires being to conduct rituals for dead family members which they had been prevented from doing during the Khmer Rouge regime.

Khmer religion consists of Buddhist rituals which require monks and a temple at which they reside. Cambodians soon set up temples in apartments, then houses and, after some years, a number of communities began constructing temple buildings. Khmer served as sponsors for monks to come to America from the Thai refugee camps, borrowed or purchased religious paraphernalia from other Buddhist countries, and held their rituals with whatever leadership was available. Today, the majority of monks came from Cambodia, and religious traditions, literature, and items pass frequently between the old and new lands.

Khmer religious thought also entails belief in spirits. Cambodians in America have devoted considerable effort to propitiating a variety of spirits, including territorial and ancestor spirits, calling on them to prevent misfortune, especially illness, and to assist in bringing them fortune and happiness. These rituals may be conducted privately in one's own home, at a public gathering, or at the temple. While many Cambodians have reduced their participation in Buddhist temple activities and spirit rites in the United States, primarily because of time and work constraints, most continue to hold to the traditional Buddhist and folk beliefs they were taught as children.

Some Cambodians conceal these beliefs by attendance at Christian churches or expressions of disbelief, but the majority of resettled Cambodians do not abandon their traditional ideas. Despite considerable obstacles—hostile American neighbors, lack of men wishing to go into the monkhood, conflict among temple participants over property ownership, and competing American religions, schedules, and interests, most Cambodians continue to practice their religion at home and at over 80 temples across the country. A major complaint by both religious leaders and followers is that Cambodian Americans, particularly the youth, do not have the time to devote to learning their traditional religious knowledge and chants.

Most Cambodians do not view successful survival in the United States and the preservation of Khmer culture as inherently opposites. Cambodians have utilized the technology of America in their efforts to preserve traditional Khmer culture. They utilized their telephones, computers, DVDs, cassettes, and vehicles, among other devices, to keep in contact with nearby temples and Cambodian stores, and to listen to the music, plays, and films of their homeland made originally in Hong Kong and California and then in numerous locations, including Cambodia. They have used whatever resources were at hand, including funding from Americans, to re-form dance troops and musical orchestras (Sam 1994, Ung 1988). College students formed discussion groups to discuss their own experiences and Cambodian politics and religion. Despite the attraction of American pop culture for most young Cambodian Americans, many are also fond of traditional Khmer food and music.

Cambodians also have been concerned about their families (Chan 2004). Americans worried primarily about increasing intergenerational conflict, domestic violence, and wayward youth among Cambodian families (Rumbaut 1995), while Cambodians—many also with the same concerns—also lamented the passing of Khmer social graces, knowledge, and custom. A gulf developed between Khmer who came to the United States as adults and will never be "Americans" by culture, and their children who tried desperately to be American. This gap continues to numerous families, between parents who continue to center their lives on Khmer tradition and their children who "just want to fit in" with their American peers.

Both Americans and Cambodians worry that Khmer children will follow less desirable models of American youth: Dropping out of school, joining gangs, using drugs. American social service programs concentrate on helping Cambodian young people stay in school, providing counseling for families suffering from generational conflict, and facilitating after-school tutoring and recreational programs. Cambodian parents concentrate instead on trying to instill Cambodian values in their children: Teaching them proper Cambodian behavior, encouraging their attendance at Cambodian Buddhist events, and cautioning them constantly about the dangers of American ways (Ledgerwood 1990a; Kulig 1991).

The loss of their children is an additional blow to Cambodians who worried that, among other things, their children would not care for them as they aged. Cambodian parents learned what immigrant parents before realized: That their children are concerned with the new land and ways, seldom the old (Steinberg 1989). While their parents struggled to retain their traditions, their children struggled to learn the new country. Since language learning ability is inversely related to age, children found it much easier than their parents to learn English and American culture. Cambodian American children, like the children of immigrants before them, experienced living in two worlds. Despite their wishes to fit in as young Americans and to please their parents, many have felt as though they belong to neither culture.

Cambodians have continued to see health as a major problem for them, due particularly to their experiences under the Khmer Rouge. Not only have they had to deal with the physical consequences of starvation, torture, and inhumane living conditions, they have struggled with trying to comprehend what happened to them and their country. Most have sought answers in their traditional religious ideas, while some have looked at alternate explanations, such as those provided by Christianity. For most, however, the enormity of the tragedies they and their parents experienced and the migration they endured have brought questions that continue to plague them: How could this have happened? Did they do something to cause what occurred to them?

Cambodian notions of being "refugees" has changed with time. Some began to find refugee status offensive, a way for Americans to pity Cambodians without listening to them, and to decide what was best for them without consulting them. Some Khmer have moved reluctantly or proudly through immigrant status, becoming permanent residents or American citizens; others are self-proclaimed "people without a country." Some Cambodians state they will always be refugees because the Khmer Rouge forced them from their land, and they do not "fit in" with Americans. Many work actively to achieve economic and social standing in America as Cambodian Americans, while others continue their dependency on social services and define themselves as refugee victims. The children and grandchildren of Cambodians who were resettled as adults may deal less with being Cambodian Americans or refugee descendants than with being a minority. For many young Cambodians, daily life reflects a migration between American life in public and Cambodian practices in private at home.

Cambodian and American ideas of "Americanness" and "Khmerness" vary. Cambodians vacillate between what they perceive to be American and what they consider to be Cambodian, utilizing whichever fits their needs at the moment. In this way, they create Cambodian responses to American realities, and reinvent their Cambodian past. Cambodians resettled as adults are aided in their recreation of identity by contrasting themselves and a "mythic" Cambodian past to

Americans and America. As their leaders in Cambodia did before them (Chandler 1990), Khmer Americans hark back to the splendors of Angkor in establishing and re-establishing their identity as Cambodians. Thus, they can speak of life as it was, as it should be, stating indirectly what is difficult to state directly: that a life without Cambodianness is not life, and that life in America is only bearable for Cambodians if they remain faithful to their cultural traditions.

Many Cambodian youth today, both in Cambodia and in the United States, are surprisingly ignorant of their parents' experiences or Cambodia's history (Münyas 2008). Some acknowledge an unwillingness to hear of the horrors of Khmer Rouge that occurred to their own family members, others pour all their efforts into "being" American, while others describe their parents' reluctance to inflict their stories and pain on their children. As a consequence, children do not comprehend the scope of their parents' loss and travail, the depth of their efforts to save themselves and their children, nor the tragedy of the Khmer Rouge. Many youth, in fact, claim the Khmer Rouge could not have been as bad as many say, and are themselves involved in efforts to excuse those who murdered and abused their own relatives. Increasing efforts are being made by both Cambodian leaders and Americans to educate Cambodian Americans about the tragedies and triumphs of their own people and the legacy to which they are heir.

A surprising number of Cambodians have returned permanently or semi-permanently to Cambodia. Many have built homes for family members still residing in Cambodia, established businesses for family members, and rebuilt temples and schools. Others have spent extended periods of time back in the homeland, engaged in business, humanitarian work, or religious activities. A number of Cambodians live part-time in Cambodia and part-time in America, saying they cannot return permanently to Cambodia because their children are now Americans. Some younger Cambodian Americans have found wives in Cambodia, and returned with them to America. Many Cambodians, primarily those who came to America as children, say they feel an obligation to return to Cambodia, at least for a time, to "pay back" their fortune in having escaped to the United States and the poverty that persists in their homeland.

In addition, since 2001 a distressing number of Cambodians have been deported back to Cambodia after being convicted of crimes in the United States (Hing 2005). The majority of these are young men who were raised in low-income, low-opportunity urban areas and drawn to gangs and illegal activities. Many never lived in Cambodia, and no longer speak Cambodian yet they are now resigned to a permanent life in a country completely foreign to them.

Conclusion

What is amazing in talking with Americans and Cambodians for three decades about their experiences of Khmer resettlement is the astonishingly different experiences people have who are in close, dependent, dramatic, and often intimate relationships with one another. Many Americans cite a multitude of reasons to explain why many Cambodians have been unsuccessful in adjusting to America: their rural backgrounds, unfamiliarity with western ways, lack of education or literacy in their own language, lack of English, and lack of employable skills in the American workplace at the time of resettlement, and the physical and mental scars of the Khmer Rouge years.

Cambodians, on the other hand, and a number of observers claim that Cambodians have been successfully adjusting to life in the United States over the past decades. Welaratna (1993) correctly notes that Cambodians are seeking to ensure the economic and emotional welfare of their families in ways that differ from Americans, placing family and social interaction above individual advancement. Those Cambodians who conclude that many of their fellow countrymen have not been successful in adjusting to America are judging Khmer success by American, rather than Cambodian, goals.

Because of their horrendous experiences under the Khmer Rouge and the traumatic resettlement they subsequently experienced, Cambodians have been forced to examine themselves and their culture, to reflect on ultimate questions, and on what is of highest priority to them (Mortland 1994). Their conclusions can be read in their strategies for living in America. These have included vigorously seizing opportunities for employment and education, utilizing traditional relationships such as family and patronage to obtain resources and services, and redefining proper behavior for Cambodians who must live in very different circumstances. In addition, they have re-established places of worship and re-asserted the value of their traditional culture and themselves as Cambodians, sought relationships with Americans and neighbors, and re-established contacts and lives in both Cambodia and the United States.

Although their worldview is now much broader than when in Cambodia, first-generation Cambodians continue to view reality in the United States through a traditional prism, through the meanings and relationships of their homeland. As American immigrants before them, they will always do so. Their children and grandchildren, however, have shifted perspective and now utilize a range of perspectives from which to view their parents' homeland, their parents' experiences, and their own experiences and future in America. Although Khmer and Khmer ways continue to affect the lives of second and third generation Cambodian Americans, their sights are increasingly turned to American culture.

Endnotes

Thanks to Jonathan H. X. Lee for including me in this project. My gratitude goes to colleagues Korath Norin, Judy Ledgerwood, and The Venerable Lok Ta Chanmony. Thanks also to Minh, Chileng, Pheng, Nghim, Paul, Phal, Bonnary, and Bunnararak, who I watched grow up in the confusion and joy of being both Cambodian and American; to my Cambodian sisters, Sithouk, Sithol, and Setha; and always to Jo and Rene.

1. A refugee is defined by the U.S. Immigration and Nationality Act as any person who is outside his or her country of nationality or with no nationality who is unable or unwilling to return to, and is unable or unwilling to avail himself or herself of the protection of that country because of persecution or a well-founded fear of persecution on account of race, religion, nationality, membership in a particular social group, or political opinion.

2. Resettlement statistics come from a variety of sources and are not always consistent with one another, depending on whether calendar or fiscal years were used in the counting and which department was responsible for reporting. Resettlement figures for 1975 through 1978 come from Gordon (1984); from 1979 and 1980 from the Office of Refugee

Resettlement, U.S. Department of Health and Human Services (Refugee Reports 1988); and for 1981 through 2004 from the Southeast Asian Resource Action Center (SEARAC) (Niedzwiecki and Duong 2004).

3. An immigrant is defined as a person who comes to a country in which he or she was not born in order to settle there.

4. An asylee is a person in the United States who is unable or unwilling to return to his or her country of nationality, or to seek the protection of that country because of persecution or a well-founded fear of persecution.

5. A refugee camp is a shelter for persons displaced by war or political oppression or for religious beliefs. Hundreds of thousands of Cambodian refugees passed through the refugee and border camps of Thailand. Some proceeded to the United States and several dozen other countries, some settled permanently in Thailand, and a great majority were eventually repatriated back to Cambodia (U.S. Committee for Refugees. 1998). Processing centers were established to hold refugees while they attended orientation, cultural skills, and English language classes before resettlement in the United States. They were intended to provide refugees with knowledge that would assist them in resettlement at a financial cost less than would have been possible in the United States. Border camps were not recognized as refugee camps: the UNHCR did not manage them or have an official connection with them. There were dozens of border camps along the Thai/Cambodian border.

References

Bach, Robert L. "State Intervention in Southeast Asian Refugee Resettlement in the United States." *Journal of Refugee Studies* 1.1(1988):38-56. Print.

Bruno, Ellen. *Acculturation Difficulties of the Khmer in New York City*. New York: The Cambodian Women's Program, American Friends Service Committee, 1984. Print.

Chan, Sachem. *Survivors: Cambodian Refugees in the United States*. Urbana: University of Illinois Press, 2004. Print.

Chandler, David P. "Songs at the Edge of the Forest: Perceptions of Order in Three Cambodian Texts." In *Moral Order and the Question of Change: Essays on Southeast Asian Thought*, edited by D.K. Wyatt and A. Woodside. New Haven: Yale University Southeast Asian Studies Monograph Series 24, 1982. Print.

Chandler, David P."Reflections on Cambodian History. Cambodia 1990." *Cultural Survival Quarterly* 14.3 (1990):16-19. Print.

Chandler, David P. *The Tragedy of Cambodian History. Politics, War, and Revolution since 1945.* New Haven: Yale University Press, 1991. Print.

Chileng, Pa and Mortland, Carol A. *Escaping the Khmer Rouge. A Cambodian Memoir.* Jefferson: McFarland & Company, 2007. Print.

Coleman, C.M. "Cambodians in the United States." In *The Cambodian Agony*, edited by David A. Ablin and Marlowe Hoods, Armonk: M.E. Sharpe, 1987. Print.

Committee for Co-ordination of Services to Displaced Persons in Thailand, The. *The CCSDPT Handbook. Refugee Services in Thailand.* Bangkok, Thailand: du Maurier Associates International Publication, 1982. Print.

Ebihara, May M. "Khmer." In *Refugees in the United States. A Reference Handbook,* edited by David W. Haines, Westport: Greenwood Press, 1985. Print.

Ebihara, May M., Carol A. Mortland, and Judy Ledgerwood. *Cambodian Culture since 1975: Homeland and Exile.* Ithaca: Cornell University Press, 1994. Print.

Eisenbruch, Maurice. "From Post-traumatic Stress Disorder to Cultural Bereavement: Diagnosis of Southeast Asian Refugees." *Social Science and Medicine* 33.6 (1991): 673-680. Print.

Hing, Bill O. "Detention to Deportation: Rethinking the Removal of Cambodian Refugees." *University of California Davis Law Review.* 2005. 38:891. Print.

Hopkins, Mary Carol. "Becoming Bicultural: Preserving Culture through Adaptation." In *Selected Papers on Refugee Issues*, edited by Pamela A. DeVoe. Arlington: American Anthropological Association, 1992. Print.

Killen, Patricia and Mark Silk. *Religion and Public Life in the Pacific Northwest: The None Zone.* Walnut Creek: Rowman Altamira, 2004. Print.

Kinzie, David. "The 'Concentration Camp Syndrome' among Cambodian Refugees." In *The Cambodian Agony*, edited by David. Ablin and Marlowe Hood. New York: M.E. Sharpe, 1987. Print.

Kulig, Judith. "Role, Status Changes and Family Planning Use among Cambodian Refugee Women." Unpublished dissertation. University of California, San Francisco, 1991. Print.

Ledgerwood, Judy. *Changing Khmer Conceptions of Gender: Women, Stories, and the Social Order.* Unpublished dissertation. Cornell University, 1990.

Loescher, Gil and John A. Scanlan. *Calculated Kindness: Refugees and America's Half-open Door, 1945 to the Present.* New York: Free Press. 1986. Print.

Mortland, Carol A. "Transforming Refugees in Refugee Camps." In *Urban Anthropology* 16.3-4 (1987): 375-404. Print.

Mortland, Carol A. "Patron-Client Relations and the Evolution of Mutual Assistance Associations." In *Refugee Empowerment and Organizational*

Change. A Systems Perspective, edited by Peter W. Van Arsdale, Arlington: American Anthropological Association, 1993. Print.

Mortland, Carol A. "Khmer Buddhists in the United States: Ultimate Questions." In *Cambodian Culture since 1975: Homeland and Exile,* edited by May M. Ebihara, Carol A. Mortland, and Judy Ledgerwood. Ithaca: Cornell University Press, 1994. Print.

Mortland, Carol A. and Judy Ledgerwood. 1987. "Secondary Migration among Southeast Asian Refugees in the United States." In *Urban Anthropology,* 16.3-4 (1987): 291-326. Print.

Mortland, Carol A. and Judy Ledgerwood. "Refugee Resource Acquisition, the Invisible Communication System." In *Cross-Cultural Adaptation: Current Approaches,* edited by Young Yun Kim and William B. Gudykunst. Newbury Park: Sage Publications, 1988. Print.

Münyas, Burcu. "Genocide in the Minds of Cambodian Youth: Transmitting (h)stories of Genocide to Second and Third Generations in Cambodia." In *Journal of Genocide Research* 10.3 (2008): 413-439. Print.

Mydans, Seth. "Long Beach Journal; From Cambodia to Doughnut Shops." *The New York Times,* May 26, 1995. Print.

Niedzwiecki, Max and T.C. Duong. *Southeast Asian American Statistical Profile.* Washington D.C.: Southeast Asian Resource Action Center (SEARAC), 2004. Print.

Haing, Ngor. *A Cambodian Odyssey.* New York: Macmillan, 1987. Print.

Nguyen-Hong-Nhiem, Lucy and Joel Martin Halpern, eds. *The Far East Comes Near: Autobiographical Accounts of Southeast Asian Students in America.* Amherst: University of Massachusetts Press, 1989. Print.

North, David and Nim Sok. *Profiles of Some Good Places for Cambodians to Live in the United States.* Washington D.C.: Office of Refugee Resettlement, U.S. Department of Health and Human Services, 1989. Print.

Office of Refugee Resettlement. *Refugee Resettlement Program. Report to the Congress. FY 1993.* Washington D.C.: Office of Refugee Resettlement, U.S. Department of Health and Human Services, 1994. Print.

Rasbridge, Lance A. and John L. Marcucci. "Reactions to Coupon Coercion. Dallas Cambodian Women's Autonomy in the Acculturative Process." In *Selected Papers on Refugee Issues,* edited by Pamela A. DeVoe. Arlington.: American Anthropological Association, 1992. Print.

Refugee Act of 1980. *Public Law 96-212,* March 17, 1980. 96th Congress. Washington D.C. 1980. Print.

Refugee Resource Center. *Cambodian Cluster Project. October, 1981 - March, 1982. Final Report.* New York: Refugee Resource Center, Committee on Migration and Refugee Affairs, American County of Voluntary Agencies in Foreign Service, 1982. Print.

Reimers, David M. *Unwelcome Strangers: American Identity and the Turn against Immigration.* New York: Columbia University Press, 1998. Print.

Robinson, Court and Arthur Wallenstein. *Unfulfilled Hopes: The Humanitarian Parole/Immigrant Visa Program for Border Cambodians.* Washington D.C.: U.S. Committee for Refugees, 1988. Print.

Rumbaut, Rubén. "Vietnamese, Laotian, and Cambodian Americans." In *Asian Americans. Contemporary Trends and Issues*, edited by Pyong Gap Min. Thousand Oaks: Sage Publications, 1995. Print.

Sam, Sam-Ang. "Khmer Traditional Music Today." In *Cambodian Culture since 1975: Homeland and Exile*, edited by May M. Ebihara, Carol A. Mortland, and Judy Ledgerwood. Ithaca: Cornell University Press, 1994. Print.

Smith, Frank. *Interpretive Accounts of the Khmer Rouge Years: Personal Experience in Cambodian Peasant World View.* Madison: Center for Southeast Asian Studies, University of Wisconsin, 1989. Print.

Steinberg, Stephen. *The Ethnic Myth. Race, Ethnicity, and Class in America.* Boston: Beacon Press, 1989. Print.

Tollefson, James W. *Alien Winds: The Reeducation of America's Indochinese Refugees.* New York: Praeger, 1989. Print.

Ui, Shiori. "'Unlikely Heroes:' The Evolution of Female Leadership in a Cambodian Ethnic Enclave." In *Ethnography Unbound. Power and Resistance in the Modern Metropolis*, edited by Michael Buraway. Berkeley: University of California Press, 1991. Print.

Ung, Chinary. "The Regeneration of Khmer Music and the Performing Arts in the United States." In *First International scholars Conference on Cambodia. Selected Papers*, edited by Russell A. Judkins. Geneseo: State University of New York at Geneseo, Department of Anthropology and the Geneseo Foundation, 1988. Print.

U.S. Committee for Refugees. *World Refugee Survey 1998.* Washington D.C.: U.S. Committee for Refugees, 1998. Print.

U.S. Department of Homeland Security. *2008 Yearbook of Immigration Statistics.* U.S. Department of Homeland Security. Web.

Welaratna, Usha. *Beyond the Killing Fields: Voices of Nine Cambodian Survivors in America.* Palo Alto: Stanford University Press, 1993. Print.

CHAPTER 10

Nature of Cambodian Gangs in America

Sody Lay

Gangs are not a social organization indigenous to Cambodia. In fact, there is no direct translation in Khmer for the English word "gang."[1] Cambodian gangs in America have patterned themselves after already existing African American and Latino gangs, acquiring from them clothing style, hand signs, and other conspicuous gang attributes. Cambodian youth gangs are generally very fluid in nature, with few rigid rules. As ethnic gangs, they are unique that they do not display the ethnocentric attitude found in many other gangs. A trend common among Cambodian American gangs is to be accepting of ethnic and racial diversity within their ranks, and other youth may often become part of the gang the same way a new person is introduced to a circle of friends.

Looseness in gang structure has both positive and negative consequences. According to John Reis, a Crime Prevention Specialist for the Rhode Island Department of Attorney General, the informal nature of Cambodian American youth gangs make it possible for gang members to fairly easily leave their gang affiliations behind should they so desire. Moreover, the informal nature of gangs allows members to freely pursue activities such as education or employment without incurring the wrath of the gang unit. In Providence, many OGs (original gangsters) have been able to acquire steady employment and start families in the very neighborhoods they used to roam as teenagers. On the other hand, the downside of loose gang structure is that members tend to be more violent than their organized counterpart. Without a formal leadership structure to issue commands and relegate antisocial behavior, members are more apt to engage in spontaneous acts of violence and crime. Because they need not answer to anyone, gang members are freer to commit crimes without having to justify their actions within a formal hierarchy.

Although there is usually little formal leadership structure, Cambodian gangs—like many mainstream gangs—do adhere to a loose hierarchical structure, with younger members given the title "juniors" and older members (usually those in their mid-twenties or so) being anointed with the title of OG. Junior members are known for their enthusiasm for violence, as they constantly seek to demonstrate their toughness and daring. Through their aggression against rival gangs, they act as the conservators of gang pride. The activities of OGs, on the other hand, shift from their youthful days of seeking danger and excitement to mostly just engaging in recreational drug use and alcohol consumption. Nevertheless, they are always prepared to retaliate if conflict should come their way. As one gang member put it, "OGs don't go lookin' for drama, they let the trouble come to them." When asked if he was still a gang member, an OG replied by lifting his shirt to reveal TRG tattooed in large gangster-style script across his back and proclaimed, "TRG for life." Yet, as mentioned earlier, many OGs, including the aforementioned, do move on, gaining steady employment and raising families.

The appearance of Cambodian youth gang members varies from region to region. In Long Beach, for instance, they tend to shave their heads bald; in Oakland, they grease up their hair and slick it back; and in Seattle, the trend is towards cornrows. Each gang also has its own personality and values. One gang may emphasize drinking and womanizing, while another, drug sales. The one common denominator of almost all Cambodian American gangs, however, is the acceptance of violence by members as an inevitable part of their lives.

The "Cambodian" in Cambodian American Gang Members

Although members have picked up the style of other gangs, many are still very much Cambodian in nature. Oak is part of a new generation of Cambodian American youth gang members. At age 16, he already has years of experience leading the gang life, having been involved with gangs since the age of 11 while residing in Oakland, Seattle, and now Providence. These days 11 is the standard age of initial membership, he informs me. His choice of dress is called "sagging," which consists of baggy pants that hang low and a loose-fitting shirt. When asked why he decided to choose the gang lifestyle, he initially had difficulty answering. After some thought, however, he offered that he was perhaps simply following in the footsteps of his uncles, members of a Cambodian gang in Oakland called Asian Street Walkers. Growing up, he had admired them for their cool attitude and fearless demeanor.

Through our conversation, Oak also revealed that his father and mother separated when he was young, with his father taking a new wife. He nonchalantly remarks that sometimes his father beat him, but mostly he just neglected him in favor of his step-siblings. While rebellion against an abusive parent may have contributed to Oak's decision to join a gang, his family life is actually not typical of other Cambodian American youth who join gangs. Many gang members live peacefully at home with their parents, and, as a gesture that can only be constructed as respect, often attempt to keep their gang affiliation hidden. According to John Reis, many parents are actually shocked when they learn that their children are involved in gangs.

The fact that many youth are even able to hide their gang affiliation from their parents perhaps reflects a more serious and pervasive problem within the Cambodian American community: the lack of communication between parents and children. Here, the aftermath of the Khmer Rouge tragedy continues to haunt individuals and families. Many Cambodian parents have difficulty coping with post-traumatic stress, recurring nightmares about the Khmer Rouge, and other mental health disorders such as feelings of exile, causing them to become depressed, irascible, and/or withdrawn. These mental health problems can make it difficult for parents to communicate with their children or even effectively perform their parental duties.

A difference between Cambodian and American culture with respect to parental interaction with children also contributes to estrangement between Cambodian American parents and their children. Cambodian culture does not generally promote overt displays of affection between parent and child in the manner children witness on American television. Cambodians view raising children to be proper as one of the most important parental duties; hence, they tend to express their love and concern for their children though instruction in and admonishment of behavior. As a result, many Cambodian American children develop the perception that their parents do not love them and complain that their parents criticize them too much.

Finally, like many second-generation immigrant youth, Cambodian children become more quickly acculturated into their new environment and acquire a new value system that clashes with their parents' traditional Khmer notions of appropriate and inappropriate behavior. The children often also develop a preference for speaking English, further compounding the already difficult lines of communication between Cambodian parents and their Americanized children. This cultural and linguistic divide increasingly pulls and pushes parents and children apart, giving Cambodian youth yet another reason to search outside the immediate family for a social support network.

Although the estrangement between parent and child is not necessarily antagonistic in nature, it does leave a void within the child's life, a void that can be filled on a variety of levels by gangs. In a gang, Cambodian American youth find those who speak a common language, older gang members who may fill the role of surrogate parents, and camaraderie with individuals who share a common experience of estrangement from parents and society at large. Gang members as individuals share that sense of being outcasts, not quite fitting in within the context of a traditional Khmer family or American society in general. Within the gang unit, they find individual acceptance but still remain outcasts collectively, an undesirable entity in poor neighborhoods.

Acculturation into the new American context, however, does not mean that Cambodian youth have rid themselves of all ethnic traits and characteristics. Although they may have acquired many American values and characteristics, most Cambodian American youth who participate in gangs are still very much in touch with their Khmer roots on a fundamental level. Even beyond overt claims of Cambodian pride (one gang actually calls itself "Cambodian Pride"), gang members display cultural characteristics that set them apart from other ethnic gangs. Many still use formal Khmer titles of respect to refer to those older than themselves (one example of the proper behavior Cambodian parents try to instill in their children). For instance, despite his five years of life as a gang member, Oak still addresses his elders politely and properly in the Khmer tradition. Even during our conversations, he and other gang members respectfully refer to me as "*Pu*" (roughly meaning "uncle") or "*Bong*" (roughly meaning "older brother"). Many Cambodian American youth in gangs also consider themselves Buddhist, a religion they accept by virtue of their Khmer heritage more than anything. Hence, although gang members may seem far removed from their traditional Khmer heritage, outward symbols of their culture emerge within the gang system itself such as expressions of respect for parents and elders, the use of honorific titles, and the acceptance of Buddhism.

The "American" in Cambodian American Gang Members

Just as Cambodian American youth gang activities have shifted, so have the motives of members for joining gangs. Although the need for a surrogate family, sense of identity, and protection may still contribute to gang membership, today there are also a host of less convoluted reasons why youth decide to join gangs. The answers given by gang members themselves to the question of why they join gangs included: "because it's cool"; "for the adrenaline rush"; "for the chicks"; and "to sell drugs and make money."

Even these seemingly superficial motives have as their foundation the unique position of the Cambodian as outcast in America. Cambodian American youth, like other youth, are interested in the opposite sex, recreation and social acceptance. These are also the values promoted by popular television stations that appeal to teenagers and young adults such as MTV. Like other Americans, many Cambodian youth would like to own fashionable clothes, attend parties, and pursue romance; unlike other Americans, however, they do not always have a culturally acceptable or financially viable means with which to attain their desires. Many Cambodian families in America are either part of the working poor or recipients of government aid and hence cannot afford the exciting lifestyles promoted by television. Cambodian culture is also extremely restrictive with regard to premarital romance; dating is not permitted, and marriages are traditionally arranged. Moreover, social interaction with the opposite sex before marriage is frowned upon. Hence, Cambodian American parents often prohibit their children from participating in activities such as parties and dances, resulting in a buildup of frustration and indignation on the part of Cambodian American youth as they witness their Anglo American, Latino, and African American counterparts engaging in these social activities.

In contrast to restrictive cultural norms and financial hardships, gangs offer Cambodian American youth the allure of romance, money, and excitement. Gangs provide a vehicle through which these youth can participate to some degree in popular American youth culture such as dating and parties. In the middle of my conversation with Oak on the front porch of a friend's home, he cavalierly waves down a car and walks over to speak with the young woman driver. After a few minutes, he comes back with a satisfied grin on his face and phone number in hand. Asked how he knew the girl, he coolly says that he had never seen her before. He just waved her down and tried his luck. His boldness in flirting with women at the age of 16 demonstrated the advantages of gang culture over traditional Khmer culture. The freedom to associate romantically is an allure of gang life that many youth, both young men and young women, find too tempting to pass up.

The particular gang with which Oak is affiliated in Providence is known for its drinking, recreational drug use, and womanizing, activities also favored by fraternities at college and universities throughout America. Although many of today's youth may drink while under the age of 21, do drugs, and seek attention from members of the opposite sex, the means to achieving these ends are not easily or equally attainable for all youth. College youth—especially those from affluent and middle-class households—have the means to drink at fraternity parties, dabble in drugs, and engage in premarital sex; for many Cambodian youth, however, these recreational options are closed, because of both their culture and class. The important difference between gangs and fraternities, however, is the willingness of gang members to commit violent crimes to achieve these ends. And as with school rivalries played out on the football field or basketball court, rivalries between gangs are an avenue for members to express bravado and interject excitement into their lives, often resulting in violence, bloodshed, and even death. It appears that when you cannot afford to be cool like Jason Priestly or Luke Perry in *Beverly Hills 90210*, you can always fall back on being cool like Marlon Brando in *The Wild One*.

"So, I continue to wander as an outcast..."

Cambodian youth in America are no different from any other youth in their desires. They feel a need for social acceptance and the weight of peer pressure. To fit in, they acquire the clothing styles, mannerisms, and values of their neighbors. At home, parental mental health problems and linguistic and cultural divides leave Cambodian American youth in various degrees alienated from their parents. At school and on television, they are exposed to values and lifestyles that are in direct contrast to the cultural and economic realities within their homes. Given these conditions, the allure of gangs to Khmer youth in America makes sense. In gangs, one finds opportunities for companionship, protection, excitement, romance, money, a sense of identity, and, not least of all, acceptance.

Nevertheless, it would be a mistake to conclude that gang membership is inevitable for Cambodian American youth, even taking into account their particular background and migration experience. Although the poor neighborhoods in which many Cambodians reside provide an environment where the temptation to choose a gang membership is all too readily available, joining a gang is still ultimately a conscious decision. Gang members fully recognize and accept this fact. That they should even attempt to hide their gang affiliations from their parents shows that they understand the undesirability of their choice. There are alternative means of acquiring companionship, protection, excitement, romance, money, identity, and acceptance—means that do not involve harm to others or invite the possibility of harm, imprisonment, and death to oneself.

Oak and other gang members are aware that they have had and continue to have options in the lifestyle they choose. In this awareness lies room for hope. Oak, for instance, asserts that he would like to make a change in his life. At 16 he sometimes feels weary of the gang lifestyle, although he still seems allured by its perks, as in the case of his brashly approaching the young woman in the car. He is aware that the gang life will lead him nowhere, and he expresses a desire to complete his high school education or work toward his GED. His mentor, and OG of approximately 30, has a wife and son and a well-paying job as a finisher at a local furniture company. His status within the gang appears to be that of semiretirement, with participation in gang life at this point mainly relegated to drinking and recreational drug use. Of course, his continued affiliation with a gang means that violence, although only intermittently now, is still a part of his life. Pointing to the porch of his home across the street, he declares matter-of-factly, "I'm gonna die on the front stoop there." Still, when asked if he wants his eight-year-old son to become a gang member when he grows up, he replies curtly and soberly, "No. He's a college boy."

Endnotes

1. English-Khmer dictionaries inaccurately translate it as Krom, a word that carries neither the negative connotation nor denotation that is usually affiliated with youth gangs in America. *Krom* simply means "group or grouping" and may be used to refer to everything from commercial companies to government councils and bureaus. Even Cambodians in America with the most limited of English-speaking proficiency will simply use the English word "gang" to refer to gangs.

References

Lee, Jennifer and Min Zhou, eds. *Asian American Youth: Culture, Identity, and Ethnicity*. New York: Routledge, 2004. Print.

Section V

Cambodian Americans
and Education

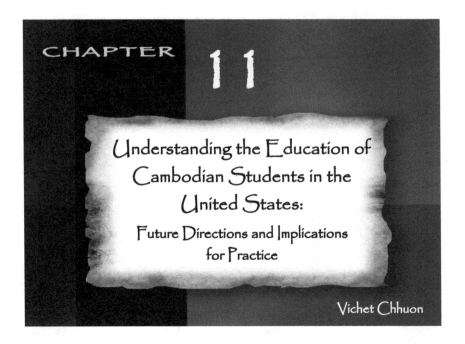

CHAPTER 11

Understanding the Education of Cambodian Students in the United States:

Future Directions and Implications for Practice

Vichet Chhuon

As one of the newest Asian groups in the United States, Cambodian students' social and educational experiences differ fundamentally from those of many other Asian immigrants, including Korean, Chinese, Filipino, and Japanese. Cambodians immigrated to the U.S. largely as a single wave of refugees in the early to mid-1980s, after enduring four years of the Khmer Rouge's communist experiment in which one to two million Cambodians lost their lives. Cambodians in the U.S. are therefore likely to have experienced an especially disorienting emigration as a result of this violent upheaval in their home country and the loss of loved ones and family members.

Unfortunately, Cambodians are often viewed within an Asian American collective that assumes all Asian Americans are succeeding educationally and economically (Ng, Lee, and Pak 2007). As well, the relatively few studies that have examined Cambodian students as a unique ethnic group tend to underscore their educational difficulties (Ngo and Lee 2007). The purpose of this chapter is to examine the extant research on Cambodian students in the United States and provide practitioners, policymakers and researchers guidance on how to better serve this unique population. The chapter is divided into three sections: the academic achievement of Cambodian students and explanations for school performance; directions for future research; and implications for school practice.

Academic Achievement of Cambodians in the United States

Given that 38.6 percent of Cambodians are under age 18 compared to 25.6 percent of the U.S. population (Reeves and Bennett 2004), Cambodians represent a growing segment of American society whose social and economic future will rely on the success of its school-age youth. However, Cambodian students in the U.S. generally exhibit low levels of academic achievement relative to other ethnic populations. For example, only 6.9 percent of Cambodians have earned a four-year college degree,[1] far below the national average for Asian Americans (44%) and the total U.S. population (24%) (Reeves and Bennett 2004).

In one of the earliest studies of Cambodian achievement, Rumbaut and Ima's (1988) report of Southeast Asian refugee adaptation in San Diego county revealed that Cambodian students in K-12 schools had notably lower achievement (as measured by GPA and reading and math scores) than other Southeast Asian groups including Lao and Vietnamese with similar incomes and parent education. More recent data from the 10-year-long Children of Immigrants Longitudinal Study revealed that first and second generation Cambodian children were underperforming compared to other immigrant groups[2] (Portes and Rumbaut 2006). Given their school performance overall, immigration scholars have argued that Cambodian children are at risk of assimilating into the lowest social and economic segments of American society (Portes and Rumbaut 2006; Zhou 1997). Research on school performance in this community has typically centered upon either cultural or structural explanations of achievement, as discussed next.

Cambodian Cultural Values

One possible explanation for a pattern of underachievement is that ethnic cultural traditions from the home country may not support academic achievement for Cambodian youth in U.S. schools. Some studies, for example, have noted that Cambodian cultural norms emphasize that parents should not intervene in the formal education of their children (Garcia Coll et al. 2002; Hopkins 1996; Um 1999). However, research with other populations clearly indicates that parental involvement in their children's education plays a significant role in children's academic success (Epstein 1992; Jeynes 2007).

Garcia Coll and colleagues (2002) investigated levels of parent involvement with second and fifth grade Cambodian, Portuguese, and Dominican immigrant student samples in New York City. They found that Cambodian families in the study scored the lowest on every parent involvement measure. In a later study with similar samples in Rhode Island, Garcia Coll, Szalacha, and Palacios (2005) reported that Cambodian families again reported much lower levels of parental educational involvement relative to Portuguese and Dominican families. Longitudinal qualitative research with Cambodian families in the Boston area found that most Cambodian parents largely preferred to defer to the teacher despite expressed desires for their children to be academically successful (Smith-Hefner 1993). Um (1999), an ethnic Cambodian scholar, has asserted that Cambodian families do not intervene in their children's education because the traditional Cambodian social hierarchy holds educators in very high regard; teachers in Cambodian society are granted a great deal of responsibility. The educational involvement of Cambodian parents is shaped by their cultural understanding of the appropriate charge and obligations of teachers, families, and students. However, educators in the U.S. might interpret this minimal involvement as a lack of care or unwillingness to support the success of their children in school.

Other data suggest that cultural beliefs regarding natural academic talents and competition might also conflict with U.S. notions of student success (Canniff 2001; Hopkins 1996; Smith-Hefner 1999). Rumbaut and Ima's (1988) report on Southeast Asian refugee adaptation in San Diego suggested low performance might be related to a cultural worldview that encouraged a passive acceptance of school performance. Though this study represented an early attempt by researchers to understand the academic struggles of Cambodians as a unique ethnic group, these data cannot clearly establish cultural beliefs as a causal explanation for achievement. The study's 20 year old sample comprised primarily foreign-born adolescents, many of whom might have had particularly traumatic experiences prior to immigration. Therefore, rather than general cultural norms, experiences related to the Cambodian genocide and forced emigration that are unique to this cohort may have played a role in families' observed attitudes of resignation.

As well, Cambodian parents tend not to push their children toward specific educational paths because of traditional beliefs about children's innate abilities and capacities for learning (Smith-Hefner 1999). Although Cambodian parents take pride in their children's academic success, they may rationalize underachievement as inevitable because everyone has natural gifts and limitations. Research with Cambodian families in the Midwest has also observed that the values of Cambodian Buddhist beliefs were largely incongruent with the competitive character of U.S. schooling, particularly as immigrant students entered adolescence. Hopkins (1996: 129) described Cambodian families' approach to schooling in this way:

> *similar to 'Latinos or asia'. Unlike East A*
>
> Parents are unlikely to try to 'make' their children study. Abil- *or*
> ity to learn academic subjects is viewed somewhat as Americans *Viet pop*
> view artistic talent—a wonderful blessing but not something
> that can be forced. A parent whose child is not doing well in
> school is likely to smile and shake their head with resignation.

Park's (2000) study of the learning style preferences of Southeast Asian students, including 71 Cambodians, found that Southeast Asians, compared with Anglo and East Asians, had a higher preference for group learning activities. She argued that Cambodian students' preference for group activities can be attributed to cultural norms emphasizing cooperation and selflessness.

Other research found that high achieving students seem to thrive in homes where some aspects of American norms and values are selectively embraced, including academic achievement, while core Cambodian cultural values and beliefs are retained (Sin 1991). Sin, an ethnic Cambodian refugee, contends that what others consider a *passive* disposition is actually a Cambodian belief in patience, an important Buddhist virtue. Maintaining a patient attitude strengthens the personal motivation and drive necessary for these Cambodians to overcome the many social, financial and educational challenges they encounter.

Some arguments cited for Cambodians' lower achievement seem consistent with an established literature positing that academic success is dependent to some extent on the alignment of the beliefs and values of a minority group with that of the dominant culture and its schools. Unfortunately, some of these findings can be interpreted as essentializing the academic experiences of Cambodian families by suggesting that their children's achievement are shaped by cultural values, similar to the model minority stereotype of Asian American success. Whereas high achieving Asian Americans are labeled the model minority because of presumed cultural values reflecting persistence and hard work, Cambodian students are low achieving because of ethnic traditions that emphasize a passive disposition and a more fixed notion of ability. These latter behaviors are perceived as incompatible with the expectations of U.S. schooling.

Structural Explanations for Achievement

While cultural values might influence educational success, structural characteristics related to social class, family composition, inner city residency, and school institutional characteristics are also significant determinants of Cambodian academic achievement (Portes and Rumbaut 2006). A comparison of cultural values and structural factors as explanations for achievement of Cambodian and Vietnamese students found structural variables related to socioeconomic status, school type (urban or suburban), and immigration patterns better predicted reading and mathematics achievement than did cultural factors. Cultural variables included items relating to sense of individuality and beliefs about family responsibility. These findings are consistent with Coleman et al.'s (1966) seminal report which argued that socioeconomic status (SES), including parental social class and educational background, is the most powerful predictor of school achievement. Other research conducted since then continues to support the importance of parental income, education, and other social class variables for children's educational success (Sirin 2005). The assumption is that, irrespective of immigrant status, parents who have had extensive schooling and possess economic resources can better provide their children with the means to achieve in school compared to families who lack these advantages

Given that a family's socioeconomic standing largely determines the schools that children attend, it is not surprising that Cambodian students often enroll in under-funded urban schools in poor communities (Kozol 2005; Portes and Rumbaut 2006). In addition, many Cambodian students grow up in single-parent homes, countering the stereotypical image of cohesive intact Asian American households. For example, Rumbaut and Ima (1988) reported that approximately half of the Cambodian households in the San Diego area were headed by a single parent. Ong's (2004) more recent ethnography of Cambodian families in Oakland similarly found that half of these homes were headed by a single parent, usually the mother, and research has documented that students living in single-parent households consistently have lower levels of school achievement than those in two-parent families (Sun 2001).

An examination of the effectiveness of bilingual education and policy for first and 1.5 generation Cambodian students in southern California (Wright 2004) found an incoherent state policy combined with poor local implementation, resulting in bilingual programs that often provided Cambodian English learners with inappropriate teaching methods and inexperienced teachers. In spite of these barriers, Wright reported that five of his 10 participants managed to go on and earn four-year degrees. In studies I conducted (with colleagues) on the experiences of highly successful Cambodian students, students often explained that their participation in enriched academic high school programs were key for their college entrance (Chhuon and Hudley 2008; Chhuon et al. 2010). Thus, school quality appears to be an important structural factor that determines academic outcomes for this population, as is true with so many students. However, the academic difficulties of Cambodian students have been obscured by the model minority stereotype (Ngo and Lee 2007). As a result, it has been difficult for educators, policymakers, and researchers to fully address the needs of Cambodian youth, who overall have not fared well in U.S. schools.

Double Perception and Identity Tensions

As mentioned, Cambodian students are typically stereotyped by the larger society as part of the Asian model minority that is academically successful, but they often endure low expectations from teachers and counselors in their local high schools (Chhuon et al. 2010; Um 2003). Local stereotypes of Cambodian students paint them as low academic achievers, delinquents, and dropouts (Chhuon et al. 2010; Um 2003). Further, some Cambodian youth believe that their ethnicity causes them to be perceived as gang members or academically at-risk by their teachers and counselors. These teachers and counselors may believe that Southeast Asian students may lack the ability to achieve in college. Further, Cambodian students have been found to perceive low expectations and little support for their higher education goals (Chhuon 2009; Um 2003).

Perceptions of teacher support and positive academic environments have been reported as important predictors of Cambodian high school students' academic achievement motivation, including school engagement and college aspirations (Chhuon, Courtright, and Carranza 2008). Cambodian youth without supportive bonds with teachers are likely to disengage from school. Aung and Yu's (2007) case-study found a disproportionately high dropout rate of Cambodian students in Lowell, Massachusetts, apparently because Cambodian dropouts were unable to connect with school adults and the school curriculum. Additionally, Cambodian students (particularly males), shared that gang and racial profiling by the local police was an important issue in their community and sometimes initiated students' involvement with the criminal justice system. Wallitt (2008) similarly reported that Cambodian high school dropouts left school early because they perceived a lack of care from their teachers and often felt invisible in their classes. Her participants stated that their teachers typically did not recognize which students were Cambodian and believed that *all* Asians were high achievers (Wallitt

2008). Thus, local negative stereotypes and lack of support for academic aspirations may also be structural factors that negatively impact Cambodian students' academic trajectories.

Some Cambodian students perceived that their school success was dependent upon academically enriched environments provided by high academic tracks including Advanced Placement and Honors classes (Chhuon et al. 2010), and small learning communities (Wallitt 2008). These contexts served as a protective buffer from the negative stereotypes of Cambodians in their community and feelings of invisibility in the classroom. At times, these environments helped foster students' positive academic identities, though perhaps at the expense of their Cambodian identity. Research has found that students coped with the negative local perceptions of their ethnic group by distancing themselves from their Cambodian ethnic identity in both their high school and their community (Chhuon 2009; Chhuon and Hudley under review; Chhuon et al. 2010). This disidentification for some Cambodian students is perhaps related to their understanding of the U.S. racial hierarchy and the pervasive power of the model minority stereotype to garner support for their academic aspirations. Unfortunately, for many students, internalizing an essentialized, albeit positive, view of Asian Americans can encourage Cambodian students to adopt negative feelings and stereotypes toward their own ethnic group. Additionally, students who embrace the model minority stereotype might feel unrealistic pressures to achieve that undermine their schooling.[3]

My study of successful Cambodian students at the university found that some participants were able to develop a positive Cambodian ethnic identity only after meeting other high achieving Cambodian students in college (Chhuon and Hudley 2008). I have recently conducted ethnographic research on Cambodian high school students' ethnic identities in Southern California and found that students in the most rigorous academic programs moved between panethnic Asian American and Cambodian labels depending upon perceived advantages associated with these identities (Chhuon 2009). However, students in rigorous classes stated that their Cambodian backgrounds were typically invisible to their teachers and some peers, and that Cambodian students in these courses were often generalized as "Chinese," if noticed at all. Their peers in less rigorous academic environments were easily identifiable as Cambodian and reported a more stable Cambodian identity. Both groups understood the differing perceptions associated with being seen as Asian or specifically Cambodian. The varied expectations attached to these identities meant that Cambodian students had to learn to negotiate these tensions and come up with sensible interpretations of what it meant to Cambodian and Asian American.

Research with Cambodian adolescents involved in community based ethnic organizations suggests that these alternative educational settings can influence students' positive identity development. For example, community based programs in Lowell, MA reported success with reaching dropouts and students at risk for dropping by providing Cambodian youth a place for mentorship, homework help, and sports (Aung and Yu 2007). Kwon's (2006) ethnography of community-based youth groups in Oakland found that these structured environments can help Cambodian students develop positive ethnic identities by engaging in social activism under the guidance of adult mentors who reflect the ethnic backgrounds of the youth with whom they work. Likewise, Reyes' (2007) work examined how an after school video-making program in Philadelphia helped Southeast Asian youth, most of whom are Cambodian, understand and defy the negative stereotypes associated with their group. This body of research suggests that opportunities to develop close relationships with role-models and mentors, and culturally relevant programming can improve Cambodian students' ethnic identity development and academic achievements.

In general, the evidence presented in this chapter points to the inappropriateness of aggregating Asian American students without regard to ethnicity and national origin when trying to understand their educational experiences. Also, much of the literature on school outcomes for Cambodian students tends to focus on either cultural or structural explanations. Unfortunately, most cultural explanations locate the problem of academic underachievement within the students and their families, similar to the model minority stereotype's reliance on individual determination and cultural values as explanation for all Asian American achievement. The studies discussed here suggest that school and structural concerns, including negative stereotypes, low expectations, and poor high school preparation are perhaps more relevant to Cambodian students' lack of academic success.

Future Directions

Few studies have addressed the experiences of Cambodian students who have done well in U.S. schools. How might successful Cambodian students reconcile cultural values that some research describes as incompatible with the norms of American schooling? While fatalistic beliefs and individualistic notions of personhood may indeed be key aspects of Cambodian culture, it is unclear how students might interpret and negotiate such values. Studies have also not accurately examined the processes and consequences of the transmission of ethnic cultural values from immigrant parents to the new second generation of immigrant children. In what ways might students interpret the cultural values of their parents, and how might these interpretations influence their schooling? Other constructs, including "responsibility," "family obligation," and "immigrant optimism," can provide additional ways for researchers to examine culture and schooling for Cambodian students (Bankston and Hidalgo 2006; Fuligni 2004). Research has addressed the construct of immigrant optimism as an influence on school achievement (Fuligni 2004; Garcia Coll et al. 2005; Kao and Tienda 1995; Zhou 1997). For example, Garcia Coll et al.'s (2005) longitudinal study of the academic pathways of elementary-age children found that Cambodian boys over time demonstrated the most positive change in attitude and achievement, despite their structural disadvantages. However, these data were inconclusive with respect to what exactly accounted for this unexpected finding. Our review has suggested that for many Cambodian students, translating their immigrant optimism into actual achievement can be a difficult process.

Further, the literature has not sufficiently examined the structural characteristics of the local contexts in which Cambodian children live, nor the opportunities for learning in the schools that Cambodian children attend. While a segmented assimilation view of

Cambodian students' achievement can help explain the increasingly divergent school outcomes of Cambodian children broadly, zooming in on the structural arrangements of schools might better reveal how academic environments matter in powerful ways for Cambodian students. Future research must examine how the institutional exclusion of Cambodian youth from enriched academic environments might shape their aspirations and achievement.

Given that the interactions between immigration, acculturation, race, class, and schooling are a dynamic process, research must examine culture and structure as complimentary rather than independent constructs that influence academic outcomes. Some research has suggested that a sociocultural perspective may be helpful in understanding how immigrants and their children negotiate unfamiliar institutions in the U.S., including schools (Monzo and Rueda 2006; Rogoff 1995). I suggest that a sociocultural approach can help the literature on Cambodian students move away from inappropriate generalizations by emphasizing students' specific activity settings and recognizing that learning is inherently multidirectional. This perspective posits that immigrants' adoption of new cultural practices and beliefs, including those learned in school, do not necessarily have to replace traditional ones from home. Rather, cultural values and beliefs can be activated according to students' differing contexts. This approach can help situate Cambodian students and their families as more active agents of their schooling, who when presented with structural opportunities, can draw on their diverse experiences to negotiate the academic demands of the American school system. Moreover, this review suggests that culturally relevant, community based organizations can serve as alternative sites for understanding the identities and academic experiences of Cambodian youth. In general, research on how ethnic identities are negotiated and shaped by students' in school and out-of-school contexts represents productive avenues for investigating ways to enhance the educational experiences of Cambodian students.

Taken together, these studies strengthen the argument that policy makers must disaggregate the experiences of Asian American students to examine differences by ethnicity. There is now a small but growing literature that has attempted to untangle the experiences of different Asian American ethnic groups by examining the within-group variation among these populations (i.e.,, Lee 2005; Lew 2006; Louie 2004; Ngo 2009; Zhou and Bankston 1998). While many Cambodian students are certainly doing well, a great many are underserved, and this diversity of experiences must be more accurately reflected in the empirical literature. Despite these limitations, some lessons can be gained from research on Cambodian students that can positively influence their educational experiences.

Implications for Practice

This chapter has emphasized that Cambodian students as a group, are not a model minority but face educational difficulties similar to other ethnic groups at-risk for school failure. Recent research on minority achievement has argued that institutionalized school structures may be more important than students' families for creating positive pathways toward academic success (Conchas 2006; Lew 2006; Wallitt, 2008). For example, students enrolled in specialized programs and academies often do not reflect the diversity of the school community (Chhuon et al. 2010; Chhuon 2009). Local school administrators must make it their explicit goal to include underserved groups such as Cambodian students. Cambodian students who attend poor and segregated schools often find themselves faced with the same limited educational opportunities experienced by other children of color (Orfield and Yun 1999). This chapter suggests that the culture of academic success fostered in various specialized programs, small learning communities, and alternative school settings can benefit Cambodian students in significant ways. These environments tend to be more personalized and rigorous and provide opportunities for students to form bonds with their classmates and teachers (Conchas 2006; Ready, Lee, and Welner 2001; Wallitt 2008). This theme resonates with other findings that student perceptions of genuine care and opportunities to build relationships are significant but uncommon aspects of effective schools (Pang 2006; Valenzuela 1999). For Cambodian students, the school environment and their contact with school personnel may be especially critical for their motivation to learn and school engagement.

In these environments, teachers should be aware of challenges Cambodian American students face on a daily basis. For example, Cambodian American students may have to juggle a number of family duties (i.e.,, work and sibling childcare) in addition to their school responsibilities. As well, research on family obligation and immigrant adolescents' academic achievement suggests that educational decisions may depend on students' perceptions of the utility of schooling for future adult roles that they will take on (Fuligni 2004). One important future role for immigrant Cambodian students is the ability to contribute to the well being of the family unit, suggesting that family relations and family support are important determinants of academic aspirations and achievement. Educators must be aware of their students' differing motivations to achieve. My own research on Cambodian students suggests that their immigrant families supported them to the fullest extent possible, and this support was perceived to be important for their success in pursuit of postsecondary education (Chhuon et al. 2010).

Schools serving Cambodian families must actively work to hire more Cambodian professionals including teachers, counselors and other institutional agents. Cambodian teachers are likely able to empathize with the struggles that Cambodian students experience in school. While non-Cambodian adults can certainly play important roles in educating Cambodian students, the presence of educated Cambodian role models sends an added positive and powerful message to Cambodian youth about ethnic identity and academic possibilities. My many conversations with Cambodian adolescents (particularly male youth) suggest that being Cambodian is often linked to stereotypes centering on poverty, low achievement, and gangs. Cambodian youth must be exposed to members from their own cultural group who are both successful and proud of their ethnic background.

Finally, schools can better serve this population by developing curricula that build on Cambodian students' values, strengths, and diverse backgrounds (Banks 1996; Pang 2006; Wallitt 2008). For example, Cambodian families in the U.S. can be viewed as a uniquely resilient population whose pre-immigration experience with genocide might provide rich topics for classroom discussion in high school. Current events including issues concerning immigration and deportation might also be relevant topics that can engage Cambodian students. Additionally, class assignments that require students to research their own family history might be a productive method to increase family involvement. Culturally relevant curriculum can be empowering for Cambodian youth and their families, particularly those who feel invisible and unsupported at school. Though many Cambodian families are immigrants who have left terrible circumstances in their home country, their children often present the same needs as many students of color who are poorly served by public education.

Pedagogy has the potential to turn cultural differences into assets and contribute to students' successful school experiences (Banks 1996; Pang 2006). Schools serving Cambodian students must examine ways in which the educational environment, inside and outside of the classroom, can foster positive ethnic identities for Cambodian youth. To better understand and teach their Cambodian students, teachers and administrators should create bridges with local community-based organizations that serve Cambodian youth. This dialogue and partnership can enhance the academic experiences of a greater number of Cambodian students. As part of the new second generation of immigrants in the U.S. (Portes and Rumbaut 2006), the education of Cambodian students is of great concern to educators, policymakers, and immigration scholars. As Suarez-Orozco and Suarez-Orozco (2001) keenly observed, "Schooling has become a high-stakes goal for the children of immigrants" (124). For Cambodian students, successful school engagement will play a critical role in the life chances of these youth and their families.

Endnotes

1. Census data revealed that of all Cambodians 25 years and older residing in the US, over half (53.3) reported attaining less than a high school diploma (Reeves and Bennett 2004).
2. In the Cambodian/Laotian sample, nearly 40 percent failed to earn a high school diploma. Other Asian immigrant groups, including Chinese, Filipinos, and Vietnamese, did significantly better academically, as measured by grade point average and high school graduation.

3. The stress involved with living up to this stereotype, for instance, can increase anxiety that can impair their performance on an exam (Steele 1997). The embrace of the model minority image can levy academic and psychological costs and may also result in ethnic identity conflict (Sue and Sue 1990; Uba 1994).

References

Aung, Khin Mai and Nancy Yu. "Does the system work for Cambodian American students? The educational experiences and demographics of Cambodians in Lowell, Massuchusetts." In *Southeast Asian Refugees and Immigrants in the Mill City: Changing Families, Communities, and Institutions Thirty Years Afterwards*, edited by Tuyet-Lan Pho, Jeffrey N. Gerson, and Sylvia Cowan. Burlington: University of Vermont Press, 2007. Print.

Banks, James A. "Transformative knowledge, curriculum reform, and action." In *Multicultural Education: Transformative Knowledge and Action,* edited by J.A. Banks. New York: Teacher College Press, 1996. Print.

Bankston, Carl L., and Danielle A. Hidalgo. "Respect in Southeast Asian American children and adolescents: Cultural and contextual influences." In *New Direction for Child and Adolescent Development* 114: 2006. 25-38. Print.

Canniff, Julie G. *Cambodian refugees' pathways to success: developing a bi-cultural identity.* New York: LFB Scholarly Publishing, 2001. Print.

Chhuon, Vichet. "How school structures influence ethnic and panethnic identities in Cambodian high school youth." Unpublished dissertation. University of California, Santa Barbara, 2009. Print.

Chhuon, Vichet, Cynthia Hudley, Mary E. Brenner, & Rroseanne Macias. "The multiple worlds of successful Cambodian American students." In *Urban Education* 45.1 (2010): 30-57. Print.

Chhuon, Vichet and Cynthia Hudley. "Factors supporting Cambodian American students' college adjustment." In *Journal of College Student Development* 49.1 (2008): 15-30. Print.

Chhuon, Vichet, Courtright, A., and Carranza, F.D. *"Factors supporting academic engagement among Cambodian high school youth."* Paper presented at the American Educational Research Association Annual Meeting, March 25-28 in New York City, NY. 2008. Print.

Chhuon, Vichet, and Cynthia Hudley. "Asian American "ethnic options": How Cambodian urban youth negotiate ethnic and panethnic identities" (unpublished manuscript).

Coleman, James S. *Equality of educational opportunity.* Washington DC: US Government Printing Office, 1966. Print.

Coll, Cynthia, Laura Szalacha, and Natalia Palacios. "Children of Dominican, Portuguese, and Cambodian immigrant families: Academic attitudes and pathways during middle childhood. In *Developmental Pathways through Middle Childhood: Rethinking Contexts and Diversity as Resources*, edited by Catherine Cooper, Cynthia Coll, W. Todd Bartko, Helen Davis, and Celina Chatman. New Jersey: Lawrence Erlbaum Associates, Publishers, 2005. Print.

Conchas, Gilberto Q. *The color of success: Race and high-achieving urban youth.* New York: Teachers College Press, 2006. Print.

Epstein, Joyce L. "School and family partnerships." In *Encyclopedia of Educational Research* (6th ed.) edited by M. Aiken. New York: Macmillan, 1992. Print.

Fuligni, Andrew. "The adaptation and acculturation of children from immigrant families." In *Childhood and Adolescence: Cross-Cultural Perspectives and Applications*, edited by Uwe P. Gielen and Jaipaul Roopnarine. Westport: Greenwood Publishing Group, 2004. Print.

Garcia Coll, C., Akiba, D., Palacios, N., Bailey, B., Silver, R., DiMartino, L. "Parent involvement in children's education: Lessons from three immigrant groups." In *Parenting: Science and Practice,* 2: 2002. 303-324. Print.

Hopkins, Mary C. *Braving a new world: Cambodian (Khmer) refugees in an American city.* Westport: Bergin and Garvey, 1996. Print.

Jeynes, William H. "The relationship between parent involvement and urban secondary school student achievement: A meta-analysis." In *Urban Education 42.*1(2007): 82-110. Print.

Kao, Grace, and Marta Tienda. "Optimism and achievement: The educational performance of immigrant youth." In *Social Science Quarterly 76.*1(1995): 1-18. Print.

Kozol, Jonathan. *Shame of the nation: The restoration of apartheid schooling in America.* New York: Crown, 2005. Print.

Kwon, Soo Ah. "Second generation Asian and Pacific Islander youth social change practices." Unpublished dissertation. University of California, Berkeley, 2005. Print.

Lee, Stacey J. *Up against whiteness: Race, school, and immigrant youth.* New York: Teachers College Press, 2005. Print.

Lew, Jamie. *Asian Americans in class: Charting the achievement gap among Korean American youth.* New York: Teachers College Press, 2006. Print.

Louie, Vivian S. *Compelled to excel: Immigration, education, and opportunity among Chinese Americans.* Stanford: Stanford University Press, 2004. Print.

Monzo, Lilia D., and Robert A. Rueda. "A sociocultural perspective on acculturation: Latino immigrant families negotiating diverse discipline practices." In *Education and Urban Society 3.28* (2006): 188-203. Print.

Ng, Jennifer C., Sharon S. Lee, and Yoon K. Pak. "Contesting the model minority and perpetual foreigner stereotypes: A critical review of literature on Asian Americans in Education." In *Review of Research in Education, 31.* 2007. 95-130. Print.

Ngo, Bic. "Ambivalent urban, immigrant identities: the incompleteness of Lao American student identities." In *International Journal of Qualitative Studies in Education 22.2* (2009): 201-220. Print.

Ngo, Bic, and Stacey J. Lee. "Complicating the image of model minority success: A review of Southeast Asian American education." In *Review of Educational Research 77.4* (2007): 415-453. Print.

Ogbu, John and Herbert D. Simons. "Voluntary and involuntary minorities: A cultural-ecological theory of school performance with some implications for education." In *Anthropology and Education Quarterly 29* (1998): 155-188. Print.

Ong, Aihwa. *Buddha is hiding.* Berkeley: University of California Press, 2004. Print.

Orfield, Gary, and John T. Yun. *Resegregation in American schools.* Cambridge: Civil Rights Project, Harvard University, 1999. Print.

Pang, Valerie O. "Asian American children: A diverse population." In *The Educational Forum 55* (1990): 49-65. Print.

Park, Clara C. "Learning style preferences of Southeast Asian students." In *Urban Education 35.3* (2000): 245-268. Print.

Portes, Alejandro, and Rubén G. Rumbaut. *Immigrant America: A portrait.* Berkeley: University of California Press, 2006. Print.

Ready, Douglas D., Valerie E. Lee, and Kevin G. Welner. "Educational equity and school structure: School size, overcrowding, and schools-within-schools." In *Teachers College Record 106.10* (2004): 1989-2014. Print.

Reeves, Terrance J., and Claudette E. Bennett. *We the People: Asians in the United States, Census 2000 Special Reports.* Washington DC: U.S. Census Bureau, 2004. Print.

Reyes, Angela. *Language, identity, and stereotype among Southeast Asian American youth: The other Asian.* Mahwah: Lawrence Erlbaum Associates, 2007. Print.

Rogoff, Barbara. *The cultural nature of human development*. New York: Oxford University Press, 1995. Print.

Rumbaut, Rubén. "Vietnamese, Laotians, and Cambodian Americans." In Contemporary Asian America: *A Multidisciplinary Reader*, edited by Min. Zhou and James V. Gatewood, New York: New York University Press, 2000. Print.

Rumbaut, Rubén G., and Kenji Ima. *The Adaptations of Southeast Asian Refugee Youth: A Comparative Study, Final Report*. Washington, DC: U. S. Department of Human Services, Family Support Administration, Office of Refugee Settlement. 1988. Print.

Sin, Bo Chum. "Socio-cultural, psychological and linguistic effects on Cambodian students' progress through formal schooling in the United States." Unpublished dissertation. University of Oregon, 1991. Print.

Sirin, Selcuk R. "Socioeconomic status and academic achievement: A meta-analytic review of research." In *Review of Educational Research 75.3* (2005): 417-453. Print.

Smith-Hefner, Nancy J. "Education, gender, and generational conflict among Khmer refugees." In *Anthropology and Education Quarterly 24* (1993): 135-158. Print.

Smith-Hefner, Nancy J. *Khmer American: Identity and moral education in a diasporic community*. Berkeley: University of California Press, 1999. Print.

Steele, Claude M. "A threat in the air: How stereotypes shape the intellectual identities and performance of women and African-Americans." In *American Psychologist 52* (1997): 613-629. Print.

Suarez-Orozco, Carola, and Marcelo M. Suarez-Orozco. *Children of immigration*. Cambridge: Harvard University Press, 2001. Print.

Sue, Derald and David Sue. *Counseling the culturally different: Theory and practice* (2nd ed.). New York: Wiley and Sons, 1990. Print.

Sun, Yongmin. "Family environment and adolescents' well-being before and after parents' marital disruption: A longitudinal analysis." In *Journal of Marriage and Family 63.3* (2001): 697-713. Print.

Uba, Laura. *Asian Americans: Personality patterns, identity, and mental health*. New York: The Guilford Press, 1994. Print.

Um, Khatharya. "Scars of war: Educational issues and challenges for Cambodian-American students." In *Asian-American Education Prospects and Challenges*, edited by Clara C. Park and Marilyn M. Chi. Westport: Praeger, 1999. Print.

Um, Khatharya. *A dream denied: Educational experiences of Southeast Asian American youth: Issues and recommendations*. Washington DC: Southeast Asia Resource Action Center, 2003. Print.

Valenzuela, Angela. *Subtractive schooling: U.S. Mexican youth and the politics of caring*. New York: State University New York Press, 1999. Print.

Wallitt, Roberta. "Cambodian invisibility: Students lost between the "achievement gap" and the "model minority." In *Multicultural Perspectives 10.1* (2008): 3-9. Print.

Wright, Wayne E. "What English-only really means: A study of the implementation of California language policy with Cambodian-American students. " In *Bilingual Education and Bilingualism* 7 (2004): 1-23. Print.

Zhou, Min. "Growing up American: The challenge confronting immigrant children and children of immigrants." In *Annual Review of Sociology 23* (1997): 3-95. Print.

Zhou, Min and Carl L. Bankston. *Growing up American: How Vietnamese children adapt to life in the United States*. New York: Russell Sage Foundation, 1998. Print.

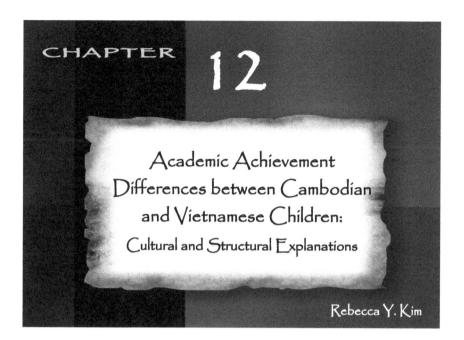

CHAPTER 12

Academic Achievement Differences between Cambodian and Vietnamese Children:
Cultural and Structural Explanations

Rebecca Y. Kim

Unlike most post-1965 Asian immigrants, Southeast Asians[1] left their homelands as political refugees fleeing war, death, and persecution, and thus lost families and contact with loved ones in the process. From such an exodus, Southeast Asians entered America as part of the largest refugee resettlement program in the country's history. As political refugees, many are dependent on government financial assistance, and they are concentrated in low-income neighborhoods. These circumstances of exit and reception and premigration characteristics make the adaptation of Southeast Asian children particularly difficult. Overcoming various social structural disadvantages, Southeast Asian children must quickly adjust to the unfamiliar U.S. school system and compete academically with native-born children. These difficulties suggest that Southeast Asians will not fare well in terms of their educational achievement—challenging the commonly told story of Asian American students' academic success (Bell 1985; Hirshman and Wong 1982; Hsia and Hirano-Nakanishi 1989).

Recent scholarship, however, complicates this story. Several studies show that, despite a variety of hardships, the children of the largest Southeast Asian group, the Vietnamese, are excelling academically and are catching up to East Asian immigrant children in terms of their educational achievement (Caplan, Choy, and Whitmore 1991; Rutledge 1992; Zhou and Bankston 1998).[2] The same level of academic success, however, is not found among other Southeast Asian children, particularly the Cambodians (Nakanishi and Nishida 1995; Portes 1996; Rumbaut and Cornelius 1995). In Kenji Ima and Rubén Rumbaut's (1995) study of six groups of immigrant and refugee children in Southern California, Vietnamese children achieved the highest GPAs and exhibited the largest number of students classified as gifted among Mexican, Filipino, Lao, Cambodian, and smaller groups of immigrant children from Asia and Latin America. In contrast to Vietnamese students, Cambodian students had the lowest GPAs among Southeast Asians and the lowest math scores of the six groups in the study. Cambodian students were also most likely to be categorized as "limited English proficient" compared to Mexican, Filipino, Vietnamese, Lao, Hmong, and other children of immigrants from Asia and Latin America (Rumbaut and Cornelius 1995). Vietnamese students also had the highest mean math scores among various Cuban, Haitian, and Mexican children of immigrants in South Florida and Southern California (Portes and MacLeod 1996). Among Southeast Asians, research shows that Vietnamese children demonstrate the highest academic performance whereas Cambodian children demonstrate the poorest performance.

Given the nature of Southeast Asian political refugees' exit, entrance, and resettlement in the United States compared to voluntary Asian immigrants, we can see why Southeast Asian children might lag behind the children of other post-1965 Asian immigrants. But it is less clear why there would be differences in academic achievement among Southeast Asians. In response, this essay examines the sources of academic achievement differences between Cambodian and Vietnamese children. This is done by applying cultural and structural explanations for academic achievement and exploring the history and settlement patterns of the two groups in the United States.

Cultural and Structural Explanations

Cultural and structural arguments are the two main theoretical explanations for understanding group differences in educational achievement among children of immigrants and refugees.

Cultural Explanations

In the most conventional accounts, cultural explanations posit that immigrants' premigration cultural values, norms, and beliefs are central to understanding ethnic differences in their educational achievement (Covello 1972; Zborowski and Herzog 1969). Such cultural perspectives present culture as a force that operates largely independently of social structure. Educational and subsequent economic achievement differences are fundamentally viewed as the product of cultural values and beliefs inherent to the group.

Cultural explanations emphasizing the importance of cultural values, beliefs, and practices have commonly been used to explain Asian American children's educational success (Caplan et al. 1991; Caudill and DeVos 1956; Kitano 1969; Rutledge 1992). Cultural values from Asian immigrants' home countries are said to be transplanted to America and are used by Asian families to socialize their children and to help them achieve academic and economic success. In particular, it has been argued that cultural values influenced by the Confucian tradition found in East Asian countries (as well as in Vietnam), that place a high value on education, hard work, and social solidarity as a means of achieving mobility, help explain Asian children's high academic achievement. Such cultural arguments have been criticized over the years. For example, the cultural argument that Chinese Confucian cultural values positively influence children's educational achievement has been challenged by studies that find that other groups who share similar values do not do well or that others who do not share similar Confucian values still do well academically (Covello 1972; Gibson 1989). Recent studies on students' beliefs about the economic payoffs of excelling in school found that there are no ethnic differences in how Asian, black, Latino, and white students value education. These students are "all equally likely to say that getting a good education will have genuine payoff down the road" (Steinberg et al 1996: 34). If other groups also value education, it is less clear why Asians would do better. If coming from a particular Asian Confucian tradition is helpful, it is also unclear why other groups that do not have a Confucian cultural tradition, like South Asians, would do well in school, taking into account social class background (Gibson 1989). Cultural explanations have also been criticized for not acknowledging the possibility that it is not the inherited cultural traits per se but the structural discrimination that Asians face in the larger society that leads them to place a high value on education and to pressure their children to work hard (Sue and Okazaki 1990). But this argument is complicated by the fact that other ethnic minorities who also face blocked mobility and discrimination do not equally turn to education as a means of mobility.

Accounting for the interactive nature of culture and structure can counter some of the limitations of traditional cultural theories. For example, in explaining the high levels of educational achievement among children of Korean and Chinese immigrants in the United States, Min Zhou and Susan Kim (2006) argue that it is really the interaction between positive cultural values for educational mobility and strong community support systems that translate to success. Positive cultural values for mobility fostered in family, peer, and community networks contribute to Korean and Chinese immigrant children's educational achievement. In particular, they highlight tangible social structures, namely supplementary educational programs like SAT preparatory programs, *buxibans*, and *hawkwons* with names like "Little Harvard," "IQ 180," and "Ivy League School" that actualize the pro-education and mobility values of Korean and Chinese immigrants (Zhou and Kim 2006: 12). Thus, culture couched in supportive social structures is what makes the difference.[3]

Min Zhou and Carl Bankston's (1998) work on Vietnamese American children's educational achievement also find the same interactive factors at play. They argue that ties to ethnic communities reinforce immigrant parents' goals of upward mobility and promote productive behaviors in schools, particularly for children in an otherwise structurally disadvantaged setting like inner-city schools.

With the assumption that ethnic communities have cultural and structural resources that can be used to assist their community members, it is expected that being close to one's ethnic community can be helpful to children's academic achievement.

Structural Explanations

More traditional structural explanations stress the premigration group characteristics of immigrant groups and the social structural conditions of the host society to explain immigrants' and their descendants' educational and occupational achievement (Steinberg 1974). Among structural variables, social class characteristics of children's families such as parents' education, occupation, and income are considered crucial for predicting children's educational achievement (Blau and Duncan 1967; Haller and Portes 1973). It is assumed that parents with higher levels of education, occupation, and income will provide their children with greater financial and social resources to succeed in school relative to those parents with lower social class characteristics (Ekstrom et al. 1986; Goldscheider and Zuckerman 1984; Kao 1995; Steinberg 1974).[4]

Although earlier waves of Asian immigrants entered with relatively low skills, post-1965 Asian immigrants came with more education and skills than native-born minorities and, in some cases, more than native-born whites (Light and Bonacich 1988; Steinberg 1989). To be sure, not all of today's Asian immigrants come with high skills and education, but a sizable portion do (Cheng and Yang 1996; Xie and Goyette 2004). Children of Asian immigrants also come from families with low rates of marital disruption (Le 2009; Xie and Goyette 2004), which has been linked to higher academic performance and aspirations (Caplan et al. 1991; Ekstrom et al. 1986; Rumberger 1983). Thus, the relatively higher socioeconomic class backgrounds coupled with the more intact family structures of recently arrived Asian immigrants can provide Asian American children with advantages in terms of academic achievement.

Unlike many post-1965 voluntary Asian immigrants who entered as wage laborers, salaried professionals or entrepreneurs, however, Southeast Asians entered as political refugees fleeing war, persecution, and death. Many Southeast Asians, such as the Hmong,

Lao, and Cambodians, came from rural backgrounds with little education, money, or skills[5] and are dependent on government financial assistance. Moreover, many Southeast Asians have disturbed family structures—they lost family members and loved ones as a result of war and the harsh refugee process. Many Southeast Asians are also concentrated in low-income neighborhoods near poorly funded minority majority schools with problems such as gang violence. In such a setting, they also face discrimination as one of the new groups of immigrant ethnic/racial minorities. These various structural factors can prove to be obstacles to the academic success of the children of Southeast Asian refugees.

A Case Study of Cambodians and Vietnamese

Cambodians and Vietnamese entered the American scene primarily due to U.S. military involvement in Southeast Asia as the United States sought to contain the spread of communism. In 1954 Vietnam was divided into North (the Democratic Republic of Vietnam headed by Ho Chi Minh) and South (the Republic of Vietnam headed by Ngo Dinh Diem) when the French army was defeated by Ho Chi Minh's forces. In an effort to quell the expansion of communism in Vietnam and the rest of Southeast Asia, the United States offered aid and sent troops to Vietnam. When U.S. troops later pulled out, however, the South Vietnamese lost ground and Saigon fell into the hands of North Vietnamese troops in 1975.

As in Vietnam, the U.S. government became involved in Cambodia in an effort to contain communism. During the turbulent wars in Vietnam in the mid-1950s and 1960s, Cambodia was neutral, but this changed in 1970 when a *coup d'état* drew the Cambodians into the Vietnam War. In the context of corruption, a failing national economy, U.S. secret bombings along the North Vietnamese/Cambodian border, and the incursion of North Vietnamese troops, the capital of Cambodia fell into the hands of the communist Khmer Rouge in 1975 (Chan 1991; Chandler 1996).

Amid this turmoil, many Cambodians and Vietnamese sought refuge in the United States. As foreigners adjusting to a new land, the Cambodians and Vietnamese faced similar difficulties. Coming from subsistence economies and traveling great cultural and geographical distances, both groups had to adjust to a postindustrial economy and U.S. culture, while also overcoming discrimination and prejudice as ethnic/racial minorities. Despite these similarities, there are cultural and structural differences that distinguish the two groups.

In terms of cultural differences, the Vietnamese have Confucianism and Mahayana Buddhism, neither of which is present in Cambodian culture.[6] Originally a religious philosophy from China, Confucianism supports a hierarchical patriarchal order and emphasizes hard work, respect for elders, discipline, and education, values that are said to encourage Asian parents to invest more in their children's education. Practiced in other East Asian countries and by over 93 percent of Vietnamese (Rutledge 1992: 47), Mahayana Buddhism is also part of Vietnamese culture and is said to esteem values that are more "social" in nature—values that can strengthen community ties and encourage Asian parents to become more involved in their children's education (Ima and Rumbaut 1995; Swearer 1981). Mahayana Buddhism teaches that humankind is intricately interrelated with others. For example, before reaching individual "enlightenment,"[7] it teaches that one must first help others to reach enlightenment. "A Mahayanist's purpose is to help others," and their salient goal is compassion to and cohesion with others (Swearer 1981: 501).

In contrast, the Cambodians have neither a Confucian nor a Mahayana Buddhist cultural tradition. Instead, the majority of Cambodians adhere to Theravada Buddhism, a school of Buddhism that is considered to be more "individual" than collective—stressing personal development and individual good behavior. In contrast to Mahayana Buddhism, Theravada Buddhism teaches that the individual must first attain enlightenment before helping others to reach enlightenment, pointing to its more "individual" character (Lester 1973).

Although not all cultural values are directly transplanted to the new country, certain values can be modified and kept, thus influencing immigrants' and their children's adaptation, including such areas as academic achievement (Zhou and Bankston 1998). For example, a recent study of Cambodian Americans found that they are more individualistic than other Southeast Asians, such as the Vietnamese who are influenced by Chinese culture and tend to be more collectively oriented (Smith-Hefner 1999). Nancy Smith-Hefner writes, "By many accounts.... Khmer are more individualistic than collective when compared with some of their neighbors, especially those influenced by Chinese tradition. Behavior among kin is less rigidly prescribed and more dependent on individual likes and dislikes" (1999: 12-13). In line with this view, others have suggested that Cambodian children may not have the same family and social pressure to achieve in school compared to Vietnamese children. Several studies have found that Cambodian "parents are unlikely to try to 'make' their children study," (Hopkins 1996: 129) believing that the mastery of various academic subjects is predetermined by a special disposition, something that all children do not possess (Ima and Rumbaut 1995). While Vietnamese parents value effort and tend to push their children in school studies, many Cambodian parents think that their children are either already specially gifted in academics or they are not, and therefore they view school studies as something that cannot be "forced" on a child. Thus, it is suggested that the Cambodians do not have the same degree of social and family solidarity as the Vietnamese and that Cambodian children may not receive the same amount of pressure to do well in school as Vietnamese children.

The Cambodians and Vietnamese also have different social structural characteristics. The Cambodians arrived largely in a single wave; the Vietnamese migrated to the United States in two waves.[8] The initial wave of the more elite Vietnamese refugees arrived shortly before the fall of Saigon in 1975. The second wave of Vietnamese, often labeled the "Boat People," followed about five years after the first wave; they arrived with little money and limited education. Unlike the Vietnamese, most Cambodians came as a single wave when Pol Pot's rule ended with the invasion of Cambodia by Vietnam in 1978 (Hopkins 1996). Because the Vietnamese immigrants included a first wave of more educated and affluent people who had arrived earlier, the second wave of more impoverished Vietnamese benefited from the economic and community structures that the first group had already established. In contrast, the Cambodians arrived in a single wave of mostly poor rural farmers; they lacked the benefit of having a more established and relatively affluent and educated first wave of settlers established as a community (most of the educated Cambodians were executed by the Khmer Rouge).

About two million Cambodians—a quarter of the country's prerevolution population—died in the three years following the fall of Saigon through starvation, execution, and disease. Jeremy Hein writes that "the hardships imposed by the new Communist regimes in Vietnam and Laos were vastly exceeded by those in Cambodia" (1995: 27). As a consequence of the severity of war experienced by Cambodians compared to other Southeast Asian refugees, more Cambodians have physically and emotionally disturbed family structures: "More than one-third of them have lost a family member or close friend, and others have witnessed atrocities" (Hein 1995: 117). Consequently, many Cambodian youth have more disturbed family structures than do Vietnamese children. With higher percentages of female headed households (with no spouse present), 56.2% of the Cambodian female headed households lived below the federal poverty level compared to 37.4% of the Vietnamese female headed households (2000 Census).

Since the Cambodians do not have an established first wave of educated and affluent coethnics and have experienced more persecution, disrupted families, and psychological wounds, their community solidarity is also tenuous (Hopkins 1996). Many distrust leadership and must also cope with the psychological scars of war. As Polin Soth, a Cambodian community leader and political historian commented, "There is no leadership in the [Cambodian] community.... People have lost faith. They don't trust leaders. They don't believe in themselves."[9] In contrast to the strong ethnic community solidarity found among the Vietnamese, Cambodians have weak community ties.

This disparity is evident in the two groups' ethnic communities in Southern California. The predominant Vietnamese community, called "Little Saigon," is located near a white suburb. Little Saigon's streets are clean, and the businesses are booming with various ethnic shops, restaurants, and shiny mini malls. In contrast, the largest Cambodian community in the country is located in the inner city with a minority majority population in Long Beach. There are no malls or shiny business complexes; the buildings are worn; and the Vietnamese, not the Cambodians, own most of the small businesses that exist.[10] Long Beach was officially designated as America's first Cambodian Town in 2007, but the goal of remaking the town into an attractive tourist and business center has yet to be achieved.[11]

The socioeconomic backgrounds of the two groups reflect these community differences. According to the 1990 U.S. Census, 40.7% of the Cambodians had less than a fifth grade education compared to 11.4% of the Vietnamese. The 2000 Census shows more favorable numbers, but differences remain. Over a quarter of the Cambodians aged 25 and over had no formal schooling compared to only 8 percent of the Vietnamese. Likewise, the median family income of the Cambodians was $35,621 compared to $47,103 for the Vietnamese. Cambodians are more likely to live below the federal poverty line; 34.8% of Cambodians live below the federal poverty line compared to 14.2% of Vietnamese (2000 Census). Cambodians are also less likely to hold managerial and professional positions than the Vietnamese.

The differences between the Cambodian and Vietnamese communities in the United States connect with the past development and present economic standing of the two countries. During the ninety years of French occupation that began in the 1860s, the French colonial government westernized and urbanized Vietnam, building roads, schools, hospitals, and industries. In the process, the Roman (Latin) alphabet was used, and many of the Vietnamese elite were educated in France. The westernizing and urbanizing influence of the French was felt among the general Vietnamese public by the 1970s (Gold 1992). On the other hand, the French did not modernize and westernize Cambodia to the extent that they did Vietnam. Because Cambodia was not considered a lucrative and strategic colony, the French did not develop systems of roads, hospitals, schools, or industries in Cambodia. And Vietnamese, not French officials, administered Cambodia, serving as a "middleman minority" throughout French Indochina. Most of the French influence in Cambodia was therefore minimal, limited to the capital city of Phnom Penh. Ordinary Cambodians "scarcely felt [the] French presence" (Hopkins 1996: 10). Outside of the capital city, villages continued to be run by Buddhist monks who refused to teach the Romanized alphabet, which the French had successfully introduced to the Vietnamese.[12]

Today, the Gross Domestic Product (GDP) of Cambodia is $28.01 billion while Vietnam is $242.3 billion.[13] In 2004, 35% of the Cambodian population was estimated to live below the poverty line compared to 14.8%[14] of the Vietnamese population. The life expectancy at birth is 62.1 in Cambodia compared to 71.6 in Vietnam. And the literacy rate (age 15 and over can read and write) is 73.6% in Cambodia versus 90.3% in Vietnam.[15]

Table 1. Cambodian and Vietnamese Americans Statistical Profile (2000 Census)

	Cambodian	Vietnamese	Total Asians	Total U.S.
Population[16]	206,052	1,223,736		
Median Age[17]	22.8	29.9	31.4	35.4
No Formal Schooling[18]	26.2%	8.0%	4.2%	1.4%
BA Degree or Higher[19]	9.1%	19.5%	42.7%	24.4%
Per Capita Income (1999)[20]	$10,215	$15,385	$21,587	$20,719
% below Poverty[21]	34.8%	14.2%	9.7%	9.2%
Female HH, no Spouse[22]	21.5%	11.9%	8.8%	11.8%
Female HH below Poverty[23]	56.2%	37.4%	27.9%	34.3%
% Professionals[24]	17.9%	27.0%	43.2%	33.6%
Median Family Income[25]	$35,621	$47,103	$59,324	$50,046
Average Family Size[26]	4.54	3.99	3.57	3.14

Conclusion

Substantial cultural and social historical differences between immigrant and refugee groups are often lost in studies that classify all Asians or Southeast Asians as a single group. In addition to the diversity in the Asian immigrant and Southeast Asian refugee populations, there is also cultural and structural diversity among Southeast Asians themselves, which can affect their adaptation, including academic achievement. Vietnamese children tend to come from higher income and more professional and more educated homes relative to the Cambodian children in the United States. Cambodian children also do not have the same supportive cultural and structural ethnic community resources compared to the Vietnamese children. The differences between the two groups in the United States are also reflected in the different historical trajectories and economic conditions of their country of origin. Any attempts to improve the educational achievement of Southeast Asian children will have to consider these cultural and structural factors that contribute to different achievement outcomes.

Endnotes

1. Southeast Asians include Vietnamese, Laotians, Cambodians, and Hmong.
2. Recent studies, however, show that Vietnamese students of the early 21st century are not doing as well as their counterparts in the 1990s. The "Vietnamese valedictorians" that were celebrated in the media over a decade ago are less common today (Zhou and Bankston 2006). Nevertheless, achievement differences among Southeast Asians clearly persist (Southeast Asian American Statistical Profile: Southeast Asian Resource Action Center, 2004).
3. Following this argument, positive cultural values toward educational achievement couched in an unfavorable social structure, an environment hostile to educational mobility, would not have the same effect.
4. Mayer (1997) provides further elaboration and critique of the influence of parents' income and education on children's education and life chances.
5. They have skills, but they are not translatable into the United States.

6. Though variations exist depending on regional and provincial nuances, Confucianism, Mahayana Buddhism, and Catholicism combine with ancestor worship to make up the Vietnamese people's unique religious culture. Among these, Confucianism and Mahayana Buddhism are the most important influences.

7. Attaining enlightenment means escaping subjection to mundane desires and "being in touch with one self."

8. In the mid-1970s, a small group of refugees from privileged segments of Cambodian society who felt most threatened by the new communist government entered America. There is also a very small group of students who came to Long Beach, California, as foreign exchange students in the 1950s and stayed in America.

9. Soth was quoted in *Los Angeles Times*, April 26, 1998, E3.

10. These comments are based on my observations in East Long Beach and Little Saigon, winter 1998.

11. The Vietnamese population is also the most sizable among Southeast Asians. The 2000 Census estimates the Vietnamese population to be 1,223,736 in contrast to 206,052 for the Cambodians (Table 1).

12. The fact that Catholicism is considered to be one of the major religions in Vietnam, but not in Cambodia, also indicates the greater cultural westernization of Vietnam relative to Cambodia.

13. In U.S. dollars, 2008 estimate; the data for both of the countries come from the *CIA, The World Factbook*: https://www.cia.gov/library/publications/the-world-factbook/geos/cb.html

14. Estimated figure for 2007, Ibid.

15. *CIA, The World Factbook:* https://www.cia.gov/library/publications/the-world-factbook/geos/vm.html

16. Asian group alone or in combination in Asian Population: 2000 (Issued February 2002) at http://www.census.gov/prod/2002pubs/c2kbr01-16.pdf.

17. "Southeast Asian American Statistical Profile" by the Southeast Asian Resource Action Center (SEARAC 2004).

18. Educational attainment of people aged 25 and over in the U.S., Ibid.

19. Ibid.

20. Ibid.

21. U.S. Census Bureau, "Profile of Selected Economic Characteristics: 2000," Summary File 4.

22. U.S. Census Bureau, We the People: Asians in the United States (December 2004), Figure 5, p. 8 at http://www.census.gov/prod/2004 pubs/censr-17.pdf.

23. U.S. Bureau of the Census, 2000 Summary File 4, DP-3.

24. Percent in management, professional, & related occupations in SEARC 2004.

25. Ibid.

26. Ibid.

References

Bell, David. "America's Greatest Success Story: The Triumph of Asian Americans." In *The New Republic,* July 15 and 22 (1985): 24-31. Print.

Blau, Peter, and Otis D. Duncan. *The American Occupational Structure.* New York: John Wiley, 1967. Print.

Caplan, Nathan, Marcella H. Choy, and John K. Whitmore. *Children of the Boat People: A Study of Educational Success.* Ann Arbor: University of Michigan Press, 1991. Print.

Caudill, William, and George DeVos. "Achievement, Culture, and Personality: The Case of the Japanese Americans." In *American Anthropologist* 58 (1956): 1102-1126. Print.

Chan, Sucheng. *Asian Americans: An Interpretive History.* New York: Twayne Publishers, 1991. Print.

Chandler, David P. *A History of Cambodia.* Boulder: Westview Press, 1996. Print.

Cheng, Lucie, and Philip Q. Yang. "Asians: The 'Model Minority' Deconstructed." In *Ethnic Los Angeles*, edited by Roger Waldinger. New York: Russell Sage Foundation, 1996. Print.

Covello, Leonard. *The Social Background of the Italo-American School Child.* Totowa: Rowman and Littlefield, 1972. Print.

Ekstrom, Ruth B., Margaret E. Goertz, Judith M. Pollack, and Donald A. Rock. "Who Drops Out of High School and Why? Findings from a National Study." In *Teachers College Record* 87 (1986): 356-373. Print.

Gibson, Margaret A. *Accommodation Without Assimilation: Sikh Immigrants in an American High School.* Ithaca: Cornell University Press, 1989. Print.

Gold, Steven. *Refugee Communities: A Comparative Field Study.* Newbury Park: Sage, 1992. Print.

Goldscheider, Calvin, and Alan Zuckerman. *The Transformation of the Jews.* Chicago: University of Chicago Press, 1984. Print.

Haller, Archibald D., and Alejandro Portes. "Status Attainment Process." In *Sociology of Education* 46 (1973): 51-91. Print.

Hein, Jeremy. *From Vietnam, Laos, and Cambodia: A Refugee Experience in the United States.* New York: Twayne Publishers, 1995. Print.

Hirschman, Charles, and Morrison G. Wong. "Trends in Socioeconomic Achievement among Immigrant and Native-Born Asian-Americans, 1960-1976." In *Sociological Quarterly* 22 (1981): 495-513. Print.

Hopkins, Mary Carol. *Braving a New World: Cambodian (Khmer) Refugees in an American City.* Westport: Bergin and Garvey, 1996. Print.

Hsia, Jayjia, and Marsha Hirano-Nakanishi. "The Demographics of Diversity: Asian Americans and Higher Education." In *Change: The Magazine of Higher Learning,* (November-December 1989): 20. Print.

Ima, Kenji, and Rubén G. Rumbaut. "Southeast Asian Refugees in American Schools: A Comparison of Fluent-English-Proficient and Limited-English-Proficient Students." In *The Asian American Educational Experience,* edited by Don Nakanishi and Yamano Nishida. New York: Routledge Press, 1995. Print.

Kao, Grace. "Asian Americans as Model Minorities? A Look at Their Academic Performance." In *American Journal of Education* 103 (1995): 121-159. Print.

Kao, Grace, and Marta Tienda. "Educational Aspirations of Minority Youth." In *American Journal of Education* 106 (1998): 349-384. Print.

Kitano, Harry. Japanese Americans: *The Evolution of a Subculture.* Englewood Cliffs: Prentice-Hall, 1969. Print.

Le, C.N. 2009. "Demographic Characteristics of Immigrants" from *Asian-Nation: The Landscape of Asian America.* Web; December 29, 2009.

Lester, Robert C. *Theravada Buddhism in Southeast Asia.* Ann Arbor: University of Michigan Press, 1973. Print.

Light, Ivan, and Edna Bonacich. *Immigrant Entrepreneurs: Koreans in Los Angeles,* 1965-1982. Berkeley: University of California Press. 1988. Print.

Mayer, Susan E. *What Money Can't Buy: Family Income and Children's Life Chances.* Cambridge: Harvard University Press, 1997. Print.

Nakanishi, Donald T., and Tina Yamano Nishida, eds. *The Asian American Educational Experience.* New York: Routledge, 1995. Print.

Portes, Alejandro. *The New Second Generation.* New York: Russell Sage Foundation, 1996. Print.

Portes, Alejandro, and Dag MacLeod. "The Educational Progress of Children of Immigrants: The Roles of Class, Ethnicity, and School Context." Unpublished manuscript. Print.

Portes, Alejandro, and Min Zhou. "The New Second Generation: Segmented Assimilation and Its Variants among Post-1965 Immigrant Youth." In *Annals of the American Academy of Political and Social Science* 530 (1993): 74-98. Print.

Rumbaut, Rubén. "Vietnamese, Laotian, and Cambodian Americans." In *Contemporary Asian America*, edited by Min Zhou and James Gatewood. New York: New York University Press, 2000. Print.

Rumbaut, Rubén G., and Wayne A. Cornelius. *California's Immigrant Children*. La Jolla, CA: Center for U.S.-Mexican Studies, University of California, San Diego, 1995. Print.

Rumbaut, Rubén G., and Kenji Ima. *The Adaptation of Southeast Asian Refugee Youth*. San Diego, CA: Southeast Asian Refugee Youth Study, Department of Sociology, San Diego State University, 1988. Print.

Rumberger, Russell W. "Dropping Out of High School: The Influence of Race, Sex and Family Background." In *American Educational Research Journal* 20 (1983): 199-200. Print.

Rutledge, Paul. *The Vietnamese Experience in America*. Bloomington: Indiana University Press, 1992. Print.

Smith-Hefner, Nancy J. *Khmer American: Identity and Moral Education in a Diasporic Community*. Berkeley: University of California Press, 1999. Print.

Steinberg, Laurence, B. Bradford Brown, and Sanford M. Dornbusch. *Beyond the Classroom: Why School Reform Has Failed and What Parents Need to Do*. New York: Simon & Schuster, 1996. Print.

Steinberg, Stephen. *The Academic Melting Pot: Catholics and Jews in American higher Education*. New York: McGraw-Hill, 1974. Print.

_____. *The Ethnic Myth: Race, Ethnicity, and Class in America*. Boston: Beacon Press, 1989. Print.

Sue, Stanley, and Sumie Okazaki. "Asian American Educational Achievement: A Phenomenon in Search of an Explanation." In *American Psychologist* 45 (1990): 913-920. Print.

Swearer, Donald. *Buddhism and Society in Southeast Asia*. Chambersburg: Anima Books, 1981. Print.

Xie, Yu, and Kimberly Goyette. *A Demographic Portrait of Asian Americans*. New York: Russell Sage and Population Reference Bureau, 2004. Print.

Zborowski, Mark, and Elizabeth Herzog. *Life is with People.* New York: Schocken Books, 1969. Print.

Zhou, Min, and Carl L. Bankston III. *Growing Up American: How Vietnamese Children Adapt to Life in the United States.* New York: Russell Sage Foundation, 1998. Print.

Zhou, Min, and Carl L. Bankston III. "Delinquency and Acculturation in the Twenty-first Century: A Decade's Change in a Vietnamese American Community." In *Immigration and Crime: Race, Ethnicity, and Violence,* edited by Martinez and Valenzuela. New York: New York University Press, 2006. Print.

Zhou, Min, and Susan S. Kim. "Community Forces, Social Capital, and Educational Achievement: The Case of Supplementary Education in the Chinese and Korean Immigrant Communities." In *Harvard Educational Review* 76:1 (2006): 1-29. Print.

Section VI

Cambodian American Dance and Music

CHAPTER 13

Cambodian Music and Dance in North America

Sam-Ang Sam

There are approximately one half million Cambodians now living in the United States. Unlike earlier Asians coming to America—such as the Chinese, Japanese, Filipinos, and Indians—Cambodians are among the more recent immigrants. On the other hand, Cambodians came to America, not for economic reasons, but for fear of harsh punishment and persecution by the torturous Cambodian Communists, better known to the world as the Khmer Rouge and Pol Pot.

Cambodia had been peaceful up until the mid-1970s. However, on April 17, 1975, the Khmer Rouge launched an aggressive attack on the Cambodian national armies and took over the country. Immediately, the Khmer Rouge began an evacuation of the cities, pushing people to the countryside, where they separated family members and put them in harsh labor camps. The Khmer Rouge systematically killed some two million Cambodians during its subsequent rule of three years, eight months, and twenty days. Among those, 80 to 90 percent of Cambodian artists, including musicians, were killed (*Kampuchea Review* 1979: 982; Jones 1987: 1; Pack 1989: J4). Since then, hundreds of thousands of Cambodians have fled the killing fields and resettled in safe havens, such as the United

States. There have been two waves of Cambodian refugees to the United States, the first occurring in 1975, which included professionals and skilled individuals. The second wave, beginning in the early 1980s, included unskilled individuals, particularly farmers and peasants who lived near the borders and could therefore flee more easily and seek refuge in Thailand before moving on to the United States and elsewhere.

In this chapter I examine the roles of music in the Cambodian community and my role as a Cambodian musician and a cultural advocate. It is difficult, if not impossible, to address issues pertaining to Cambodian music in North America without reference to the music in Cambodia since musicians in Cambodia have different musical priorities from those in the United States due to context, situation, environment, and pressure; they are, however, interrelated. In Cambodia musicians are more concerned with the loss of culture and their music is directed at cultural revival and preservation of dying traditions, as well as further developing the culture and restoring pride. On the other hand, Cambodian musicians in the United States are more concerned with identity crisis, peer pressure, cultural sharing, ethnic solidarity, restoration of pride, ensuring continuity, upholding traditional ceremony, as well as expressing homesickness and providing entertainment. Indeed, it is a strong response to the Khmer Rouge radical and utopian policies to uproot Cambodian culture.

Unlike other Asian music ensembles in America, which tend to be academic-based, Cambodian ensembles are almost entirely community-based—primarily due to a lack of awareness and familiarity of the general public as well as the priorities of the Cambodian American community: revival, maintenance, development, and promotion. Indian and Indonesian music, for example, were introduced to the American public many decades ago and the American public is aware of the style and familiar with the sound.

Cambodian music ensembles can be found in virtually every Cambodian community in America. However, only a few musicians lecture, do workshops, perform, and serve in residencies in schools. Most perform for community social functions: weddings, New Year celebrations, and social gatherings. Connecticut College and the University of Washington had Cambodian ensembles during the 1980s and 1990s, created primarily to enable me to teach American students. After I left those institutions, the ensembles were discontinued.

Current Practice

Cambodians in America practice art forms that are functional and most familiar to them, including folk dance and court dance. In addition, two forms of theater are occasionally staged—*yike* (folk theater) and *basakk* (theater of Chinese origin). Among the approximately two dozen music ensembles, *kar* (wedding), *pinn peat* (court), and *mohori* (entertainment) ensembles are found prominently in current practice. The most popular form of all is modern urban (or popular) music, primarily ballroom dance music and pop songs.

A New Trend:
What Is American About It?

In an effort to keep Cambodian traditional modes of artistic expressions alive in our Cambodian American community, and in reaching out to a wider audience in a changing world, Cambodian music is, by and large, more observatory than participatory. Americans seem reluctant and shy away from participation in new things, at least at first. This is perhaps because Cambodian music is so new to America—unfamiliar. There are few advocates, and we, as a people, are facing different problems from other Asian American ethnic communities. Additionally, Cambodian musical instruments are difficult to learn compared to other instruments. Indeed, it takes years to become a virtuoso in any tradition.

Cambodian culture in America is firmly based in its traditional Cambodian form. Democratic principles of inclusiveness, gender, context, and repertory change over time. Are these changes good or dangerous for Cambodian culture? Finding meaningful ways to keep Cambodian music alive, accessible, and viable in America is a difficult task and, thus far, the end results in America are, at times, worrisome. Today, there is confusion about the male-female traditions. Traditionally, Cambodian court dance is known to be a female tradition, in which women perform all roles and characters—king, prince, queen, princess, and demon—except the role of monkey, which is played by a man. Some fifty years ago, however, even the monkey role was performed by a woman. There have been situations in which musical pieces have been shortened. Many musicians play the *chhing* (small finger cymbals) in a reversed manner. The generally poor performance quality in Cambodian communities in America is due to a lack of knowledge of the true quality of art that can be attained, although indeed, some good and professional groups exist as well. The professionals have often been criticized for being narrow-minded; their "narrow-mindedness" can perhaps be attributed to their fear of losing their culture and diminishment of the artistic quality. For instance, a dance troupe in California performs the "Coconut Shell Dance" using ashtrays instead of actual coconut shells. Do we call this a new idea? Is this new idea creative? Is it alright to do that? Many Cambodians view this as an insult and disgrace to their culture and tradition.

Connection to the Homeland

Maintaining cultural ties with the homeland is crucial to cultural continuity and the assurance of high quality in the arts. Although some students have traveled to Cambodia to study traditional arts, opportunities for learning from dedicated and professional musicians and dancers who teach and perform in America have recently increased with professional artists from Cambodia coming to the United States. This began when five dancers defected from the troupe after a tour to the Los Angeles Festival in 1990. This trend of Cambodian artist defection continued, exemplified by the 2001 *Dance: The Spirit of Cambodia* and 2005 *Seasons of Migration* tours of the United States. Other artists have reached the United States through marriages to Americans or Cambodian Americans and, thus far, have not returned to Cambodia. They are currently teaching students in their localities.

This connection and exchange provide nourishment to traditional art forms and are vital to the continuity and the success of Cambodian culture—the more one knows about the tradition, the more engaged one becomes. The authenticity these performers bring to their art form definitely has an effect on form and tradition. For the performers, a quality performance or presentation is evidence of great work and a source of pride. Professional musicians become very discouraged by mediocre performances.

Transcending Boundaries

What motivates young men and women to study Cambodian music? It begins with parental encouragement of music classes to expose their children to Cambodian culture. Further, for peer socialization and courtship, Cambodian youngsters attend cultural events on their own initiative. Artists who are raised in America need to express their creativity—commitment, sincere desire to learn, dedication, responsibility, sensitivity, and most importantly, "respect" for the tradition enhances their learning and participation, regardless of race and background.

Large Cambodian communities in the United States are concentrated in two locations: Long Beach, California, and Lowell, Massachusetts, although smaller Cambodian communities can be found in Washington, D.C., Seattle, Chicago, and Philadelphia. Cambodian communities tend to maintain traditional customs and observe as many of their religious and national festivals as possible. As with most immigrant groups, however, the younger generations now coming of age in North America are strongly inclined to adapt to their new environment and culture, although a small minority have strived to maintain the artistic traditions of their homeland.

The maintenance of Cambodian culture in North America depends on the geographical proximity of balanced groups of musicians, singers, and dancers—dependent upon free time and appropriate contexts for performance. All have been and continue to be problematic. In the case of village ensembles, substitutions have either been impossible or dissimilar (i.e., using an American banjo in place of the *chapey dang veng* [long-necked lute]). Popular music requires a distribution system of media materials (cassette tapes, compact discs, DVDs, and videos), but Cambodian shops are difficult to find outside of Cambodian communities.

With the fall of the Cambodian monarchy in 1970 (albeit, restored in 1993 when Prince Sihanouk returned as King Sihanouk), the court traditions ceased to be exclusive. Court musicians and dancers living in the refugee camps began teaching their arts to interested commoners. Because the court arts were seen to embody the very soul of Cambodian culture, they quickly came to represent the Cambodian heritage that gave all individuals grounding. Court musicians and dancers, having had near-sacred status before 1975, came to have a kind of spiritual status after 1979. Their restoration represented the restoration of the Cambodian soul. Consequently, the court arts in North America have been entirely democratic, open to anyone willing to learn. These became part of the healing process of a people deeply scarred by events so terrible that those who have not personally experienced them can never even imagine the horror. Court arts were not merely elegant, sophisticated, and exotic, but became fundamental to maintaining and expressing Cambodian national identity. We are very proud of the fact that the Khmer court dance (also called Royal Ballet) was proclaimed a Masterpiece of the Oral and Intangible Heritage of Humanity by UNESCO on November 7, 2003.

The classical repertory underwent numerous changes in North America to accommodate missing instruments and the limitations of the performers. These include:

1. The *pinn peat* ensemble, traditionally comprised of *sralai* (shawm), *roneat* (xylophones/metallophone), *korng vung* (circular frame of gongs), *chhing* (small finger cymbals), *sampho* (small double-headed barrel drum), *skor thomm* (large double-headed barred drums), and *chamrieng* (vocals), now also includes *tror* (two-stringed fiffles), *krapeu* (three-stringed zither), *khimm* (hammered dulcimer), and *khloy* (duct flute) to compensate for the lack of musicians and appropriate instruments. Some of these modified *pinn peat* ensembles also use the Western flute or recorder instead of the *khloy*.

2. Because of the absense of *sralai* players, *pinn peat* ensembles have the *roneat ek* (high-pitched xylophone) player perform the traditional and well-known "Salauma," normally played on a *sralai*.

3. Lacking *skor thomm* players, the *sampho* player now plays both parts, resulting in a decline in timbre variability.

4. Male dancers now dance male and demonic roles in the *lkhaon kbach* instead of the traditional female dancers.

5. Because of inadequate knowledge of repertory of both music and dance, substitutions and abbreviations of classical pieces occur. For example, musicians may substitute a simpler and more familiar piece for the correct one. Sometimes when musicians cannot play all the sections of a traditional piece, they simply repeat what they know instead.

Young Cambodians often feel that their parents and older relatives are too conservative, old-fashioned, and even backward. They perceive Cambodian music, song, and dance as too slow and, therefore, boring. Nonetheless, a few young Cambodians do seek out lessons in traditional arts and attend performance events.

Cambodian associations in some communities, such as Cambodian-American Heritage and Khmer Buddhist Temple in Maryland, offer classes in the traditional performing arts.[1] Some students have little interest in learning these arts, but they come to music and dance classes for their social value, especially to meet members of the opposite sex. Sometimes courtship failures lead to a student's dropping the class. There is also the problem of commitment; some come to class once and are never seen again. In addition, community arts and outreach groups (i.e., the Cambodian Network Council in Washington D.C., Portland Performing Arts in Portland, Maine, Country Roads: Refugee Arts group in Boston, New England Foundation for the Arts, and the Jacob's Pillow Dance Festival in Massachusetts) actively seek and work with Cambodian artists to offer master classes, document traditional pieces on film, and sponsor concerts and festivals.

Although young Cambodians have had opportunities to study the musical and theatrical arts of their parents, it is necessarily on an informal and sporadic basis, depending on the availability of teachers and spare time. More often young Cambodian Americans praise and adopt Western popular culture and discredit their own. They wish to be integrated into American rather than Cambodian culture—to fit in rather than stand out as possibly exotic. Their preferred instruments are guitar, keyboard, and drums. During breaks from their study of Cambodian music, which they often characterize as boring or slow, they are inclined to form small groups to rap, dance the "electric slide" or the "macarena." Few choose to express themselves in Cambodian form.

The classical tradition has been maintained albeit in an incomplete form. A full *pinn peat* ensemble has not been possible until recent years, making incomplete or ad hoc mixed ensembles the norm. Some of the older musicians possess an imperfect knowledge of repertory, but younger, possibly more knowledgeable, musicians are prevented from correcting their elders by customary standards of behavior. Work schedules often conflict and, even in those rare circumstances where there are enough musicians in a given area, it is challenging to schedule practice times and performances. Not surprisingly, many of the traditional ceremonies that would require music in the homeland now omit it in the United States. Others have been simplified and shortened, such as the wedding ceremony. What used to be three days and three nights is now shortened to one day, responding to the new social, economic, and logistical realities. Many Cambodian artists wish to remain faithful to their ancestral culture, but the challenges are daunting and temptations to give in to the popular culture of North America are overwhelming.

Popular Music

Popular music has long been a part of Cambodian life, although before American influence became dominant, it was French music that Europeanized Cambodians enjoyed. International styles of ballroom dance and its music (bolero, cha cha, foxtrot, and rumba) were, and continue to be, popular both in Cambodia and in North America. Cambodian youth often form rock and pop bands that are engaged for many kinds of community events. Some have managed to produce cassettes, compact discs, DVDs, and video tapes—sold in Cambodian and other Asian groceries stores.

Cambodian rock bands use Western instruments such as the electric guitar, electric bass, keyboard, and drums. Most of this music is intended for dancing. The bands play popular songs composed by various groups and artists, including the Beatles, Rolling Stones, Bee Gees, Credence Clearwater Revival, Santana, Lionel Richie, Michael Jackson, Lobo, Brian Adams, Rod Stewart, Madonna, and Celine Dion. They also play Cambodian popular songs in traditional Cambodian rhythms, such as *roam vung, roam kbach,* and *saravane.* These dance gatherings are attended mostly by the young (Chap 1962; Sam and Campbell 1991; Chen et al. 1993).

Personal Experiences and Efforts

For more than two decades and through various projects, I have been dedicated and committed to the preservation, maintenance, development, and promotion of traditional Cambodian music in America. It is encouraging and at the same time challenging for me to take the initiative and lead in this venture, although leadership is definitely needed in my Cambodian community. Having succeeded academically, I am often perceived of and expected to be a role model. In many circumstances, I serve as a link between the Cambodian community and the general community. In this context, I have been the focal point for coordination, referral, and resources. The burden is heavy, but I never hesitate to carry it as I often look back to my predecessors, who carried even heavier burdens.

As the result of my consistent endeavors, I have made possible some important works, including publications,[2] video productions,[3] compact discs,[4] DVDs,[5] live performances of dance and theater,[6] and cultural exchanges between Cambodian artists in Cambodia and America.[7]

Because Cambodians were resettled in widely scattered areas, it has been difficult to form coherent ensembles and assemble performances. My wife, Chan Moly Sam, and I having lived and worked in the United States for many years, working tirelessly to reunite ensembles and troupes, produce teaching materials and archival documents, and offer workshops and residencies, supported primarily by an array of private and public foundations and agencies. As a result, a number of young artists, some born in the United States, have learned the traditional arts of their homeland.[8]

Conclusion

Despite cutbacks in public spending for the arts in the United States, there is still hope for traditional Cambodian music to continue to be performed. However, much work and energy must still be invested. Traditional musicians must strive hard to increase musical activity to encourage, train, and produce more professional musicians, and to remain ever competitive. The road to the future will indeed be rough, with no free rides. Musicians must continue to create, perform, making themselves indispensable at all times. Increased funding from diverse means is a necessity and important strategy for the survival and continuity of the traditional culture and cultural programming. The community must participate and share this burden.

More collaboration is necessary to empower ourselves. A connection with Cambodia must continue. We must continue to produce high-quality work. We should seek further support from the community, and involve our communities in cultural activities to take ownership of the community projects. In this way, we would feel responsible for maintaining the quality and the ongoing continuity of these traditional expressions of Cambodian art forms.

Endnotes

1. Community-based organizations play a vital role in the preservation and promotion of Cambodian culture, sponsoring classes, workshops, and performances. These include: the Cambodian Network Council (District of Columbia), Cambodia-American Heritage (Maryland), Cambodian Studies Center (Washington), Khmer Studies Institute (Connecticut), United Cambodian Community (California), and Cambodian Association of Illinois (Illinois). Cambodian Buddhist temples in different parts of America also offer similar programs.

2. Through my efforts and those of a core group of friends, several books on Khmer culture have been published within the past decades. These publications are intended to encourage and promote native scholars and scholarships, rather than to entrust Cambodian scholarship to foreigners alone. There is a recent consensus among Cambodian scholars that we must research, study, write, and publish our own works. Several works have already been produced as a starting point toward reaching these goals and objectives.

3. I have produced a professional video entitled *Khmer Court Dance* (1992), featuring four dances and a dance drama, with an introduction to the history of Cambodian court dance—a project supported by national Endowment for the Arts.

4. Several compact discs on traditional Cambodian music have been released and made available to the public by Tower Records, World Music Institute, Music of the World, Cambodian Network Council, Center for the Studies of Khmer Culture, and Cambodian Business International. These are good resources for music lovers, musicians, and particularly for dancers who cannot afford live music and need good pre-recorded musical accompaniment for their performances.

5. In 1993 the National Initiative to Preserve American Dance (NIPAD) funded a film project to document a dozen of the Cambodian court dances and dance dramas. The project includes interviews with dance masters and musicians, as well as teachers and students at Royal University of Fine Arts in Phnom Penh.

6. In the United States, performances of dance, music, and theater are regularly staged. Cambodian dancers and musicians participate in cultural festivals across the country.

7. There have been cultural exchange programs for approximately three decades now. Exchanges have taken place between Cambodian dancers and musicians in the United States and Cambodia. We have been working very closely with the Ministry of Culture and Fine Arts, the Royal university of Fine Arts, the Department of Arts and Performing Arts, the Amrita Performing Arts, the Silapak Khmer Amatak, and Khmer Arts Academy in Phnom Penh.

8. In some cases, there have been innovative projects, especially involving dance, such as those at the Portland Performing Arts in Maine (July, 1996) and the Jacob's Pillow Dance festival in Massachusetts (October, 1996). The latter included collaborations with the English dancer, Jonathan Lunn, and the American dancer, Gwyneth Jones.

References

Cambodian Mohori: Khmer Entertainment Music. 1991. World Music Institute (WMI 015). CD.

Cambodia: Traditional Music, Volume 1. Folkways Records (FE 4081). CD.

Cambodia: Traditional Music, Volume 2. Folkways Records (FE 4082). CD.

Chap, Pin. Danses *Populaires au Cambodge.* Phnom Penh: Editions de l'Institut Bouddhique,1962. Print.

Chen, Vivien, Magaly Jarrad, and Chan Moly Sam. "Sharing Common Ground: Social Dancing in the U.S.A.," In *Smithsonian Institution Festival of American Folk Life* (1993), 63-68. Print.

"Chheng Phon and Others Address Drama Day Ceremony," *Kampuchea Review* (1982), H1. Print.

Court Dance of Cambodia. 1995. Cambodian Network Council and Cambodia Association of Illinois (AVL95001). CD.

Ebihara, May et. al., eds. *Cambodian Culture since 1975: Homeland and Exile.* Ithaca: Cornell University Press, 1994. Print.

Echoes from the Palace: Court Music of Cambodia, performed by the Sam-Ang Sam Ensemble. 1996. Music of the World (CDT-140). CD.

Giuriati, Giovanni. "Khmer Traditional Music in Washington, D.C." Unpublished dissertation. University of Maryland, 1988. Print.

Jones, Clayton. "Cambodians Revive Classical Dance after Near Destruction of Heritage," *Christian Science Monitor* (1987), 1. Print.

Khmer Court Dance, produced by Sam-Ang Sam and Naomi Bishop. 1992. Khmer Studies Institute and Media Generation. Video.

Mohori: Khmer Music from Cambodia, performed by the Sam-Ang Sam Ensemble. 1997. Latitudes (LAT 50609). CD.

Music of Cambodia, performed by the Sam-Ang Sam Ensemble. 1989. World Music Institute (WMI-007). CD.

Pack, Susan. *"Cambodian Odyssey," Press Telegram* (1989), J1-J5. Print.

Patriotic and Traditional Khmer Songs. 1990. Cambodian Business Corporation International (PTKS90-SS-NT001). CD.

"Phnom Penh Report Membership of New KNUFNS Central Committee," *Kampuchea Review* (1979), H1. Print.

Sam, Sam-Ang. *"The Pinn Peat Ensemble: Its History, Music, and Context."* Unpublished Dissertation. Wesleyan University, 1988. Print.

Sam, Sam-Ang and Patricia Campbell. *Silent Temples, Songful Hearts: Traditional Music of Cambodia.* Danbury: World Music Press, 1991. Print.

The Great Legacy Lives On: The Mengs and Phleng Kar and Mohori, produced by Sam-Ang Sam and Natalie Chhuan. 1998. (GLLO99-SSNC-ND001). CD.

Traditional Music of Cambodia. 1987. Center for the Study of Khmer Culture (TMC-SS-NR001). CD.

CHAPTER

14

A Transnational Hip Hop Nation:
praCh, Cambodia, and Memorialising the Killing Fields

Cathy J. Schlund-Vials

Within Asian American Studies, the Cambodian American experience occupies a similar, yet by no means identical, discursive position as that of Holocaust survivors within Jewish/Jewish American cultural production. Cambodian American cultural production is shaped by a period of time more widely known as "the Killing Fields," an era dominated by the horrific policies enacted by Pol Pot and the communist Khmer Rouge. Between 1975 and 1979, over two million Cambodians perished due to execution, starvation, disease, and forced labour. This number represents approximately 15 to 25% of the contemporary Cambodian population. The memory of this genocide, along with the documentation of it, is the primary referent for the Cambodian American identity within the United States. It has been documented cinematically in the 1984 Academy-Award-winning film, *The Killing Fields*, which is arguably the most well-known cultural production about the genocide.

"A Transnational Hip Hop Nation: Prach, Cambodia, and Memorialising the Killing Fields," *Life Writing, Vol. 5*, No. 1, Copyright © 2008 Taylor & Francis Group. Reprinted by permission of Taylor & Francis Group, http://www.informaworld.com.

But *The Killing Fields* is not the only narrative about the genocide. In 2000, during the Cambodian New Year celebrations in Long
Beach, California, Cambodian American rapper praCh distributed
Dalama: The End'n Is Just the Beginni', a hip hop CD produced not
in the studio but in his parents' garage.[1] praCh sampled Khmer
Rouge propaganda speeches, rapped in English and Khmer, and
based his lyrics on stories told to him by family members who had
survived the Killing Fields.[2] The album featured members of Northstar Resurrec, a hip hop group begun in 1996 which included praCh
and other Cambodian American rappers sparC da Polar, doZer, and
Toeum Tom Chan.[3] A hip hop memoir, *Dalama: The End'n Is Just
the Beginni'* was by no means a financial success in the United States.
In Cambodia, however, praCh was a phenomenon. Unbeknownst to
the rapper, a copy of his CD made its way to Cambodia, was played
on Phnom Penh radio, and its popularity increased through bootleg
copies.[4] Renamed *Khmer Rouge Rap*, praCh's work was incredibly
popular among Khmer youth, who connected with lyrics about the
Cambodian genocide and Cambodian American life after the Killing
Fields.[5] Although praCh had not been back to his homeland since he
was a toddler, he became the number-one music artist in Cambodia.

Unintentionally, praCh created a transnational hip hop nation
through his music, connecting Cambodian American and Khmer
youth cultures. This connection is the entry point for this essay,
which examines how Cambodian American youth memorialise the
Killing Fields in a manner that is transnational and diasporically specific to the refugee experience. *Dalama: The End'n Is Just the Beginni'*
is the initial album in a trilogy, followed by *Dalama: The Lost Chapter* (2003). The primary title "dalama" reflects praCh's desire to auto-
biographically combine drama and trauma, and he "made up his
own word and turned that into the story of his life"(May 77). The
final album in the trilogy, *Dalama: Memoirs of an Invisible War*, is
according to praCh, "a very dark album…about political turmoil,"
and is slated for release in 2007 (May 81).

Focusing on praCh's second album, *Dalama: The Lost Chapter*
(hereafter *The Lost Chapter*), I assert the rapper, through the interdisciplinary idiom of hip hop, negotiates individual, familial, and
communal stories grounded in Cambodian refugee and Cambodian

American experiences.[6] The four basic elements of the form—djaying, mcing (rapping), breakdancing, and graffiti—are auditory and visual signifiers of identity and location. Fundamental to hip hop is its potential to serve as a site of wisdom and a space of knowledge.[7] In praCh's work, knowledge takes the form of a genocidal history consistently relegated to the margins. However, praCh's role as knowledge producer goes beyond the reclamation of history. This reclamation intersects with a contemplation of how this history continues to impact a generation who are "children of the Killing Fields" living in the United States.[8]

Identity and location—dominant themes in hip hop—are complicated with regard to the transnational Cambodian American refugee experience, which is problematised given U.S. foreign policy in Southeast Asia during the Vietnam War. U.S. bombings of the Cambodian countryside destabilised an already fragile postcolonial government, paving the way for the Khmer Rouge takeover of Phnom Penh, which signaled the start of the Cambodian genocide. For the Cambodian American refugee subject, the United States is a paradoxical site responsible for dislocation from the country of origin yet it also serves as a significant place of refuge. Although Cambodian refugees have not exclusively relocated to the United States, aforementioned political actualities make the United States a potentially provocative space for examination. Furthermore, the passage of the 1980 Refugee Act facilitated the migration of over 100,000 Cambodian refugees to the United States. One of the largest Cambodian refugee communities is in Long Beach, California, which incidentally is praCh's home location. Cambodian American citizenship, circumscribed by particular dominant ethno-racial logics, U.S. foreign policy, and U.S. domestic policy, raises the question not only of American identity, but what it means to be Cambodian and Cambodian American in light of a genocidal history.

The memory of genocide is undeniably traumatic. Acts and projects of memorialisation attempt to negotiate trauma through remembrance and reconciliation. The negotiation of trauma through this two-sided process characterizes praCh's hip hop project. praCh memorializes the Killing Fields in his work, and this memorialisation is geographically and culturally located in the United

States and Cambodia. As the history of Cambodian memorialisation efforts (or rather, lack thereof) illustrates, praCh's albums engage contemporary issues of Cambodian selfhood and nationhood. Moreover, praCh's hip hop project, domestically produced and globally consumed, embodies what editors Gillian Whitlock and Kate Douglas suggest is a relatively under-examined and unexplored transit of testimony. The notion of transit—connotative of a journey or passing—is literally apparent in the global migration of praCh's debut album from Long Beach, California to Phnom Penh, Cambodia. This concept characterizes the transits or journeys embedded in praCh's artistic project. *The Lost Chapter* thematically and artistically highlights Cambodian genocidal history, foregrounds the impact of this history on Cambodian American refugees, and recuperates Khmer artistic forms largely destroyed during the Khmer Rouge reign.

The memory of the Killing Fields and its legacy haunts *The Lost Chapter*. The genocide gives rise to multiple forms of traumatic memory within the narrative fabric of the album; images of death coexist with repeated directives to remember that past. The song, "Stories," is emblematic of this negotiation. Its early placement in the album (as the second track) and chorus illustrate the album's central historical focus:

> "Stories told by our parents to us / Before we go to bed about the field revolution / and two millions that are dead / Is in our head / And it's hard to let go / but instead-a shedding tears / we're here to let you know / about the Killing Fields / not long ago" (*The Lost Chapter*).

praCh's lyrics emphasise the source of the traumatic story—"our parents"—directly referencing the Killing Fields and its human cost. The use of collective pronouns establishes that the auditory narrative which follows, rooted in the trauma of the genocide, is familial and communal. The temporal frame suggested—that the genocide did not happen "long ago"—reminds the listener of the contemporary and historically relevant nature of praCh's narrative. praCh's lyrics highlight a more active subject position not predicated on "shedding

---

Courtesy of praCh Ly. Reprinted with permission.

tears" but instead marked by the assertion that "we're here to let you know...about the Killing Fields." Thus, the revelation of this genocidal history through testimony is cast as an act of power and agency.

With a total of twenty-one tracks, *The Lost Chapter* uses samples from American and Cambodian films, documentaries about the Killing Fields, and political speeches, including the address given by President George W. Bush following the September 11th attacks.[9] The majority of the compositions are in English, yet certain tracks feature Khmer and other pieces are bilingual (Khmer and English). In addition to compositions that privilege praCh as the primary mc, Cambodian American rappers and fellow Northstar Resurrec members doZer, Toeum Tom Chan, and sparC da Polar headline four tracks. Selected beats and background vocals are provided by the Universal Speakers, a pan-Southeast Asian American female trio.[10] praCh's father, Seng Ly, who speaks in Khmer, is also included in the album. Ho C. Chan, a pin peat musician living in the United States, figures keenly in the album's audioscape. Thus, praCh's *The Lost Chapter* is a polyvocal and intergenerational production very much embedded in familial and communal Cambodian/Cambodian American frameworks.[11] The inclusion of this polyvocal sensibility echoes one of the founding principles of hip hop as a form inextricably linked to community awareness and engagement.

This polyvocal sensibility, a multidisciplinary fusion of Khmer and U.S. musical traditions, is politically significant to Cambodian genocidal history. For example, pin peat is a traditional Khmer music style that includes three singers, two bamboo xylophones, a flute, suspended brass pots, a two-headed drum, a large kettle drum, and a quadruple-reed instrument.[12] Based in Indian and Javanese traditions, Cambodian pin peat emerged during the Angkor era (c. 842- c. 1431 CE). It was revived as a music form during the twentieth century and was a cultural staple of the Khmer royal court. Pin peat also accompanied Cambodian Buddhist religious ceremonies. The form, along with classical Khmer ballet and Buddhism, was outlawed during the period of Democratic Kampuchea. Artists and religious practitioners were executed as part of the Khmer Rouge strategy to return the nation to "year zero" through cultural, religious, and political obliteration.

Traditional Khmer music and dance artists were viewed as enemies of the communist Democratic Kampuchea state because of their affiliation to Prince Norodom Sihanouk and the Khmer royal court:[13]

> As a revered symbol of Khmer culture, the musicians and dancers…were singled out by the new regime for elimination. They buried some instruments, costumes, and masks, and tried to escape detection by pretending to be workers in the rice fields. A few survived this way; most were put to death. ("America Provides Refuge" 37)

The obliteration of traditional Khmer art forms was thus related to a larger, nationally-sponsored project of erasure. The inclusion of pin peat as a musical foundation in praCh's *The Lost Chapter* is significant given its connection to the genocide. Such inclusion reflects a conscious attempt by the rapper to revive the tradition and create a markedly different Cambodian American hip hop form.[14] Most importantly, the focus on pin peat music in *The Lost Chapter* connects to a culturally-specific and pre-genocide Khmer identity. Concomitantly, praCh's use of pin peat challenges the Khmer Rouge intent to erase the past. This challenge is apparent in the instrumental composition, "Pin Peat's Resurrection," which showcases pin peat master artist Ho C. Chan. The title of the track suggests the form's reemergence and continued livelihood, yet it also reads metaphorically as a marker of Khmer identity and culture. Simultaneously, the "resurrection" suggests the agency of the Cambodian/Cambodian American to reconstruct a sense of selfhood in the face of overwhelming genocidal obliteration.

praCh supplements his use of traditional Khmer cultural forms with the improvisational theatrical form ayai. In ayai, one singer poses a question or rhyme, and the other singer responds in kind. The second singer typically answers with the last line sung. praCh maintains,

> Ayai is sort of like rap music, but in a Cambodian way. Ayai is like one poetry master to another poetry master going out on stage or in front of a village and competing with their wisdom, their knowledge about certain subjects, like their land, but it

has to continuously rhyme. So basically—rap. Not all rap is about streets and drugs and partying. There's every variety of rap. With Cambodian ayai, it's sort of like that too. (May 80-81)

Traditionally accompanied by musicians, ayai can also be sung acappella. In *The Lost Chapter*, ayai echoes the tenets of rap, which is predicated on rhymes and repetition. praCh foregrounds ayai in the composition entitled, "refleXion," spoken in Khmer. Alongside pin peat, the appearance of ayai within the album's Cambodian/Cambodian American imaginary reinforces the transnational nature of *The Lost Chapter*. This style is analogous to pin peat with regard to cultural reclamation and memory, and functions as yet another marker of Cambodian/Cambodian American selfhood and agency.

The artistic fusion of multiple music forms within the auditory imaginary of *The Lost Chapter* collapses multiple sociopolitical identities within the creative space of the album. National, familial, and individual traumatic narratives are embedded within the narrative framework of the album. The album's structure reflects the traumatic history of Cambodian refugees and Cambodian Americans in that it is organised chronologically from past to present. Historically, the initial compositions address the Khmer Rouge takeover of Phnom Penh (1975); the album's setting then shifts to 1979, the year of praCh's birth. The remaining pieces, which reference September 11th and the PATRIOT ACT, are, for the most part, located in the present.[15]

Structurally, the album is divided into three primary sections, including an intro (subtitled "invasion"), an intermission ("RULES..."), and an "outro" ("p e a C e") (*The Lost Chapter*). *The Lost Chapter* begins with a brief traditional flute composition that is interrupted with an excerpt from the film, *The Killing Fields*. The cinematic sample is taken from a conversation between an American reporter, a member of the U.S. military, a Cambodian soldier and a Cambodian interpreter.[16] This scene concludes with an explosion, establishing for the listener Cambodia's war-torn landscape prior to the period of the Killing Fields. Entitled, "Invasion," the sample takes the listener to 1975, presumably days before the Khmer Rouge takeover of Phnom Penh. The cinematic sample is followed by a second hip hop introduction featuring rapper doZer, who, in the midst of an electronic baseline, starts the aforementioned "Stories" with a detailed account of Khmer Rouge occupation and subsequent evacuation of Phnom Penh. This account reveals national history, highlights familial anecdotes of disruption, and stresses individual trauma (subjects faced with incredible violence and under constant fear of death). The inclusion of a multimedia format—which combines samples from cinema, hip hop compositions, and traditional Khmer music—is replicated throughout the album.

Next, the album moves to an excerpt from the documentary, *Year Zero: The Silent Death of Cambodia* (1979), narrated by Australian journalist and documentary filmmaker John Pilger.[17] praCh interrupts the documentary narrative with a rap about the political landscape of Democratic Kampuchea in a song entitled, "Power, Territory, and Rice." praCh recounts the evacuation of Phnom Penh through a hip hop narrative, providing another lens through which to consider Cambodian national history. In the chorus, praCh connects the evacuation to a larger political agenda which includes war, destabilisation, and power, along with its inevitable cost: "It's about Power, Territory, and Rice, / And of course that comes with a hefty price. / Whenever there's war, there's always sacrifice, /And it's usually the innocent who lose their life" (*The Lost Chapter*).

Furthermore, praCh examines in "Power, Territory, and Rice" the generational impact of the Killing Fields, asserting, "No one was told who was running the country but ah, / Only that those in power was called "Angka."/ Children's was brainwash into believing in them, / They was taught that: "there's no such thing as parents" (*The Lost Chapter*). The focus on children and erasure is relevant to contemporary Khmer youth, who, as the reception of praCh's first album illustrates, have little to no knowledge of the Killing Fields. Moreover, Cambodian American cultural production is largely characterised by a resistance to forget the past despite the Khmer Rouge directive to disremember, reinforced by the lack of sustained memorialisation efforts in contemporary Cambodia.

The Lost Chapter's subsequent pieces enumerate the experiences of Cambodians during the time of the Killing Fields. For example, track six, entitled "The Great Escape," focuses on praCh's familial story of flight. After "The Great Escape," the album shifts to a more contemporary contemplation of the Cambodian refugee and the Cambodian American in the United States. Nonetheless, this contemplation—which for the most part dominates the remaining fifteen tracks of *The Lost Chapter*—explicitly and implicitly references the initial history of the Killing Fields. This connection is manifest in direct mentions to the Killing Fields and is suggested in the use of Khmer as a significant linguistic foundation in the album. Repeatedly, praCh's compositions stress national and familial history, Khmer culture, and Cambodian American identity.

The auditory elements of the album are visually replicated in praCh's album cover, which features Cambodian architecture, an American cityscape, and a ship. Together, these images signify the journey from Cambodia to the United States, reminding the listener of the transnational experience of the rapper. Given the communal stresses in the album's lyrics and artistic collaborations, the images reflect a larger Cambodian/Cambodian American migration history. praCh is also mindful of individual history, apparent in two other images that appear on the album's cover—a tree and a hut. These two images are significant given the location of praCh's birth. According to the rapper, in 1979 "…my mom was pregnant with me. She had me in a hut. Later, my parents went back to Cambodia and videotaped the tree I was born under, but the hut's no longer there" (May 73). This birth location is confirmed in the previously mentioned "The Great Escape," which opens with the assertion that praCh "was born in a hut / umbilical cord cut" (*The Lost Chapter*).

The revelation of praCh's origins quickly gives way to the trauma which accompanies the Cambodian subject who attempts to cross into the Thai border. The composition, which includes an almost violin-like backbeat, implicitly stresses the drama of the situation and reminds the listener of the danger this journey entails. This danger is confirmed lyrically in the chorus, when praCh states, "watch out! / for boobie traps and land mines, / ain't no time to take breaks, / death is close behind, / night or day it's not OK! /gotta stay awake! / no matter what it takes, / we gotta make / the Great Escape!" (*The Lost Chapter*). The refugee subject is cast in a manner that acknowledges the trauma of "the great escape" while simultaneously highlighting the degree to which this same Cambodian subject is empowered precisely because of the struggle. praCh asserts,

> when there [is] total silence, / you know danger ahead. / and when the bomb goes off / then you know someone is dead. / but forward ahead. / we gotta make it further. / no matter what it takes / we gotta make it across the border. / we lost our heart, but found the strength in our soul, / words can't describe, / but the stories must be told. / the fields, the jungles, / the mountains of death. / the struggle continues, / but we're gonna make it! (*The Lost Chapter*)

The above excerpt suggests that, despite the loss of homeland and in the face of "the mountains of death," the collective "we"—in this case praCh's family—still finds strength that "words can't describe" to enact "the great escape." This characterisation stresses a familial narrative and confirms the articulation of a Cambodian agency embedded in a difficult, dangerous, and unimaginable journey to the border.

Moreover, in "The Great Escape," praCh alludes to his own project, maintaining that "stories must be told," and anticipates the next rap composition, entitled, "I Just Want You to Understand." This eighth track is preceded by "Pin Peat's Resurrection." Unlike previous tracks on *The Lost Chapter*, "I Just Want You to Understand" combines, in the space of the composition, traditional Khmer music styles and hip hop. The song begins with a digitised pin peat beat and combines contemporary hip hop with traditional Khmer music. The pin peat beat is supplemented by an additional electronic bass line, reinforcing a transnational musical fusion between Khmer and American forms. The composition takes an autobiographical turn when praCh begins to rap. praCh states that he is:

> a messenger, a writer, inspired by the truth / take you behind the scenes like Fox 10 o'clock news / firsthand experience a living proof / 100% special delivery to you / when I first started off it was just for fun / now I'm doin' it cause they say it can't be done / I love narration tellin' my story that's my hobby / if money wasn't involved I'd probably do it for free / not for publicity or fame / cause all I want is for people to understand. (*The Lost Chapter*)

praCh enunciates a form of selfhood linked to his ability to provide the listener with a "behind the scenes...firsthand experience" embedded in a "love of narration." Most importantly, praCh's revelation of a significant historical truth through "firsthand experience" facilitates a transit of testimony which allows Cambodian Americans to reclaim their past and continue as active agents in the present. This role of praCh as a cultural broker and knowledge producer is illustrated in the song's chorus, when the rapper maintains, "I just want you to understand / it must be taught / history must be told / I just want you to understand / the past is unlocked / we played a key role" (*The Lost Chapter*). The emphasis on a collective "we," coupled with a mention of a past "unlocked," connects Cambodian/Cambodian American communal modalities to the official narrative of nationhood through history. Thus, praCh begins from an individualised position as a "messenger of truth" who then connects his work to a larger Cambodian/Cambodian American sense of agency and selfhood.

Returning briefly to structure, it is admittedly difficult to divide the album into geographically or politically distinct sections. For example, the song, "S-21 (Tuol Sleng)," about the infamous prison in Phnom Penh, is rendered in Khmer, and is placed rather late in the album (as the eighteenth track). Its placement, coupled with its linguistic characteristics, reminds the listener that the album is rooted in an ongoing contemplation of the Cambodian genocide. Concomitantly, with a piece entitled, "TUES," which examines the attacks of September 11th, praCh blurs the lines between simplistic nation-state affiliations, claiming that he is both Khmer (Cambodian) and American. In this piece, praCh raps about the traumatic memory of September 11th. This composition reiterates in content and form to the album's reification of national identity through trauma. praCh articulates a transnational sensibility that traverses multiple borders and collapses the space between Cambodia and the United States.

Thus, praCh creates through the inclusion of traditional Cambodian music, samples from Khmer movies, *The Killing Fields*, and documentaries, and rhymes spoken in English and Khmer, a transnational Cambodian American subjectivity that resists a singular location in one geographic place or historical place. Instead, this subjectivity follows the trajectory of Cambodian American youth from the Killing Fields of Cambodia to the streets of Long Beach to the INS lines in a post-September 11th United States. The culmination of this transnational trajectory is apparent in praCh's "Art of Fact," a composition that combines artistically and thematically the album's primary motifs. What precedes this nineteenth track is the aforementioned rap about "S-21," rendered in Khmer. What follows is a spoken portion entitled, "out-tro," spoken in Khmer by Seng Ly, praCh's father, who states, ""We shouldn't argue about race. We are all one. We must learn to live together." The inclusion of his father's voice reinforces the intergenerational transit of testimony within *The Lost Chapter*'s imaginary.

The transnational meditation on Cambodian/Cambodian American identity is confirmed in "Art of Fact." This contemplation is reflected in the fusion of Khmer and American music styles reminiscent of "I Just Want You to Understand," and the song's initial instrumentation echoes that of a traditional pin peat flute. Further, its lyrics and rhythms suggest a fusion of Cambodian and Cambodian American identities. The piece blends R & B, a Cambodian pin peat beat, an electronic bass line, and a traditional Cambodian flute. praCh reminds the listener of his refugee past, beginning with the assertion that:

> Beyond the killing field, / a quarter of a century after the genocide. / after 2 million people murdered, / the other 5 million survive / the fabric of the culture, / beauty drips the texture, / I find myself in Long Beach, / the next Cambodian mecca.... / There's a gap in our generation, / between the adults and kids, / but since I'm bilingual / I'ma use communication as a bridge

praCh mentions the two million lost alongside the five million who survived, and the song stresses need to communicate in order to reconcile the past. This sense of communication becomes intergenerationally significant with praCh's claim that he is "bilingual," intent on, as the lyric continues, "knock[ing] down the walls/between me and my parents," a subject who "listens to their stories on all/ without interference" (*The Lost Chapter*). praCh articulates a transnational location for Cambodian/Cambodian American identity through the declaration that he is in "Long Beach...the next Cambodian mecca" while underscoring a generation gap that prevents dialogue between "adults and kids." His assertion of bilingualism is a solution to this gap, and the song repeatedly returns to praCh's agency as a Cambodian American rapper.

Hence, praCh complicates this transnational solution with an acknowledgement of life in the United States, and the composition shifts to this particular location. Critical of "the American Dream," praCh stresses the experience of Cambodian American youth who must face "terrorist and INS deportation" due to a U.S. policy of "one strike and you're out" (allusions to the 1996 Immigration Reform and the PATRIOT Act, which allowed for the deportation of 1,600 Cambodian/Cambodian Americans in 2001 and 2002) and gang life ("code of the streets"). praCh is not only critical of the promise of the United States as a place of possibility; he reminds the listener of the history of the Killing Fields. It is this history, reiterated throughout the album and throughout the song, which partially contextualises the experiences of Cambodian American youth. praCh includes a political critique of the United States; he then addresses generational tension and shifting family values ("fixing up marriages" and commodity fetishes in the form of "fast cars"). This layering lyrically echoes the layering of musical texts, establishing the transnational and conflicted (at times conflicting) experiences of Cambodian American youth in the United States.

In a recent interview, praCh stated:

Hip hop to me is the voice of the youth. Telling how one really feels about their way of living and how they are living. Their surrounding[s], their environment, or just one's story....It's not just talking into the mic, it's talking to the world. As for me growing up, it was all around me. Hip hop, rap, breakdancing, graffiti art. It's not just music, it's the culture I grew up in. But as an Asian, Cambodian, I had to tell my own story because no one else was going to tell it for me. Once I was able to record my voice I knew what I was going to say. I can only talk about what I know best. And that is my history. And my history is in my family and me. We lived and went through it.[18]

Within *The Lost Chapter*, praCh is the carrier of the Cambodian past and the embodiment of a Cambodian American who proudly maintains he is "Khmer" and "refuse[s] to let his culture die." praCh provides an avenue of resistance through hip hop rooted in the past yet negotiates the present. His lyrics are matched by the transnational structure and content of the album with regard to language, culture, and tradition. praCh firmly articulates a Cambodian American subjectivity that uses, as the title of the song suggest, "art" to address "fact," creating, in the process, a memorial to the history and legacy Killing Fields and a monument to Cambodian American identity.

praCh's cultural work is more significant when contextualised against the lack of memorialisation in Cambodia and the paucity of such memorials in the United States. In Cambodia, the primary sites for memorialisation—Tuol Sleng (S-21) and Choeung Ek—were constructed during the Vietnamese occupation of Cambodia in the early 1980s. Paul Williams observes that although "survivors of the DK [Democratic Kampuchea] regime have constructed seventy-eight genocide memorials in towns and rural districts," Tuol Sleng and Choeung Ek are the only two government-sanctioned sites that exist in the nation (247). These memorials privilege a politicised narrative of liberation, wherein the Khmer Rouge regime is cast as an enemy of the Vietnamese-liberated state. No culturally and politically-specific Cambodian space exists within such memorials. Nor is there space for a Cambodian narrative of the Killing Fields that problematises the potentially imperialistic position of the Vietnamese not as liberators but as occupiers. Because of the degree to which Cambodian cultural and political life was obliterated between 1975 and 1979, Cambodian funding for such memorials and the creation of these memorials is still not feasible.

After the 1988 Vietnamese withdrawal, the continued presence of the Khmer Rouge in sociopolitical realms prompted the Cambodian government to seek political reconciliation through a peace process. Cambodians were asked to forgive Khmer Rouge leaders and forget the genocide. In 1996, the Cambodian government emphasised national reconciliation. Upon making pledges of peace, former Khmer Rouge fighters were welcomed back into the Cambodian government. Three years after Pol Pot's death, in December

2001, Prime Minister Hun Sen called for the restoration of current memorials and the future memorialisation of other burial sites. Additionally, the prime minister called for the construction of a memorial museum that would facilitate a national reconciliation. However, the construction of such a museum has yet to occur. Just as there has been no nationally-sanctioned and funded memorial effort, no consistent policy for reconciliation exists in Cambodia.[19] This brief history of memorialisation efforts in Cambodia illustrates the weight which falls upon praCh and other Cambodian American cultural producers who negotiate the problematic past in their work.[20]

As a Cambodian American cultural producer, praCh creates a particular transnational transit of testimony, wherein the history of the Killing Fields travels across nation-state borders. praCh's work memorialises the genocide and generationally intersects with the work of other 1.5 generation Cambodian Americans. "1.5 generation Cambodian Americans" refers to those who were born in Cambodia but who left prior to their teens. It is this group who has recently taken on the task of memory work with regard to the Killing Fields. This memory work is largely literary and autobiographical, and such narratives are often written from the perspective of those who survived the Killing Fields as children.

The titles of three full-length autobiographies that have recently been published are illustrative: Buth Keo's *The Stones Cry Out: A Cambodian Childhood, 1975-1980* (originally published in 1986 and republished in 1999), Chanrithy Him's *When Broken Glass Floats: Growing Up Under the Khmer Rouge* (2000), and Luong Ung's *First They Killed My Father: A Daughter of Cambodia Remembers* (2000). Keo, Him, and Ung each begin with a brief account of life before 1975 (the year the Khmer Rouge came to power), recount life under the Khmer Rouge, and examine life after the Khmer Rouge (usually from the position of a refugee in a camp or in the United States). The narrative emphasis of each work revolves around coming of age under the regime of the Khmer Rouge.

The impulse to memorialise Cambodian history connects praCh's work to that of other Cambodian American cultural producers who transnationally re-imagine Cambodian nationhood and selfhood.[21]

Unlike praCh, these authors do not explicitly focus on the journey from Southeast Asia to the United States, nor is there a sustained exploration of Cambodian American identity. Rather, the narrative is located primarily in Cambodia, and the focus is not on Cambodian American but Cambodian subjectivity and selfhood. Despite the overwhelming presence of the genocide as a historical, social, and political foundation in *The Lost Chapter*, praCh also emphasises Cambodian American identity, artistically mapping the journey from traumatised subject to empowered agent. It is the multisided contemplation of Cambodian/Cambodian American identity—wherein praCh is a child of the Killing Fields and a product of an American upbringing—which signals a particularly Cambodian American transit of testimony between Cambodia and the United States. The memorialisation of the Cambodian genocide exists alongside articulations of a Cambodian American who must, because of sociopolitical actualities, re-imagine the country of his birth from the country of settlement.

Thus, praCh's hip hop exploration of Cambodian American subjectivity through a double-sided resistance against erasure and marginalisation disrupts the "traditional" Killing Fields narrative largely set in Cambodia and Southeast Asia. Furthermore, the degree to which praCh focuses his hip hop project on questions of empowerment, assertions of ethnic pride, and critiques of policies that in fact target Cambodian American youth signal a significant departure from other 1.5 generation Cambodian American literary productions. The multiple forms of testimony in *The Lost Chapter*—wherein Cambodian history and culture are mediated in the same artistic space of Cambodian American experience and culture—force a transnational consideration of trauma connected to Cambodian and Cambodian American identity. *The Lost Chapter* militates against essentialised contemplations of unilateral selfhood, problematises notions of belonging, and revises conceptualisations of nationhood.

In conclusion, politics of representation—including questions of authenticity, notions of narrative authority, and ideas of what constitutes a "valid" Cambodian selfhood—are vital to scholarly examinations of Cambodian/Cambodian American cultural work in which political, social, and personal affiliations are imagined vis-à-vis the genocide, supporting a particular solidarity built on trauma and resistance. praCh's work complicates Killing Fields remembrance in that it explicitly negotiates the Cambodian past alongside the Cambodian American present. Additionally, praCh's *The Lost Chapter* functions as a transnational text in form and content, which is haunted by the trauma of the Killing Fields yet paradoxically uses this trauma as the basis for a Cambodian American form of selfhood linked to resistance and remembrance. Nonetheless, praCh's project is also linked to other Cambodian American cultural producers who consistently return to memorialisation as a thematic focus in their work. Such memorialisation and the negotiation of trauma intersect with constructions of nationhood and contestations over national memory. Ernest Renan's notion of historical amnesia, fundamental to nation-building in the twentieth and twenty-first centuries, is relevant to a post-genocide Cambodian nationalism that liminally exists between memory and erasure.[22] And, within Cambodian American cultural production, impulses to remember coexist with desires to never forget.

Endnotes

1. "praCh" is the stage name for Prach Ly. For the remainder of this essay I will refer to the rapper by his stage name. According to praCh, "The meaning of *praCh* is "advisor to the king" or "person who talks a lot." But my parents didn't name me praCh because of that. The area where I was born was called Veal Srae K'rach: farmland of K'prach…They [his parents] didn't know what to name me when I was born at the camp place, so they just named me praCh" (May 73). The "C" in "praCh" is capitalized to emphasize the rapper's connection to his Cambodian roots. praCh was born in 1979 near Battambang, Cambodia. For consistency, I will use the following spelling: "hip hop."

2. For the debut album, praCh used a karaoke machine, microphones, and a tape player. CDs bought from local record stores provided the basis for beats and instrumentation on the album, and the album was produced in three months (May 77). Tracks in the debut album include: 1) "Intro: The Temple of Peace—Takeover"; 2) "The Letter (Prisoner of War)"; 3) "Skit: Start anew, nuth'n has gone before"; 4) "The YearZero!" 5) "Interlude: Peak of Light"; 6) "Welcome"; 7) "Interlude: New Hope";

8) "Out-tro: The Burden of Power—The Countdown 3, 2, 1..."; 9) "NorthSide (We High)" (featuring Toeum); 10) "Walk-a-Block" (featuring Northstar Resurrec); 11) "War on the Street"; 12) "Knowledge, Nix-Mo"; 13) "Ah-Ye (Khmer Rap!)"; 15) "Make Money Take Money; 16) "Zip (Da N Nite)" (featuring doZer and Pinner; and 17) "Take Your Time." praCh's second album, *Dalama: The Lost Chapter*, utilises a similar structure with regard to sections.

3. According to *Khmer Connection* reviewer Poli Bou, praCh was the first Cambodian American rapper to complete a full-length hip hop album. Bou provides a useful overview and comprehensive summary of praCh's *Dalama: The End'n Is Just The Beginnin'* (http:khmer.cc/channels/0,8,7,01,4438.html) (accessed May 14, 2007).

4. Although unsure as to who transported the album from Long Beach, California to Phnom Penh, Cambodia, praCh suggested in a 2003 interview that "DJ Sop, a well-known deejay in Cambodia" was at the 2000 Cambodian New Year celebration and may have been responsible for its play on Cambodian radio (May 78).

5. According to praCh, in the Cambodian reproduction, "The cover was gone. The artwork was gone. My name was gone. The credits were gone. Gone out the window" (May 79). It was not until the rapper was contacted by Gina Chon, a reporter for *Asiaweek* and *Cambodian Daily*, that praCh was aware of his success abroad.. Shortly after Chon's story was published in *Asiaweek*, praCh's work was featured in periodicals including the *Los Angeles Times, Newsweek*, and the *New York Post*. He was the focus of the American television program, *Frontline*, and interviewed in the American radio broadcast, *Voice of America*. I mention these publications and shows because they are referenced in praCh's song, "I Just Want You to Understand," from his second album.

6. Although the debut album is certainly of interest with regard to its distribution history, and lyrically adheres to praCh's larger goal to memorialise the Killing Fields in his work, this initial production relies heavily on other artists' work for instrumentation and beat. *The Lost Chapter* is more original production with regard to instrumentation and beat production. As praCh maintains, "I think *Dalama Two* is more—I don't want to say creative, but I gave it its own life. It's not a duplication of the first album. It bears a similarity because it's an autobiography too. But at the same time, it holds its own ground. I mixed Cambodian traditional music with rap; I created a Cambodian hip-hop beat. And this time, I was really proud to say, all the beats and instrumentals were ours" (May

80). *The Lost Chapter* allows for a more multidisciplinary consideration of Cambodian American hip hop that accommodates an examination of lyrics and music.

7. Hip hop, as an interdisciplinary form of resistance, has not escaped scholarly attention within the United States. Jeff Chang and Nitasha Sharma have written extensively and provocatively about hip hop as a form in which to examine racial and ethnic construction. Chang's *Can't Stop, Won't Stop* (2005) is a useful introduction to the history of the form from the 1970s to the present. Sharma's work examines hip hop through a comparative ethno-racial frame that brings together African American and South Asian American cultural producers. S. Craig Watkins's text, *Hip Hop Matters* (2005) highlights the contradictory nature of hip hop as a terrain of commodification and a significant site of resistance. Other useful examinations of the form include Tricia Rose's *Black Noise: Rap Music and Black Culture in Contemporary America* (1994), *Droppin' Science: Critical Essays on Rap Music and Hip Hop Culture* (1995) by William Eric Perkins, Russell A. Potter's *Spectacular Vernaculars: Hip Hop and the Politics of Postmodernism*, (1995) and *The 'Hood Comes First: Race, Space, and Place in Rap and Hip-Hop* (2002) by Murray Forman.

8. "Children of the Killing Fields" is a line from praCh's "Resurrect" from his debut album.

9. What follows is an ordered listing of the nineteen tracks which constitute *Dalama: The Lost Chapter.* 1) intro ("invasion"); 2) STORIES (featuring doZer); 3) skits, "the YearZero and One" (documentary sample); 4) "Power, Territory, and Rice"; 5) skits, "the aftermath" (documentary sample); 6) "The Great Escape!"; 7) "Pin Peat's Resurrection (featuring Khmer traditional musician Ho C. Chan); 8) "I Just Want You to Understand!"; 9) "D'eBreeZZe" (featuring sparC da Polar); 10) "Min-Tom-Ie-Da"; 11) Sox-Si-Bie; 12) intermission (RULES...); 13) "refleX-tion"; 14) "Wisc's That"; 15) "Neutral (before the war)"; 16) "Tues"; 17) "s.i.c."; 18) "S-21" (tuol sleng); 19) "Art of Fact"; 20) out-tro and 21) ("p e a C e").

10. According to www.muestic.com, the Universal Speakers, who include Cambodian American, Laotian American, and Thai American female singers, combine reggae, hip hop, and R&B in their music (accessed May 3 2007).

11. The inclusion of Ho C. Chan is of particular note because of his connection to traditional Khmer music (pin peat).

12. The Khmer names for the instruments enumerated are as follows: *reneat* (bamboo xylophones), *gong vong* (brass pots), *kloy* (flute), *sampho* (two-headed drum), *skor thom* (a large kettle drum) and *srlai* (the oboe-like instrument).

13. Prince Sihanouk, following the death of his father in 1960, became the Cambodian head of state. In 1963, he forcibly changed the Cambodian constitution so that he would remain head of state for the remainder of his life. He was deposed in 1970 by then prime minister Lon Nol.

14. In addition to his own work, praCh is also a music producer. Among his current projects is an album of traditional pin peat music. praCh asserts, "I really want to help revive that. There are only about four Cambodian master musicians left in the United States, and Mr. Chan Ho [Ho Chan] is one of them. He plays all the instruments. I was privileged to have him play interludes on traditional instruments for *Dalama Two*. There's also some traditional music with me rapping over it; his son played that" (May 80).

15. THE U.S.A. PATRIOT Act (Uniting and Strengthening America by Providing Appropriate Tools Required to Intercept and Obstruct Terrorism Act of 2001) was passed following the September 11, 2001 attacks. A 342-page document, the act was linked to national, state, and local anti-terrorist initiatives. Much more can certainly be written with regard to the act's impact on civil liberties and law enforcement, but what is most relevant is that the act reconfigured the authority of the Immigration and Nationality Service (INS) and was used to facilitate the deportation of individuals who had committed "aggravated felonies." Such felonies lacked concrete definition, and crimes that fell under this rubric ranged from writing bad checks to murder. 1,500 Cambodian/Cambodian Americans living in the United States were threatened with deportation, and this story is mentioned in praCh's "Art of Fact."

16. *The Killing Fields* (1984). Dir. Roland Joffe. The film was based on the experiences of Cambodian journalist Dith Pran during the period of the genocide. Dr. Haing S. Ngor portrayed Pran in the production, and won the American Academy-Award for Best Supporting Actor in 1985. Dr. Ngor died in a gang-related shooting in 1996.

17. Pilger's film highlights the extent to which the genocide in Cambodia was met with indifference on the world stage by various governments. It includes interviews with survivors and footage of Cambodia during and after the period of the Killing Fields.

18. Interview conducted 24 November 2006.

19. The lack of a nationally-sanctioned memorial in Cambodia is reflected by the absence of justice for victims of the Killing Fields on the world stage. It was not until March 2003 that the United Nations reached a draft agreement with the Cambodian government for the formation of an international criminal tribunal to try former Khmer Rouge leaders. Such an effort occurred after five years of negotiation and twenty-four years after the Khmer Rouge were driven out of power. The rules for the tribunal were recently codified in March 2007. According to Ek Madera, "Pol Pot, the "Brother Number One" of the government which spawned the "Killing Fields," died in 1998. But "Brother Number Two" Nuon Chea, former head of state Khieu Samphan and ex-Foreign Minister Ieng Sary are all living free in Cambodia and are due to face trial. The only senior Khmer Rouge figure in detention is Duch, head of the notorious Tuol Sleng interrogation center, a former school in Phnom Penh where at least 14,000 people were tortured and executed before a Vietnamese invasion ended their rule in 1979" (*Reuters*, 16 March 2007). In August 2007, news that Duch would testify against the Khmer Rouge to an UN-backed international war crimes tribunal was released.

20. In the United States, the Khmer Institute and the Cambodian American Heritage Museum in Chicago have created virtual memorials to the Killing Fields. To draw briefly from James Young's work, these virtual sites, along with other cultural productions, provide the significant spaces "where groups of people gather to create a common past for themselves" and construct "constitutive narratives" (6).

21. Marianne Hirsch's work on postmemory provides a useful entrée into a discussion of memory in 1.5 generation Cambodian American youth. Hirsch draws from the traumatic memory of the Holocaust and its continued position as a referent for familial memory for children of survivors. Hirsch asserts that postmemory "characterises the experience of those who grow up dominated by narratives that preceded their birth, whose own belated stories are evacuated by the stories of the previous generation shaped by traumatic events that be neither understood nor recreated" (*Family Frames* 22). However, Cambodian American youth and their respective cultural productions do not fit neatly into Hirsch's rubric. Such productions reflect the experiences of those who, as children, lived during the genocide yet have left their country of origin prior to their teens. The narrative of the Killing Fields is one that is intimately linked to childhood remembrance.

22. Renan, Ernest. "What is a Nation?" (1882). Written at a time of shifting global dynamics and in light of large-scale colonial projects, Renan dis-

misses racial and linguistic foundations for nationhood. According to Renan, "A nation is a soul, a spiritual principle. Two things, which in truth are one, constitute this soul or spiritual principle. One lies in the past, one in the present. One is the possession in common of a rich legacy of memories, the other is present-day consent, the desire to live together, the will to perpetuate the value of the heritage that one has received in individual form....Where national memories are concerned, griefs are of more value than triumphs, for they impose duties and require a common effort"(*Becoming National: A Reader* 52-53) (Lecture at Sorbonne, 11 March 1882 in Discours et Conferences, Paris, Calman-Levy, 1887, pp.277-310; also in Geoff Eley and Ronald Grigor Suny, ed. 1996. *Becoming National: A Reader.* New York and Oxford: Oxford University Press, 1996: pp. 41-55.)

References

"America Provides Refuge for an Imperiled Art." *Music Educators Journal.* Vol.69. (1983 May): 37-38. Print.

Hirsch, Marianne. *Family Frames: Photography, Narrative, and Postmemory.* Boston: Harvard University Press, 1997. Print.

May, Sharon. Interview with praCh. "Art of fact." In *Manoa.* 16.1 (2004): 73-82. Print.

praCh. *Dalama: The End'n Is Just the Beginnin'.* Long Beach, California. Mujestic Records, 2000. CD.

_____. Dalama: *The Lost Chapter.* Long Beach, California: Mujestic Records. 2002. CD.

Renan, Ernest. "What is a Nation?" In *Becoming National: A Reader.* New York: Oxford University Press, 1996. Print.

Williams, Paul. "Witnessing Genocide: Vigilance and Remembrance at Tuol Sleng and Choeung Ek." In *Holocaust and Genocide Studies* 18.2 (2004): 234-255. Print.

Young, James. *The Texture of Memory.* New Haven: Yale University Press, 1993. Print.

Section VII

Cambodian American
Literature

CHAPTER 15

Trauma and Transformation:
The Autobiographies of
Cambodian Americans
(1980-2010)

Teri Shaffer Yamada

Autobiography is an uncommon genre in Cambodia (Jacob 1996). During the 1950s and 1960s in the urban centers of Phnom Penh and Battambang, there were many modern writers producing romantic novellas, detective fiction, short stories, poetry, and essays for newspapers and magazines, but not autobiography or biography (Yamada 2009). Most of these modern writers lost their lives during the Pol Pot era (1975-79).[1] A few were studying abroad prior to 1975; others were able to relocate to France, Australia or other countries during the late 1970s or early 1980s, where they took up residence as refugees of the Cambodian diaspora. It is among these refugee Cambodians that the genre of testimonial autobiography emerged as the most popular literature of the diaspora.[2] In this essay I will focus on the historical context, distinctive qualities, and cultural significance—in terms of politics and the formation of identity—of this new literary form of testimonial discourse, predominately among Cambodian Americans.[3]

As a new genre, Cambodian refugee autobiographies grew out of the experience of tragedy and displacement caused by the Pol Pot era (Jackson). They share a sense of collective cultural identity caused by a horrific, shared experience (Gerber). This is summarized by, Loung Ung in *First They Killed My Father* (2000):

> From 1975-1979—through execution, starvation, disease, and forced labor—the Khmer Rouge systematically killed an estimated two million Cambodians, almost a fourth of the country's population.... This is a story of survival: my own and my family's. Though these events constitute my experience, my story mirrors that of millions of Cambodians. If you had been living in Cambodia during this period, this would be your story too (ix).

These autobiographies also reveal the need to "bear witness" to an "unthinkable" experience or give voice to an "unspeakable" atrocity; Cambodians were silenced, while being forced to steal and lie in order to survive. Psychologically, this need to bear witness can be attributed to "survivor's guilt" framed as "Why did I live while so many others died?" There is a sense of the miraculous at having been spared death as seen in Daran Kravanh's *Music through the Dark: A Tale of Survival in Cambodia* (2000), combined with complex feelings of deep sorrow, guilt, and gratitude.[4] And beyond these emotions, there is the need to "honor" those who died in this tragedy by remembering their suffering, recognizing their bravery and sacrifice, and ultimately seeking justice for them and for Cambodia itself (Dy). This complex set of emotions is reflected in Sophal Leng Stagg's statement from *Hear Me Now: Tragedy in Cambodia* (1998): "I cannot completely explain my reasons for the need to write about these experiences except as a testimony to those whose lives were lost and who can no longer speak for themselves" (5).

In short, these autobiographies arise from complex feelings. They derive from a desire to change public perception of Cambodia to one not solely framed by the tragedy of the Killing Fields, to heal oneself and other survivors, to honor the dead, to seek some form of justice for those who experienced this atrocity, and finally to facilitate a cultural restoration of Cambodia.

The Development of a Genre

Since 1980, Cambodians have written over twenty-three autobiographies published in English,[5] at least fifteen authored by Cambodians in America.[6] Over eight Americans, some of them professional writers and academics have authored biographies or ethnographic studies of Cambodian survivors.[7] The tragedy of the Cambodian experience has been a compelling story, driven partly by indignation over the stark impunity for leaders of the Pol Pot regime who caused this dystopic experience. The need for justice is a concern for many of the Cambodian American autobiographers as they advocate for a Khmer Rouge tribunal or some type of criminal prosecution for crimes against humanity, typically in closing comments at the end of their narrative.

The majority of these autobiographies have been written by urban dwelling Cambodians. Structurally, they share a similar temporal-spatial frame, formatted into three parts.[8] The first part typically begins with a short portrayal of urban life in Phnom Penh before 1975 as the city steadily devolves into chaos through the violence of a civil war spreading from the north towards Phnom Penh. The second part begins on April 17, 1975 and spans the nearly four-year reign of Pol Pot's Democratic Kampuchea until the country was invaded by Vietnam in January 1979. On April 17, 1975 black-clad, Khmer Rouge cadres began to empty Phnom Penh of its residents. They violently implemented a forced march to the countryside while telling the frightened citizenry that Americans would soon be dropping bombs on the city; intellectuals, government and military officials were specifically targeted and executed along the way.

Over the next several years, city people, referred to as "new people" by the Khmer Rouge, were progressively starved to death as they were moved relentlessly around the countryside and forced to work on various labor-intensive projects, such as building dikes, growing rice for export, or clearing malarial forest land. Children were isolated from their parents and placed in separate communal work teams; loved ones were disappeared by "Angkar," the "Organization." This second part is the longest section of the autobiography as it explores the horrific experiences endured during this period. The third part of the autobiography is essentially a coda. The author describes his or her escape and ultimate arrival to the United States after the Vietnamese invasion of Cambodia in 1979 and ends the narrative without much discussion of the experience of acculturation.[9]

The prototype of this three-part format appears to be journalist Sydney H. Schanberg's 1980 *New York Times Magazine* article, revised and published as a book in 1985 under the same title *The Death and Life of Dith Pran*, which became the basis of the movie *The Killing Fields* (1984). Schanberg's article begins with the fall of Phnom Penh during his assignment as a reporter there in 1975 and describes his despair at being unable to save his close friend, Cambodian photographer Dith Pran, from the Khmer Rouge. Schanberg traces Pran's torturous experience, daring escape to a Thai border camp, and ultimate relocation to the United States where the reportage ends. Although most Cambodians have neither read Schanberg's *New York Times Magazine* article nor *The Death and Life of Dith Pran,* nearly all have seen *The Killing Fields*.[10]

Haing Ngor, who played the role of Dith Pran in *The Killing Fields,* authored one of the first autobiographies by a Cambodian relocated to the United States. His *Haing Ngor: A Cambodian Odyssey* (1987), more like a memoir than the typical three-part autobiography that would become the standard during the following twenty years, provides a clue to the ideological and political subtext to this literature. Providing an emotional context for his survival story, Ngor begins with a comment on the unthinkable reversal of fortune he and other Cambodians experienced during 1975-1979.

> I am a survivor of the Cambodian holocaust. That's who I am. . . . To keep the Khmer Rouge soldiers from killing me, I had to pretend I was not a doctor. They had already killed most of my family. And my case was typical. By destroying our culture and by enslaving us, the Khmer Rouge changed millions of happy, normal human beings into something more like animals. They turned people like me into cunning, wild thieves (1).

At the time of these early autobiographies in the 1980s, many Cambodian intellectuals in the diaspora felt outrage at the lack of international attention to this horrific historical event. Sophal Leng Stagg echoes this continuing frustration in her 1996 *Hear Me Now: Tragedy in Cambodia*:

> This holocaust, while well documented in such treatments as the movie *The Killing Fields* and in the autobiography by Haing Ngor, has been almost totally ignored outside of Southeast Asia. If, however, we have learned nothing in the continuing struggle of man's inhumanity to man, we can confidently state that such 'lessons' in history will be repeated as long as they are overlooked by the world community. The continuing reliance upon witnesses to such events serves as a constant reminder of the need to bring them to our attention (1).

This advocacy for justice at an international level becomes a recurrent theme throughout the decades' history of these testimonial autobiographies. And as Stagg reflects, the quest for justice takes on a deeper dimension: to record it is to remember and remembering may create the necessary condition for such atrocities to be stopped. That is the hope.

Recording Atrocity

The first Cambodian to write of his Khmer Rouge experience, Pin Yathay, is only one of two autobiographers to date able to escape during the Khmer Rouge regime.[11] After fleeing in 1977, Pin, an educated professional, immediately went to France where he arranged a series of press conferences with Western reporters in an attempt to inform the world about the atrocities occurring in Cambodia.[12] In 1978 he spoke in "Paris, Brussels, Montreal, Ottawa and Washington demanding Western action against the Khmer Rouge" (236). He was greeted with polite concern and inaction.

Pin's demand for action initiates us into the ideological and political dimension of these autobiographies: the audience is international in scope; the topic is human rights violations; the historically accurate, testimonial autobiography becomes symbolically evidentiary in its ability to substantiate the crime.[13] For Cambodians relocated to America, this broad internationalist, human-rights perspective requires a positionality that is situated on an interstice of the national/international.[14] On the national front, the autobiographers position themselves within the geographical safety of the United States, the ideological land of "liberty and justice for all," and from this base address an international audience, including the United Nations, in their plea for human rights and justice for all Cambodians. For some autobiographers this positionality, which requires an appreciation of both a national and international stage, deploys America's own ideology of justice against itself. It reveals the hypocrisy of America's machiavellian National Security State policy, which supported Pol Pot as the official representative of Cambodia in the United Nations during the Vietnamese occupation of Cambodia (1979-1989); and it may be used to lobby the United States' administration for a rectification of its past wrongs symbolized, in this case, by its current weak support for a United Nations sponsored, war-crimes tribunal.[15] On the other hand, a number of autobiographers, such as Loung Ung, Oni Vitandham, and Sichan Siv, advocate for the rebuilding of Cambodia without much political critique of U.S. involvement in Cambodia during the 1970s.

Haing Ngor illustrates the complex ideological position of an advocate in exile. Towards the end of his memoir he relates how the Cambodia Documentation Commission (1985-1990) has been trying to arrange for the trial of top Khmer Rouge leaders before an international tribunal:[16] "It is seeking to bring those responsible to justice in the World Court, under the terms of the UN Convention on the Prevention and Punishment of the Crime of Genocide" (464). Once again Ngor's activist memoir reveals the resonance between Cambodian American autobiography as proof of "crimes against humanity" and the politics of international human rights. It reveals the need for justice, symbolized by a trial, which officially recognizes that atrocities have been committed, thereby moving toward punishment of the perpetrators and, theoretically, some closure for their victims.

Cambodia would remain under Vietnamese governance until 1989 with democratic elections finally held during 23-28 May 1993 under the auspices of the United Nations[17] (Asian Human Rights Commission). Pol Pot would remain in a Khmer Rouge camp along the Thai border free from indictment until tried in July 1997 by rival Khmer Rouge forces at their jungle base in Anlong Veng in a "people's tribunal." On April 15, 1998, Pol Pot died, supposedly of a heart attack (Becker). Given this historical context, unrequited justice has become a subtext of these autobiographies. The need for evidence to substantiate Khmer Rouge atrocities and the desire for international justice continued to be major factors propelling the production of Cambodian autobiographies through the 1990s. What links these two decades of autobiographical productivity—1980s and 1990s—is the growing political power of the Cambodian Documentation Commission and Yale University's Cambodian Genocide Program.[18]

The Cambodian Documentation Commission mentioned by Haing Ngor in his memoir would ultimately achieve its mission: the collection of documents in preparation for a war crimes trial. Its efforts were institutionalized by the United States with the 1994 Cambodian Justice Act that provided the political recognition and the economic basis for the collection of evidence. Yale University's Cambodian Genocide Program (CGP) was the result. The CGP's mandate is "to help implement 'the policy of the United States to support efforts to bring to justice members of the Khmer Rouge for their crimes against humanity committed in Cambodia between April 17, 1975 and January 7, 1979'" (1). Their 1995 report states: "Until now, no detailed picture has existed of specific atrocities, victims and perpetrators of the Cambodian genocide. The Cambodian Genocide Program has made major strides in assembling the documentation necessary to prosecute the authors of the Cambodian genocide" (1). An excellent example of the synergy between this historical project and the production of testimonials is Dith Pran's anthology *Children of Cambodia's Killing Fields: Memoirs by Survivors* (1997). Pran, who worked for the Cambodian Genocide Program (CGP) during the 1990s, describes the 29 autobiographical vignettes in his anthology as "testimonials." Kim DePaul, the executive director of The Dith Pran Holocaust Awareness Project, explains their significance:

> The testimonies...bear poignant witness to the slaughter the
> Khmer Rouge inflicted on the Cambodian people...They speak
> on their bewilderment and pain as Khmer Rouge cadres tore

their families apart, subjected them to harsh brainwashing, drove them from their homes to work in forced-labor camps, and executed captives... (http://www.dithpran.org).

These testimonies also refute the forced confessions written by prisoners in S-21, a former school turned into an interrogation-torture center during the Khmer Rouge regime.[19] Thousands of fabricated confessional documents were created at S-21, often linking the victim's life history to involvement with the American CIA. S-21's archive of forced confessional documents and photographs was discovered during the early 1980s by a number of U.S. western Cambodia scholars (Chandler 1999: 1-13). Cornell University then established a documentation project in cooperation with the museum curator at S-21 to photograph and catalogue the archives. David Chandler, who studied the confessions for over a decade, contextualizes their historicity: "I hoped initially to use the archive as the basis for a narrative history of opposition to the DK. I soon discovered, however, that the truth or falsity of the confessions, along with the innocence or guilt of the people who produced them, could rarely be corroborated" (ix). In *A Cambodian Prison Portrait: One Year in the Khmer Rouge's S-21,* Vann Nath describes how false confessions were a prisoner's attempt to free him or herself from the various unthinkable tortures devised by the "truthseekers" associated with S-21. Haing Ngor laments how most Cambodians were forced to prevaricate for survival, turned into liars for self-preservation (1). Therefore, the truthfulness of Cambodian autobiography has a double significance. It becomes politically significant as evidentiary proof in an effort to restore justice to the homeland Cambodia and the victims of the Khmer Rouge through a trial of crimes against humanity; and it becomes personally significant as a means of transforming the trauma caused by the Khmer Rouge.

Transforming Trauma

The autobiographical act contains both a political and personal dimension and becomes one public means for the transformation of public and personal trauma. Most Cambodians are no strangers to trauma. They have been doubly inscribed as victims: once in

Cambodia under Pol Pot, and once in the United States under the social service bureaucracy (Ong 1995). Many Cambodians never fully recover from the multiple-traumas of the Pol Pot years. Obsessive reflections, regret, sorrow, and depression are common emotional states experienced by a significant number of Cambodian refugees. One Western interpretation is that these symptoms persist for the first generation Cambodian refugee because of traditional cultural restraints on self-expression as a healing modality (Morelli: 128). And trauma can be passed down within a family for generations. Many older Cambodians feel that it is inappropriate to publicly reveal such deep, painful feelings, or feel incapable of verbalizing an experience of such horror.[20] Words simply fail to communicate the experience. Ironically, symptoms for many Cambodians with post-traumatic stress disorder are sometimes exacerbated by a disclosure of these feelings simply because the experience is relived. Western "talking" therapy is often ineffective in the case of Cambodians (Silove, Chang and Manicavasagar). Nevertheless, many Cambodian autobiographers seem to appreciate this possibility. They use this genre as a form of therapeutic self-disclosure. Writing becomes a political and personal act which has the potential to transform trauma. This movement from victim to advocate for justice—an action signified by the rupture of an imposed silence—informs most Cambodian American autobiographies.

This objective—personal and social transformation—is exemplified by Chanrithy Him in her autobiography *When Broken Glass Floats* (2000).

It is reiterated again in her 2004 letter to Representative Henry J. Hyde enjoining him to support the Khmer Rouge Tribunal:

> Like many survivors, I am a living symbol of suffering of innocent war victims. As a woman and a U.S. citizen, I spent painful years writing my autobiography, *When Broken Glass Floats: Growing Up Under the Khmer Rouge* (W.W. Norton).
>
> Since its publication, I have devoted my heart and soul and whatever energy I have, to educating and inspiring our world about the triumph of the human spirit in the worst of times, especially after September 11. Psychologically and emotionally, it has been quite taxing to speak on such subject. But as a child

survivor and a citizen of this world, I oblige myself to play this role to make a difference.

Mr. Hyde, it is *time* that the remaining top Khmer Rouge leaders be brought to justice for committing crimes against humanity. Cambodia needs closure and so do survivors in the Khmer diaspora. Bringing these leaders to justice will be one of the key factors, which I believe, will help us heal (Him 2004).

A lineage of Cambodian autobiographers whose intention is to make a difference by fighting for justice on an international stage begins with Someth Mey in 1986. It extends through others like Haing Ngor and Dith Pran, ending with Loung Ung and Chanrithy Him, and now culminates in 2010 with the actual Khmer Rouge Trials. These controversial trials finally began in the Extraordinary Chambers of the Courts of Cambodia during February 2009 with the Khmer Rouge official Kaing Guek Eav ("Duch").[21] This special court had been established by a joint resolution of the United Nations and Cambodia in 2003 with the task to try "senior leaders and those most responsible for serious violations of Cambodian and international law committed during the Khmer Rouge rule" (UN News Center). Ngor and Pran's untimely deaths in the United States have precluded them from observing these trials in Cambodia, the goal of so much effort and sacrifice.

Hybrid Identity

Cambodians are the only Southeast Asian refugees in America to have experienced a form of cultural genocide before relocation, making their experience of Americanization even more problematic. They have been caught in the dilemma of an acculturation/assimilation process, which requires the abandonment of traditional norms while simultaneously needing to reconstruct these norms as the basis for healing the kind of trauma they have endured (Goodwin). Moreover, many Cambodian refugees who relocated to the United States have found themselves experiencing the same pattern of abject or binary "identity" paradox as other Asians in America, making genuine assimilation an illusive prospect.

The author's development of a distinct hybrid identity, which balances or accommodates Americanization with the heritage culture, is illustrated as a subtext in many of these autobiographies even though it is not the author's main objective.[22] The three-part format, shared by so many of these autobiographies, can obfuscate this difference. Chris Higashi's review of Loung Ung's *First They Killed My Father* and Chanrithy Him's *When Broken Glass Floats* illustrates this tendency to homogenize:

> These survivors hope to help others to heal by giving voice to those who did not survive and those who still suffer but cannot speak for themselves. They honor their parents, family, friends, and Cambodians who lost their lives. They work to alter the world's perceptions of Cambodia based on images of the brutal Khmer Rouge (4).

Indeed, Him and Ung's autobiographies appear very similar. They both conform to the three-part format. Both focus on survival under the Khmer Rouge; both are written by 1.5 generation Cambodian Americans, both authors are female; both were young children under the Khmer Rouge; both relocated to the United States where they grew up attending public schools and ultimately achieved college degrees; both have experienced the recurrent nightmares associated with post-traumatic stress disorder (PTSD).

To some degree both Him and Ung share similar patterns of a hybrid identity, or in Aihwa Ong's terms "self-positioning and social agency" (1993: 755). Both have made the requisite double movement: rehabilitating and accommodating what it means to be Cambodian, given the traumatic experience endured under the Khmer Rouge, while developing a "successful" hybrid American identity. Other autobiographies also illustrate the difficulties encountered in this process of hybrid identity formation, especially Oni Vitandham in *On the Wings of a White Horse* and Loung Ung in *Lucky Child*. Nor is it easy to adjust in other countries as Vannary Imam illustrates in *When Elephants Fight* from her experience in Australia. The rehabilitation of a Cambodian cultural identity—the reclaiming of what is positive about 'traditional' culture and the desire to restore it—clearly takes place through the autobiographical act, by describing and comparing pre- and post-Khmer Rouge Cambodia and the extent of cultural devolution that took place during 1975-1979.[23]

This rehabilitation symbolizes a psychological movement away from the cultural abjection created by Cambodia's autogenocide. It comes full circle when the author returns to Cambodia to uncover lost relatives or to become reunited with family survivors. For many autobiographers the ultimate personal restoration is working to rebuild Cambodia, whether serving as an advocate for the Khmer Rouge trials or by establishing social service projects such as the building or schools or the construction of wells in rural villages.

The structuring of a hybrid identity through becoming a politically or socially active subject-citizen in the United States is common among these autobiographers. In Him's case, her socially active "Americanness" occurs through her work in Portland, Oregon with Cambodian refugees, especially adolescents suffering from PTSD; her participation in international conferences on this issue; and her published autobiography which decries the atrocities caused by this trauma while seeking "justice" for its victims. In a somewhat parallel pattern, Ung has served as a national spokesperson for the Campaign for a Landmine Free World, a program of the Vietnam Veterans of American Foundation. She has traveled to Cambodia several times on landmine issues. Both Ung and Him have constructed an individualized hybrid identity that intersects the national/international. This focus on reparations for Cambodia is a common pattern seen in the lives of many other autobiographers such as Oni Vitandham and Dith Pran.

Irrespective of such similarities, Ung and Him's paths to hybrid identity differ; each develops through their own process of cultural negotiation. The difference in their socio-economic position in Cambodia—for example, Ung's upper-class social status and cultural identification as "Chinese" Cambodian in Phnom Penh compared to Him's more rural, middle-class status and identification as ethnic "Cambodian"—partially explains their different perspectives about Cambodian culture and the Khmer Rouge.[24] Their experience of America upon relocation, whether isolated within an American community or buffered by a small refugee Cambodian community, also makes a difference. Their different ideological sensibilities about the United States and its role in Cambodian politics during the 1970s may be due to this relocation experience and the area in which they resettled. It is symbolized by their divergent maps of Cambodia found in their autobiographies.

Him's map displays a conscious concern about the historical veracity of her autobiography, *When Broken Glass Floats*, which also reveals ideological complexity. Her map of Cambodia includes the 1969-70, B-52 "Menu" targets, the sites of America's illegal bombing of Cambodia, along with the route of her family's forced relocations in the countryside after their evacuation from Phnom Penh in 1975. In contrast, Ung's map contains the different Khmer Rouge zones and names of the provinces. Him, without overtly criticizing U.S. covert policy towards Cambodia in her autobiography, does so indirectly through dialogical complexity. Narrating her story in both first person and historically omniscient voices, she also incorporates "historical records" in the form of newspaper quotations at the beginning of a number of chapters. Chapter Two "B-cinquante-deux" begins with an 18 July 1973 excerpt from an article by *New York Times* correspondent Seymour M. Hersh:

> Washington, July 17—United States B-52 bombers made at least 3,500 secret bombing raids over Cambodia in a 14-month period beginning in March, 1969, Defense Department sources disclosed today...sources did confirm...that information about the...raids was directly provided to President Nixon...and his top national security advisers, including Henry A. Kissinger [25](38).

Him successfully establishes for her American readers a visceral connection between "historical fact" and "personal experience." The bombing and subsequent Vietnamese skirmishes destroyed her family's rural life, forcing them to Phnom Penh. Without polemic, she nudges historically amnesiac American readers towards recognition of their government's complicity in an unpleasant history. Through this interweaving of the historical and personal, Him's autobiography provides a multi-faceted ideological positioning which both covertly applauds and embraces America's "human rights advocacy" while indirectly criticizing the United States' actual policy of illegal bombing and subsequent support of the Khmer Rouge. She exploits the gap between ideology and reality.

In contrast to Ung's *First They Killed My Father*, Him also provides a more historically complex and nuanced representation of the Khmer Rouge: some were brutal, others saved her life. Ung, who identifies as "Chinese" Cambodian, associates Khmer Rouge brutality with anti-Chinese ethnic cleansing and repeatedly describes the deep hatred they generate in her; an emotion of such intensity, it may well have saved her life: "I stand in my corner with more conviction than ever to kill these soldiers, to avenge the blood that drips from my brother's skull. Someday, I will kill them all. My hatred for them is boundless" (118-9). Ung was five and Him was eight in 1975, which may explain some difference in their recollections and experiences. Both rely upon relatives' memories to reconstruct their stories. Ung also explores in dreams and fantasy (italicized passages), speculation on the fate of her disappeared father and other relatives, thus reflecting less concern for historical veracity and a more "American" approach to autobiography which accommodates fictive elements. Daran Kravanh's *Music through the Dark* (2000) is also very interpretive and provides a nuanced representation of the Khmer Rouge.

In contrast to Him, Ung is more ideologically pro-American in her autobiography (2000, 12). There are no B-52 bombing sites on her map of Cambodia (xv), though she does mention the U.S. bombing: "The war in Vietnam spread to Cambodia when the United States bombed Cambodia's borders to try to destroy the North Vietnamese bases. The bombings destroyed many villages and killed many people, allowing the Khmer Rouge to gain support from the peasants and farmers" (40). Relocated from a Thai border camp, Ung's geographical site of resettlement in America became Vermont in 1980 at age eight, where she grew up in the town's only Cambodian family. Rejecting anything Cambodian, she became as American as possible and only seriously began to explore and reclaim her Cambodianness in college, all the while suffering from nightmares common to Cambodian PTSD. She explains her different experience of Americanization:

When Meng and I came to America, I did everything I could to not think about them [sic her relatives who remained in Cambodia]. In my new country, I immersed myself in American culture during the day, but at night the war haunted me with nightmares.... As the Ethiopian crisis faded from the screens and Americans' consciousness, I was even more determined to make myself a normal American girl. I played soccer. I joined the cheerleading squad...I cut and curled my hair. I painted my eyes with dark makeup to make them look more round and Western. I'd hoped being Americanized could erase my memories of the war (2000: 235-6).

In contrast, Him's site of relocation in the United States was Portland, Oregon, where she grew up in a community with other Cambodian refugee children who attended the same public schools. Compared to Ung, she did not go through such a deep personal rejection of her Cambodianness although learning how to balance two cultures was stressful:

To me, I'm American, Cambodian-American. I don't know what it means...there was still Cambodian culture being thrust on me by my elders and aunts and uncles early on in college, and it was really stressful dealing with this living between two cultures (Frontline World).

Him's experience of growing up in a Cambodian enclave may explain the care she takes in the historical veracity of her autobiographical reconstruction; she absorbed the mainstream understanding of the Cambodian refugee, intellectual community represented by Haing Ngor, Dith Pran and others, regarding the historical importance of testimonial discourse.

Proof of this is the publication of her experience, "When the Owl Cries," in Pran's *Children of Cambodia's Killing Fields: Memoirs by Survivors* several years before the publication of her own autobiography (147-154). In contrast, Ung, who was more culturally isolated from a Cambodian community while growing up as a teenager in the United States, was probably unaware of any intellectual concern over the historical and cultural accuracy of Cambodian American autobiographies. Towards the end of her publicity tour in 2000, she was severely criticized by some members of the Cambodian community, specifically a cohort of 1.5 generation intellectuals, for misrepresenting their experience while being promoted as their spokesperson (Lay; Phim 2007: 79-80).

Regardless of these factors, both Chanrithy Him and Loung Ung exemplify how the trajectory from a passive to active Cambodi-anness during resettlement serves as one path toward the construc-tion of a more resilient hybrid identity in America. Both have become college educated professionals in the United States, dedi-cated to rebuilding Cambodia. Him's circumstances, having reset-tled in a small Cambodian refugee community in Oregon, must have contributed to her focus on improving mental health for Cam-bodians now living in the United States, while Ung's resettlement as the lone Cambodian family in her Vermont community finally led to her focus on landmines in Cambodia. Their hybridity is not homogeneous; rather, in the terms of Stuart Hall, it "lives with and through, not despite difference" (80).

Loung Ung has also become part of those Cambodian Ameri-can autobiographers who have gone beyond a focus on the Pol Pot experience. In *Lucky Child: A Daughter of Cambodia Reunites with the Sister She Left Behind* (2005), written as a sequel to *First They Killed My Father*, she breaks with the typical three-part format found in most Cambodian American testimonial autobiographies. In *Lucky Child* she compares her resettlement experience in America from 1980-1995 to her sister's life in Cambodia as the country struggles under reconstruction during the same period. The cultural contrast between life in Cambodia and the United States is strikingly por-trayed in juxtaposed chapters. Ung ends *Lucky Child* with her expe-rience of returning to Cambodia in 2003, when she reunited with her sister and remaining family, by disclosing the emotional upheaval and subsequent healing caused by this experience.

Many Cambodians in diaspora experience this reconciliation when they return to the homeland for the purpose of meeting sur-viving relatives or rebuilding Cambodia through temples, schools, and water wells, or to participate in other social services (Siv 273; Ung 2005: 246-264). Many build better homes for their relatives. This need to return and assist in reconstruction is found in many other autobiographies. Oni Vitandham has been the driving force behind the Progressive United Action Association Incorporated (PUAAI) foundation for Cambodia, established in 1995 to con-struct schools with trained teachers throughout Cambodia. She too has advocated for a global criminal tribunal to prosecute crimes against humanity and genocide in Cambodia.[26] Theary Seng, now a lawyer, describes how she always felt compelled to return to Cambodia to assist in its reconstruction in her autobiography *Daughter of the Killing Fields: Asrei's Story* (2005: 254).

Several other more recent autobiographies illustrate the complexity of being a Cambodian American: Navy Phim's *Reflections of a Khmer Soul* (2007) and Oni Vitandham's *On the Wings of a White Horse* (2005) reflect issues of acculturation in the Cambodian community that emerged in Long Beach, California. They also reflect the specific challenges of growing up during the 1990s within the Long Beach Cambodian community.[27] In contrast Sichan Siv in his *Golden Bones* provides an ideologically pro-American story of remarkable accomplishment in the United States. For all of these authors, however, a new hybrid identity—both Cambodian and American—is accomplished through service to the Cambodian community, whether here in the United States or in the homeland.

The impassioned ideological and political subtext as well as the tragedy and transcendence of Cambodian American autobiography provides one explanation why during the past several decades there has been more life writing by or about Cambodians than any other Asian ethnic cohort in the United States. Although, each individual's life story reflects a similar hologram of tragedy bounded by the time period April 17, 1975-January 1979, the intent of writing and the results may often be different. The prison-camp trope, which links these autobiographies, is the organizing principal that determines their format, a quality different from other ethnic, refugee, or immigrant American autobiographical forms. Yet as Stuart Hall reminds us about a subject's position of enunciation, the identity of these authors is complex and fluid; it shifts with the very act of writing as self-representation in the search for meaning (1989).

Endnotes

1. On this period of history see Chandler (1991) and Kiernan (1996).
2. For information on the early cultural experience and adaptations of diasporic Cambodians in the United States see Ebihara, Mortland and Ledgerwood (1994); Ebihara (1985). Compared to other Asians in

America see Hong (1993) and Ma (2000). For how this earlier form of Cambodian American autobiography is different from "standard" auto-biography see Olney (1972, 1980), Stone (1972); and Marcus (1994). For information on how it differs from Vietnamese refugee literature, see Truong (1997); Cargill and Huynh (2000); Christopher (1992); Elliott (1999); Freeman (1989); and Tran (1992). For a comparison to the Hmong experience in the U.S. see Faderman and Xiong (1998), Fadi-man (1997), Chan (1994, 1991) and Mattison (1994). For a compari-son to ethnic autobiographies see Boelhower (1982) and to other Asian American literature see Koshy (1996) and Wong (1993). On Cambodian American literature see Bunkong Tuon (2009).

3. For a further elaboration of this term "testimonial discourse" see Yamada (2005).

4. Kravanh's *Music through the Dark* is described as a "literary account of a personal experience told by one person and written by another with all the interpretations of such a transfer" and not a "translation, an oral his-tory, or an autobiography" (viii).

5. Two were first published in French then later translated into English and published in the United States: Pin Yathay, *Stay Alive My Son* (1987); Molyda Szymusiak, *The Stones Cry Out: A Cambodian Childhood* (1986). There are probably Cambodian French autobiographies published in French, unknown to me at this time. Two autobiographies were first pub-lished in Great Britain: Var Hong Ashe, *From Phnom Penh to Paradise: Escape from Cambodia* (1988); Someth May, *Cambodian Witness: The Autobiography of Someth May* (1986, 1987). Vannary Imam's *When Ele-phants Fight* (2000) was published in Australia where she resettled and Vann Nath's *A Cambodian Prison Portrait: One Year in the Khmer Rouge's S-21* (1998), was published in Thailand. In 2001 an English translation of Svay Ken's autobiography *Painted Stories: The Life of a Cambodian Family from 1941 to the Present* was published by Reyum in Phnom Penh. There is also a compilation of life writings edited by Dith Pran, *Children of Cambodia's Killing Fields: Memoirs by Survivors* (1997) and Carol Wagner's reportage in *Soul Survivors: Stories of Women and Chil-dren in Cambodia* (2002) on the incredible resiliency of Cambodians who have undergone this horrendous experience.

6. Haing Ngor, *Haing Ngor: A Cambodian Odyssey* (1987); Ma Vany, *Life in Danger* (1996); Sophal Leng Stagg, *Hear Me Now: Tragedy in Cambo-dia* (1998); Physa Chanmany as told to Catherine Lawton. *No More Fear: From Killing Fields to Harvest Fields* (1999); Loung Ung, *First They*

Killed My Father: A Daughter of Cambodia Remembers (2000); Chanrithy Him, *When Broken Glass Floats* (2000); Bree Lafreniere and Daran Kravan, *Music through the Dark: A Tale of Survival in Cambodia* (2000), Ly Y, *Heaven Becomes Hell: A Survivor's Story of Life under the Khmer Rouge* (2000); Sokreaksa S. Himm, *The Tears of My Soul* (2003); Loung Ung, *Lucky Child: A Daughter of Cambodia Reunites with the Sister She Left Behind* (2005); U Sam Oeur, *Crossing Three Wildernesses: A Memoir* (2005); Oni Vitandham, *On the Wings of a White Horse: A Cambodian Princess's Story of Surviving the Khmer Rouge Genocide* (2005); Theary C. Seng. *Daughter of the Killing Fields: Asrei's Story* (2005); Navy Phim, *Reflections of a Khmer Soul* (2007); Sichan Siv, *Golden Bones: An Extraordinary Journey from Hell in Cambodia to a New Life in America* (2008).

7. During the same period, American ethnographers, journalists, or acquaintances have written at least eight biographies or life writings on behalf of or about Cambodians. These include Martin Stuart-Fox and Bunheang Ung, *The Murderous Revolution* (1985); Gail Sheehy. *Spirit of Survival* (1986); JoAn D. Criddle, *To Destroy You Is No Loss: The Odyssey of a Cambodian Family* (1987); Sharon Sloan Fiffer. *Imagining America: Paul Thai's Journey From the Killing Fields of Cambodia to Freedom in the U.S.A* (1991); Nancy Moyer, *Escape from the Killing Fields: One Girl Who Survived the Cambodian Holocaust* (1991); JoAn D. Criddle. *Bamboo & Butterflies: From Refugee to Citizen* (1992); Usha Welaratna. *Beyond the Killing Fields: Voices of Nine Cambodian Survivors in America* (1993); Adam Fifield, *A Blessing Over Ashes: The Remarkable Odyssey of my Unlikely Brother* (2000); Carol Wagner, *Soul Survivors: Stories of Women and Children in Cambodia* (2002). For the politics of this see Clifford and Marcus (1986); (Journalist Jon Swain writes about his experience of Cambodia in *River of Time: A Memoir of Vietnam and Cambodia* (1995), and Spaulding Gray gives an overview of the experience in his autobiographical monologue *Swimming to Cambodia* (1987).

8. Those that follow this pattern include Ung, *First They Killed My Father* (2000); Him, *When Broken Glass Foats* (2000); Vitandham, *On the Wings of a White Horse* (2005); Szymusiak, *The Stones Cry Out* (1986); Pin, *Stay Alive My Son* (1987); Seng, *Daughter of the Killing Fields: Asrei's Story* (2005); Kravanh, *Music through the Dark* (2000); Ly, *Heaven Becomes Hell* (2000); Himm, *The Tears of My Soul* (2003).

9. Some authors first escape to either Great Britain or France and then relocate to the United States.

10. Schanberg's format is followed in subsequent Cambodian autobiographies: Molyda Szymusiak's *The Stones Cry out: A Cambodian Childhood* (1984) mentions *The Killing Fields* in her preface. Someth May's *Cambodian Witness: The Autobiography of Someth May* (1986), Haing Ngor's *Haing Ngor: A Cambodian Odyssey* (1987) and Pin Yathay's *Stay Alive My Son* (1987) follow it as do four subsequent autobiographies published in 2000 to commemorate the 25th anniversary of the fall of Pol Pot.

11. Pin Yathay's *Stay Alive My Son* was self-published in French in 1980 as *L'utopie meurtrière,* revised and republished in 2000 as *Tu vivras, mon fils: l'extraordinaire récit d'un rescapé de l'enfer khmer rouge.* It was published in English translation in 1987, then revised and published with a foreword by David Chandler by Cornell University Press in 2000. A Tagalog translation was published in the Philippines in 1989; a Japanese translation was published in 2009. The other Cambodian autobiographer to escape within a year of the Khmer Rouge takeover was Sichan Siv, who recently published *Golden Bones* (2008).

12. The preoccupation with the homeland for exilic intellectuals is well illustrated by Said.

13. Cheah provides an interesting critique on the international positioning of human rights discourse.

14. On Asians and the transnational see Lim, Smith and Dissanayake (1999) and Chow (1993).

15. The U.S. government is still reluctant to support these trials, which finally got underway in 2009. For a good analysis of the U.S. position see Lum (2007). The actual efficacy of these trials has been a controversy itself. On the failure of the international community to stop this atrocity and forestall justice see Maguire (2005); for an introduction to the trials see Office of Public Affairs, Extraordinary Chambers in the Courts of Cambodia (2006); in defense of the trials and some history about their complexity see Fawthrop and Jarvis (2004).

16. Cambodian refugees, human rights, legal, and Cambodia specialists established the Cambodian Documentation Commission (1985-1990). "Associates of the Documentation Commission have conducted numerous research investigations in Cambodia and Thailand, analyzed phenomena of repression, translated Khmer language documents into English and international human rights declarations and conventions into Khmer, made human rights appeals to Cambodian political leaders and UN member states, made oral and written interventions at the UN

Commission on Human Rights, testified to committees of the U.S. Congress, and monitored the Cambodia debates at the UN General Assembly and international conferences on Cambodia. The Director of the Documentation Commission is David R. Hawk, Associate of the Columbia University Center for the Study of Human Rights." http://rmc.library.cornell.edu/EAD/htmldocs/RMM04499.html, February 23, 2003.

17. The United Nations Transitional Authority in Cambodia (UNTAC) was established by the United Nations Security Council on 29 February 1992 "to ensure the ensure the implementation of the Agreements on the Comprehensive Political Settlement of the Cambodia Conflict, signed in Paris on 23 October 1991." http://www.un.org/Depts/dpko/dpko/co_mission/untac.htm, February 23, 2003.

18. Corresponding with this period of intense documentation work by the CGP is the second period of Cambodian American autobiography. These 1990's autobiographies, whose precedent is Molyda Szymusiak's *The Stones Cry Out: A Cambodian Childhood*, 1975-1979, are predominately by young women of the 1.5 generation:[18] Sophal Leng Stagg, *Hear Me Now: Tragedy in Cambodia* (1996); Loung Ung, *First They Killed My Father: A Daughter of Cambodia Remembers* (2000); Chanrithy Him, *When Broken Glass Floats: Growing Up Under the Khmer Rouge* (2000). They all employ the same three-part format as the male autobiographers in the 1980s. Unlike the male autobiographers, however, they were young children during the Khmer Rouge regime. In contrast, the 1980s' male autobiographers (Ngor, Pran, May, and Yathay) were mature professionals when the Khmer Rouge forced them to flee Phnom Penh. Their longer life experience within traditional Cambodian culture before the rupture is revealed in the depth of their analysis about the Khmer-Rouge impact on traditional Cambodian culture and family structure. The 1990s' female autobiographies express less ethnographic depth. They foreground a "traumatic" childhood under the Khmer Rouge, including forced separation from parents, witness to torture and death, indoctrination into Khmer Rouge ideology and, in Loung Ung's case, instruction in how to kill. What links the 1980s and 1990s autobiographies are the similar testimonial structure, the human-rights subtext, and the quest for an international audience.

19. Among other documents, the archives contained over 4,000 typed or handwritten confessions of one to several hundred pages in length (Chandler viiii).

20. Karen Brown's radio documentary, "Trauma and Recovery: A Cambodian Refugee Experience" updates some of the problems and successes in treating PTSD in Cambodian refugees. The successes include a recognition that PTSD symptoms never go away completely but can be dealt with more successfully over time. Healing modalities include combined cultural modes that incorporate Cambodian spirituality and cultural sensitivity with western forms of talking therapy and medication. Cognitive psychological approaches have been somewhat successful. See also Farrell (1998); Somasundaram, van de Put, Eisenbruch and de Jong (1999); Caruth (1996).

21. On Duch see Fawthrop and Jarvis, 266-268.

22. On the issue of hybrid identity see Judith Butler (1995); Lisa Lowe (2000); Palumbo-Liu (1999, 2001).

23. This is certainly not the only means for reconstructing a "positive" Cambodian culture. Him also studies and performs traditional Cambodian dance.

24. The differences in their experience related to ethnic identification in Cambodia can be compared to Vannay Imam's ethnic identification as a Vietnamese Cambodian and the difference in treatment she attributes to that dual identity; see *When Elephants Fight* (2000)

25. For Kissinger's complicity in the illegal bombing of Cambodia refer to Hitchens (30).

26. http://www.onistory.com/index.html, February 16, 2010.

27. The "rural background, lack of education, limit of opportunities" in this community within Long Beach, which also happened to be the largest cluster of Cambodians within the United States made acculturation more difficult (U.S. Committee for Refugees). On this community see Needham and Quintiliani (2008) as well as Shaw (1989) and Wright (1998).

References

Ashe, Var Hong. *From Phnom Penh to Paradise: Escape from Cambodia*. London: Hodder and Stoughton, 1988. Print.

Becker, Elizabeth. "Pol Pot: Life of a Tyrant." BBC News (Friday, 14 April 2000). Web.

Boelhower, William. *Immigrant Autobiography in the United States (Four Versions of the Italian American Self)*. Verona: Essedue edizioni, 1982. Print.

Brown, Karen. "Trauma and Recovery: A Cambodian Refugee Experience." Radio documentary. Web.

Butler, Judith. "*Collected and Fractured: Response to 'Identities'.*" In *Identities*, edit by J. Anthony Appiah and Henry Louis Gates, eds. Chicago: University of Chicago Press, 1995. Print.

Cargill, Mary, and Jade Quang Huynh, eds. *Voices of Vietnamese Boat People: Nineteen Narratives of Escape and Survival*. New York: McFarland, 2000. Print.

Caruth, Cathy. *Unclaimed Experience: Trauma, Narrative, and History*. Baltimore: John Hopkins University Press, 1996. Print.

Chan, Sucheng, ed. *Hmong Means Free: Life in Laos and America*. Philadelphia: Temple University Press, 1994. Print.

———. *Asian Americans: An Interpretive History*. Boston: Twayne Publisher, 1991. Print.

Chandler, David. *The Tragedy of Cambodian History: Politic, War and Revolution since 1945*. New Haven: Yale University Press, 1991. Print.

———. *Voices from S-21: Terror and History in Pol Pot's Secret Prison*. Berkeley: University of California Press, 1999. Print.

Cheah, Pheng. "Posit(ion)ing Human Rights in the Current Global Conjuncture." In *Transnational Asia Pacific: Gender, Culture, and the Public Sphere*, edited by Lim, Shirley Geok-lin Lim, Larry E. Smith and Wimal Dissanayake. Urbana: University of Illinois Press, 1999. Print.

Chow, Rey. *Writing Diaspora: Tactics of Intervention in Contemporary Cultural Studies*. Bloomington: Indiana University Press, 1993. Print.

Christopher, Renny. "Blue Dragon, White Tiger: The Bicultural Stance of Vietnamese American Literature." In *Reading the Literatures of Asian America,* edited by Shirley Lim and Amy Ling. Philadelphia: Temple University Press, 1992. Print.

Chu, Patricia. *Assimilating Asians: Gendered Strategies of Authorship in Asian America*. Durham: Duke University Press, 2000. Print.

Chun, Gloria Heyung. *Of Orphans and Warriors: Inventing Chinese American Culture and Identity*. New Brunswick: Rutgers University Press, 2000. Print.

Clark, Thekla. *Children in Exile: The Story of a Cross-Cultural Family*. Hopewell, N.J.: The Ecco Press, 1998. Print.

Clifford, James, and George Marcus, eds. *Writing Culture: The Poetics and Politics of Ethnography*. Berkeley: University of California Press, 1986. Print.

Criddle, JoAn D. *Bamboo & Butterflies: From Refugee to Citizen.* Dixon, Ca: East/West Bridge 1992. Print.

———. *To Destroy You Is No Loss: The Odyssey of a Cambodian Family.* Dixon: East/West Bridge, 1987. Print.

Dy, Navy. "The Tragedy of My Homeland." In *Children of Cambodia's Killing Fields: Memoirs by Survivors,* edited by Dith Pran. New Haven: Yale University Press, 1997. Print.

Ebihara, May. "Khmer." In *Refugees in the United States,* edited by David W. Haines. Westport: Greenwood Press, 1985. Print.

Ebihara, May, Carol Mortland and Judy Ledgerwood, eds. *Cambodian Culture since 1975: Homeland and Exile.* Ithaca: Cornell University Press, 1994. Print.

Elliott, Duong Van Mai. *The Sacred Willow: Four Generations in the Life of a Vietnamese Family.* Oxford: Oxford University Press, 1999. Print.

Faderman, Lillian, with Ghia Xiong. *I Begin My Life All Over: The Hmong and the American Immigrant Experience.* Boston: Beacon Press, 1998. Print.

Fadiman, Anne. *The Spirit Catches You and You Fall Down: A Hmong child, Her American Doctors, and the Collision of Two Cultures.* New York: The Noonday Press, 1997. Print.

Farrell, Kirby. *Post-traumatic Culture: Injury and Interpretation in the Nineties.* Baltimore: John Hopkins University Press, 1998. Print.

Fawthrop, Tom, and Helen Jarvis. *Getting Away with Genocide? Elusive Justice and the Khmer Rouge Tribunal.* Ann Arbor: Pluto Press, 2004. Print.

Fifield, Adam. *A Blessing Over Ashes: The Remarkable Odyssey of my Unlikely Brother.* New York: Avon, 2000. Print.

Fiffer, Sharon Sloan. *Imagining America: Paul Thai's Journey From the Killing Fields of Cambodia to Freedom in the U.S.A.* New York: Paragon House, 1991. Print.

Fong, Timothy P. *The Contemporary Asian American Experience: Beyond the Model Minority.* Upper Saddle River: Prentice Hall, 1998. Print.

Freeman, James A. *Hearts of Sorrow: Vietnamese-American Lives.* Stanford, CA: Stanford University Press, 1989. Print.

Gerber, Lane. "We Must Hear Each Other's Cry: Lessons from Pol Pot Survivors." In *Genocide, War, and Human Survival,* edited by Charles B. Strozier and Michael Flynn. London: Rowman & Littlefield, 1996. Print.

Goodwin, Fred, narrator. "Voice of Experience: Cambodian Trauma in America." In *The Infinite Mind* radio program. New York: March 2003. Print.

Gray, Spalding. *Swimming to Cambodia.* Australia: Cinecom Pictures, 1987. Print.

Hall, Stuart. "Cultural Identity and Cinematic Representation." In *Framework*. 36 (1989): 68-81. Print.

Him, Chanrithy. "Letter to Representative Henry J. Hyde." University, Cambodian Genocide Project. Web; January 2010

_____. *When Broken Glass Floats: Growing Up Under the Khmer Rouge*. New York: W.W. Norton, 2000. Print.

Himm, Sokreaksa S., with Jan Greenough. *The Tears of My Soul*. Oxford: Monarch Books, 2003. Print.

Hitchens, Christopher. *The Trial of Henry Kissinger*. New York: Verso, 2001. Print.

Hong, Maria, ed. *Growing Up Asian American: An Anthology*. New York: William Morrow and Co., 1993. Print.

Hughes, Caroline. "Trying Pol Pot on the International State." Paper presented at the annual meeting of the *Association for Asian Studies*, Chicago, Illinois.

Imam, Vannary. *When Elephants Fight: A Memoir*. St. Leonards, Australia: Allen and Unwin, 2000. Print.

Jackson, Karl D. *Cambodia 1975-1979: Rendezvous with Death*. Princeton: Princeton University Press, 1989. Print.

Jacob, Judith M. *The Traditional Literature of Cambodia: A Preliminary Guide*. London Oriental Series. Vol. 40. Bath: Oxford University Press, 1996. Print.

Kravanh, Daran, and Bree Lafreniere. *Music through the Dark: A Tale of Survival in Cambodia*. Honolulu, University of Hawai'i Press, 2000. Print.

Kiernan, Ben. *The Pol Pot Regime: Race, Power, and Genocide in Cambodia under the Khmer Rouge, 1975-79*. New Haven: Yale University Press, 1996. Print.

Koshy, Susan. "The Fiction of Asian American Literature." In *The Yale Journal of Criticism* 9 (1996): 315-346. Print.

Lay, Sody. "The Cambodian Tragedy: Its Writer and Representations." In *Amerasia Journal* 27.2 (2001): 171-182. Print.

Lee, Rachel C. *The Americans of Asian American Literature: Gendered Fiction of Nation and Transnation*. Princeton, New Jersey: Princeton University Press, 1999. Print.

Lim, Shirley, and Amy Ling. *Reading the Literatures of Asian America*. Philadelphia: Temple University Press, 1992. Print.

Lim, Shirley Geok-lin, Larry E. Smith and Wimal Dissanayake, eds. *Transnational Asia Pacific: Gender, Culture, and the Public Sphere*. Urbana: University of Illinois Press, 1999. Print.

Lowe, Lisa. "Heterogeneity, Hybridity, Multiplicty: Marking Asian American Differences." In *Contemporary Asian America: A Multidisciplinary Reader*, edited by Min Zhou and James V. Gatewood. New York: New York University Press, 2000. Print.

Lum, Thomas. "Cambodia: Background and U.S. Relations." CRS Report for Congress. Washington D.C.: Congressional Research Service, July 18, 2007. Print.

Ly Y. *Heaven Becomes Hell: A Survivor's Story of Life under the Khmer Rouge*. New Haven: Yale University Southeast Asian Studies, 2000. Print.

Ma Sheng-Mei. *The Deathly Embrace: Orientalism and Asian American Identity*. Minneapolis: University of Minnesota Press, 2000. Print.

Ma Vany. *Life in Danger*. Pittsburgh: Dorrance Publication, 1996. Print.

Maguire, Peter. *Facing Death in Cambodia*. New York: Columbia University Press, 2005. Print.

Marcus, Laura. *Auto/biographical Discourses: Criticism, Theory, Practice*. Manchester: Manchester University Press, 1994. Print.

Mattison, Wendy, et al., ed. *Hmong Lives From Laos to La Crosse: Stories of Eight Hmong Elders*. La Crosse: The Pump House, 1994. Print.

May, Someth. *Cambodian Witness: The Autobiography of Someth May*. New York: Random House, 1986. Print.

May, Someth, *Cambodian Witness: The Autobiography of Someth May*. New York: Random House, 1987. Print.

Mollica, Richard F, Grace Wyshak and James Lavelle. "The Psychosocial Impact of War Trauma and Torture on Southeast Asian Refugees." In *American Journal of Psychiatry* 144.12 (1987): 1567-1572. Print.

Morelli, Paula Toki Tanemura. "Trauma and Healing: The Construction of Meaning Among Survivors of the Cambodian Holocaust." Unpublished dissertation, University of Washington, Seattle, 1996.

Moyer, Nancy. *Escape from the Killing Fields: One Girl Who Survived the Cambodian Holocaust*. Grand Rapids, Michigan: Zondervan, 1991. Print.

Nath, Vann. *A Cambodian Prison Portrait: One Year in the Khmer Rouge's S-21*. Thailand: White Lotus, 1998. Print.

Needham, Susan and Karen Quintiliani. *Images of America: Cambodians in Long Beach*. Chicago: Arcadia Publishing, 2008. Print.

Ngor, Haing S. *Haing Ngor: A Cambodian Odyssey*. New York: Macmillan Publishing, 1987. Print.

Office of Public Affairs, Extraordinary Chambers in the Courts of Cambodia. "An Introduction to the Khmer Rouge Trials." Cambodia: Secretariat of the Task Force for the Khmer Rouge Trials, 2006. Print.

Olney, James, ed. *Autobiography: Essays Theoretical and Critical*. Princeton: Princeton University Press, 1980. Print.

_____. *Metaphors of Self: the Meaning of Autobiography*. Princeton: Princeton University Press, 1972. Print.

Ong, Aihwa. "On the Edge of Empires: Flexible Citizenship among Chinese in Diaspora" In *Positions* 1.3 (1993): 744-778. Print.

_____. "Making the Biopolitical Subject: Cambodian Immigrants, Refugee Medicine And Cultural Citizenship in California." In *Social Science and Medicine* 40:9 (1995): 1243-1257. Print.

Palumbo-Liu, D. "Modeling the Nation: The Asian/American Split." In *Orientations: Mapping Studies in the Asian Diaspora*, edited by Kandice Chuh and Karen Shimakawa. Durham: Duke University Press, 2001. Print.

_____. *Asian/American: Historical Crossings of a Racial Frontier*. Stanford: Stanford University Press, 1999. Print.

Phim, Navy. *Reflections of a Khmer Soul*. Tucson: Wheatmark, 2007. Print.

_____. *"First They Killed My Father: A Daughter of Cambodia Remembers."* Web; January 2000.

Physa Chanmany. *No More Fear: From Killing Fields to Harvest Fields*. Fulton: Cladach Publishing, 1999. Print.

Pin Yathay, with John Man. *Stay Alive, My Son*. New York: The Free Press, 1987. Print.

Pran, Dith. *Children of Cambodia's Killing Fields: Memoirs by Survivors*. New Haven: Yale University Press, 1997. Print.

Said, Edward. "Intellectual Exile: Expatriates and Marginals." In *The Edward Said Reader*, edited by Bayoumi, Moustafa Bayoumi. New York: Vintage, 2000. Print.

Somasundaram, Daya J., Willem A.C.M. van de Put., Marice Eisenbruch, and Joop T.V.N. de Jong. "Starting Mental Health Services in Cambodia." In *Social Science & Medicine* 48 (1999): 1029-1046. Print.

Schanberg, Sydney. *The Death and Life of Dith Pran*. New York: Penguin, 1980. Print.

Seng, Theary C. *Daughter of the Killing Fields: Asrei's Story*. London: Fusion Press, 2005. Print.

Shaw, Scott. *Cambodian Refugees in Long Beach, California: The Definitive Study*. U.S.: Buddha Rose Publications, 1989. Print.

Sheehy, Gail. *Spirit of Survival*. New York: William Morrow, 1986. Print.

Silove, Derrick, R. Chang, and V. Manicavasagar. "Impact of Recounting Trauma Stories on the Emotional State of Cambodian Refugees." In *Psychiatric Services* 46.12 (Dec. 1985): 1287-1288. Print.

Siv, Sichan. *Golden Bones: An Extraordinary Journey from Hell in Cambodia to a New Life in America*. New York: Harper Collins, 2008. Print.

Stagg, Sophal Leng. *Hear Me Now: Tragedy in Cambodia*. Tampa: Mancorp Publishing, 1996. Print.

Stewart-Fox, Martin, and Bunheang Ung. *The Murderous Revolution: Life and Death in Pol Pot's Kampuchea*. Bangkok: Orchid Press, 1998. Print.

Stone, Albert. "Autobiography and American Culture." In *American Studies* 11.22-26 (1972): 22-36. Print.

Svay Ken. *Painted Stories: The Life of a Cambodian Family from 1941*. Phnom Penh: Reyum, 2001. Print.

Swain, Jon. *River of Time: A Memoir of Vietnam and Cambodia*. New York: Berkeley Books, 1995. Print.

Szymusiak, Molyda. *The Stones Cry Out: A Cambodian Childhood, 1975-1980*. Linda Coverdale, trans. Bloomington: Indiana University Press, 1999. Print.

Takaki, Ronald. *From Exiles to Immigrants: the Refugees from Southeast Asia*. New York: Chelsea House Publishers, 1995. Print.

Tobin, Joseph J. "(Counter) transference and Failure in Intercultural Therapy." In *Ethos* 14.2 (1986): 120-143. Print.

Tran, Qui-Phiet. "From Isolation to Integration: Vietnamese Americans in Tran Dieu Hang's Fiction." In *Reading the Literatures of Asian America*, edited by Shirley Lim and Amy Ling. Philadelphia: Temple University Press, 1992. Print.

Truong, Monique T.D. "Vietnamese American Literature." In *An Interethnic Companion to Asian American Literature*, edited by King-Kok Cheung. Cambridge: Cambridge University Press, 1997. Print.

Tuan, Mia. *Forever Foreigners or Honorary Whites? The Asian Ethnic Experience Today*. New Brunswick: Rutgers University Press, 1998. Print.

Tuon, Bunkong. "Cambodian American Literature." In *Asian American History and Culture: An Encyclopedia*, edited by Huping Ling and Allan W. Austin, eds. Armonk: M.E. Sharpe, 2010. Print.

U Sam Oeur. *Crossing Three Wildernesses: A Memoir*. Minneapolis: Coffee House Press, 2005. Print.

U.S. Committee for Refugees. "Los Angeles's Cambodian, Ex-Soviet Jewish, and Vietnamese Refugee Communities: A Profile." In *Refugee Reports*, XV.11 (Nov. 30, 1994): 9-12. Print.

Ung, Loung. *Lucky Child: A Daughter of Cambodia Reunites with the Sister She Left Behind*. New York: Harper Collins, 2005. Print.

_____. *First They Killed My Father: A Daughter of Cambodia Remembers*. New York: Harper Collins, 2000. Print.

Vany, Ma. *Life in Danger*. Pittsburgh: Dorrace Publishing, 1996. Print.

Vickery, Michael. "Cultural Survival in Cambodian Language and Literature." In *Cultural Survival Quarterly* 14.3 (1990): 49-52. Print.

Vitandham, Oni. *On the Wings of a White Horse: A Cambodian Princess's Story of Surviving the Khmer Rouge Genocide*. Mustang: Tate Publishing, 2005. Print.

Wagner, Carol. *Soul Survivors: Stories of Women and Children in Cambodia*. Berkeley: Donald S. Ellis, 2002. Print.

Welaratna, Usha. *Beyond the Killing Fields: Voices of Nine Cambodian Survivors in America*. Stanford: Standford University Press, 1993. Print.

Wong, Sau-ling Cynthia. *Reading Asian American Literature: From Necessity to Extravagance*. Princeton: Princeton University Press, 1993. Print.

Wright, Wayne. "The Education of Cambodian American Students in the Long Beach Unified School District: A Language and Educational Policy Analysis." Unpublished MA thesis. California State University, Long Beach, 1998.

Yamada, Teri Shaffer. "Modern Short Fiction of Cambodia: A History of Persistence." In *Modern Short Fiction of Southeast Asia: A Literary History*, edited by Teri Shaffer Yamada, ed. Ann Arbor: Association for Asian Studies, 2009. Print.

_____. "Cambodian American Autobiography: Testimonial Discourse." In *Form and Transformation in Asian American Literature*, edited by Xiaojing Zhou and Samina Najmi. Seattle: University of Washington Press, 2005. Print.

CHAPTER 16

Crossing the River and Ocean:
A Review of Cambodian American Literature for the Young

Lorraine Dong

In Cambodian American fiction and non-fiction for the young, Cambodian refugees are the most popular subjects and have a formulaic refugee-turned-American storyline: The narrative begins as a cultural ambassador to explain Cambodian history and culture during peaceful (and colonized) times. This ends with the brutal regime of Pol Pot and the Khmer Rouge. The period from 1975 to 1979 is described with the death of the character's family, torture in labor camps, and escaping across the Mekong River. Once the border is crossed, he/she lives in Thai refugee camps under dismal conditions until an airplane takes him/her across the ocean to America. The story ends with the Cambodian's adjustment to a new country and becoming an American citizen.[1]

From the above formulaic storyline, two basic universal themes in literature emerge: overcoming obstacles in life, which involves courage and survival under extremely difficult conditions, and adjusting to a new environment with its different values. Due to the black-and-white presentation of Pol Pot's tyrannical communist regime versus America as a free country, the message of freedom and peace are also strong in literature about Cambodian refugees arriving in America.

Cambodian Americans in Children's Picture Books

There are four picture books with Cambodian American main characters. One of them is a biography of Arn Chorn-Pond (b. 1966). Another is a photo-journal documenting a Cambodian American family celebrating New Year. Only two books among the hundreds of Asian American children's picture books are fictional with Cambodian American characters.

Michelle Lord's *A Song for Cambodia* (2008) belongs to the non-fiction genre of biography. It begins with eight-year-old Arn, who loses his family with the arrival of the Khmer Rouge. Arn is forced into a children's work camp, where he undergoes tortuous conditions until he "volunteers" to play revolutionary songs. He manages to break away after four years, undergoing another horrific three months of escaping to Thailand, where he stays in a refugee camp to await resettlement. The climax comes when Arn is literally rescued by the Reverend Peter Pond in a flood and is later adopted by the Reverend. In the last few pages, Arn adjusts to his American life, using music to heal.

Arn's rescue and adoption have the semblance of a "white savior" theme, but this child protagonist is not weak. Besides surviving on his own in Cambodia, Arn is the one who proactively asks the Reverend to get him musical instruments to help with his healing process. There is nothing passive about Arn; he is a victim of history but he makes decisions and resolves conflicts by himself. Lord has manipulated the formulaic refugee-turned-American storyline into a narrative with strong characterization and a plot that successfully engages children.

A Song for Cambodia excels in another literary way. Since music is Arn's life, Lord skillfully uses sound and silence throughout the book. The story begins with an idyllic life of "whispering grasses" and the sounds of gongs, birds singing, and children laughing ([6]). When the Khmer Rouge arrives, Arn's heart beats fast and loud like a drum until songbirds stop chirping, monks are silenced, and music disappears from the people's lives ([9-11]). In camp, the silence is "deafening," with only the shouts of soldiers and the rumbling of Arn's empty stomach ([13-15]). He gets a small reprieve from this silence when he plays the khim for the soldiers ([20]). In his escape, he follows the "chattering sounds" of a monkey family and sleeps to the "sounds of nature" ([23]). Language becomes the next sound or the absence of it. Arn's relationship with the Reverend begins in silence because of an obvious language barrier, so they "talk" with hand signals and smiles. Arn's adjustment in America involves communication through his Cambodian music. Music is the core of the biography when the reader finally comprehends what Arn's real father meant when he tells his son: "...Cambodian music existed only in memory. Songs were passed down from a parent to a child or from a master to a student. There were no written compositions" ([17]). This statement is helpful to understanding the character whose country and culture will always exist in his/her memory and in the transmission from one generation to the next, regardless of the fact that everything tangible has been destroyed by the Khmer Rouge.

The second picture book that is based on real-life Cambodian Americans is entitled *Sokita Celebrates the New Year: A Cambodian American Holiday* (2004), written by Barbara Lau and Kris Nesbitt and photographed by Cedric C. Chatterley. This book is part of a larger exhibition project, *From Cambodia to Greensboro: Tracing the Journeys of New North Carolinians*.[2] The authors are folklorists and the photographer has extensive experience documenting folklore traditions. The book is less a work of literature and more a work to document the folklore of Cambodian Americans as well as to document one of America's newest citizens in North Carolina.

Ten-year-old Sokita is the only daughter in the Ksa family of six. There is no formulaic refugee storyline, only the mention that the family had to leave because it was "not safe" ([4]). The bulk of the book serves as a cultural ambassador, describing all the preparations and rituals involved with the Cambodian New Year. Of note is that Sokita and presumably her four-year-old brother are born in Greensboro. The cultural ambassador goal of the book to educate America is now intertwined with the goal of transmitting Cambodian culture to the American-born Cambodian generation.

Dara's Cambodian New Year (1992) is written by Sothea Chiemruon and illustrated by Dam Nang Pin, both born in Cambodia. This holiday picture book has the expected cultural ambassador lessons, but characterization and plot are just as evident, which makes it more a work of literature than *Sokita*. There is also no formulaic refugee storyline, just the simple mention of being forced to leave because of war and "terrible times" (2). The story begins with Dara rushing home to tell his family that he has won first place in school for his painting of a Cambodian countryside. When he hears how homesick his grandparents are for Cambodia, Dara decides not to mention the award but comes up with an idea to solve his grandfather's unhappiness. He asks his grandfather for help to finish his New Year paintings. His works are incomplete pictures of Cambodia and the grandfather immediately cheers up when he begins to tell Dara how to authenticate the paintings. Cultural ambassador lessons are provided every time the grandfather tells his grandson what is missing. This process gradually leads to Dara's award-winning painting. Grandfather finds nothing missing in it and says, "I have never seen the countryside of Cambodia look more beautiful. It is just as I remember it…it is just as I want to remember it" (21). Dara gives it to him and the grandfather ends the story by saying, "Come, let us share your beautiful pictures with the rest of the family. After all, it is the beginning of the New Year" (21). In order for the grandfather to accept and be happy with the New Year (i.e., a new beginning in America), the grandfather realizes that Cambodian culture is not lost with the next generation. Dara can draw Cambodia exactly right and sometimes with a little assistance from an elder. A strong Cambodian American child has helped to resolve an elder's sense of loss in America.

Ethnic holiday books in children's literature are often published and used, in the name of promoting diversity and multiculturalism, to inform mainstream America of other cultures. Most books present these holidays as alien and outside the United States. This is acceptable if the goal is to promote the understanding of global multiculturalism among nations. However, if the goal is to promote domestic multiculturalism within the one country of the United States, then presenting Asian holidays as non-American becomes problematic. In a few progressive books, an Asian holiday would be acknowledged and accepted in America as equal to other European holidays like Valentine's Day, Halloween, and Christmas. The Cambodian New Year is an alien holiday in *Dara's Cambodian New Year*. Twelve years later, *Sokita* boldly presents it as an American holiday, as evidenced in its subtitle. This book mentions a few differences on how people in two countries celebrate the Cambodian New Year, the most obvious being Cambodia celebrates it for a week while it is celebrated for only one day and usually on a Sunday in Greensboro.

The last picture book with a Cambodian American character serves as another type of learning tool. *Who Belongs Here? An American Story* (1993) is written by Margy Burns Knight and illustrated by Anne Sibley O'Brien. The goal is for children to explore the "human implications of intolerance" with the usage of anecdotes from American history and culture as counterpoints to Nary's story (inside front jacket flap). Every page in the book is split in two: the top portion is Nary's story and the bottom portion has anecdotes to lead the reader into critical thinking moments. For example, when the storyline is about Nary's difficulties in learning English, the anecdote mentions that 350 languages are spoken in the United States and that many English words come from other languages ([10]). And, when Nary admires photojournalist Dith Pran's courage, the anecdote counterpoints this with another activist, Dolores Huerta ([15]). In the end, readers learn who is a "real" American and that everyone is an American; hence a Cambodian refugee's story is "an American story."

Who Belongs Here? follows the formulaic refugee-turned-American storyline: Nary's parents and family are killed by the Khmer Rouge. He escapes to Thailand with his grandmother carrying him on her back because his feet are bleeding with blisters ([5-6]). Cultural adjustment involves Nary eating rice, and enjoying pizza and ice cream as well. Also emphasized is that Nary likes his "new freedom" and is learning about the U.S. Constitution ([17]).

Knight avoids an ideal portrayal of adjustment for Nary. Discrimination and racism are themes raised when two classmates call Nary "chink" and "gook," and tell him to "get back on the boat and go home where you belong" ([18; 24]). Nary is "mad and hurt" and talks about it with his grandmother. On his own he asks his classmates to leave him alone because he does not want to be afraid to go to school and because he does not like to be called names ([24; 26]). In addition, he goes to his teacher to plan a lesson for their social studies class to teach everyone what it is like to be a refugee ([29]).

Nary's classmates ultimately understand and accept him as an American and his adjustment is complete without forgetting his Cambodian roots:

> Nary is working hard to make the U.S. his home....Nary has learned to write Khmer so he can keep in touch with relatives. He wonders if there will ever be peace in Cambodia. He also hopes people in his new country can learn to get along. ([33])

The finale of Nary's story focuses on peace and getting along.

These four picture books serve as learning tools about Cambodian history and culture, and about tolerance and differences in America. Only one of the books is written and illustrated by Cambodians, and *A Song for Cambodia* is the most artistically written and illustrated in terms of literature. Sokita stands out because she is born in the United States and has two parents. The boys in the other three picture books begin as refugees with broken homes, having one parent (Dara), no parent (Arn and Nary), and/or later an adoptive parent (Arn). Sokita's book functions mainly as a cultural ambassador, so her story barely has plot or character growth. She passively participates in the New Year festivities and in the end, she is "already thinking about next year's holiday. She can't wait" because she had so much fun this year ([30]). Unlike many Asian American characters in past literature, the three Cambodian American boys in the picture books are strong and do not need adults to move their lives. Nary's story is the most daring because the character confronts racism directly. Two of the books do reveal America's gradual acceptance of Cambodian refugees as Americans. A major progressive step is taken in Sokita's story when Cambodian New Year is acknowledged as an American holiday.

Cambodian Americans in Young Adult Novels

During recent decades, American educators and publishers have focused on girls and women because of gender disparities in the K-12 educational system. As a result there is increased K-12 literature highlighting female protagonists and role models. However, out of the four Cambodian American picture books above, only one has a female main character. This imbalance is changed in the genre of young adult novels.[3] There are two fictional novels with strong female Cambodian American protagonists: *Children of the River* (1989) by Linda Crew and *Chantrea Conway's Story: A Voyage from Cambodia in 1975* (2001) by Clare Pastore. Both follow the formulaic refugee-turned-American storyline. The latter does not match the literary qualities of the former that has received at least four recognitions and awards almost immediately after its publication.[4]

Chantrea Conway's Story is the third novel written by Pastore in The Journey to America series for grades 5-8.[5] Falling in line with the intent of the series—to show the hardships girls in the past had to overcome when coming and adjusting to America—the refugee-turned-American formula dictates the main storyline. Approximately 60% of the novel is devoted to the horrors experienced by thirteen-year-old Chantrea and her grandparents under the Khmer Rouge. There are the usual senseless, indiscriminate killings (the mother is killed), the torture and starvation in the camps, and the escape, hiding in caves and among the roots of a one hundred foot banyan tree. Chantrea loses two teeth during this ordeal. The Author's Note reinforces the terror of the time with more details that liken Pol Pot's regime to that of Hitler. The remainder 40% is about the Mok family adjusting to America.

Chantrea Conway's Story is unique because the main character is of mixed heritage. Born and raised part-American by her father in Cambodia, she does not have the cultural conflicts that are more visible in the other characters. However, due to Chantrea's "American blood," her identity becomes an issue when it jeopardizes her life in

Cambodia. To avoid execution, she covers her mixed heritage-looking face, changes her surname to Mok, and does not speak English.

Chantrea's mother Dara Mok is Cambodian and her father Seth Conway is Caucasian American. Her parents met and married when Seth was stationed in Cambodia as a photographer for the *American World View* magazine. Their interracial relationship is presented simplistically in the novel. Attention is not on the couple but on the families. Grandfather Meng is a retired school teacher who taught English. His educational level is revealed by his home library of books written in Khmer, Chinese, French, and English, so he can easily adjust to having Seth as his son-in-law, except perhaps for a brief note in the narrative that says he is "just a few years older than Seth" (6). There is no outward expression of Grandmother Teva disapproving her daughter's marriage, except the reader is constantly informed of her dislike of anything "Western." As for the Conway family, Chantrea observes that in a brief visit to America, Grandpa Joey and Grandma Laura did not like Dara or their son's marriage to a Cambodian (7). Any tension over this interracial marriage is quickly resolved when the Mok family resettles in Columbus, Ohio and the two families learn to know each another better. Teva becomes more accepting of "Western" ways and Laura is "ashamed" of how she treated Dara in the past, citing being "afraid" as the reason (142).

There are the obligatory cultural ambassador moments in the novel when the reader is introduced to Chantrea's Cambodian heritage that coexists with her American heritage as represented by her love for baseball and rock and roll music. Upon her arrival in America, Chantrea does not reveal any cultural clash, while the Moks and Conways interact with cultural clashes. Her biggest adjustment is living a life that is relatively more affluent, like having enough to eat, sleeping on a good bed, watching television, and wearing shoes for the first time. She readily accepts the "American" culture of hot dogs, apple pies, Thanksgiving, and Christmas with no hesitation.

Prayers are a good example of how Chantrea has no contradiction living with two cultures. The Mok family is Buddhist and the Conways are Christians. In asking for her father's safe return, Chantrea prays to both Buddha and Jesus when she is in Cambodia.

In Ohio, she prays to only Buddha one time (135) and in another occasion there is no mention of to whom she is praying (144). Both prayers yield no results. But when she prays to Buddha and Jesus together again (153), she receives news immediately that her father has been found and will be home by Christmas (159). An Asian deity has shared equal credit with a Christian god for the safe return of a Christian father to celebrate a Christian holiday. Without any reason to think that she must choose between Buddha and Jesus, Chantrea's non-existing religious conflict equates to her non-existing cultural conflict.

Although Chantrea does not exhibit cultural conflict, she does face racism that is specific to her adjustment and identity as an Asian American of mixed heritage. Like the almost perfect Conway family with whom she and her grandparents are living, her classmates and teachers are also ideally friendly and accepting. The one exception is blond-hair Alex Colfax who calls her "half-breed" and "dirty slant-eyes," tells her to "go back to Vietnam," and says men marry Asian women and dump their "half-breed babies" (138-39). Chantrea's classmates and the Conway family immediately come to her defense. Alex's attitude is resolved with the typical literary technique of having the teacher create a curricular activity to teach the class about a country from where refugees come. After Alex learns about the military in Cambodia, he is no longer hostile to Chantrea (170). As with the case of Laura's dislike for Dara, this conflict is resolved easily.

Chantrea has no issue becoming an American because of her mixed heritage background. However, Pastore ends with more details to finalize the character's Americanization process. Chantrea's Thanksgiving dinner is served with ansamcheks next to pumpkin pie and cranberry bread, and her father gives her an autographed Cincinnati Reds baseball for Christmas.[6] Chantrea has been playing baseball with her father ever since she was a little girl in Cambodia. Now she will continue with this all-American sport in the United States and might possibly become the first female baseball player in her school. Yet, her Americanization is not totally Eurocentric when both Cambodian and "American" food are served on the dining table for a representative, all-American holiday.

In *Children of the River*, the refugee-turned-American process for seventeen-year-old Sundara Sovann is complex and more skillfully presented as literature. Only the first chapter takes place in Cambodia; the remaining 96% of the book is devoted to Sundara's conflict between being Cambodian and American in Willamette Grove, Oregon, 1979. Chapter 1 introduces the reader to Sundara's Cambodian background: Sundara is sent away by her mother to help take care of Aunt Soka's newborn baby in Réam. When the Khmer Rouge takes over Phnom Penh on April 17, 1975, she escapes with Soka's family. While at sea for three weeks with seven hundred starving on board, the baby dies in Sundara's arms. It is later revealed that they were at sea for a total of six to seven weeks, escaping to Thailand, then Malaysia, Indonesia, and the Philippines before arriving in California.

With the whereabouts of her family unknown, Sundara lives with her aunt, uncle, two cousins, and the uncle's mother. They are a family that upholds traditional Cambodian values while representing the work ethics of the Asian American "model minority." After four years of hard work, Soka and her husband Naro manage to purchase their own house and drive a new Ford. Despite Sundara's imperfect English, she becomes a straight "A" student and has ambitions to be a doctor because her family wants her to go back to Cambodia to help "her people" (42). In addition to the formulaic refugee-turned-American storyline, the novel has a parallel story involving the interracial relationship between Sundara and blond-hair, blue-eye Jonathan McKinnon. This relationship is complicated by Sundara's love for Chamroeun who does not leave Cambodia for patriotic reasons and promises her that they will reunite in the future (125-26).

Sundara's main conflict deals with choosing between Cambodia and America. She resolves this in three ways. The most obvious involves the romantic decision between Chamroeun who represents Cambodia and Jonathan who represents America. Next is settling her strained relationship with Soka who also represents Cambodia. The third calls for Sundara's change in attitude regarding the difference between life on the Mekong River in Southeast Asia and life on the Willamette River in America.

Written for ages twelve and up, *Children of the River* is marketed as a romance novel about "forbidden love," which caters to the young female adult reader. From page 71 of the novel, the back cover of the novel highlights Sundara's "thrill of temptation" to be with Jonathan. The reader is told that "Such secret feelings would have to be guarded with utmost care, heaven protect her, for this certain someone was white, he was American, he was absolutely forbidden" (68).

Sundara's aunt is adamantly opposed to the relationship with Jonathan for cultural reasons: dating is not allowed, marriages are arranged by parents, and women do not talk to men (29; 70; 84). These reasons are reinforced by universal parental convictions that children should focus on school and not "fool around." The opposition is compounded further by the fact that the two families come from different racial/ethnic and socioeconomic backgrounds.

The attraction between Sundara and Jonathan is mutual. On the surface, Cambodian tradition, as represented by Soka, is preventing them from being together. The relationship is complicated by Sundara's conflicting love for two boys (and countries). On the last night Sundara spends with Chamroeun, who is determined to stay in Cambodia to fight the Communists, he promises her that they will be together again: "I will come find you wherever you are. Someday when the war's over" (126). These last words stop Sundara every time she feels an attraction for Jonathan, a football star who is also a classmate in her honors social studies class: "And surely being faithful did not mean involving herself with an American boy. Shame. Was this the way to honor Chamroeun after the promise he'd made?" (126). Sundara's guilt intensifies when she learns that Chamroeun is dead, his neck chopped with a hoe when he got up one night to desperately find something to eat (143). She believes his death is caused by her unfaithful attraction to Jonathan. When she learns that Chamroeun was killed at age sixteen, Sundara is freed to love Jonathan: "Chamroeun's fate could not possibly be her punishment for allowing herself to care for Jonathan, as she had imagined in her first, guilty grief. Now, calmer, she reminded herself that Chamroeun had been killed long before she'd looked up to find Jonathan's blue eyes upon her" (142).

Sundara's inner turmoil regarding Americanization reaches a turning point when Jonathan is hospitalized after being hurt in a football game and Sundara dreams in English for the first time:

> Strange, yesterday she'd thought only of Chamroeun and the past, both lost to all hope. But this fear of Jonathan had wrenched her back to the present, sparked her to life again, cut short her private mourning [for Chamroeun]. Did this do Chamroeun dishonor? Heaven protect her, she couldn't help it. She was alive and had to move on. Chamroeun was the past, but Jonathan was right now, and suddenly, right now mattered very much. (150)

Although Cambodia/Chamroeun is the past and dead because of Pol Pot, Crew hints that Cambodia is not forever lost in Sundara because Chamroeun's last words say he/Cambodia will find her wherever she is when the war is over (126). Meanwhile, Sundara has accepted America/Jonathan as her present and she must think of the future which hopefully will be her return to Cambodia as a doctor.

The next literary technique used to finalize Sundara's Americanization process involves her relationship with Soka. Again, on the surface, the aunt is depicted as an obstacle; she represents traditional Cambodian values that contradict American values. The root of this strained relationship lies deeper—in the death of Soka's baby who represents Cambodia's future. Allowing the baby/Cambodia's future to die while escaping alive has convinced Sundara that Soka/Cambodia hates her. It is not until the guilt-ridden Sundara suffers a "breakdown" that the aunt/Cambodia admits to feeling guilty for personally being too weak to nurse her baby/Cambodia's future (191-93). This "confession" frees Sundara's guilt and desire to become American. She realizes she is not responsible for killing or betraying the baby/Cambodia, thus releasing her from a life-owing obligation to Soka and the country.[7]

Rivers are used to complete Sundara's Americanization process. There are two rivers in Sundara's life, the Mekong and the Willamette. The Mekong symbolizes Sundara's childhood and roots; as her poem says, Cambodians are the "children of the Mekong" (10). Her river changes when she resettles in Oregon.

In the beginning, Sundara is both a fatalist and Buddhist in her feelings about life. She says the following to Jonathan:

> "We [Cambodians] think of life more like a river. Think of it that way, maybe you right I have no choice. On a river it is not so simple as just choose which way to go. On a river we try to steer a good course, but all the time we getting swept along by a force greater than ourselves.
>
> "A road can go anywhere,"…"and then it stop. But a river never stop. All the river flow together and become one. This is more like life, don't you think so? Because then it begin all over again." (146)

Towards the end of the novel, a strong family friend named Moni awakens Sundara by saying, "I think I must learn to steer my own boat down this river, Little Sister. I must take care of myself now" (204). Finally, with Jonathan by her side, Sundara accepts a new river with a new perspective:

> "…I never dream that someday I stand on the bank of a river so far from the Mekong, holding the hand of an American boy. So who can ever tell about the future?"
>
> The future was a long time, she thought, all the way down the river.
>
> Sometimes it would be a river of deep whirlpools and treacherous shallows; she'd come too far not to know that.
>
> But now she saw that it could also be like this, a river stretching before them clear to the horizon, broad and inviting, shimmering with hope. (213)

Sundara still acknowledges that a river inevitably flows to the ocean, but now she sees the river differently as a future with an end that no one can see or predict, but "shimmering with hope" where she can steer her own boat. By viewing the American river more positively, she has grown to be more hopeful of life. Instead of Chamroeun/Cambodia, Jonathan/America is the one with Sundara as "children of the river."

Crew has presented, in complicated multi-layers, the internal process that Cambodians might undergo to relieve themselves of any uncertainty, shame, or guilt associated to becoming an American. In the end, Soka realizes that being a U.S. citizen does not equate to betraying one's ancestral roots:

> Maybe their [Soka's and other Cambodians'] mistake was in feeling they had to choose, fearing they couldn't be American without giving up being Khmer. Why couldn't they be both? In the end, after all, what was more American than coming from someplace else, bringing another culture with you? (188)

Chantra Conway's Story and *Children of the River* have the formulaic refugee-turned-American storylines. The two female protagonists have an almost identical past, except Chantrea is of mixed heritage. Both undergo horrific conditions when Pol Pot took over Cambodia and both are resolved and happy to be American in the United States. They are victims of the Khmer Rouge with one or maybe both parents killed, but they exhibit courage and strength in their ability to survive extreme conditions. Once they arrive in the United States, Chantrea is not as strong and becomes almost passive when her classmates stand up for her against Adam Colfax. Unlike Nary in *Who Belongs Here?* Grandma Laura is the one who goes to the social studies teacher and suggests a classroom activity to teach the class about Cambodia.[8] Being more complex, Sundara is the stronger of the two adolescent characters; she agonizes in deep conflict, and comes to her own decisions and resolutions.

Looking beyond the River and Ocean

The current trend in Cambodian American literature for the young is dominated by formulaic refugee-turned-American stories—the more horrific, the better—to impress upon young readers how fortunate they are to be in the United States. The literature also functions as a cultural ambassador to teach about Cambodian culture, with most books presenting Cambodian culture as alien and not American. The stories in these books are mainly American success stories with strong themes of courage to provide positive role models for the youth.

Since Cambodian Americans are rarely seen in picture books and young adult novels, it is encouraging that most of the characters in the current literature are not depicted as passive. However, the six books reveal patterns that can potentially lead to stereotypes if more books are not published in the future to provide a diverse picture of Cambodian Americans. For example, with the exception of *Sokita Celebrates the New Year*, all the characters are refugees with broken or incomplete homes because of the war. Among the six main characters, Sokita is the only one who is American-born. Forever labeled as refugees and alien, the elders in the stories are often depicted as resistant to Americanization and deep in nostalgic yearning for the return of their true home, Cambodia. Also important to note is the lack of Cambodian American writers and illustrators for children and young adults. Just one of the six books is written and illustrated by a Cambodian. Huy Voun Lee, who is an Asian American of mixed heritage (part Khmer and part Chinese), has eight picture books published. However, they are not about the Cambodian American experience.[9] Cambodian American writers are needed to be the voice of Cambodian America.

Cambodian American literature for the young is still in its infant stage. At present too much attention is on the refugee experience, always crossing the Mekong River and the Pacific Ocean. As the population continues to grow and mature, there will be more diverse characters and stories, especially with themes reflective of the emerging American-born generation. When the time comes, the Cambodian American community will express for themselves a more refined definition of what it means to be an American of Cambodian ancestry.

Endnotes

1. The most well-known Southeast Asian American groups in literature for the young are those with origins from Vietnam and Laos. The third most written about are the Cambodians. People from other Southeast Asian countries barely make a presence in literature. Generally, the formulaic refugee-turned-American storyline is used to tell the stories of all Southeast Asian Americans.

2. The project was sponsored by the Greensboro Historical Museum, the city of Greensboro, and the Center for Documentary Studies at Duke University in collaboration with the Greensboro Buddhist Center.

3. This paper will focus on two fictional novels. There are at least five Cambodian refugee-turned-American biographical/autobiographical novels written for the older adolescent and adult reading audience. The last three listed here are memoirs of Cambodian American women: Sharon Sloan Fiffer, *Imagining America: Paul Thai's Journey from the Killing Fields of Cambodia to Freedom in the U.S.A.* (New York: Paragon House, 1991); Haing Ngor, with Roger Warner, *Haing Ngor: A Cambodian Odyssey* (New York: Macmillan Publishing Company, 1987); Chanrithy Him, *When Broken Glass Floats: Growing Up under the Khmer Rouge* (New York: W.W. Norton and Company, 2001); Loung Ung, *First They Killed My Father: A Daughter of Cambodia Remembers* (New York: Harper-Collins, 2000); and Loung Ung, *A Daughter of Cambodia Reunites with the Sister She Left Behind* (New York: HarperCollins, 2005).

4. Crew earned the following recognitions for *Children of the River*, her first novel: Honorable Mention, the Fifth Annual Delacorte Press Outstanding First Young Adult Novel; the International Reading Association Children's Book Award (Older Reader Category); the Society of Children's Book Writers' Golden Kite Honor Book; and the American Library Association Best Book for Young Adults.

5. The Journey to America series publishes stories on the journeys of girls coming to America. The first novel is about a girl from Ireland in 1849 and the second is about a girl from Poland during World War II.

6. The choice of using the Cincinnati Reds as the team for the story is an interesting play on words when considering "rouge" in "Khmer Rouge" means "red."

7. Chantrea also suffers a similar guilt and breakdown. While in camp, Chantrea spends all her time volunteering to care for the sick and becomes physically strained. When Grandmother Teva tells her to stop, Chantrea says, "I have no right to be happy and healthy. Who am I to be so lucky?" Teva finally relieves Chantrea from her guilt of being alive by saying, "Who are you to question why Buddha does what he does?...Yes, you are lucky. Be glad of it. It is not your fault what happened to those others" (105).

8. Using a curricular activity to resolve issues of racism is a common technique used in literature for the young. Crew also has a similar curricular activity in *Children of the River*: Jonathan is assigned to study Cambodia

in the social studies class, which triggers his initial communication with and interest in Sundara. Other popular curricular activities used in class-rooms and literature to resolve cultural/ethnic conflicts are the international potluck and the show-and-tell where students share their different backgrounds and objects in class.

9. The titles are: *At the Beach* (1998), *Cardinal and Sunflower* (1998), *In the Park* (1998), *1,2,3, Go!* (2000), *In the Snow* (2000), *In the Leaves* (2005), *Honk, Honk, Goose! Canada Geese Start a Family* (2009), and *Fire Drill* (2010).

References

Chiemruon, Sothea. *Dara's Cambodian New Year.* Illus. Dam Nang Pin. New York: Half Moon Books-Simon & Schuster, 1992. Print.

Crew, Linda. *Children of the River.* New York: Delacorte Press-Bantam Doubleday Dell Publishing Group, Inc. 1989. Print.

Knight, Margy Burns. *Who Belongs Here? An American Story.* Illus. Anne Sibley O'Brien. Gardiner: Tilbury House Publishers, 1993. Print.

Lau, Barbara and Kris Nesbitt. *Sokita Celebrates the New Year: A Cambodian American Holiday.* Photographs by Cedric N. Chatterley. Greensboro: Greensboro Historical Museum, 2004. Print.

Lord, Michelle. *A Song for Cambodia.* Illus. Shino Arihara. New York: Lee & Low Books, 2008. Print.

Pastore, Clare. *Chantrea Conway's Story: A Voyage from Cambodia in 1975.* New York: Berkley Jam Books, 2001. Print.

Section VIII

Cambodian American
Economic Integration

CHAPTER 17

Khmer Cultural Values and Economic Behavior

Nancy Smith-Hefner

In contrast to the Sino-Khmer pattern, the consensus among most Cambodians, both ordinary and Sino-Khmer, is that ordinary Khmer are less single-minded in their dedication to business affairs and more reluctant to assume economic risks. The clearest example of this distinctive difference, one frequently remarked upon by Khmer and Sino-Khmer alike, is the tendency of ethnic Khmer who have acquired some savings to place the purchase of a home above the opening or expansion of a business. Sino-Khmer business owners were quite emphatic that they felt it wiser to defer the purchase of a home until their businesses were on a firm financial ground. Conversely, several ordinary Khmer shop owners linked their financial difficulties to their home mortgage bills. One female grocery store owner explained how after paying her mortgage and utilities bills on her home and the rent and utilities on her store, she had no more capital to invest in new stock. She acknowledged that this had

Reprinted from *New Migrants in the Marketplace: Boston's Ethnic Enterprises*. Copyright © 1995 by Marilyn Halter and published by the University of Massachusetts Press.

been a serious miscalculation on her part. And yet, though less single-minded in their commitment to business investment, non-Chinese Khmer are regarded as significantly more concerned with an array of nonbusiness social investments related to one's standing, or "face," in the community. This preoccupation is notably different from that of their more independent-minded Sino-Khmer counterparts. For ethnic Khmer a key feature of one's standing in the community is the ability to make generous contributions to the temple and to sponsor expensive religious and life-cycle ceremonies that serve to increase not only one's prestige in this life but also one's store of merit for the next. In his detailed study of Theravada Buddhism in Southeast Asia, Robert Lester underscores this association between merit and social status among Khmer Buddhist: "In general, the more merit a man 'makes,' the greater is his social status. The power and prestige which one holds are the result of past merit-making; likewise, the maintenance and enhancement of status depends on continued merit-making." In this way many ordinary Khmer believe that, "one's merit potential is his social mobility potential" (Lester 1973: 147).

The difference between Khmer and Sino-Khmer social investments is related, in part, to the difference in religiousness. Although Sino-Khmer typically adopt Theravada Buddhism, for many it involves little more than a nominal involvement, with aspects of Chinese Buddhist religious practice and ancestor worship also maintained.[1] In virtually every Sino-Khmer business, for example, one observes a small Chinese altar with a statue of the Buddha, candles, incense, food offerings, and an inscription in Chinese characters on red paper. One young Sino-Khmer male explained the religious participation of Sino-Khmer in the following terms: Real Cambodians probably go to the temple more often than Chinese because the Chinese work too hard to go. "But I give food for temple celebrations if they come to my place to ask. I do that for the good feeling and because it is my tradition too…because I am Cambodian. As for beliefs like destiny, reincarnation, well, most Cambodians believe in that; Chinese, maybe only 1 percent believe and the rest believe in hard work. I don't believe that if you go to the temple you will have a long life or better life. I go because it's part of my tradition."

Again, this contrast highlights what is perhaps the most fundamental difference between Sino-Khmer and ordinary Khmer. Ordinary Khmer expend significantly more time and energy, as well as surplus capital, on merit-making endeavors and status-generating activities. A preoccupation with issues of destiny, face, and reincarnation, as well as social standing within the community, results in a significantly different attitude toward business endeavors among non-Chinese Khmer.

For these ordinary Khmer, the idea of taking one's capital and risking it in a deferred and highly uncertain investment—especially uncertain given the widespread recognition that ordinary Khmer lack the entrepreneurial skills of their Sino-Khmer counterparts—strikes many as perilous at the very least. One Khmer widow whom I knew quite well confided that she had dreams of opening a small market someday. But she immediately added that she would never consider telling any of her friends or acquaintances about her aspirations. If she did tell them of her plans, she said, and then the store did not materialize, she would be called a lair (*kohoc*) and the community would judge her badly. When I asked how anyone can possibly make plans for the future if they are constantly afraid of losing face should their plans fail, she said, "You just don't dare talk about it until you are sure. You can only talk with your family and depend on your family for advice. Then, when you open the restaurant everyone is very surprised and they will say, 'she didn't say anything about that; that's a good lady'." The cautious attitude displayed here in social relationships and the sharing of confidence as regards future projects is vividly captured in a well-known Khmer saying, "The less often you open your mouth, the fewer mistakes you make."

The concern for public opinion, the absence of mutual aid associations, and the lack of precedent for joint-venture enterprise make ordinary Khmer extremely hesitant to call on friends and associates for economic assistance. The result is that what economic partnerships there are are effectively limited to family relationships or, in rare cases, the few non-kin who, by virtue of long-standing social ties, have been elevated to the status of fictive kin. Khmer frequently say that they are too ashamed (*ien*) to ask their friends to loan them money. They express the fear that if they ask a friend for money and he refuses, the real problem is that the person is not really a friend but "looks down on you as if you are lower status." Whatever the case, the seriousness with which Khmer take their standing in the community makes it difficult to interpret such failed initiatives as anything other than a loss of face, which is to say, a loss of that which most Khmer regard as most integral to their social being.

Unassimilated Chinese who lived in Cambodia are themselves aware of this basic difference between Chinese and Khmer. One first-generation Chinese shop owner, raised in Cambodia, summed up the contrast with the rather dry observation that "Cambodians are less interested in money than in status because they believe that power is bigger than money. They say, 'if you have money with no power you can do nothing. If you have power you can make money easily'." Of course, non-Chinese Khmer summarize the contrast differently, emphasizing that the Chinese may be economically savvy, but it is at the cost of being so thoroughly money-grubbing as to lack the cultural sensitivity required for dignified social standing. A similar contrast—between Chinese as hard-nosed and independent to the point of social disesteem and non-Chinese Southeast Asians as status-and power-conscious to the point of being economically inefficient—has been widely noted in other parts of Southeast Asia (cf. Jay 1969; Keeler 1986).

This contrast is again related to aspects of Cambodian history. In prewar Cambodia, power and high social standing were typically obtained through government employment. Although the majority of ordinary Khmer in the Boston area had been farmers in Cambodia, they were familiar with and, to a certain degree, endorsed the ideal of the Khmer middle class—to become or to have their children become a white collar functionary in government. According to this ideal, it was sufficient that a single individual, the head of the family, work to support his whole family. The wife, then, could devote her free time to religious and social activities; she might also open a small business on the side. In some cases, the father's bureaucratic position might even be used to finance quite extensive business arrangements, but these were viewed as subsidiary to the father's central bureaucratic role and status.[2]

Under the influence of the new homeland, Khmer notions of status and economic mobility are, of course, changing. As one interviewee aptly commented, "In Cambodia if you hold a government position you are set for life, but here, they always try to throw you out." Nonetheless, many Khmer in the United States still hold to a version of this middle-class, bureaucratic ideal. Rather than looking to government, however, upwardly mobile Khmer in the United States look toward the credentialed professions as the most appealing avenue for realizing a modified version of this ideal pattern—a strategy that has only limited success among lower-class Khmer (Rumbaut and Ima 1988; Smith-Hefner 1990, 1993). In any case, the practical consequences of this modified ideal and other social constraints are quite real. Few Khmer regard independent business activity as an attractive or feasible option for upward movement into their new host society.

Emergent Patterns of Khmer Entrepreneurship

Though its actual dimensions are small, there are nonetheless several interesting aspects to business activity among non-Chinese Khmer in the Boston area. First and most notably, primary ownership of a good number of enterprises (especially hair and nail salons, but also small stores) lies in the hands of Khmer women, while their husbands, if there is a husband at all, play a secondary, supportive role. This matrifocal pattern in part reflects the traditional dominance of women in the domestic economy, as well as their predominant role in small-scale marketing (Ebihara 1968). It is perhaps remarkable that in Sino-Khmer families this same pattern obtains, in notable contrast to the patriarchal pattern of economic control in many Chinese families.

Second, even where ordinary Khmer engages in enterprise, there is an important difference in the way they invest their profits compared with most Sino-Khmer. Sino-Khmer tend to reinvest a greater proportion of their profits back into their business endeavors than do ordinary Khmer. Among Sino-Khmer, in particular, one finds a widespread pattern of economic expansion, in which a business owner slowly establishes several related business endeavors. For example, the Sino-Khmer owner of a successful photography business rents traditional and Western-style wedding clothing and jewelry to customers, as an option in the various photo service packages he offers for weddings. His business also rents Asian film videos (dubbed in Khmer) and offers videotaping services for special occasions. Most recently, he has added a courier service to Cambodia for the delivery of video messages, photos, small goods, letters, and money to friends and relatives left behind. The courier returns with handicraft items made in Cambodia, including fabrics, religious statues, carvings, and musical instruments, which are for sale in the shop. In some cases such expansions may become separate enterprises, which are then placed in the hands of different members of the owner's extended family. A Sino-Khmer video store owner, for example, opened a second shop for his younger brother when the youth graduated from high school. He has plans to open a third, he says, to be managed by a nephew who has recently arrived from the camps. By contrast with this pattern of Sino-Khmer business expansion, ordinary Khmer tend to invest a large proportion of their profits in goods and endeavors that enhance their social capital within the community without directly enhancing their business capital. Such events include sponsorship of ritual festivals, the purchase of a new home, or travel to Cambodia to visit relatives. Though all these investments help to establish one's standing in the community, most are also expensive, not just of capital but of time and social energy as well. As Sino-Khmer business people readily observe, whatever their social benefits, such activities divert capital away from business enterprises and may undermine the long-term success of a business.

Whatever the salience of this contrast between Sino-Khmer and non-Chinese Khmer business people, my research among the two groups in the Boston area revealed that on one point they show an unexpectedly similar attitude. A large number of the small business owners I interviewed, Khmer and Sino-Khmer alike, volunteered the opinion that they would prefer to be doing something else other than running their own business. These individuals view their business enterprises as preferable to the other type of low-status employment available to them, but the great majority did not regard their businesses as satisfying ends in themselves. They complained of the long hours associated with their work (typically ten to twelve hours a day, seven days a week), and lamented the never-ending stress and uncertainty. Many said quite bluntly that their business had become an obstacle to a satisfying family and social life. One would suspect that, rather than reflecting the reproduction of pre-migration values here in the United States, this critical attitude toward business may be new, and strongly influenced by business owners' awareness that, here in the United States, there are avenues to social autonomy and economic success other than through business enterprise.

Few business owners, for example, said they expected or wanted their children to succeed them in their businesses. Most were quite deliberately encouraging their children to pursue credentialed professional positions in health care, computers, or engineering. They regarded these "soft" professions as more economically attractive, and less demanding of time and energy than ownership of a small business. Here again, one suspects, is a broadening of economic horizons that reflects quite clearly the changed employment opportunities in the United States. A commitment to business ideals remained, nonetheless. Though most business owners hoped their children would go into more comfortable professions, they quickly added that, should their children fail to obtain a degree or to secure professional employment, there would be a place for them in the family enterprise.

The patterns of business activity seen among Sino-Khmer are not surprising, given what is known about business activities among overseas Chinese in East and Southeast Asia. Gordon Redding (1990), for example, has described the way in which business among overseas Chinese is characterized by a predominance of family firms, in which parents and children are deeply and often obsessively involved in joint enterprise. Redding similarly emphasizes the way in which extra-family relationships of language, clan, and community provide important measures of trust and confidence in business interaction, all of which serve to facilitate Chinese business endeavors. What is surprising, perhaps, is the degree to which some of the key features associated with Chinese ethnicity have been diluted or weakened among many Sino-Khmer. Nonetheless, this assimilation process appears to have stopped short of diluting the distinctive economic advantage Chinese enjoy over ordinary Khmer.

Viewed from the perspectives of non-Chinese Khmer, the pattern is perhaps a bit less familiar, but it is quite intelligible. Where ethnic Khmer sought upward mobility they turned to bureaucratic positions, not business. This pattern reinforced the Khmer cultural bias toward social and political standing rather than pure wealth as a determinant of status. The pattern was further reinforced by the force of ethnic rivalries between Khmer and Sino-Khmer, though, by Southeast Asian standards, these were moderate and rarely escalated to the extreme levels of open hostility seen elsewhere (Willmott 1967: 40). Through this process of ethnic differentiation, money-mindedness came to be regarded as a feature of Chinese identity, while ritual consumption and social largesse remained markers of Khmer ethnic identity.

In the United States, the basic pattern has been perpetuated, but with the additional twist that upwardly mobile Khmer here look not to government but to education and the professions as their vehicle for social advancement. Despite this ideal, most Khmer have not been particularly successful in obtaining professional positions in the United States, and many Khmer children are struggling in American schools (Rumbaut and Ima 1988; Smith-Hefner 1993). Nonetheless, it is interesting to note that those Khmer individuals who do succeed at upward mobility often move so thoroughly into a new social universe, an American one, that they end up far removed from the embedded social communities from which they or their parents might have come, and more thoroughly adopt the economic and cultural customs of their host country. In so doing, some of these successful Khmer end up so distant from the integral Khmer community that they disappear from its horizons entirely.

This, one suspects, may remain the pattern for some time to come: more and more successful Khmer assimilated into American culture. But if the experiences of Chinese and Japanese are any model, as this community of successful Khmer American grows, it may rediscover and reinvent, albeit in a fashion that reflects their

American circumstances, aspects of their ethnic culture. Such a process may have important implications for Khmer identity in the United States. However, it seems unlikely to transform the basic pattern of Khmer economic activity: the avoidance of risky enterprise in favor of expansive social investments and, for upwardly-mobile Khmer, higher education, through which one moves into the professions rather than business.

Endnotes

1. Willmott (1967: 38-39), writing about the situation of Chinese in pre-war Cambodia, states that religious behavior is "a clear index of ethnicity particularly with regard to participation in the support and activities of the temples."

2. Reports of those community members who have visited friends and family living in California or Washington, D.C. indicate that a similar pattern is being followed by at least some of the remaining Khmer elite who have obtained positions in government-supported refugee programs. A similar ideal apparently holds among middle-class Vietnamese as well (Gold 1992; Kibria 1989).

References

Halter, Marilyn, ed. *New Immigrants in the Marketplace: Boston's Ethnic Entrepreneurs*. Amherst: University of Massachusetts Press, 1995. Print.

CHAPTER 18

The Doughnut Emporium

Aihwa Ong

America is a miraculous country.
Ted Ngoy, the *"Father of Doughnut Entrepreneurialism"*

In recent years, Californians have noticed that more and more doughnut shops are being operated by Cambodian Americans. By the late 1990s, the Winchell's Donut House chain was being replaced in many places by independent doughnut shops owned by Cambodian Americans.[1] The story has it that a Ted Ngoy—identified as a former Cambodian ambassador to Thailand or a former Cambodian army officer (or both)—found refuge with his family in Orange County, where he first encountered an American doughnut. Ngoy applied for a job as a trainee in a Winchell's shop. After a year, he borrowed money to buy his own shop, Christy's (named after his wife), in La Habra. By the mid 1980s Ngoy owned a chain of fifty doughnut shops, stretching from San Diego to San Francisco, and a luxury home on a private lake in Mission Viejo. "America is a miraculous country," Ngoy told the *Los Angeles Times* in 1989. He has since returned to Cambodia to "enter politics."[2] Ngoy is credited with training hundreds of his countrymen. He made loans available to workers to help them start their own shops. By spawning an ethnic industry, he came to embody the Cambodian American success story.

What this legend underplays is that Ngoy was a Sino-Cambodian, one of the old Phnom Penh social and economic elite who survived the Pol Pot slaughter. Among the Cambodian refugees, they are perhaps the best able to take advantage of the American economic scene. Before 1970, Sino-Cambodians composed one-third of the population in Phnom Penh, and were also found in Battambang and Kampot. They controlled the rice trade, retail trade, and import-export businesses.[3] With their background in running family businesses and experience at pooling resources, Sino-Cambodians felt that they did need to rely on American institutions in order to find their legs in this country.

In the San Francisco Bay Area, including Stockton, there were in the 1990s 120 doughnut shops operated by Cambodian Americans, 80 percent of whom were Chinese ancestry. Sino-Cambodians also opened shops in Modesto (eleven) and Sacramento (eight). Cambodian Americans operated doughnut shops in Los Angeles and New York as well. Many have pointed out that it was in some ways an ideal business for newcomers: one did not need to know good English to learn to make pastries; the job required only hard work, and a willingness to work odd hours and accept being apprenticed at little or no pay to the shop owner. A Cambodian American manager of Donut Star in San Francisco was quoted as saying, "Getting hired at a place where your boss and colleagues speak Chinese was a real incentive for my wife and I to take on this work five years ago. The prospect of working without language barriers and amongst the comfort and familiarity of our own folk is attractive."[4] These family businesses did not need to bother with union rules, and apprentices were trained for up to a year without pay, often working at night. Shops depended on unpaid or underpaid family labor.

The combination of opportunity to learn from one's ethnic compatriots, apprentice system, hard work, and fortuitous circumstances enabled displaced Sino-Cambodians to take on an established restaurant chain and reenact the classic American story of immigrant family labor. But is this a classic American story of the mom-and-pop enterprise, or is it a tale of nepotism in a "family business" that grew into a franchise chain?

I interviewed Randy Yu, because his doughnut shop was on my way as I went to pick up my daughter at school. It took me a couple of phone calls to fix a date with Yu, because he was always busy traveling among his many different shops. As I waited in one of his shops, nursing a cup of standard American coffee, Yu drove up in a red Cadillac. Practically the first thing he said to me was that he usually drove a green pickup truck, but that day he was using his wife's Cadillac. The car had been his gift to her for working so hard to help him get started in the business. Now that he had succeeded, she could stay at home or go shopping. These are new Cambodian American figures—the entrepreneur and his consumer wife, a Cambodian woman who drives her own flashy car.

Yu said that 30 percent of Cambodian refugees in the United States were ethnic Chinese, and that they were the ones who were in business. Sino-Cambodians, he said, quickly took over the doughnut business because it was "too hard work for the 'natural Cambodians'." In Phnom Penh, the Chinese commercial elite had a leisurely life, attended by servants. But the Pol Pot time changed everything. Having spent two years in Khao-I-dang, Yu noted that many people from privileged families like his learned to make money there. "During the war, people got very smart, smuggling goods across Khmer Rouge lines and selling them in Khao-I-Dang. They worked very hard, not like before." Yu went on to describe how he became a minor doughnut king.

Yu and his wife used to work sixteen-hour days, and for years spent nights in doughnut shops, taking turns every other night. He apprenticed himself to a friend for six months with no salary to learn everything—mixing batter, baking, setting out the wares, sales, and the financial end of the business. Then, in 1983, Yu bought his first store for twenty-five thousand dollars, using loans from family members. Next, he bought a shop in Albany, near Berkeley, and trained his half-brother, Joe's father, to be the baker—a job that required him to come in at two in the morning to prepare that day's batch of doughnuts. Yu said that for a family man, owning and operating two shops is the optimal strategy, because if you have more than that, labor costs and the amount of time each spouse has to spend at each shop (ten hours a day) will be too much to make the enterprise truly profitable.

At this point, the by-the-bootstraps family operator transformed into the mobilizer of an ethnic labor pool for building up a chain of businesses. Yu started loaning money and training relatives to operate shops in other towns. When he ran out of relatives, Yu recruited individuals from other minority groups whom he partially absorbed into his kin-based business network. The sales clerk in his Albany shop was a Laotian teenager. He employed a Hispanic man in the same capacity for another shop he recently bought in Daly City. By the time I met him, he was the owner of a least ten doughnut shops.

Yu's story echoes the stereotype of the mobilization of family labor, the recruitment of relatives or pseudo-kin, and the circulation of money in the making of a traditional American ethnic family enterprise. As newcomers with no credit history, Cambodian Americans—like other impoverished people—could not rely on American banks. Sino-Cambodians mobilized cash and savings from their relatives and friends through a rotating credit system called *hui* in Mandarin and *thong thing* in Khmer. A typical lending circle is made up of relatives and friends. Meeting once a month, the club awards a loan sometimes to the bidder with the highest interest rate, and at other times to the bidder with the greatest need. In this way, small-timers can get startup capital of twenty thousand dollars or so to make a down payment on a shop, and then they pay back the lenders from earnings each month. By the late 1990s, it cost fifty thousand to sixty thousand dollars to establish a doughnut shop, but twice as much in cities such as San Francisco.

Here we have a classic American family business, making and selling doughnuts in the neighborhood, but with a twist. There are Cambodian American family-operated doughnut shops, but the rotating credit system allows a mom-and-pop operation to expand into a franchise system. As Marilyn Strathern has argued, commodification allows the money that sticks to a family to circulate beyond the immediate family, within the wider kinship group.[5] Entrepreneurs like Yu become the capitalists who seed new business units that are partially based on exploiting the unpaid labor of relatives and minority friends. Yu would establish a shop, then sell it after a year or two to a relative or friend who had worked for a while without pay, while Yu would move on to a bigger shop. This way, thousands of Cambodian American families in California managed to set up family doughnut businesses, and many more are running units in franchise chains owned by energetic fellows like Yu. These chains, based on nepotism and kinship networks, eventually allowed Cambodians to control the doughnut industry in the state.

The very circumstances that led Cambodian Americans to carve out an economic niche for themselves in the doughnut business also produced a similar success story among Vietnamese, who have come to dominate the nail-salon industry. Like doughnut making, doing nails offers an easy entry point for hardworking immigrants without a good education. Vietnamese immigrants in Southern California first opened nail salons as a sideline employment for young women (between the ages of twenty-one and thirty-five). By the late 1990s, the nail manicure industry had grown into a more than $6.5 billion industry, with half of the nation's manicurists being of Vietnamese descent. In many cases, nail salons are family-operated affairs, with mothers teaching daughters and cosmetology certification tests administered in Vietnamese. Fathers or husbands may own the family salons and have shares in other nails shops. Kim, a licensed manicurist in San Francisco's Pacific Heights, said, "The younger people, they go to school and learn English. They don't want to do nails. They work in offices."[6]

After having learned to operate doughnut shops, many Cambodian families wanted to try other American mom-and-pop businesses, such as running gas stations or hamburger joints or Cambodian-cuisine restaurants with names like Angkor Wat and Battambang. For Yu, however, doughnut shops are a better business than restaurants, because restaurants are even more labor-intensive. And besides, there is "loss from sales tax, about eighty dollars per thousand, that works out to three thousand dollars per year for the government!" In doughnut shops, most of the business is take-out. Nevertheless, he pointed out, "Doughnut shops are finished now as a way to make good money." There were too many in the Bay Area, and the cash price to buy an existing business had risen to a hundred thousand dollars. He had already turned his entrepreneurial energy in another direction: "Better to buy a house—a couple hundred thousand, and wait for the value to rise before selling it. In five years it will make a lot of difference." Pause. "I am always thinking about making more money," he said with a big grin. He confessed that he was in debt again, having borrowed money from relatives to buy eight houses for rental.

Yu's story is a wonderful example of how different these contemporary mom-and-pop operations are, because they go beyond being stand-alone family enterprises. Instead, they are units in a chain that develops from the entrepreneur's use of nepotism to mobilize unpaid and overworked labor to build an empire within the ethnic labor niche. Yu is a small-time homo economicus who has been able to leverage value garnered in a low-status take-out business into the higher-yielding, more prestigious sector of real estate. Already, Cambodian franchise chains of doughnut shops are moving to cities such as Detroit—"The auto workers, they want lots of doughnuts." Cambodian doughnut king Ning Yen has a multimillion-dollar business that includes the principal distributorship of doughnut-making ingredients and equipment to his compatriots' shops.[7] He plans to introduce the pastries to China and South Korea.[8]

The next generation may not want to invest in the labor ability of relatives, or to circulate money among a circle of pseudo-kin as a way to make a family business. They may want to stress the individual acquisition of knowledge and become highly paid professionals, more like the now-standard image of Asian Americans, or they may prefer to become a different kind of businessman. Joe confessed that his childhood was spent living in different Cambodian enclaves around the West, as his father moved from doughnut shop to doughnut shop to learn his trade. Yu gave him the best pay, so he decided to work full-time in the Albany shop. The family moved a lot because Joe's parents did not think that children should be limited by the local conditions of ghettos. Observing how hard his dad worked, however, Joe did not see a future for himself as a doughnut king. He wanted to go to business school and later operate a launderette instead, "because this would be easier than the doughnut shop; the laundry machines do the work. Besides, you get cash immediately from the machines." His goal was to be a different kind of American entrepreneur, operating a chain of cleaner businesses, perhaps.

The Helping Professions

The majority of Cambodian Americans could afford to take few risks, and, like other poor immigrant and minority communities, they still relied on a range of helping professions to get their needs translated and wants met. This demand for social services provided an opening for a small group of Southeast Asians—working as translators and aides in schools, hospitals, and government offices—to ascend to the middle class. Phauly Sang's career trajectory is fairly representative of how educated Cambodian Americans climbed into the middle class. After she arrived she tried to get a hospital job as a lab technician, but local hospitals would not accept her Phnom Penh license. She learned to drive and to type, and soon became a public-school bilingual teacher's aide. Still on welfare, she moved on to a part-time job in family planning, teaching Southeast Asian women how to use birth-control devices she herself had never used. A few months later, Phauly found a full-time job as a translator in a prestigious hospital, and bought herself a nice car. For the next few years, she and her relatives pooled money to buy a house, and she devoted much of her energy to sponsoring relatives still in refugee camps to come to America. Because she signed an agreement with the INS that those relatives would not depend on government support after they arrived, Phauly started a home business, in addition to keeping her hospital job. She converted her living room into a workroom putting her newly arrived relatives to work sewing pieces for Chinatown's garment factories. While her pressing financial needs were understandable, she became in effect an agent in supplying cheap exploitable labor for the sweatshop economy.

Like many Cambodians in the helping professions, Phauly came to reflect deeply on how her actions mediated between her community and the dominant institutions and how they shaped norms within her own community. This mediating role engendered profound personal ambivalence…. [Cambodians in the helping professions]…were supposed to instill the very normative regimes among their compatriots that they themselves were still uncertain about, and they recognized that they were disciplining instruments for remaking their own people into appropriated kinds of American subjects. The ethical uncertainties associated with being a helping professional were compounded when they felt that their community was the brunt of antiwelfare criticisms, and that they had to explain and justify the needs of terribly helpless people to receive welfare. Phauly was also upset when newspapers claimed that 65 percent of Cambodian refugees were "depressed"; she protested that in her experience, this was not true, and that such branding of Cambodians was part of a range of tactics on the part of intractable individuals mental-health clinics aimed at obtaining more funds.

At the same time, Cambodian social workers were learning their craft from established American professionals, those specific intellectuals who were often the very source of the biased perceptions, categorization, and stereotyping of what being a Cambodian American should mean. Thus, as bilingual, mediating second-tier professionals, Phauly Sang, Mr. Eam, Peter Thuy, and Sam Ngor were crucial to the human technologies for constituting autonomous subjects, but were also promoting values that they were not entirely in accordance with. In their conversations, they occasionally criticized what they saw as the extreme individualism and selfishness of American culture. Phauly, for instance, who had lost her husband in the war, would not consider marrying a non-Cambodian man despite the interest she had attracted from male coworkers, because she was not convinced that long-resident Americans shared Cambodians' cherishing of human relationships. Even so all of them felt that they were doing extremely gratifying, if frustrating, work that gave them the chance to provide necessary resources, help, and culturally sensitive comfort to their countrymen, especially to the weak, the confused, and the elderly.

Perhaps it would not be wrong to say that contemporary neoliberal capitalism progressively divests society of its moral obligations by evacuating institutions of moral purpose, and by forcing more and more social institutions such as the family to serve the economy, and not the other way around. In late 1999 Bill Clinton, a Democratic president, cut back on social programs and pushed needy families onto workfare, saying that "Work is more than just a weekly paycheck. It is, at heart, our way of life. Work lends purpose and dignity to our lives, instills in our children the basic values that built our nation."[9] But dignity now demands greater sacrifice, because working people have fewer claims on the state than before, and must turn to their families and community for support to make ends meet. As neither industry nor the state seems invested anymore in the working poor, their acute vulnerability can be shielded only by access to a variety of family and social networks that sustain individuals one paycheck away from being homeless. It is the job of immigrants employed in the helping professions to regulate their compatriots, who may not yet realize their impending loss of entitlements, and move them off welfare.

Work as the centerpiece of an American ideology of respectability takes on new meanings in such circumstances, as institutions formerly endowed with moral purpose—such as the welfare state and family—are either stripped down or forced to perform as economic ventures. At the same time, the entrepreneurial figures who deploy nepotism to mobilize unpaid or underpaid labor within ethnic enclaves build business chains they can extend to their home countries.

Transnational Cambodians

There is a tiny community of elite Cambodian Americans—aristocrats, professionals, and students, many of whom arrived before the refugee wave who link their notion of the American way (democracy and market freedom) to the reconstruction of their home country. An estimated six hundred successful Cambodian Americans, who come largely from the Seattle area, have gone back to "strengthen democracy and liberalism in Cambodia."[10] Working people and college students have sought employment with social-service agencies with names like CANDO that aim to teach Cambodians the basics about democracy, elections, voting, and political responsibility.[11] Some of the more prominent returning Cambodian Americans have run for political office, mainly supporting opposition political parties. As mentioned earlier, doughnut king Ngoy returned to Cambodia, while another former doughnut entrepreneur, Noeun Kim Ou, became Prime Minister Hun Sen's defense minister. Some Cambodian Americans ran for office as independents, including a woman from Oakland who closed her restaurant to participate in the elections, but lost. Yu was cynical about Cambodian Americans who returned to engage Cambodian politics: "Why? Because they were in the government before. Also to make money through the government connection. But most lost all their money."

Cambodian Americans who wish to share their notion of American citizenship—representative government, fair elections, and entrepreneurialism include businessmen who want to build business parks in Phnom Penh, but doing so would entail relocating squatters who not so long ago were war refugees like themselves. Many simply returned to provide economic resources to relatives and the hometown, and perhaps in the process also scout out business opportunities. Yu returned to Cambodia three times with friends to "help the poor," including relatives, and to rebuild a Chinese school in Battambang. He believed that Cambodia would prosper in the future, and then perhaps he would return to set up business there. He had been reluctant to sponsor two surviving brothers to come to America because, he said, the wait for siblings was about ten years. But he may also have been thinking about employing them as local agents for his future transnational business ventures. Like many Cambodian American tourists, Yu had no intention of living in Cambodia, but wanted to maintain kinship, cultural, and economic connections. Indeed, Cambodian Americans are considered no longer "pure" Khmer, because they are cut off from their Cambodian spiritual home;[12] but even so, many are attracted by the idea of promoting a combination of American democracy and transnational ethnic enterprises.

Despite the street glamour of Southeast Asian gangsters, the majority of Cambodian Americans are employed workers, service providers, and small businessmen. Doughnut entrepreneurship represents the emergence on a small scale of transnational ethnic networks that build on nepotism and labor mobilization among kin and ethnic labor markets. They are modest operations, however, compared to Asian managers and professionals from Taiwan, Hong Kong, and India, who have forged transnational business networks in the high-tech industries and other venues of power. The varied insertions of Cambodian and other Southeast Asian immigrants into the globalized economy have had a splintering effect on the concept of Asian American identity, reflecting their differential positioning along the black-white continuum.

Endnotes

1. The number of independent doughnut shops operated by Cambodian Americans was estimated to be between 2,450 and 5,000 in California. As a result of the Cambodian American entry into the doughnut business and of competition from fast-food outlets, by the late 1980s the Winchell's chain had shrunk from 450 to 120 shops in the state; see Jonathan Kaufman, "How Cambodians Came to Control California Doughnuts," *The Wall Street Journal*, Feb. 22, 1995.
2. John Flinn, "Success the Old-Fashioned Way," *San Francisco Chronicle*, April 30, 1995.
3. William E. Willmott, *The Chinese in Cambodia* (Vancouver, B.C.: University of British Columbia Publications Center, 1967).
4. Debbi Gardiner, "Donuts Anyone?" *Asian Week*, June 22, 2000, p. 18.
5. Marilyn Strathern, "New Economic Forms: A Report," in her *Property, Substance and Effect* (London: The Athlone Press, 1999), pp. 89-116.
6. Janet Dang, "A Hand for Vietnamese Americans," *Asian Week*, Nov. 29, 1999, pp. 13-14.
7. Kaufman, "How Cambodians."
8. Ibid.
9. Jason DeParle, "Bold Effort Leaves Much Unchanged for the Poor," The *New York Times*, Dec. 30, 1999, A1. Inquiries among welfare recipients

in Wisconsin revealed that they considered the workfare requirement of a thirty-hour week to be "insulting" for welfare recipients, because women formerly on welfare could make more if they worked full-time at a regular job. The crux of the problem was getting employed in steady jobs and finding child-care support, so that mothers could go out to work.

10. Puala Bock, "Phnom Penh Connections," *The Seattle Times*, July 1, 1999.

11. Kathryn A. Poethig, *Ambivalence Moralities: Cambodian Americans and Dual Citizenship in Phnom Penh,* Ph.D. diss., The Graduate Theological Union, 1997.

12. Poethig, *Ambivalence Moralities*, pp. 174-177, 190-191, 205-206

References

Ong, Aihwa. *Buddha is Hiding: Refugees, Citizenship, and the New America.* Berkeley: University of California Press, 2003. Print.

CHAPTER 19

Cambodian Americans and Welfare Reform as Social Control

Michael H. Truong

One of the central aims of the contemporary American welfare state is to instill self-reliance among its citizen-subjects. Accordingly, recent welfare reforms have focused on cultivating self-sufficient capabilities among those who are a public charge of the state. However, after three decades of being in the United States, many Cambodian Americans continue to struggle to become economically independent and get off welfare rolls. The obvious question then is what happens when the welfare state fails to cultivate self-reliance among its citizen-subjects? How does the welfare state deal with citizen-subjects who are incapable of economic self-sufficiency? What methods of governance are employed by the state to make public recipients 'earn their keep'? This article attempts to address these questions. Structured in three parts, this article will first discuss how the passage of the *1996 Welfare Reform Act* represented in many ways a triumph of liberal governance, whereby the American welfare state exerts control over the bodies of its citizen-subjects vis-à-vis the imposition of work and normative family ethic. How this regime of liberal governance has operated in the specific case of Cambodian Americans on welfare rolls is taken up in the second part of this paper. I identify the scrutiny employed by the state and illustrate how Cambodian welfare recipients negotiate these attempts to impose disciplines upon their lives. The third part will discuss some of the material and ideological implications of liberal governance in general and specific regimes of discipline in particular. I focus on what it means when public assistance shifts from being a source of economic support to being a regulating mechanism for social control. This paper draws heavily from in-depth interview data, especially from public assistance-receiving Cambodian American families living in Southern California.[1]

Welfare Reform and the Triumph of Liberal Governance

On August 22, 1996, President Clinton signed into law the *Personal Responsibility and Work Opportunity Reconciliation Act* (PRWORA), ushering in the most significant and wide-sweeping welfare reform since the New Deal of the 1930s. Clinton's campaign to end "welfare as we know it" brought about fundamental changes to the American welfare state. The act effectively functioned to discourage, denigrate, and, in many cases, deny citizen-subjects who have been on public assistance from further dependence by reducing their support, restricting their access, and/or removing them from welfare rolls altogether. PRWORA represented the confluence of a key ideological current: the shift in the mission of welfare programs from economic support to social control (Delgado and Gordon 2002).

These draconian reforms under PRWORA are part and parcel of the triumph of the American welfare state and its strategies to 'govern at a distance' (Rose 1996). Instead of directly imposing its authority, the American welfare state since the 1960s has undergone what is known as devolution, or the relinquishing of state powers, granting authority to professionals who are licensed and empowered by the state to create norms of individual conduct, make judgments, and administer policies.

While there are many strategies employed by the welfare state to govern its citizen-subjects, I highlight what I believe are the two most fundamental: the imposition of work and the insistence of a normative family ethic. These two dictates are worthy of focus because they both deal with the disciplining of the bodies of citizen-subjects. Tactics such as the use of time-limits, sanctions, and diversions may interfere with welfare recipients' behaviors, but coerced labor and controlled reproductive/marital rights actually give the welfare state legal control over the bodies of its citizen-subjects, rendering them more like 'subjects' than 'citizens'.

Imposing Work

One way the American welfare state governs its citizen-subjects is by imposing work. What makes coerced labor under the new welfare system possible is the assumption that recipients of public assistance are 'lazy' and 'unmotivated' in getting a job, leading them to develop an unhealthy dependence on welfare. One historian argued that the passage of the PRWORA was achieved on the assumption that long-term "dependency" was the crux of the welfare problem, and that it could be resolved by changing welfare to promote work and individual "self-sufficiency" (O'Connor 2001). It was believed that the underdevelopment of the work ethic was the fundamental problem of those on welfare rolls.

The campaign to impose 'work' led to the slashing of longtime federal cash assistance program, Aid to Families with Dependent Children (AFDC). AFDC recipients were transferred to a downgraded program called Temporary Aid to Needy Families (TANF). Among its many new restrictions, TANF capped a lifetime eligibility limit at five-years and required recipients to participate in work or work-related activities (i.e., English classes, job training, job search, participation in government workfare programs, etc.) in order to continue receiving cash aid. Even though TANF allows recipients to enroll in English language classes and job skills training for non-English-speakers and low-skilled workers, the main thrust is narrowly focused on getting recipients into a job, any job, as soon as possible. Essentially, public assistance has come to be a regulatory mechanism of the welfare state for the imposition of work and discipline on its citizen-subjects.

One national study by the Urban Institute showed that 'over 75 percent of former recipients who left welfare rolls for jobs earned less than $8 dollars an hour in jobs where there are no benefits, no stability, and no opportunities for advancement. Most welfare leavers who are now working find themselves unable to pay rent, utility bills, or for other basic necessities.

A key feature of the 1996 act included a welfare-to-work (WTW) component, whereby public assistance recipients are assigned to service projects. These assignments are meant to serve a useful community purpose and afford opportunities for the development of marketable skills. However, due to the nature of how WTW program was administered, it created an involuntary labor force used to fill low-wage and dead-end jobs (Hawkesworth 2001). Not only do forcing WTW participants into unskilled and low-paying jobs diminish their chances of obtaining employment that affords sufficient income to escape poverty, but in the case of Cambodian Americans, it does little to resolve their overall economic plight. A Director of Refugee Services for Catholic Charities (CC) in Southern California has been working with Cambodian Americans on welfare rolls for over a decade pointed out that the welfare system assumes that getting a job is the "magic bullet" for lifting people out of poverty. However, the jobs that most welfare dependent individuals qualify for are typically low-wage, and after paying for transportation and childcare, they are often worse off than simply staying on welfare dole. In summary, the American welfare state is able to govern at a distance because it makes work a condition for public assistance participation, shifting the ultimate responsibility for the economic well-being of citizen-subject from the welfare state to the individual. Thus, if a needy individual is not receiving public assistance, it is not the fault of the government; rather, it is because the individual lacks effort in finding a job.

Legislating Normative Family

The insistence of a normative family ethic is another way the American welfare state governs welfare recipients. A dominant myth exists within welfare discourse that purports a lack of family planning in general and single-parenting in particular causes poverty, and thus welfare dependency. Moreover, it is believed that poor life choices (having more children while on public assistance or while unmarried) are not only immoral but also harmful to both the individual and society.

Therefore, a close reading of the PRWORA makes it clear that the intent of the lawmakers was to champion normative family values in general and promote marriage in particular, encouraging the formation and maintenance of two-parent families. PRWORA's language begins with statements about how "marriage is the foundation... [and] an essential institution of a successful society which promotes the interests of children." The law went on to describe the problems of teenage pregnancy, out-of-wedlock births, children raised in single-parent homes, fathers who fail to pay child support, and irresponsible parenting. Indeed, a reading of this statement of the law's intent would lead one to believe that the problem of poverty itself is the direct result of failures to live up to the family ideal (United States Congress 1996). Although there are no sound evidence for the direct correlation between single-parent household and poverty, such intense focus on the out-of-wedlock births and pregnancies have not only led to PRWORA's overwhelming passage but also incited a number of measures designed to penalize unwed mothers and their children.

One way the welfare state has demonstrated its commitment to curbing single-parenthood is the prohibition of mothers under the age of eighteen from receiving welfare benefits for any child born out of wedlock, regardless of when the aid is sought for the child. The only way she could qualify for welfare assistance is either to marry the child's father or someone who adopts the child.

Within PRWORA, there is also a provision entitled 'family cap' that bars all non-marital births to existing mothers on public assistance from receiving additional aid. The underlying logic is that women who consider becoming pregnant while on welfare will know that their progeny would be ineligible for benefits and hence will think twice before having more children. Here, we see how existing welfare policies attempt to determine and distinguish between 'legitimate' and 'illegitimate' births by providing the former and denying the latter of benefits. Such social engineering leads to questions of basic women's rights and the constitutionality of government-funded programs' attempt to penalize some women for exercising their right to reproductive choice (Mink 1998).

While the majority of Cambodian Americans on welfare come from two-parent households, there is a small, but growing group of single-parent caseloads. One social worker who works with many single-parent households, including Cambodian Americans, noted that "rewarding or punishing certain groups based on whether or not they have two parents in the house is ridiculous." In other words, the economic need of a household is independent of whether the household has one or two parents. By privileging two-parent households as more 'deserving' of support, the new welfare system unfairly discriminates against single-parent households simply because they do not measure up to the normative family ascribed by the framers of PRWORA.

Like the imposition of work, the use of a normative family ethic (married, two-parent household) allows the American welfare state to govern at a distance. Demarcations like 'single-parent households', 'unwed-mothers', and 'illegitimate births' are used to justify the denial or the reduction of benefits for some needy citizen-subjects; while, labels like 'two-parent households', 'married couples', and 'legitimate births' are used to reward others because they reinforce the normative family ethic. In the next section, I show how the dictates of work and family ethics operate in the daily context of Cambodian Americans receiving public assistance.

Disciplining Cambodian American Bodies

How has the regime of liberal governance under PRWORA impacted welfare recipients at the individual level? What has life been like for those who remained on public assistance in the post-welfare reform era? In this section, I attempt to answer these questions by providing three mini vignettes, drawn from fieldwork and interviews with the Cambodian American community in Southern California. I illustrate how the welfare state has attempted to govern their lives by imposing various forms of disciplines. These case studies, selected because of their illustrative and informative qualities, offer important insight into how the lives of families and individuals have been impacted since the 1996 act. These case studies also reveal the insidious nature of liberal governance disguised as welfare reform. While these case studies are neither representative nor exhaustive of how the American welfare state disciplines its citizen-subjects, they, nevertheless, help capture the intricate and dynamic character of Cambodian American experiences on public assistance—traits that tend to remain submerged in statistical descriptions of the group.

Cheapening Labor

In the rhetorical buildup to welfare reform, it was uniformly assumed that a job was the ticket out of poverty and that the only thing holding back welfare recipients was their reluctance to get out and get one. Since the passage of PRWORA, there is no shortage of popular accounts touting the success of moving people off welfare and into full-time work. On the surface these stories may appear impressive, but upon closer examination, the reality is that those who work full-time are still unable to lift themselves and their family out of poverty. There is a strong ideology in the United States that assumes that hard-work leads to success, but for many former welfare recipients, they are working hard—harder than they could ever thought possible—and still find themselves sinking ever deeper into poverty and debt.

Take the case of Mr. Pheng, 50 years old, who works full-time and is still unable to earn enough for his family's basic needs. Three years ago when Mr. Pheng was in the middle of his internship program to be a program producer at a local Cambodian television studio, he received a letter notifying him that his benefits might be terminated if he does not fulfill the work-requirement. His eligibility worker told him that he needed to work at least 35 hours in order to keep his welfare benefits. To ensure the livelihood for his wife and four children (ages 16, 14, 9, and 7), Mr. Pheng had no choice but to quit his training program at the studio. After a few weeks, he found an advertisement for a full-time security guard position at a local manufacturing company. Since the position was a "contract position" through a temporary employment agency, his job offered no medical benefits, retirement plans, job security, or career advancement. Mr. Pheng is paid $6.75/hour, the state's minimum wage, earning him a monthly wage of $1080 a month before taxes. Since his monthly salary falls substantially short of the poverty level for a family of six ($1974), set by the federal government, he and his family qualifies for public assistance, including TANF, food stamps, and medicare. Even though Mr. Pheng works full time and his family receives welfare, he still struggles monthly to make ends meet.

For Mr. Pheng and many other poor Cambodian Americans, working in minimum-wage and dead-end jobs has become the only viable option. When asked about his security guard job, he sees it as a necessary inconvenience. While the job has no possibility of advancement in pay or position, he continues to work because it's a necessary condition for his family to receive benefits. Mr. Pheng's expression, "I work because I have to," in many ways suggests that he has resigned to the imposition of work placed upon him by the welfare state. Despite the daily grind of doing non-fulfilling, dead-end work, Mr. Pheng tolerates it because he has no choice.

Curtailing Reproductive Rights

Government-funded programs for the poor have historically interfered with the reproductive rights of poor women (Mink 1998; Gordon 1994; Abramovitz 1988). The 1996 welfare act was no different. The systematic and institutionalized curtailing of reproductive freedom has been a central component in recent public assistance programs to aid the poor (Roberts 1997). Plans to distribute birth control, laws to penalize women for bearing children, and welfare reform measures to cut off assistance for children born to unwed welfare mothers all point to the same message: The key to solving America's welfare dependency is to curtail the fertility of welfare mothers. For three decades, Cambodian mothers have faced attempts by the welfare state to regulate their bodies and limit their reproductive rights, but the loss of their children to starvation, disease, and war during the Khmer Rouge years has only increased their desire to have more children in the United States. Thus, there is a constant struggle between Cambodian mothers on welfare wanting to exercise their reproductive rights and their eligibility workers who want to curtail those rights.

The average number of children among the Cambodian American families I interviewed was five, with two being the fewest and eight being the most. When Mr. and Mrs. Chea were first sponsored by Catholic Charities to come to the U.S. in 1981, Mrs. Chea had only one child, the one that was still in her womb. Now, twenty-two years later, in addition to her own six children, Mrs. Chea also has custody of her oldest daughter's two sons, making her a 'supermom' of eight, ranging between 2 and 24 years of age. Like many other Cambodian families in the area, the Chea are now in their third consecutive decade of reliance on public assistance. Except for the oldest son who joined the Army a few years ago and the oldest daughter who is currently in the east coast, Mr. and Mrs. Chea live with their four children and two grandchildren in a modest two-bedroom apartment, located in a complex of mostly African American and other Cambodian American tenants. Mrs. Chea told me that her eligibility workers have repeatedly told her to stop having children after her first two kids, but she simply did not listen because her children was an important source of her livelihood.

In her study of how the modern welfare state attempts to curtail the reproductive rights of Cambodian mothers vis-à-vis refugee medicine, Aihwa Ong showed how Cambodian families negotiated the imposition of family planning. While repeatedly discouraged from having more children by their social workers, Khmer women were able to "maintain official connections" with the state but at the same time passively resist "family planning pressures" by keeping their silence and by disregarding medical advice (Ong 1995). Through their passive posture, they were able to exercise their liberty in reproductive rights and redefine what 'family planning' means. In this manner, the Chea family, under the guise of the welfare state, have subtly negotiated a space that has allowed them to define family planning on their own terms.

Mrs. Chea's concerns and hopes for her children's future well-being speak volumes about her desire to exercise her motherhood. She explained, 'Our [she and her husband] relationship with the children are peaceful...We want to raise our children the best we can...We want them to have good jobs...We want them to have the best life possible.' Like any loving and caring mothers (welfare or non-welfare), Mrs. Chea and her husband want the best for their children, but due to their shrinking welfare support, their ability to fulfill those wishes are increasingly uncertain.

Condemning Single-Parenting

When Ms. Sharon Nin came to the United States 15 years ago, she was 14 years old. She was the oldest of four siblings, so she had to take care of her younger brothers and sisters while her parents worked in sweatshops. Due to the financial responsibilities placed upon her by her parents, Ms. Nin was only allowed to finish high school and had to go into the workforce upon graduation. While working at a retail store, she met her future husband. They got married within a few months, and in their first three years of marriage, they had two children. When the youngest son turned one, Ms. Nin's husband suddenly abandoned her and their two children. Since Ms. Nin depended on her husband's salary to raise her two children, when he left, she was economically devastated, not being able to support her family. She was unsuccessful in getting alimony from her husband because he was nowhere to be found. Left with two children to support, she had no other option but to resort to applying for welfare.

Currently, her two sons are ages 6 and 8. The younger one just started first grade and the older one is in third. When asked what life is like raising two children as a single-parent on welfare, Ms. Nin expressed feelings of shame and guilt because she doesn't have the resources to provide for her kids or give them a better future. She agrees that getting off welfare and working is much better by far, but since she has limited education and employable skills, finding a job with decent wage is difficult. As a result, she is unable to improve her family's economic situation, making her feel like a "bad" mother who does not care about her family. Ms. Nin informed me that many poor Cambodian families she knows have expressed similar frustrations. In fact, she tells me that there is a popular saying known among the Cambodian American neighborhood. It says,

"Chinese parents want to help their kids, but Cambodian parents don't." She explained, "It's not that Cambodian parents don't want to help their kids, but they simply can't. They are too poor to do anything for their kids."

Being a single-mother on welfare brings much social stigma, and Ms. Nin has personally experienced her share of the harassment, especially from her social worker. Every time she meets with her social worker, she is treated as a delinquent parent and incompetent adult. She is asked demeaning questions, such as do you physically abuse your kids or do you use your welfare check to purchase liquor. Moreover, she is constantly reminded and criticized for not being employed like other productive citizens in society. When her social worker conducts home visits, Ms. Nin informed me that he often criticizes how her apartment "stinks" and accuses her of not taking "good care" of her children. Ms. Nin genuinely believes that her social worker is not there to help her achieve economic independence, but rather, he is there to tell her how poorly she is living her life.

Ms. Nin shared that her social worker is a traditional Cambodian American man, and he does not seem to approve of her position in life as a single-mother. On more than one occasion, he has told her to find someone to marry, assuming that marriage is the solution to her life's problems. However, she is still traumatized by her separation from her former husband, and she feels if she is going to marry, it has to be for the right reasons, and not just for economic support. She wants to focus on improving her English and eventually finding a good job, so she can raise her children well. Ms. Nin gently reminded me that the reason she is in her current plight is because she got married to the wrong person. She intends to not make the same mistake twice.

As law professor Dorothy Roberts argued, the imposition of marriage upon single-mothers on welfare rolls might trap victims of domestic violence in their situations due to their economic dependence upon the husbands (Roberts 1997). The push for this type of normative family is so strong that various state governments have enacted "bridefare" programs, whereby single-mothers are given monetary rewards for marrying. When public assistance is tied to the imposition of marriage and normative family, single-parents, especially unwed mothers, and their children become the greatest victims.

As clearly seen in the case of Ms. Nin's situation, being a single-mother on welfare has a high social and emotional cost. She has to continually defend and prove herself to her caseworker, who often accuses and criticizes her for being a "lazy" person and a "bad" mother. Her "deservedness" of government support is constantly questioned. Ms. Nin did express desire to withdraw from welfare to avoid the harassment of her social worker, but apart from finding a livable-wage job, she knows there is no viable alternative for economic support.

Liberal Governance and Its Consequences

The mini case studies above clearly reveal that recent welfare reform is less concerned about economic support than it is about social control. According to welfare advocate Gary Delgado and Rebecca Gordon of Applied Research Center, PRWORA has transcended its original purpose of providing support for poor women and their children to become a purely ideological and disciplinary instrument driven more by moral than economic considerations. The 1996 act replaced a system of entitlement to financial benefits based on economic need with one that provides limited aid, contingent on recipients' state-mandated responsible behavior (Delgado and Gordon 2002). This new regime of liberal governance has resulted in major material and ideological consequences, namely the overall reduction of welfare rolls and the redefining of the terms of social welfare.

Dramatic Welfare Caseload Reductions

Through work requirements, restrictive eligibility, sanctions, time limits, diversion programs, and other disciplinary strategies, PRWORA has been extremely effective in helping reduce welfare rolls. When the act passed in 1996, there were 12.6 million individuals receiving cash-based public assistance. By 1999, just three short years after its passage, the number of recipients was cut by 50 percent, down to 6.2 million recipients. By 2003, only 4.9 million individuals were receiving welfare—a total of a 61 percent overall reduction since 1996.

In a very short amount of time, between 1996 and 2003, over 7.7 million welfare recipients lost their benefits. What happened to those seven million people? According to a national study, 61 percent of those who left welfare found jobs, but among them, only 21 percent of the households had earnings above the poverty line (Delgado and Gordon 2002). The situation in California closely aligned with national trends. Six years after the passage of PRWORA, the total number of CalWORKs (California's version of TANF) recipients in the state of California plummeted by half from 986,710 in 1996 to 479,174 in 2002—a 51.4 percent drop. During the same period, the total number of Asian welfare cases also decreased by half (51 percent) from 85,016 to 41,616. Southeast Asian cases (40% of which is consisted of Cambodians) decreased from 53,805 in 1996 to 31,155 in 2002—a 42.1 per cent drop.

According to an important study published by the Asian Pacific American Legal Center (APALC) of Southern California, PRWORA created four major barriers that have kept Southeast Asians from receiving the aid they need (Asian Pacific American Legal Center of Southern California 2001). First, the changes under PRWORA created a complex and confusing labyrinth of rules and regulations. As a result, many Southeast Asian recipients who were unable to comply with new requirements (i.e., filling out the appropriate forms) were dropped from public assistance rolls.

Second, the report stated that participants with limited English skills are significantly disadvantaged when it comes to accessing welfare-to-work activities and supportive services. As seen in the case studies above, many Cambodian American recipients were unable (due to limited English) of taking advantage of job training/search services, leaving them vulnerable for assignment to demeaning job.

Third, the report found that over 83 percent of Southeast Asians were placed into low-wage industries, including food service (i.e., fast food restaurants), service sector (i.e., janitorial, beauty industry, grocery, restaurant), light manufacturing (i.e., garment), and low-skilled healthcare (i.e., homecare)—industries that are characterized by part-time work, high turnover rates, no or little benefits, limited opportunities for improving employment skills, and high incidence of labor law violations. The case of Mr. Pheng, who worked as a security guard, resembled this trend.

Lastly, the study also indicated that many Southeast Asian welfare recipients had difficulty working with their caseworkers, as typified by Ms. Nin's overcritical caseworker. The report found that many caseworkers provided incorrect and inconsistent information and were often abusive and intimidating. Consequently, caseworkers were often ineffective in helping their clients properly access available services, or clients were so frustrated that they simply gave up and stopped seeking government aid.

In short, the APALC report concluded that through the use of these insidious strategies, PRWORA in general and CalWORKs in particular have effectively and systematically reduced the overall number of Southeast Asians on welfare rolls. Moreover, due to the failure to recognize the unique needs and concerns of the Southeast Asian welfare population, PRWORA has done little to help current Southeast Asian recipients achieve long-term and lasting economic self-sufficiency.

Redefining Social Welfare as Social Control

Liberal governance has resulted not only in the reduction of welfare rolls but also in the redefinition of the terms—from "social welfare" to "social control." Prior to the 1996 act, public assistance served as an economic safety-net available for anyone who simply exhibited a need (whose income was below the poverty line). Since the passage of PRWORA, participation in public assistance is contingent not only on one's income but also on a whole host of other factors, including acceptable family ethic, willingness to engage in workfare activities, mandatory job training, and other commitments. In the words of one welfare administrator, 'PRWORA offers no free lunches'—welfare recipients are expected to 'earn' their benefits by adhering to a regimented list of requirements and activities."

This ideological shift is reflected in the funding structure of public assistance. In 1996 over three-quarters (76 percent) of the entire public assistance budget ($32.4 billion) went to cash-payments. By

2000 the cash-payment component dropped to 41 percent (of the overall budget of $26.4 billion) (Weil 2002). The reduction of cash-payment as a percent of public assistance spending has resulted in the reshuffling and redirecting of funding, mainly into systems that support paid employment and family support, including transportation vouchers, tax credits for low-income families, and programs to promote marriage or reduce non-marital pregnancies. PRWORA's shifts in funding priorities reflect a "work first" and "family first" welfare system. Consequently, the new system is designed to achieve "rapid labor force attachment, with less emphasis on skills development or long-term education" as well as to discourage "teenagers from having children, non-marital child-bearing, and sex before marriage' (Weil 2002). These funding measures go beyond addressing the economic plight of individuals to modifying and controlling their social behaviors.

As one theorist argued, once social welfare becomes a form of social control, recipients of public assistance cease to exist as free individuals and become "subjected" and "normalized" citizen-subjects.

> The individual who has been subjected does not ask questions about what kinds of work might be fulfilling, more interesting or more conducive to the development of one's full potential. The subjected individual obeys. The individual who has been 'normalized' does not conceive of work as means of achieving dignity or as a means of expressing creativity; work is accepted as a form of discipline which extorts the body's forces in order to optimize the capacities which society finds useful (Hawkesworth 2001, 275).

Conclusion

In *Welfare's End*, sociologist Gwendolyn Mink (1998) claimed that the 1996 welfare act essentially moved poor families from the welfare state to a police state. Under the new regime, families on public assistance are denied not only income security but also basic civil rights. They are subjected to stringent and intrusive moral and social regulations in exchange for meager and temporary assistance.

As I have illustrated in this article with the situation of Cambodian families on public assistance, the contemporary welfare 'police' state is focused on governing the social behaviors of its citizen-subjects and disciplining their bodies in hopes of decreasing welfare rolls. I also showed how the hegemonic regulations faced by recipients of public assistance are stifling their liberty and freedom to live as they choose. In short, the American welfare state through its various strategies—whether it is to push them into dead-end jobs (through work-requirement), to expel them (through time-limits), to penalize them (through sanctions), or to harass them (through abusive case workers)—have succeeded in reducing the number of public assistance caseloads. However, at what cost to the individuals who now have to face poverty without the help of the government?

Endnotes

1. Interview data included in this article comes from a larger project, whereby I interviewed a total of 50 public assistance recipients (from 12 different families) from Southeast Asian backgrounds living in Southern California over a course of a two-year span, starting February 2001. The families chosen for this study were a result of referrals from refugee resettlement organizations, community organizations, personal contacts, and subsequent referrals from interviewed individuals themselves (snow-ball sampling). Often, I was introduced to these families as a "student" working on "a school project about poverty and welfare." Here, I chose to focus on the Cambodian families living in Long Beach (a suburb of Los Angeles County) exclusively because they were the majority of the interviews, and they constituted a good sample for a case study. Interviews with these families were conducted in their native language for the most part with the help of translators. Frequently, the English-speaking, American-born/raised children of these families helped translate, explain, and clarify what their parents were trying to express to me. The interviews were informal, relaxed, and conversation-based. The individuals who were ultimately included in the study were those who were most willing and open to talk with me and share about their experiences of being on public assistance and those whose insight were directly relevant to the topic at hand. As with any projects that involve interview data, there is always more information collected than can be used. The interview materials included below are selectively chosen primarily

because of their usefulness in illustrating key concepts and ideas concerning how recent welfare reforms discipline the bodies of its citizen-subjects. Thus, there were many interesting but less integral issues raised from interviews that were eventually omitted from this final report.

References

Abramovitz, Mimi. *Regulating the lives of women: Social welfare policy from colonial times to the present.* Boston: South End Press, 1988. Print.

Delgado, Gary, and Rebecca Gordon. 2002. Oakland, CA: Applied Research Center.

Gordon, Linda. *Pitied but not entitled: Single mothers and the history of welfare, 1890-1935.* New York: Free Press, 1994. Print.

Hawkesworth, Mary. "Workfare and the imposition of discipline." In *Philosophy and the problems of work: A reader,* ed. K. Schaff, New York: Rowman and Littlefield, Inc., 2001. Print.

Mink, Gwendolyn. *Welfare's end.* Ithaca, N.Y.: Cornell University Press, 1998. Print.

O'Connor, Alice. *Poverty knowledge: Social science, social policy, and the poor in twentieth-century U.S. history.* Princeton, N.J.: Princeton University Press, 2001. Print.

Ong, Aihwa. "Making the biopolitical subject: Cambodian immigrants, refugee medicine and cultural citizenship in California." In *Social Science Medicine,* 40.9 (1995): 1243-57. Print.

Roberts, Dorothy E. *Killing the black body: Race, reproduction, and the meaning of liberty.* New York: Pantheon Books, 1997. Print.

Rose, Nancy E. Governing "advanced" liberal democracies. In *Foucault and political reason: Liberalism, neo-liberalism, and rationalities of government,* edited by Andrew Barry, Thomas Osborn, and Nikolas Rose. Chicago: University of Chicago Press, 1996. Print.

United States Congress. *Personal responsibility and work opportunity reconciliation act* (PRWORA) of 1996. United States Congress. PL 104-193. Washington, D.C, 1996. Print.

Weil, Alan. *Ten things everyone should know about welfare reform* (Series A, No. A-52). Washington, D.C.: The Urban Institute, 2002. Print.

CHAPTER 20

Cambodian American
Women and the Politics
of Welfare Reform

Lynn Fujiwara

On August 22, 1996, President Clinton signed the "Personal
Responsibility and Work Opportunity Reconciliation Act"
(PRWORA) that not only "ended welfare as we know it" but repo-
sitioned immigrants ("legal permanent residents") as further ineligible for various forms of public assistance. At the time of its passing,
PRWORA barred most non-citizens from Supplemental Security
Income (SSI)—cash assistance for the blind, elderly, and disabled—
and food stamps.[1] Likewise states were granted the option to provide
Temporary Assistance to Needy Families (TANF) to immigrants, as
well as other locally-funded benefits. The politics of welfare reform
were intricately tied to an anti-immigrant movement that charged
non-citizens as overusing an over-generous welfare system.[2]

For Cambodians, especially Cambodian American women in
the U.S. the consequences of welfare reform proved devastating
because it (re)traumatized a community that had yet to heal. Cambodians joined other Southeast Asians and immigrant communities
to fight for many provisions that were ultimately rescinded through
mass mobilization campaigns for immigrant rights in the aftermath
of the harshest welfare cuts. According to the 1990 Census, at the

time of PRWORA's passing, 47 percent of Cambodians were officially impoverished. Thus, the loss of major forms of assistance would prove devastating to Cambodians living in poverty and struggling to keep their families afloat.

Before moving on to the specific factors that shaped the impact of welfare reform on Cambodian American families, I will discuss the forces that shaped the rationalization for cutting benefits to noncitizens, and provide a schematic outline of the specific provisions that affected legal permanent residents—Cambodian American women—most directly.

The Racial and Gender Politics of Welfare Reform

Throughout the 1980s and early 1990s, the welfare reform movement paralleled the anti-immigrant movement, culminating with the convergence of an integrated 1996 immigration and welfare social policy. The convergence of these two political movements found synergy in the demonization of both welfare users and immigrants alike; thus, immigrant welfare recipients were deemed to be a group that should be excised from public support without question. The racialized and gendered constructions of the *welfare queen* and the *hyper-fertility* of undocumented Mexicana migrants crossing the border to give birth to American citizens were joined by the elderly Asian immigrant mothers (of well-to-do model minority Asian American children) scamming the system to receive SSI based upon their elderly and disabled status, while enjoying all the comforts of a middle class lifestyle supported by their children.[3] The image of Asian immigrants, sponsored to the U.S. by their children specifically to receive public benefits stuck in the minds of legislators. Politicians and anti-immigrant advocates based their arguments to exclude immigrants from public assistance on the premise that welfare was the magnet attracting immigrants to America, rather than jobs or family reunification.

PRWORA operated on the assumption that those residing within the U.S. without citizenship status occupy an "alien" position as outsiders to American membership. Little thought was given to the preponderance of immigrants who were here to work and be with their families, or who had resided in this country for decades but were unable to fulfill the requirements for citizenship or, until this point, had had no compelling reason to naturalize. Nor did Congress consider the fact that a large proportion of non-citizens utilizing public assistance came to this country as refugees. In fact all legally residing non-citizens were classified as "legal aliens" regardless of the conditions that had brought them here. Rather, Congress argued that they possessed a "compelling government interest to enact new rules for eligibility and sponsorship agreements in order to assure that aliens be self-reliant in accordance with national immigration policy" (P.L. 104–193, Title IV, Sec. 400). The immigrant provisions clearly tied eligibility for basic public benefits to citizenship status.

Thus, although immigrants utilize public benefits at rates comparable to U.S. citizens—about 5 percent—cuts to immigrant communities accounted for 44 percent of the overall estimated federal savings from the *Personal Responsibility Act*.[4] The elimination of coverage for immigrants saved an estimated $23.7 billion over the first six years, constituting the 44 percent savings of the total $53.4 billion savings package.[5] By the time 1996 rolled around, this broad-sweeping cut to immigrants had been shaped and legitimized through the anti-immigrant campaign that defined immigrants as outsiders, foreign threats, and leeches to scarce public resources. The construction of the immigrant threat successfully targeted the most vulnerable non-citizen populations: women, children, and the elderly.

When President Clinton signed PRWORA, the extent of the law was broad-sweeping in that it altered public assistance in multiple realms, including aid for the elderly and disabled, food stamps, and completely dissolved the program we have known as Aid to Families with Dependent Children (AFDC)—a guaranteed family assistance program meant to prevent families from falling into complete destitution. Under PRWORA, non-citizen immigrants and legal permanent residents were no longer eligible for SSI and food stamps unless they became naturalized citizens or could show documented proof of formal employment for at least 40 quarters (ten years). This proved impossible as many worked in the U.S. in the informal economy or invisible labor sector. Non-citizens could also continue their SSI and food stamp benefits if they were U.S. military veterans or the wives or children of veterans, however, this became a problem for most Southeast Asian and Filipino veterans who were not initially granted veteran status. For Asian immigrants and refugees the requirements for eligibility had a direct gendered impact.[6] Approximately 72 percent of the immigrants scheduled to lose their SSI benefits were women. Hence, citizenship as a filter through welfare reform particularly affected women, leading to a disproportionate difficulty for women and their children.

September 1, 1997, was the expected date for those non-citizens to lose their SSI if they could not show proof of U.S. citizenship, 40 qualified quarters of employment, or demonstrate their U.S. veteran's status. An estimated 500,000 non-citizens were expected to lose their SSI benefits, and nearly 1 million lost their federally funded food stamps. For a substantial proportion of immigrant recipients, losing SSI would mean losing life-sustaining support needed to continue convalescent care, skilled nursing facilities, in-home health care, and basic nutrition. Families began to flood social service agencies and community organizations, panicked about how they were going to take care of their physically or cognitively disabled elderly parents. Immediately, reports of suicides by elderly and disabled immigrants sprang up across the country; three Southeast Asian women, an elderly man from China, and an elderly man from Mexico left behind messages that they did not want to burden their families.[7]

The crisis that ensued led to nation-wide grassroots mobilization and visibility campaigns with the intent to gain public attention and make legislators aware of the immediate and potentially far-reaching harm created by welfare reform to the nation's politically disenfranchised. Despite the forces allied against poor immigrants, community organizational efforts were initially successful. On August 4, 1997, just a few weeks before SSI cut-offs were scheduled, SSI was restored so that immigrants who were receiving benefits before the passing of the Personal Responsibility Act would not lose their benefits even if they did not meet the exemptions.[8] While the partial restoration of SSI did not benefit all impacted immigrants, immigrant rights organizations still viewed the policy changes as a victory, given the dire level of human suffering that was to unfold if all 500,000 elderly and disabled immigrants were to lose their assistance.

The Impact of Welfare Reform on Cambodians in the U.S.

For Cambodians utilizing welfare in the U.S., it is first critical to clarify the difference between the title, refugee, as an "identity" of experience, as opposed to a status of eligibility for social services. Most Cambodians utilizing welfare as of 1996 were not eligible for refugee assistance. Although the vast majority of Cambodians relying on welfare at the time of the law's passage were refugees, their status in the eyes of PRWORA was of "legal aliens"—subjected to all the changes that all legal immigrants found themselves.

As the cut-offs of SSI and food stamps neared, the fear and panic that disabled and elderly "legal aliens" would soon be losing their life-sustaining benefits resulted in public outcry. A public statement by the staff at the Khmer Health Advocates of the Cambodian Health Network decried the re-traumatizing effects that welfare reform inflicts on an already traumatized refugee community. The following are excerpts taken from their public statement:

> Cambodian survivors of the Mahantdorai, the Cambodian Holocaust, are among the most traumatized people in the world today. They have experienced a quarter of a century of destruction that has included civil war, the massive secret bombing by the United States, and years of captivity in the Pol Pot Regime. They have endured torture, starvation, slave labor, brainwashing, and exposure to atrocities and disease. Those who escaped Cambodia experienced years of isolation, deprivation, and abuse in refugee camps; with little more than the clothing on their backs, came to the United States, which had no established Cambodian communities and few resources for dealing with the culture, language, and trauma of these new arrivals.

Courtesy of Khmer Health Advocates, Inc. Reprinted with permission.

Today, Cambodian adults have one of the highest disability rates in the United States. The Urban Institute reports that 22,460 Cambodians were receiving Social Security Income [sic. Supplemental Security Income] as of December 1995. At least 15 percent of Cambodians, age 16 to 64, are disabled, more than 4 times the rate of the general population of the United States. Forty two percent of Cambodian families are living below the poverty level compared to 13 percent of the general population, and more than 50 percent of Cambodian adults are not in the workforce.

These dramatic numbers should have been a signal of a health crisis in the Cambodian community. Instead, they were used by lawmakers as the rationale for denying financial aid and health care to elderly and disabled refugees. Lawmakers who were conferees on the final version of the *Welfare Reform Bill* had full knowledge of the health problems of Cambodians when they removed them from eligibility for SSI and health care. They did this by simply changing their name from refugee to legal alien, as if the title of alien could wipe out three decades of history.

The 1990 census documents 147,400 Cambodians in the United States. Of this number, 70,000 are children or adolescents; 22,460 are elderly or disabled, the remaining 55,000 Cambodian adults include 12,000 widows with children. More than 36,000 adults have had less than an elementary school education and are able to communicate only marginally in English. Thirty seven percent of Cambodian households make less than $12,000 a year and 47 percent make less than $20,000. These figures clearly show that it is beyond the realm of possibility for Cambodian families to provide health care or financial support for the approximately 22,460 disabled or elderly in their communities who will lose their financial aid and health care within the next year.

Khmer Health Advocates believes that the *Welfare Reform Act* in its present state will be responsible for the deaths of untold numbers of Cambodian holocaust survivors. Deaths will be due to a critical increase in stressors in people who have already expended their reserves of endurance. They will also be due to a loss of medication and treatment for hypertension, anxiety, depression and PTSD and numerous other health conditions that are a direct result of trauma. Cambodian Survivors face the terrible reality of being sick and disabled in a society that is fascinated by violence but bored by suffering. The United States Congress without conscience legislated the abandonment of a people who have known suffering beyond human comprehension. They did this without discussion or plans for transitional services that could avert tragedy. The moral and psychological implications of these actions are sure to haunt a nation that has clearly made a commitment to "never again" tolerate genocide. And yet, without health care, the genocide of Cambodians will continue with the American people as unwitting participants.

This statement demonstrates the intense emotions that followed the cruelty of the provisions laid out for non-citizens. Posted on their website, and circulated amongst advocacy groups, these public statements became a prominent force in the movement to rescind the SSI cuts for "legal aliens." Most scholars of welfare reform focus primarily on the transition from Aid to Families with Dependent Children (AFDC) to Temporary Assistance to Needy Families (TANF), without realizing the multifaceted impact welfare reform had on the wide range of public assistance immigrants rely on. The cuts to SSI for "legal aliens" proved so devastating that Congress restored the nearly 500,000 existing non-citizens scheduled to be cut-off—just months before the expected date. Testimony by Cambodians and Southeast Asian refugees were instrumental in the fight to restore these benefits.

A feature story in the *San Francisco Weekly* published in the February 1997, "Immigrants Desperately Seeking Citizenship," highlighted the unforgiving challenges primarily elderly and/or disabled Southeast Asian women were facing as they tried desperately to naturalize before their benefits were cut off. The devastating history of torture, malnutrition, and terror that many refugees from Cambodia experienced resulted in a community with very high levels of disability and mental health problems. The article appeared six months after the passing of the *Personal Responsibility Act* and about seven months before SSI cut-offs were to begin. The article focused on the 17,000 elderly, disabled, and blind legal immigrants in San Francisco, of whom 60 percent were Asian, who depended on federal aid. Visiting a civics and English class at the North of Market Senior Services in the Tenderloin, author Tara Shioya reveals the grave situations women faced in trying to learn and comprehend the basic U.S. civics that is required by INS for citizenship:

> [On a]…gray Thursday morning in January, Tuan Van Dang is setting out to accomplish…an impossible task. He is trying to teach women old enough to be his grandmothers…who can't read, write, or speak English—the civics fundamentals the INS requires for citizenship. Dang's deadline is tight—and, like the law…unforgiving.[9]

According to Janet Griffiths, the director of the citizenship project at the North of Market Senior Center, "Only a fortunate few of the center's male clients—and almost none of the women—are literate in their native Vietnamese, Chinese, Khmer, or Lao" (Shioya 1997). Griffiths explained that many of her students have taken years of English as a Second Language (ESL) classes with little success. Griffiths argued that the new citizenship requirement is unrealistic. "How can you expect them to pass an interview when they don't have the language skills to be able to remember or understand what someone is asking? They try, but they just can't remember."[10]

The inhumane process elderly and disabled women were forced to endure is exposed in Shioya's article, which focused on the traumatic experiences of Cambodian refugees. Shioya notes, Kiev Lim's story. Lim is a 79-year-old former refugee from Cambodia with basic elementary English skills. She lives alone in low income housing in the Tenderloin district of San Francisco. She has unsuccessfully taken the citizenship test five times. Lim said she was scared and nervous about taking the exam. Lim says, "Even before the examiner asked me anything, I was already shaking."[11] The article reflects the level of trauma imposed by U.S. military operations in Southeast Asia, and the second level of trauma imposed by U.S. legislation, now denying the benefits once promised to those who sought refuge due to American military actions. The stress of having to prepare for an interview with an American INS agent, and having to respond to any one of a hundred possible questions, created a crisis situation with few mechanisms for coping, which is enough reason for some to commit suicide. The story of Kiev Lim reveals the intense level of anxiety spawned by a harsh welfare policy that purposely chose to exclude her because of her citizenship status.

Sarouen Meas, a 65-year-old refugee from Cambodia, became a public figure in the outcry against the SSI, Medicaid, and food stamp cuts. At an immigrant rights media event held on the one-year anniversary of President Clinton's signing of the welfare bill, Meas spoke publicly before a group of reporters. His story was printed by the Associated Press that states:

> Meas fled the killing fields of Cambodia.... Disabled from torture and malnutrition, Meas and his wife now struggle to raise their five teenage children. Worried by the loss of $350 in food stamps a month, Meas said through an interpreter, "I now fear my children will suffer starvation as well," (Mittlestadt 1997).[12]

In an interview with the Meas family for the PBS *Online News Hour* dated October 13, 1997, the interviewer, Elizabeth Brackett, explains that the Meas family lost their food stamps because they were not citizens. Already lessening the amount of food they purchase, they were also struggling to learn English and study for the citizenship test. While some states were supplementing the lost federal food stamps through state programs, the Meas lived in Illinois, a state that did not restore food stamps.[13]

Thirteen years after the passing of PRWORA, immigrant communities continue to assess the impact of the broad-sweeping changes for non-citizens, as well as the political impact such vitriolic anti-immigrant sentiment had on the comfort level within immigrant communities to seek any form of assistance at all. Social service agencies and policy analysts refer to the broader hesitation for immigrants to seek public assistance as "chilling effects." A primary reason for these chilling effects was due to the redefinition of the Public Charge provision simultaneously passed and enforced through the *Illegal Immigration Reform and Immigrant Responsibility Act* (IIRIRA), passed just one month after PRWORA. A "public charge" is defined as "an alien who has become (for deportation purposes) or is likely to become (for admission or adjustment of status purposes) primarily dependent on the government for subsistence, as demonstrated by either the receipt of public cash assistance for income maintenance, or institutionalization for long-term care at government expense."[14] Since its implementation, the Public Charge provision has stirred enormous confusion for both immigrants and immigration officers overseeing determinations. The fear of public charge as a mechanism for deportation or denial of naturalization resulted in dissuading immigrants from seeking public benefits they were, in fact, eligible for and, in some cases, from applying for naturalization for fear of repercussions. Stories of deportation cases ensuing from use of public assistance spread throughout immigrant communities.

In addition to the Public Charge provision, the mass confusion over eligibility was intentionally complex in its creation of new categories of qualifications: differentiating among particular programs, governmental levels, and alien categories; the creation of many exceptions; the insertion of "grandfather" clauses; and the presence of special transition rules. According to Peter Schuck, "This crazy-quilt pattern is not accidental . . . the federal government has now made a clear comprehensive policy choice, albeit one confusing in its details, in favor of a national policy to discriminate against aliens in its federal programs, and to either require or permit the states to do so in their programs."[15]

The Persistence of Poverty among Cambodian American Women and Welfare-to-Work

In addition to the major changes in SSI, Medicaid, and food stamps, the welfare-to-work mandate central to the implementation of Temporary Assistance to Needy Families (TANF, the previous AFDC—Aid to Families with Dependent Children) had major consequences for Cambodian families. Already surviving on less support due to cuts in SSI and food stamps, Cambodian families had to negotiate an entirely new TANF structure. TANF block-grants to states put the regulatory mandate back into the hands of states and local governments, while establishing mandatory work requirements (or engagement in work related activities), and a maximum five-year lifetime limit of eligibility regardless of economic need. Likewise, PRWORA granted states the option to exclude non-citizens from TANF altogether.[16] TANF operated under the idea that people needed to take personal responsibility to pull themselves out of welfare into self sufficiency—with work incentives and welfare-to-work programs. While we have seen a drastic drop in welfare roles, this is, in large part, due to people being pushed out into more exploitable conditions, rather than their actually moving out of poverty.

By 2000 the poverty rate among Cambodians was 29.3 percent, while the national average was 11.3 percent. The median family income for Cambodians was $35,621, while the median family income for all families was $50,046.[17] As of 2004, education levels for Cambodians 25 years and older was 26.2 percent for those who had no formal education (31.6 percent for Cambodian women), while the U.S. national average was 1.4 percent.[18] Before the *Personal Responsibility Act*, poor and working class families utilized AFDC to supplement their inadequate wages to support their families. With the implementation of TANF we see greater restrictions, stricter and stingier calculations of grant amounts, and a sanctioning system for "non compliance"—that has been characterized by welfare scholars studying the impact of welfare reform as new forms of "disciplining."[19]

The larger disciplining by the welfare state can be seen in the day-to-day struggles Cambodians face with their local social service offices. Welfare-to-Work programs were constructed and implemented county-by-county, but most followed general models of work appraisal, assessment for "barriers to work," and a professionalizing model of "job readiness." Once a TANF client signs his contract, his 5-year lifetime limit clock starts ticking, and he must begin his mandatory work requirements in order to receive assistance. The process of becoming job-ready often involves required "professionalizing" activities, classes, and skill workshops referred to as "Job Club."[20]

As a result of mandatory work participation rates, a more elaborate and strictly enforced sanctioning system and practice by local welfare agencies for "non compliant" clients has contributed to the large drop of participants in TANF—and contributing to the high rates of welfare leavers. If a recipient does not meet his mandatory work requirement the state is required to reduce the amount of family assistance or terminate assistance altogether. Several studies have shown that women of color have higher sanctioning rates than white recipients.[21] For immigrant women, sanctioning is even more prevalent, given confusion, inaccessible language problems, and lack of culturally appropriate child care. Sanctioning has been imposed for a range of infractions (i.e., tardiness to job training, lack of necessary work activity hours, or missing an appraisal appointment), usually at the complete discretion of the case worker.

California—Los Angeles in particular—is home to the largest settlement of Cambodians in the U.S. California's TANF program, California Work Opportunities and Responsibility to Kids (CalWORKs) must accommodate the nation's largest non-citizen demographic. As soon as CalWORKs went into operation, numerous problems pertaining to non-citizen recipients became evident. Language accessibility was the most immediate problem, and one which still has not been fully addressed. The initial notification letters were sent to recipients without proper translation; thus, in the transition from AFDC to CalWORKs, where 5-year time limits began for all remaining eligible recipients, mostly non-citizen clientele in some counties failed to attend their initial interviews to begin their TANF contracts. Under the new rules, this entire population would have been sanctioned off, thus ending their eligibility to receive benefits.

A study by Karen Quintiliani examines the day-to-day realities for 11 first- and 1.5-generation Cambodian CalWORKs recipients, demonstrating the particular challenges both groups of women face as low-skilled mothers trying to conform to the work-related activities and work requirements. All recipients work directly with Greater Avenues for Independence (GAIN), which is the employment-related services arm of CalWORKs in Los Angeles County. GAIN caseworkers oversee a person's efforts to acquire employment, and assess one's compliance in fulfilling the requirements. Quintiliani's study found that first-generation Cambodian women experienced major challenges to meeting their requirements. Representative of the majority of first-generation Cambodian women refugees, most of the women in her study had no formal education, and only three had taken English classes for two years or less. With few marketable skills, limited English abilities, and little to no education, the only types of jobs available to them are highly exploitable, part-time, low-skilled, low-paying jobs without health benefits. Thus, it became impossible for these women to find employment. The disabled women in this study had lost their SSI, regardless of Congress' restoration in 1997. For these first-generation Cambodian American women, who had experienced trauma, death, and escape, losing their welfare benefits was akin to death.[22]

While the 1.5-generation Cambodian American women in Quintiliani's study had greater language acquisition, they still found it very challenging to fulfill the mandatory work requirements. While their experiences of terror, trauma, and escape occurred in their childhood, they were still greatly affected by the loss of loved ones, and the suffering they witnessed their parents endure. In addition, their resettlement experiences as children negotiating the public schools, racial tensions within their neighborhoods, and the persistent poverty in their families, resulted in lack of educational attainment, because many dropped out before acquiring their high school degrees. In addition, many faced early motherhood and the added pressure of caring for their aged and disabled parents who had lost their SSI benefits. Two of the women found opportunities through literacy training programs in their young children's preschools and elementary schools. Because they did not have high school diplomas their GAIN caseworkers counted their literacy training and volunteer time in their children's schools toward their work activities. As a result of better and more appropriate training, these two women were eventually hired as teaching assistants. Other women, however, found themselves in low-wage, unskilled work in fast-food restaurants earning $5 an hour, while also enduring racial and ethnic tensions from other employees and supervisors.

Overwhelmingly, most welfare studies show the challenges women endure to meet their mandatory work requirements in order to receive little, but much-needed assistance. Without an honest recognition of the low-wage economy, lack of jobs, and the added challenges of housing costs, childcare, transportation, education, and so on, welfare recipients tend to utilize the programs as much as they can until their time expires or they are sanctioned off. Unfortunately, once they are timed out, the only forms of assistance remaining are general workfare programs or general assistance. Workfare is another form of work-required assistance—to receive a grant, workfare participants must "work off" their support. Workfare jobs are usually county- or city-based public jobs, such as cleaning parks, city buses, county hospitals, and the streets. This is a form of exploitation because people are basically working wage-jobs for no wages.

To challenge existing forms of exploitation and degradation of their parents, Cambodian and Vietnamese American youths in the Bronx engaged in a community-based protest at the local welfare office. In *Eating Welfare*, a documentary, the Youth Leadership Project of the Committee Against Anti-Asian Violence (CAAAV) organized the occupation of the local welfare office in the Bronx, insisting on a meeting with the director to demand adequate translation services for the high population of Cambodians and Vietnamese, to make assistance more accessible, and to find meaningful work for their mothers rather than the degrading jobs of picking up trash at local parks and playgrounds around the city.

The film documents the depth of their poverty and the day-to-day humiliations their parents deal with as they struggle to get assistance under the new rules and conditions. The youth themselves have become intermediaries and translators at very young ages to help their parents communicate with impatient welfare agents. They are forced to miss school, put into embarrassing positions with invasive questions, and must deal with their own parents' shame as they are forced into menial workfare wage-less jobs to receive their assistance.

A narrative that weaves throughout the documentary is a daughter's quest to see what her mother does all day to earn her welfare check. As someone who has not found employment, the mother participates in the city's workfare program. The daughter follows the mother as she opens the gates to a small community playground and begins picking up trash very early in the morning. Hour after hour her mother picks up trash with a stick with a nail on the end. She has no contact with anybody. When she first started the job, she did not have the gloves or the poker stick necessary for the job. With her daughter translating, the mother, who appears to be in her mid-fifties, tells how humiliating and dirty the work is, and how it is not providing any kind of training to find a better job. With her lack of English and employable work skills, and her low-level education, this mother will be unable to find employment by the time she reaches her five-year lifetime limit; thus she will be shuffled onto General Assistance and will remain part of the largest workfare program in the country. In the end, the youth group succeeded in their demands that children not be relied upon to act as translators, and managed to persuade the director to discontinue some of the worst workfare conditions.

Possibilities for Change?

While TANF has undergone numerous reauthorization measures, very little has changed. Even in times of economic crisis, welfare reform is not a political priority. The economy continues to occupy concern, yet mainly in the direction of the ever-increasing falling middle class. Massive housing foreclosures, bankruptcy, and credit scandals supersede the needs and dire circumstances of the nation's poorest. Immigration reform has re-entered the political debate, but these issues are primarily centered on comprehensive immigration reform for undocumented immigrants, and draconian deportation measures instituted in the mid 1990s and greatly magnified in post-9/11 Bush years. Welfare reform for the nation's poor remains a silent issue. For Cambodian refugees, significant change has corresponded with demographic changes. As more second-generation Cambodian Americans grow into adulthood, they will shift the overall economic picture of their communities. Yet, the drastic changes in SSI, food stamps, Medicaid, and TANF, have had devastating consequences that bespeak a need for improvement as too many continue to struggle on too little, and family members will continue to face the job market with few employable skills and more burdens to carry.

Endnotes

1. SSI is a federal assistance program for the poor elderly, blind and disabled.

2. In earlier works, I chart the racial and gendered politics that shaped the provisions of PRWORA that systematically worked to exclude most non-citizens from public benefits, and resulted in a drastic drop in welfare use despite persistent levels of poverty within immigrant communities. For earlier versions of this work see Lynn Fujiwara, *Mothers without Citizenship: Asian Immigrant Families and the Consequences of Welfare Reform*, Minneapolis: MN, 2008; Lynn Fujiwara, "Mothers without Citizenship: Asian Immigrant and Refugees Negotiating Poverty and Hunger in Post Welfare Reform," Race, Gender, Class, 12 (2) pgs. 121–141, 2005; Lynn Fujiwara, "Immigrant Rights are Human Rights: The Reframing of Immigrant Entitlement and Welfare" *Social Problems*, 52(1), pgs. 79–101, 2005.

3. William Wong, "Asian-Americans and Welfare Reform: The Mainstream Press perpetuates Images but Fails to Report on Real Experiences," *Nieman Foundation for Journalism at Harvard University* 53(2) (Summer 1999).

4. See "Devolution's Drastic Consequences: Welfare Reform Devastating to Immigrants" by Angie Wei and Sasha Khokha. *National Network for Immigrant and Refugee Rights.*

5. Bill Ong Hing, "Don't Give Me Your Tired, Your Poor: Conflicted Immigrant Stories and Welfare Reform," *Harvard Civil Rights-Civil Liberties Law Review*, 33(1), Winter 1998, p. 159.

6. At the time of the law's passing, there were more foreign-born Asian Pacific American women than men (71.8 percent of women compared to 69.7 percent of men are over age 65), and among foreign born, 26 percent of the women rely on public assistance, compared to 18.5 percent of the men.

7. Community based agencies implemented suicide hotlines with language accommodations for suicidal immigrants.

8. In the Balanced Budget Act of 1997, Congress agreed that non-citizens who resided in the U.S. on or before August 22, 1996, should not lose their life-sustaining benefits.

9. See Tara Shioya, "Immigrants Desperately Seeking Citizenship," *SF Weekly*, February 12–18, 1997 pp. 12–15.

10. Bill Ong Hing, 12–15.

11. Ibid., 12–15.

12. Mittlestadt, M. (1997). Nearly 1 Million Noncitizens Lopped Off Food Stamp Rolls. *Associated Press*, August 24, 1997.

13. Through various other subsequent policies under both Clinton and the Bush presidencies, food stamps were gradually replaced to different categories of immigrants, until they were restored to legally residing immigrants who have lived in the U.S. for at least five years. However, the piecemeal restoration of benefits has still left a legacy of confusion and fear, and non-citizens continue to under-utilize the benefits they are entitled to, and need.

14. U.S. Department of Justice, Immigration and Naturalization Service, Fact Sheet "Public Charge." http://www.rapidimmigration.com/www/news/news_237.html. Retrieved 8/9/05.

15. Ibid.

16. Alabama turned out to be the only state that has excluded "legal aliens" from TANF.

17. Terrance J. Reeves and "We the People: Asians in the United States," *Census 2000 Special Reports*.

18. 47.1 percent of Cambodians had a high school degree or higher (approximately 53 percent had less than a high school degree), but only 9.1 percent had a bachelor's degrees or higher (for Cambodian women 39.5 percent had high school degrees and 6.7 percent had college degrees; the national average 80.4 percent had high school degrees and 24.4 percent had bachelor degrees). Education data are drawn from the Southeast Asian Resource Action Center, "Southeast Asian American Statistical Profile" 2004.

19. Aiwha Ong's study of the Cambodian community in Oakland California pre-welfare reform is an excellent example of how Asian welfare recipients were racialized through particular ideologies of "personal responsibility." Ong's book, *Buddha is Hiding*, is important for a better understanding of how Cambodians were affected by welfare reform a decade later. In her ethnographic exploration of Cambodian refugees negotiating the welfare system, Aihwa Ong demonstrates the way social service agency workers perceived and treated their Cambodian clients as particularly unworthy of welfare benefits and in need of more direct disciplining to move towards self-reliance and accountability. Ong argues that already embedded in a racialized system, Southeast Asian refugees who fail to "fit into" a perceived model minority image, are further racialized as not only racial others but as deviant in their foreignness that

requires a limit on their entitlement. Immigrant and refugees dealing with welfare agencies must engage in this process with minimal English, fewer marketable labor-force skills, as well as with traumatic historical backgrounds of war and displacement.

20. Recent studies show a host of indignities that non-citizens experience due to language barrier, cultural insensitivity, and racist behaviors by social service officers who hold more power over their eligibility through their determination of the welfare recipients' compliance and conformity.

21. Kenneth J. Neubeck and Noel A. Cazenave, *Welfare Racism: Playing the Race Card against America's Poor*, (New York: Routledge, 2001), 182.

22. Karen Quintiliani, "Cambodian Refugee Families in the Shadows of Welfare Reform." *Journal of Immigrant and Refugee Studies*, 7:129–158, 2009.

Section IX

Cambodian American Identity Formations

CHAPTER 21

Cambodian American Ethics of Identity Formation

Jonathan H. X. Lee

"The past is irretrievable yet I can never be free from it."
Andrew Lam, 2000

"Being a spectator of calamities taking place in another country is a quintessential modern experience...."
Susan Sontag, 2003

Introduction

Since 1975, there has been an influx of Cambodian and ethnic Chinese Cambodian refugees entering the United States. Thirty-five years later, the younger of these refugees, known as the 1.5 generation (refugees having arrived when they were knee high), are now adults in their thirties and forties. Having grown up in America, they have married, have established families of their own, and their kids are now entering college. A common phenomenon among these Americanized Cambodian Americans is their unfamiliarity with the historical developments in Cambodia that led to their elders' flight from their homeland. This is partly due to the elder refugees' reluctance to talk about—and hence relive—the horrors that they faced, and partly a reflection of the quality of historical education in America's public schools. This chapter examines how 1.5-generation and second-generation Cambodian Americans learn about the Killing Fields, and how they reconcile historical awareness with a sense of self. It is a reflection on what I call the ethics of identity formation, and an acknowledgment of Cambodia's history and how it is deeply connected to their contemporary lives as Americans. An ethic of identity formation requires that students wrestle with the Killing Fields and their families' histories. In the process, healing, both individual and collective, may occur. An ethic of identity formation requires that Cambodian Americans know their history, not just as Americans, but as Cambodians, thus allowing them to negotiate the multiple sources of their identity, and begin the process of creating a mosaic from fractals of history and memory.

My father was born in Siem Reap, to a Chinese father and Cambodian-Vietnamese mother. His birth marked the fourth generation of my paternal family lineage in Cambodia. In 1949, when my mother was nine years old, she immigrated to Phnom Penh with her family from China. I was born in Hue, Vietnam in 1976, when my family was forced to flee from Phnom Penh. Fearing for their lives, my parents gathered my sisters and brother and left. Their extended family stayed behind. None of them survived. In 1981, we came to the United States as refugees. Since then, neither of my parents have mentioned Cambodia, spoken a word of Khmer, nor talked about their families. It was not until the summer of 2002 that I became aware of my family's history and its connection to Cambodia. I wrestle with my own subjectivity and agency as I begin to self-identify as part Cambodian. Simply saying and ascribing to being part Cambodian American was not enough for me. I proceeded to study and learn about my Cambodian history, but did so consciously and conscientiously, with deference for my parents' feelings, and for the community that I wanted to be a part of.

History is powerful. History can be enlightening and, at the same time, dark. It can cause fragmentation and destabilize the past and present state of one's sense of self, thus disrupting one's present life. Therefore, many survivors, Cambodian refugees, who experience life-changing losses—material, spiritual, psychological, cultural, emotional, and physical—have willfully "forgotten" recent historical events in their lives. There are cases of survivor-refugees who willfully damaged their own eyes, choosing to become blind, so as not to confront the reality of their recent past and present state of ambivalence. Caught in the process of historical forgetting, Cambodian refugees who grew up in America, occupy an *in-between* space among multiple worlds. Not fully American, yet not fully Asian, their identities are fraught with complications and uncertainties. Living as subjects without historical awareness, or knowledge of their heritage and ancestry, they grow up in America with shallow roots, and an incomplete sense of self. At some point, for some, when they encounter their history, they struggle to make sense of their identity and personhood. How should they react to the historical knowledge that is newly acquired? What responsibility do they have, to history, to their family, and to themselves vis-à-vis their recent historical awareness?

This chapter seeks to examine these questions. It argues that with an awareness of history, a self conscious process of identity reflection takes place and requires ethical responses. This in turn informs the process by which 1.5 and second generation Cambodian Americans transform and construct their identities in light of historical knowledge. The 1.5-generation, and second-generation Cambodian Americans are responsible for internalizing and processing the emotional baggage that their elders have long kept hidden, not just for their own self awareness, but as a means of healing, equally at an individual, familial, and collective level. At the same time, their parents, grandparents, uncles and aunts share in the responsibility, because they shape and inform the creation of Cambodian American identity. At this moment, they are forced to confront history, and question their subjectivity, as Cambodian, as American, and as Cambodian American.

Historical Awareness

I became aware of my family's connection to Cambodia in my early twenties, as a result of my mother's religiosity. Most Cambodians are Buddhist, and believe that people who die and are not properly cared for after death, become hungry ghosts, who can potentially haunt and harm the living. According to my mother, our Cambodian family members all became hungry-ghosts, and lived in America as refugees. They haunted her. They visited her dreams and followed her around.

My mother reconciled her loss and her lot in life on a basic understanding of Buddhist *karma*. The concept of *karma*, is the belief that one's actions in previous lives, and the merit that one has accumulated, determines one's current life situation and destiny. This is also informed by the principle belief in reincarnation, the belief that every individual is at a certain stage of rebirth. Many Cambodian refugees will invoke their understanding of *karma* to make sense of their realities, and social inequities, injustices, and collective suffering. Poor or unfortunate people, for example, explain their unfortunate life circumstances as a consequence of their misdeeds in their previous lives. Present suffering also results from the spectral presence of hungry-ghost relatives, who are awaiting their future rebirth out of hell.

To placate the hungry-ghosts of the relatives who haunted my mother, she made them offerings of food, merit, material goods, and paper money. However, she felt that doing this in our backyard in Los Angeles, California was not enough to save them. In June 2002, my mother decided to go back to Cambodia to perform merit transfer ceremonies (*thvoeu bon*), to deliver them all out of hell. Her success depended on the willingness of the ghosts to accompany her back to Cambodia.

In deciding to join my mother on her journey, I finally discovered that I was, indeed, part Cambodian and therefore, part Cambodian American. What does it mean to be Cambodian American, or even part Cambodian American? Traditional indicators of ethnicity: language, religion, cultural practices, and food—ways that reinforce being Cambodian are foreign to me. Acknowledging and wanting to be part Cambodian American requires that I fulfill duties and responsibilities with that name. Confucians call this process the "rectification of names." The ethics of my identity formation as part Cambodian American require that I acknowledge and fulfill my duties and obligations as a member of the community. I need to be Cambodian American, actively, not passively.

Coming Face-to-Face with Death

In Cambodia, I came face-to-face with death. I met survivors of the Killing Fields and heard their stories of torture and suffering. I visited the site where countless souls died, suffered, continued to suffer, and ultimately waited for their suffering to end. The Killing Fields and its victims were not completely dead, because they continued to haunt the landscape and the lives of the living.

I went on guided tours of the *Tuol Sleng Genocide Museum* Security Prison 21 (S-21). I was struck by the ironic contrasts *Tuol Sleng* exhibited: The peacefulness of the sun-soaked compound with horrific exhibits on display; whitewashed classrooms, with cheery yellow and white tile floors, containing instruments of torture; the beauty of two plumeria placed on an iron bed that was once used for torture; children now playing outside the buildings with a backdrop of mug shots of past children en route to their death.

The children's eyes in the mounted mug shots seemed to follow me as I walked through the museum. Knowing as I did—and as they perhaps did not—that every one of them was facing death when the photographs were taken, I was unnerved by these photos, these faces. As I walked through and took pictures of mug shots, of faces facing death, I insulated myself from becoming personally connected to their spirits, by viewing them through the lens of my camera. I went from one face to the next, clicking away, trying not to make eye contact with any of them. The sound of my camera clicking, of my film automatically advancing, assured me that I was safe, and that they were just faces on a wall. Why should I want to get to know these faces? Do I want to know why #399 has a friendly smirk? Could #1 be my cousin? Could #396 be my aunt with her baby? Coming face-to-face with the harrowing photographs from S-21 haunted me. I was attempting to recall the possibilities of the historical past, and the events that influenced not only my life, but the lives of my entire family. Yet at the same time, my act of remembering was based on a selective creative reconstruction of my family's past. Questions abound. What is the ethical limit of my historical reconstruction? What role does historical authenticity play in my historical recovery? Am I projecting to much of myself and my family's history into these mug shot photographs—these snapshots of death? Further, do I need to address the real and immediate pain of loss: my own and those represented by the photos? But, would pain impede my ability to translate the images and experiences of torture into words?

Repeatedly, I come face-to-face with the repetitive facts and faces of death. When dealing with the culture of S-21, it is tempting to rush to the conclusion that evil takes place elsewhere, that what happened was awful, and that it happened long ago to some other people. I was reluctant to come face-to-face, to become intimate, with the victims of torture. Does intimacy mean taking responsibility for death and misfortune? Does intimacy explain my parents' survivor's guilt?

If I now consider myself to be Cambodian and American, what are my responsibilities to history, especially to the group of Americans who identify as Cambodian Americans? By extension, what is my responsibility, not only with respect to the history of the Killing Fields, but to my own family's history in Cambodia? Kwame Appiah has suggested that our engagement with history, that is to say, our collective and individual identities, are responses to something outside ourselves, and are not under our control (2005: 19). Similarly, the process by which Cambodian Americans assume citizenship, both literal and figurative, is just as inherently social, contradictory, and complex (Ong 2003). Is my self-ascribed identification as part Cambodian American outside of my control? Does the social aspect of *becoming* Cambodian American require that I be a part of the Cambodian American community? Am I born a Cambodian American, or do I become one?

For many Cambodians, the reality of the Killing Fields is not history. My mother did not want to accompany me to the S-21 museum. "It's haunted!" she said. "Why do you want to go? People died there, that's all. It's haunted! I don't think you should go." The Killing Fields are alive. It has lived in my mother's mind, memories, and with her spirit, for twenty-seven years. It suddenly occurred to me that it was the spectral fields and faces of dead relatives that caused her dis-ease and dis-comfort in our California home, an ocean apart, and a world away.

For decades my parents did not have a chance to properly grieve the loss of our relatives, because they were so busy just trying to stay alive—trying to keep my sisters, brother and me alive. They had no time to grieve. Grieving was something people did when they had the luxury to do it. My parents were not able to grieve the death of my fourth sister, who died before I was born while the family was en route to refugee camps in Thailand and Hong Kong.

However, my mother finally had a chance to grieve the loss of our family the summer we returned to Cambodia. She experienced joy walking and eating on the streets of Phnom Penh, again, and showing me our old house. These joys were coupled with the joy of finally being able to cry. I realized grieving requires knowledge of personal histories. I never knew about the murder of my grandparents, aunts, uncles, and cousins. I simply grew up never knowing them, so grieving for them seemed strange. As a Cambodian American who did not experience the Killing Fields first hand, what do I do? How can I grieve? What are my responsibilities? To whom am I held responsible and for what?

Ethics of Identity

In my twenties, I had come to identify as being part Cambodian, and hence, part Cambodian American. How do I *live* as a Cambodian American? *Living as* a Cambodian American is a blueprint for "identity." Therefore, to speak of *living-as* is to speak of identity. Nancy Smith-Hefner has argued that to be "Khmer is to be Buddhist" (1999: 23). Thus, to be Khmer American is to live life in America guided by Buddhist doctrines, morals, and ethics. Ethically living as a Buddhist, informs what it means to be Khmer American. But, this is not as simple as it may seem, because Khmer Buddhist morals and ethics of selflessness, compassion, and community, clash with American values of individualism and materialism (Smith-Hefner 1999; Ong 2003). Smith-Hefner points out that the collective, the social body, is key to the construction of self, identity, and ethics; this, too, is fragile in the Khmer American community because there is a scarcity of religious institutions and monks who transmit and reinforce the moral and ethical order of Khmer sociality and society (1999: 96).

The "self" constructs the frame of authenticity for this life as a Cambodian American, even if it is just partial and not a fully self-ascribed identification. The (re)discovery of history thus fragments and (re)creates the authentic experience of *living-as* a Cambodian American. Echoing Smith-Hefner, Appiah argues, "The idea of identity has built into it a recognition of the complex interdependence of self-creation and sociability" (2005: 17). More importantly, Appiah also notes the role of creativity in the process of constructing one's self-identity, saying, ". . . self-construction, creating one's self-identity is a *creative response* to our capacities and our circumstances . . ." (Appiah, 19; emphasis added). This creative response may be exemplified in Smith-Hefner's documentation of Cambodian elders who use Bernardo Bertolucci's *Little Buddha* to transmit Buddhist beliefs and teachings to Khmer American children. This creativity is exemplified by Cambodian American writers, artists, and musicians who create identity through recording history in memoirs, hip-hop, and visual arts. Teri Shaffer Yamada documents how Cambodian American writers employ memoirs as a way to not only record history and tell their stories, but to transform trauma from pain and terror to socially engaged efforts to demand justice for survivors of the Killing Fields (Yamada 2005; 2010). Similarly, Cathy Schlund-Vials (2008) writes about praCh, a Cambodian American hip-hop artist who employs Khmer musical styles and techniques, movies about the Killing Fields, and family narratives, to construct not only an identity as Cambodian American, but a transnational subjectivity that situates the self in a vexing position between two worlds: America and Cambodia. 1.5-generation and second-generation Cambodian Americans will creatively employ the works of Cambodian American writers, artists, and musicians, coupled with their own family narratives, to recreate, (re)discover their history, and construct a self that is simultaneously consciously, and conscientiously, Cambodian and American.

The process of historical recovery for 1.5-generation and second-generation Cambodian Americans, is marked with responsibility. Identity is defined only through things that matter: history, material condition, and social relationships. For Cambodian Americans, identity includes the history of the Killing Fields, family relationships, and emerging Cambodian American communities. The idea of finding one's self—of discovering and recovering one's history by means of reflection, memory work, and creative construction of self-identity—requires a careful attention to the world and one's history. Becoming a Cambodian American necessitates confronting dark history and memories. Forgetting, or willful amnesia of history, is not an option—at least not for 1.5-generation and second-generation Cambodian Americans. Perhaps active denial of painful historical events has been the only salve of the first generation refugees, a salve that is quickly fading now that the 1.5 and second generation Cambodian Americans are coming of age. Perhaps the new generation will be able to better lead the way to inter-generational recovery, since they did not directly face the horrors of the Khmer Rouge like their parents did, and can therefore more easily confront the past and move through it.

Since arriving in America in 1981, my father has not spoken a word of Khmer. Is his memory loss a matter of neglect, a display of non-filial behavior, or a means of a carefully crafted way to, according to Michel Foucault, "care for the self" in modernity? My relationship to my father has been shaped by his relationship to history. As a teenager in Cambodia, my father was in a band, he was an artist—a photographer—carefree and creative. In America, he quietly struggled. He negotiated survivor's guilt, destabilization and fragmentation of self, tremendous grief, and the need to care for himself and his family—quietly. To what degree, in what ways, can I comfortably and without guilt, echoing Susan Sontag, regard the pain of my father? What are the responsibilities that come with regarding that pain?

Teaching to Heal, Teaching to Grieve

Since 2002, I have included the topic of the Killing Fields and Cambodian Buddhism in my Asian religions, global religions, and Asian American history courses.[1] In so doing, I discovered that many younger generation Cambodian Americans are not fully aware of the Killing Fields, nor of their personal connections to Cambodia. Unlike my experience, many of them know something about Cambodian cultural traditions, and some are able to speak Khmer, but in general, their knowledge of their family history, of how and why their parents came to America, remains dim.

By identifying with my refugee status, and my Cambodian heritage, I am responsible for bringing to public attention the unspeakable events that occurred during the Democratic Kampuchea era. I accomplish this in the classroom, with my students. For Cambodian American students, this process is transformative: allowing history to potentially change from a source of haunting, to a source of healing, transformation, and subject making. For my non-Cambodian students, they gain knowledge about Cambodian history and the Cambodian American experience. They cultivate empathy for individuals and communities who are trying to settle their roots on America's soil. Once Cambodian American college students figure out the process of establishing stability and balance in their identity, they are then able to engage their parents and elders in oral history, and begin their historical recovery. In this way, old wounds are made public and, by being recognized, given a chance to mourn and hopefully heal. This allows the silent suffering to come to an end, and the acknowledgement of pain to begin. The children of this generation will discover, in turn, where they come from and thereby gain a vision of where to go in the future.

Endnotes

1. Before teaching about the history of the Killing Fields, I cover Cambodian civilization and history. Pol Pot's regime and the Khmer Rouge are not the center of the lesson plan; rather, they are examples of global historical conditions. The events of the Killing Fields must be accounted for in terms of global history and ideological battles, specifically between perceived protectors of democracy and the red scare. This must be anchored in a discourse on global nationalist movements that marked the end of European colonization. The purpose of this is to illustrate to students that the plan in Cambodia under the Khmer Rouge is not a localized event that erupted in Cambodia, and stays in Cambodia. Rather, global ideological conflicts that originated at the end of World War II, struggles against colonization, and competing visions of nationalism collided, not just in Cambodia, but China, Viet Nam, and Korea, as well as in Africa and Latin America.

References

Appiah, Kwame. *The Ethics of Identity.* Princeton: Princeton University Press, 2005. Print.

Chandler, David. *Voices from S-21: Terror and History in Pol Pot's Secret Prison.* Berkeley: University of California Press, 2000. Print.

Foucault, Michel. *The Care of the Self: The History of Sexuality.* Volume 3. New York: Vintage Books, 1986. Print.

Lam, Andrew. "Child of Two Worlds." In *San Francisco Examiner*, 2000. Print.

Ong, Aihwa. *Buddha is Hiding: Refugees, Citizenship, and the New America.* Berkeley: University of California Press, 2003. Print.

Schlund-Vials, Cathy J. "A Transnational Hip Hop Nation: praCh, Cambodia, and Memorialising the Killing Fields," in *Life Writing*, Vol 5, No. 1 (April 2008). Print.

Smith-Henfer, Nancy. *Khmer American: Identity and Moral Education in a Diasporic Community.* Berkeley: University of California Press, 1999. Print.

Sontag, Susan. *Regarding the Pain of Others.* New York: Farrar, Starus and Giroux, 2003. Print.

Yamada, Teri Shaffer. "Trauma and Transformation: The Autobiographies of Cambodian Americans (1980-2010)," in Jonathan H. X. Lee, ed., *Cambodian American Experiences: Histories, Communities, Cultures, and Identities.* Dubuque: Kendall/Hunt, 2010. Print.

_____. "Modern Short Fiction of Cambodia: A History of Persistence," in Teri Shaffer Yamada, ed. *Modern Short Fiction of Southeast Asia: A Literary History.* Ann Arbor: Association for Asian Studies, 2009. Print.

_____. "Cambodian American Autobiography: Testimonial Discourse," in Xiaojing Zhou and Samina Najmi, eds. *Form and Transformation in Asian American Literature.* Seattle: University of Washington Press, 2005. Print.

Narratives of "Khmerness" and Cambodian American Identity

Christine M. Su

> I am proud to say
> "I'm a Khmer" with pride.
> because I, praCh,
> refuse to let my culture die!
>
> -praCh ly, Cambodian American rap artist

Introduction

For a few days during the third week of April, Cambodian American families and friends gather early in the morning to pray, chant, and make offerings to Buddhist monks dressed in saffron robes. In the afternoon, many of them adorned in beautiful silks or other traditional clothing, begin to dance, sing, perform dramas and comedic skits, play traditional games, and eat delicious Khmer food well into the night. The days or even weeks leading up to the festivities are filled with housecleaning, decorating, preparing special dishes and sweets, and buying or making new clothes that will be worn for the

---

Courtesy of praCh Ly. Reprinted with permission.

celebrations. For many, these occasions are much like those they experienced back in Cambodia, out in the countryside, sounds of Khmer music filling the air, sharing good food and conversation.[1] For others, the events are associated solely with their lives in the United States, the only country they have ever known as their homeland, but they are indelibly linked to their identity as Khmer.[2] The annual Khmer "New Year" (*chol chenam thmey*) holiday celebrates the end of the harvest season, and is appreciated by Cambodian Americans either because they lived the traditions and customs, or have listened to countless stories about them recounted by community elders.

These stories tell of times before war and political repression in Cambodia, for which the small Southeast Asian nation has become infamous. These were times before the Khmer Rouge—the Communist regime which overtook Cambodia from 1975-1979—during which their beloved traditions were banned, and their stories hidden deep within their hearts.[3] Given the upheaval Cambodian refugees endured in leaving Cambodia, however, and the feelings of helplessness, guilt, fear, loneliness, and sadness they felt as they attempted to comprehend their changed lives in a new American homeland, it is not surprising that they look to the past—or at least, to life before war—to define "traditional" Cambodian culture.

Certainly, Cambodia itself has grown and transformed in the years since 1979, and Cambodian society is neither the same as it was during nor before the atrocities of war.[4] While much of the population still lives in rural areas as rice farmers in small villages, Cambodia has kept pace with the modern world in many ways: students at all levels have the opportunity to study not only Khmer and English, but Japanese, Korean, and Chinese as well, and to meet and exchange ideas with others from around the globe; cell phones abound, even in much of the countryside; young Khmer generate Facebook pages and blogs discussing current events. Expat Khmer travel back and forth to Cambodia from the United States, Australia, France, and other countries to which they were relocated, and hundreds if not thousands of refugees repatriated to Cambodia in the 1990s to open businesses and schools and reunite with family members.[5]

Long since the waves of refugees arrived on American shores, too, a new generation of Khmer has been born and raised in the United States, and members of this generation live "Americanized" lives. Parents and grandparents lament that their youth have become *too* American, speaking slang English, eating American fast food, and wearing trendy Western clothing, for example. Yet when asked the question, "What is a Khmer?", Cambodian Americans of all ages tend to refer to the same customs, traditions, and stories, whether or not they conduct themselves in accordance with the codes and conventions related and espoused therein. More than 30 years later, the perception of what it truly is *to be Khmer* for Cambodians in the United States is still significantly informed by (idealized) memories and accounts of life in pre-war Cambodia, whether or not this perception reflects the reality of life in Cambodia today.[6] While it is important to resist essentialist notions of Khmer culture as something static, it is as important to acknowledge and respect what Ebihara, Mortland and Ledgerwood call survivors' "need to recreate an orderly universe," by returning to events, traditions, and practices that connect them to and mitigate the world around them (8). To explain who they are, Cambodians in the United States impart stories—narratives—about what it is that comprises Khmer identity, what makes them Khmer. As shall be discussed below, I call these *narratives of "Khmerness."* Cambodians in the United States use these narratives of Khmerness to determine or measure the extent to which one is, in their view, truly Khmer.

Narratives of "Khmerness"

In their introduction to *We Are a People: Narrative and Multiplicity in Constructing Ethnic Identity*, Paul Spickard and W. Jeffrey Burroughs write that "ethnicity—that powerful bond of peoplehood—is one of the most important forces organizing individual understandings of reality and the grouping and dividing of peoples in the world today" (1). Indeed, ethnicity helps us to situate ourselves and others, and define our relationships to each other; we form bonds because of it, fight wars over it, make and break laws concerning it. Yet importantly, the authors continue, "it is also true that no one seems to understand very well how ethnicity works." That is, what *is* ethnicity? Scholars have oscillated between interpretations of ethnicity as rooted in biology (ancestry and physical characteristics), society (group interests and institutions), and psychology (individual experience), and "there is at present no satisfactory theory that unites the field" (ibid.) Sociologist Stephen Cornell suggests that ethnicity might be more easily ascertained through *narrative(s)*, stories that peoples tell about themselves that somehow capture central understandings of what it means to be part of that (ethnic) group (42). Cornell writes that a narrative "is a story that can be told in many ways, but ultimately it can be reduced to something along the lines of 'we are the people who...'." Below I explore some of the *narratives of Khmerness* that Cambodians in the United States use to establish Khmer identity for themselves and communicate it to their progeny.[7] Through these narratives, Cambodians of varying generations and ages in the United States navigate and convey their knowledge of a cultural system that encompasses specific hallmarks, norms, rituals and rules that tell people they are Khmer.

I add one ancillary note to preface this section: particularly interesting about Cambodian identity is that it is, for the most part, not rooted in physical attributes. This is not to say that phenotype does not inform Cambodian identity, as there are some general or common physical traits that are expected of one who identifies him or herself as Khmer; however, one's identity is informed more consistently by the extent to how one manifests the *state of being Khmer*—one's "Khmerness."[8] I find this to be true in the United States as well as in Cambodia.

Narrative 1. *To be Khmer is to love Cambodia and its heritage.*

Above all else, Khmer love their country, and other Khmer. While Cambodia's physical and political borders have shifted, its officials designated and deposed, and its people scattered, there is still a discernable devotion to "Cambodia." In his seminal work on nationalism, Benedict Anderson wrote that the concept of a nation "is imagined because the members of even the smallest nation will never know most of their fellow-members, meet them, or even hear of them, yet in the minds of each lives the image of their communion" (5). There is something, some superlative shared sense of belonging, that binds hundreds of thousands of Khmer people together, whether urban or rural, rich or poor, male or female. Thus, Khmer in diaspora—be they young students studying at Japanese universities, repatriated Khmer raised in Europe, or generations of Cambodians living in the United States—remain linked to other Khmer by their fierce love of country, whether or not that "country" refers to an idealized Cambodia, and not necessarily to the nation-state and civil society as it currently exists.

Inherent in this expectation of love for country is knowledge of and admiration for the greatness of ancient Cambodia—the vast Khmer Empire of centuries past, and the culture and customs associated with it. In asking Cambodians the question, "What is a Khmer?,"9 their responses nearly always reference Cambodia's early history—and in particular, the Angkor period (the massive Angkor Wat temple, a monument to the Hindu god Siva, was built in the 12th century). Indeed, one would be hard pressed to find a Cambodian American home that does not have at least one painting or photograph of Angkor Wat hanging on its walls.

The walls of the Angkor monuments are covered with bas-reliefs of the stories of powerful kings and deities from Khmer mythology, and for Cambodians, Angkor hearkens back to a time of greatness, a time of strong kings who consolidated disparate territories throughout the Mekong Delta region into a vast Khmer kingdom. Thus to be Khmer is to recognize and acknowledge that Cambodia was once a dominant kingdom with vast landholdings and exceptional, godly leaders and builders.

Furthermore, the bas-reliefs of Angkor are lined with dancing *apsara*, beautiful celestial nymphs who in Cambodian cosmology danced and sang to mediate between humans and gods, and stone carvings of Cambodian musical instruments and ensembles, commemorating the importance of music and dance in Cambodian life. For hundreds of years, melodies and performance methods such as those chronicled at Angkor were passed on from one generation to the next, with master teachers transmitting Cambodian culture to eager pupils through movement and song. Khmer history and legends were often told through dance and music as well as through literature. To be Khmer is to love Khmer arts, dance, song, and music—with particular reverence for those of the eras described above, as these skills and traditions were passed down from generation to generation for centuries.

As a result, when nearly all of the artists died during the Khmer Rouge years, an integral part of Khmerness was lost. Those who spent much of their childhoods in the Khmer Rouge camps were deprived of traditional Khmer dance, music, literature, theatre, and crafts, such as textile weaving and metalwork. Thus it is not surprising that in seeking to rebuild their culture, Khmer in the United States seek out the arts, pooling resources to form dance troupes and music groups, for example; even for those who do not participate in the arts individually, they recognize their significance for Khmer identity. The act of listening to or playing Khmer music, for example, evokes a sense of connectedness to other Khmer. While many Cambodian Americans live on meager incomes and struggle to make ends meet (according to the 2000 U.S. Census, nearly 30 percent lived below the poverty line), they readily contribute their resources to support the arts in their communities. They raise funds to support visiting artists from Cambodia who survived the Khmer Rouge regime, and enroll their children in arts classes. There are Cambodian dance troupes in most if not all of the U.S. cities with significant Cambodian populations (i.e., Long Beach and San Jose, CA; Washington, D.C.; Lowell, MA; Philadelphia, PA; Seattle, WA, to name a few), and even those with relatively small populations (i.e., Honolulu, HI). Indeed, to be Khmer (American) is to love Cambodia and its heritage.

Narrative 2. *To be Khmer is to be Buddhist.*

Several noted scholars of Cambodian American life as well as Khmer history and culture have noted that "To be Khmer is to be Buddhist" (i.e., Smith-Hefner; Ebihara, Mortland, and Ledgerwood; Lee). The significance of Buddhism in traditional Cambodian life cannot be overstated. Theravada Buddhism came to dominate Cambodia in the 13th century. Theravada Buddhism teaches the writings of

Siddhartha Gautama, an Indian prince born into wealth and status in the 5th century BC, who renounced his right to the throne to become a religious seeker early in his life. He first sought out and studied the meditative and ritual practices of Brahman and other spiritual teachers, but attained "enlightenment" of his own volition, while meditating underneath a Bodhi tree. After reaching enlightenment, or *nirvana*, he became known as the Buddha, and became a spiritual teacher.

Buddhism teaches that one must proceed through a series of lives before he or she can reach nirvana, because of karma (*kam*), "the notion that one's actions in previous lives and the resulting store of merit (*bon*) that one has accumulated determine one's current life situation" (Smith-Hefner: 34). The late Venerable Maha Ghosananda, a renowned Khmer Buddhist monk, suggested that Khmer are reincarnated up to sixteen times before reaching nirvana. Cambodians in the United States continue to believe in *kam*, and perform rituals and participate in ceremonies to earn merit, which will help them in their journey toward nirvana.

In (pre-Khmer Rouge) Cambodia, the Buddhist *wat* (temple) served as the center of Cambodian life, as the nucleus of education, religion and spirituality, and local politics. The monks, followers of the Buddha and his teachings, disseminated cultural knowledge to the community at the *wat*, through Pali chants, the *chbap* (didactic verses), the *Gatiloke* (folktales), and epics such as the *Reamker* (the Khmer version of the Ramayana story). As with their support of the arts, Cambodian Americans have gone to great lengths to build temples within their communities—often erecting two or three within one community (Mortland: 171). They put Buddhist icons and designate areas of their homes for worship, and even build makeshift temples. In Hawai'i, for example, where there is neither a large community (according to the 2000 U.S. Census, there were fewer than 400 Cambodians there) nor a temple, community members spent countless hours constructing a temple out of scrap wood and donated materials in a secluded area, and it was regularly used for several years before permitting difficulties caused it to have to be dismantled. Some Cambodian Americans set up shrines in their homes, which then become "de facto" community temples (Lee: 115).

When asked when or in what situations they feel "very" Khmer, Cambodian Americans often mention going to and making offerings at the temple during different Buddhist holy days, which punctuate the Khmer calendar and give meaning to their lives. "In Khmer American communities," writes Lee, "Buddhist temples become repositories of Khmer culture, brokers in cultural adaptation, and centers of community solidarity and Khmer identity" (116). Indeed, to be Khmer (American) is to be Buddhist.

Narrative 3. *To be Khmer is to speak Khmer.*

When asked about their identity, Cambodians in the United States will often assert, "I know I am Khmer because I speak Khmer." While upon first reading this relationship between one's language and one's identity may seem obvious, note that Americans do not necessarily say, "I know I am American because I speak English" (i.e., native English speakers can be English, Canadian, Australian, New Zealander, etc.).

But for Cambodian Americans, *piasa-khmae* (Khmer language) is a source of great pride and a source of hope for retaining their culture, as it plays an essential role in shaping traditional Khmer life. The language is comprised of 33 consonants, 31 vowel configurations, and 14 "independent" vowels, plus a complex system of subscripts and diacritics (Huffman: 6-8). It is also very important to speak Khmer well, with proper syntax and intonation.

Perhaps most importantly, the structure and syntax of *piasa khmae* inform social interaction. The traditional Khmer speaking system reflects the Buddhist view that gods rank above humans and humans rank above animals, and this hierarchy is reflected in forms of address, honorifics, and special vocabularies, and also in the verb choices Khmer speakers make. Selection of pronouns and verbs is based primarily on age, but also on familial relationship, gender, status, and wealth. A sampling of terms of address appears in the following chart.

Figure 1. Terms of Address[10]

Term of reference	Used with	Additions to further classify the relationship	Used with
Bang	Those older than or relatively close in age to the speaker respectful)	Bang pros	Older male (formal)
		Bang srey	Older female (formal
P'aun	Those younger than or relatively close in age to the speaker (subordinate)	P'aun pros	Younger male (formal)
		P'aun srey	Younger female (formal)
Pu	Males slightly older than speaker but generally younger than or approximate age of one's father	Lok-Pu	Male, slightly older than speaker but younger than one's father (formal)
Ming	Females slightly older than speaker but generally younger than or approximate age of one's mother	Neak-ming	Females slightly older than speaker but generally younger than or approximate age of one's mother (formal)
Ohm	Males older than speaker and generally older than one's father	Lok ohm	Males older than speaker and generally older than one's father (formal)
Ohm	Females older than speaker and generally older than one's mother	Neak-ohm	Females older than speaker and generally older than one's mother (formal)
Neak	"you"; used with those of parallel status, usually only among friends	Neak eyeng or eyeng	"you"; used with those of parallel or subordinate status (casual); may be considered derogatory

Notably, one can change from *bang* to *p'aun* to *neak* to *pu* in the course of a single conversation among several people, depending upon who is speaking to whom. Indeed, when the Khmer Rouge attempted to eliminate most hierarchical speech, forcing people to call each other "comrade," rather than by the appropriate traditional pronouns, this caused Cambodians great distress.[11]

In addition to pronouns, there are also verbs specific to status, as below.

Figure 2. Variations of the verb "to eat"

King/royalty	Monks	People of higher or equal status (polite)	People of equal or lower status (informal/ also regional)	Animals		Khmer Rouge directive (for all—regardless of age or previous status)
Saoy	*Chan*	*Nyam*	*Hope*	*Si*		*Hope*

Older generations of Cambodian Americans do not see their ranked system of speaking as demeaning or confining; on the contrary, it enables one to know what to say and how to say it. Moreover, the "loss" of Khmer language to English is the source of much lament among Cambodian Americans, and as a result, Cambodian American communities support language classes, no matter how informal, to keep their Khmerness alive. In the United States, where "Southeast Asians" tend to be grouped together, even in studies about Asian Americans, *piasa khmae*, Cambodians say, differentiates Khmer from others: it is atonal, in contrast to the tonal dominant languages of Thai and Vietnamese, and all languages have culture-specific terms that cannot easily be translated, and are therefore uniquely Khmer. There are also dialectical variations that allow one to determine what part of Cambodia a person (or his or her family) comes from. Anecdotally, when meeting others for the first time (particularly members of the younger generation who may have been raised in the United States), how well he or she speaks Khmer is used to ascertain that individual's Khmerness. Often, if one speaks Khmer well, he or she is referred to as a *kaun khmae* (child of Cambodia), a term of endearment in praise of one's Khmerness. To be Khmer (American) is to speak Khmer.

Narrative 4: *To be Khmer is to be respectful, polite, patient, modest, and humble.*

Khmer believe there is something special and exemplary about their attitudes and behavior, and so too do Cambodian Americans believe and want to maintain this narrative of Khmerness. One's deportment is extremely important in determining one's "Khmerness." In pre-war Cambodia, Khmer children were taught the *chbap*, a set of moral codes emphasizing humility, patience, honesty, modesty and respectfulness both from their families and in schools, and Cambodians see their children's good behavior as a source of pride. In the United States, elders still use folktales and proverbs to teach accountability and responsibility; more often, proper Khmer behavior is discussed among community members and wayward actions chided, particularly when someone's behavior is deemed to run counter to Khmerness.

Respect for elders is particularly encouraged. For example, it is viewed as very important for Khmer to offer each other the *sompeah*, a gesture of respect in which an individual's hands meet in front of the face, often accompanied by a slight bow and the phrase, "*chumreap sour*" (a very polite form of hello). Traditionally, those of lower status take the initiative to *sompeah* those of higher status, who *sompeah* in return. Correspondingly, younger individuals *sompeah* older individuals, and the elderly are especially reverenced, with the hands meeting higher up on the face.[12] Cambodian American parents can often be seen teaching young children to *sompeah* their elders.

Another important element of this narrative is politeness and respect for others' feelings. Such qualities bring merit not only to oneself, but also to one's family (Keo: 10). One should act such that he or she will not anger others. Ideally, angry or loud face-to-face confrontation is to be avoided at all costs. One of the most despised acts a Khmer can commit is to *thvoe reuk*, to act overly proud or arrogant. Khmer often act to avoid becoming *khmas ke* (shamed by others) and also, to avoid making others *mien khmas ke* (made to feel ashamed).

The onus of this narrative often falls on the shoulders of Khmer women, and Cambodian American women are expected to be the culture-bearers of this ideal as well. Khmer women's narrative of Khmerness obliges them to be quiet, deferential, and modest. While in reality Cambodian women have exercised considerable independence and authority (women typically managed family finances, for example), the narrative is connected to visions and expectations of humility and timidity. Folktales, songs, and proverbs assert the merits of appropriate conduct and the dreadful consequences of inappropriate conduct. As one example, in 2010 a young Cambodian American woman appeared on an episode of "The Bachelor," a reality show in which an unmarried man chooses a bride from a group of women who try to woo him. In her attempts to court him, she made a very flirtatious (some might say uncouth) comment in Khmer language. Immediately Cambodians in the United States began to gossip amongst themselves, speaking of the inappropriateness of her behavior (some spoke not only of her comment, but of the fact that she participated on the show in the first place), the embarrassment she caused the Cambodian American community, and how her behavior was "not Khmer."[13] To be Khmer (American) is to be respectful, polite, patient, modest, and humble.

Narrative 5: *To be Khmer is to be flexible, to understand the impermanence of things, and thus to readily adapt to change.*

This "final" narrative is possibly the most vital. Actually, it is perhaps better described as a component of the other narratives. Thus, in as much as the narratives seem to dictate or limit "Khmerness," they actually allow for more expanded conceptions.

The much-loved Khmer history narrative, for example, is replete with illustrations of how what is "Khmer" is flexible, and through time has incorporated change. Southeast Asia for centuries served as a "crossroads of the world," with traders and explorers from across the globe landing in the area, bringing with them new materials, new ideas, new beliefs (Neher). Indian civilization spread into

Cambodia early on (some say as early as the first century BC), and Chinese travelers mention Cambodia as early as the 7th century. Cambodian culture has been influenced by a myriad of cultures, including Thai, Vietnamese, Portuguese (missionaries landed in Cambodia in the 15th century), French, Australian, British, and American.[14] Angkor, as discussed above, is an iconic representation of Khmerness. The Angkor complex itself, however, reflects different belief systems and monuments to various deities: Angkor Wat is a temple dedicated to Siva, the Hindu god of power and destruction, but the Bayon, built several centuries later, is a Buddhist temple. Moreover, the arts depicted on the temple were not (and are not) the only arts of Cambodia: folk music and dance have been created and practiced far from Angkor, and these, too, contribute to the narrative of Khmerness. In stating that "to be Khmer is to love Cambodia," certainly these "folk" arts are included in that which is considered Khmer.

Khmer Buddhism itself, deemed essential to Khmerness, is a merged religion. When King Jayavarman VII made Buddhism the state religion, it had already incorporated elements of Hinduism and Khmer animistic beliefs. For centuries, Buddhist ceremonial offerings have been made to the *neak-ta*, spirits associated with hills or trees, where they take up residence (Mabbett and Chandler: 108). Furthermore, Buddhism teaches that life is impermanent (that is, we are caught in a cycle of birth and death and reincarnation, often changing forms from human to animal or vice-versa), and thus, what we "know" as truth is always changing. Only when we let go of the desire to know and accept impermanence and uncertainty can followers reach *nirvana*.

Khmer language reflects early Cambodia's diverse history and influences as well. *Piasa khmae* is laden with numerous Sanskrit and Pali words, and the Khmer borrowed and indigenized many French words introduced during the colonial period, as well as Chinese, Vietnamese, and English words, altered to fit Khmer pronunciation and intonation. In short, Khmer language is a fascinating conglomerate reflective of Cambodia's colorful past. Yet it is most definitely a signifier of Khmerness.

Finally, regarding proper Khmer demeanor and behavior: certainly, as various travelers arrived on the shores of the Khmer Empire, the Khmer had to adopt customs and manners that differed from their own in order to be respectful to their visitors. Intermarriage between Khmer and Chinese and other ethnicities was not uncommon, and certainly, some of the customs of these cultures were incorporated into "Khmer" behavior. The narrative of Khmerness about women's "proper" behavior, too, which is depicted in the didactic *chbap srey* as follows: "women are to walk slowly and softly, be so quiet in their movements that one cannot hear the sound of their silk skirt[s] rustling..." also acknowledges that women are capable, "industrious" members of Khmer society. Indeed, the Chinese emissary Zhou Daguan, who visited Cambodia in the 13th century, commented on the entrepreneurial prowess of Khmer women, writing that "in Cambodia it is the women who take charge of trade. For this reason a Chinese, arriving in the country, loses no time in getting himself a mate, for he finds her commercial instincts a great asset" (Siam Society: 43).

Here we see that the so-called "limitations" implied in the narratives also allow for (indeed, encourage) flexibility. To be Khmer (American) is to be flexible, to understand the impermanence of things, and thus to readily adapt to change.

New Ambassadors

While the narratives of Khmerness in their narrowest interpretation call to mind an idealized pre-war Cambodia, in reality Cambodians in the United States have, both of necessity and opportunity, developed broader answers to the question, "What is a Khmer?" As they have in the past, the narratives will bend to accept societal norms as well as to try to shape them. Importantly, changing narratives (or perhaps more accurately, making changes within the narratives) do not negate one's identity as Khmer. Rather, while the narratives can still be used to inform Khmerness, Cambodian Americans, recognizing that the narratives are constantly being revised and changed, need not use them to control it. Cornell notes that "as groups' understandings of themselves and others change, so do the narratives in which those understandings are encapsulated and through which they are given substance" (Cornell 44). Thus, as Cambodians continue to navigate their lives in the United States, they may in the present and future, as they have in the past, revise their narratives of Khmerness.

Moreover, as the narratives change, so too may their ambassadors. In the epitaph to this article, young Cambodian American rapper praCh ly's lyrics express his desire to keep Cambodian culture alive. While his work is in a format perhaps unfamiliar to the older generation of Khmer, he too participates in and contributes to narratives of Khmerness. And while the medium for his message is worlds apart from the classical dances of Angkor Wat and the traditional folktales told by his elders, his intentions are the same. His lyrics reflect Cambodian (American) life, and while respecting the value of erstwhile narratives, he is also helping to revise them. He is a new ambassador, a culture-bearer—and perhaps most importantly, a narrator.

> I inherited all of this,
> the knowledge of the facts.
> Being a Khmer that I am,
> I feel the weight on my back.
> But look what we're building,
> right here in Long Beach -
> a Cambodian Town,
> down Anaheim Street.
> The seed has been planted,
> the foundation has been laid,
> all it takes is time. . .
>
> from "Art of Fact," *Dalama...the lost chapter.*
> praCh ly, 2003

Endnotes

1. While in the 21st century many Khmer in Cambodia celebrate the new year in the cities, urban dwellers usually go to the countryside during Khmer New Year, either returning to their native villages or, if they were brought up in Phnom Penh, accompanying rural-born friends to their home villages. As a commemoration of the end of the rice harvest, new year (*chol chenam thmey*) is a celebration of rural life.

2. The term *Khmer* is the phrase the people of Cambodia use to refer to themselves. In native language, it is pronounced "khmae," the "r" being silent. "Cambodian" is an Anglicization of *Cambodge*, the French term for Cambodia, and *les cambodiens/cambodiennes*, their term for the people of *Cambodge*. In this essay, I use "Khmer" and "Cambodian" interchangeably.

3. Certainly, the Khmer Rouge regime (1975-1979) serves for many Cambodians as the watershed period or dividing line between "normal" life and the nightmare of the killing fields and subsequent upheaval as refugees. However, civil war in the early 1970s also disrupted many Cambodian lives, and often, when speaking about what they believe to be the "true" Cambodia, they are referring not only to pre-1975, but also the pre-1970 (pre-war) period.

4. See, for example, *Tradition and Change: Khmer Identity and Democracy in the 20th Century and Beyond* , my study of contemporary society in Cambodia (University of Hawai'i, 2003).

5. In 1989, the Vietnamese, who had occupied Cambodia since late 1979, left Cambodia, which looked toward independent governance. With the aid of the international community, national Cambodian elections were held in 1993, followed by additional, domestically-managed elections in 1998 and 2003. Whether Cambodia is a truly democratic country is the subject of much scholarly (and grassroots) debate, but most would agree that Cambodia became much more open, especially by the late 1990s, than it had been for the past several decades.

6. There is insufficient space here to more fully discuss the dissonance between what Cambodians in the United States believe "Khmerness" is versus the reality of life in a changed Cambodia. For an excellent analysis of this issue, see Carol A. Mortland's "Legacies of Genocide for Cambodians in the United States," in *Cambodia Emerges from the Past: Eight Essays*, edited by Judy Ledgerwood (2002: 151-175).

7. Cornell's analysis focuses on narrative as stories about events. He writes that narrative's "primary idiom is *events*: the things the group does or did or will do or had done to it" (42, emphasis mine). I interpret the term "events" quite liberally, to include participation in belief systems, customs and traditions, rather than only large-scale historical events (while certainly not excluding these). For example, certainly being Khmer for many Cambodians includes the narrative of genocide/the Khmer Rouge regime. However, I also use narrative to refer to stories about how *to be Khmer is to be Buddhist*. Narrative reflects what a people believe and how they act, as well as situating them as participants in specific historic events.

8. Sherri Prasso asserts that in Cambodia, as in some other Asian countries, there tends to be a preference for lighter complexions, and anecdotally, I have also found this to be the case; however, in more in-depth surveys I conducted, "true" Khmer were described as dark- as well as fair-complexioned, yellow-complexioned, and "bean-color" complexioned. This is indicative of Khmer awareness of a mixed and varied heritage, and that in determining Khmerness, physical characteristics, if mentioned at all, were certainly less important than other attributes.

9. In 2009, I conducted a preliminary survey of approximately 200 members of the Cambodian Community of Hawai'i and compiled the results. Among the list of questions included in the survey was "What does it mean to be Cambodian/Khmer?" and "How do you know whether or not someone is Khmer?" Hundred percent of the respondents mentioned reverence for Angkor Wat and what it represents (i.e., Khmer greatness) as an element of Khmer identity. While the responses should not be viewed as representative of all Cambodian Americans or even Cambodians in other states, anecdotal evidence with Cambodians in various cities across the United States also supports this assertion. For more information on the survey, please contact the author.

10. This is just a sampling, not an exhaustive list, of Khmer pronouns, and the chart is certainly not definitive. Some will undoubtedly disagree with my categorizations. However, I very humbly introduce it here only as a tip-of-the-iceberg example to provide insight as to how Khmer language informs interactions, and how for Cambodian Americans, at least speaking (if not also reading and writing) Khmer language well is an indicator of "Khmerness."

11. The Khmer Rouge overturned the hierarchical language system, insisting people call each other *mit* (comrade) rather than using pronouns that

reflected age, gender, and status. This overturned Cambodians' understanding of social order, and how individuals should related to each other.

12. Some Khmer point out that there are a number of specific styles of *sompeah*. Moul Jetl, for example, writes the following: 1) *angkuoy baott cheung sompeah cham pee muk*, which literally translates as "sitting on the
legs which are folded, feet to one side, with a salute by placing both
hands together palm to palm in front of a person; 2) *angkuoy boatt cheung sompeah pee cham-hieng*, which translates as sitting on the legs which
are folded, feet to one side, with a salute by placing both hands together
palm to palm to the side of a person; 3) *lut chung-kung sompeah*, which
translates to kneeling and saluting by placing both hands together palm
to palm in front of or to the side of a person; 4) *Angkuoy choang-hoang
sompeah*, literally translated as sitting on one's heels in a hunched-down
manner with a salute formed by placing both hands together palm to
palm in front of a person.

13. Personal communications, January 2010. Of note is that when I mentioned to a few Cambodian Americans that I was including this incident
in this article, they asked me not to reveal exactly what was stated by the
young woman, as it would "make us look bad"—a negative reflection on
Khmerness.

14. Jan Knappert rightly states, however, that Southeast Asians "were not
merely the passive recipients of ideas, practices and materials from outside the region," but rather "adapted, reworked, and transformed the raw
material[s] with which there were presented" (paraphrased in King, vi-
vii). Thus, the Khmer entertained new things, and if they felt they were
appropriate, incorporated them into Khmer culture.

References

Anderson, Benedict. *Imagined Communities: Reflections on the Origin and
Spread of Nationalism*. London: Verso, 1983. Print.

Chou, Ta-Kuan. *The Customs of Cambodia*. 2nd edition. Trans. Paul Pelliot
of Chou's Chinese original by J. Gilman d'Arcy Paul. Bangkok: The
Siam Society, 1992. Print.

Cornell, Stephen. "That's the Story of Our Life." In *We are a People: Narra-
tive and Mulitiplicity in Constructing Ethnic Identity*, edited by Paul R.
Spickard and W. Jeffrey Burroughs. Philadelphia: Temple University
Press, 2000. Print.

Ebihara, May, Carol A. Mortland, and Judy Ledgerwood, eds. *Cambodian Culture Since 1975: Homeland and Exile*. Ithaca: Cornell University Press, 1994. Print.

Keo, Sopheap. "Child Rearing and Discipline among Cambodian Americans." Khmer Institute, 2003. Web; 12 April 2010.

King, Victor T. "Foreward." In *Mythology and Folklore in South-East Asia*. By Jan Knappert. New York: Oxford University Press, 1999. Print.

Lee, Jonathan H.X. "Religion, Cambodian American." In *Asian American History and Culture: An Encyclopedia*, edited by Huping Ling and Allan Austin. Armonk: M.E. Sharpe, 2010. Print.

Ly, PraCh. "Art of Fact." *Dalama...the lost chapter*. PraCh Ly, 2003. CD.

Mabbett, Ian, and David Chandler. *The Khmers*. Chiang Mai, Thailand: Silkworm Books, 1996. Print.

Mortland, Carol A. "Legacies of Genocide for Cambodians in the United States." In *Cambodia Emerges from the past: Eight Essays*, edited by Judy Ledgerwood. DeKalb: Southeast Asia Publications, 2002. Print.

Moul, Jetl. "Sampeah: Khmer Salutations." In *Leisure Cambodia*. May 2002. Vol. 2 (5). Web; 12 April 2010.

Neher, Clark D. *Southeast Asia: Crossroads of the World*. DeKalb: Center for Southeast Asian Studies, Northern Illinois University, 2000. Print.

Prasso, Sherri. *Violence, Ethnicity, and Ethnic Cleansing: Cambodia and the Khmer Rouge*. Cambridge: University of Cambridge, 1995. Print.

Smith-Hefner, Nancy. *Khmer American: Identity and Moral Education in a Diasporic Community*. Berkeley: University of California Press, 1999. Print.

Spickard, Paul R., and W. Jeffrey Burroughs. "Introduction." In *We are a People: Narrative and Mulitiplicity in Constructing Ethnic Identity*. Philadelphia: Temple University Press, 2000. 1-19. Print.

Su, Christine M. "Tradition and Change: Khmer Identity and Democracy in the 20th Century and Beyond." Unpublished dissertation. University of Hawaii, Manoa, 2003.

Section X

Cambodian American Families, Genders, and Sexualities

CHAPTER 23

Khmer American Marriage Arrangements and Morality

Nancy Smith-Hefner

Khmer parents have deep anxieties about the marriages of their children. To understand these anxieties, one must look closely at the much debated issue of marriage arrangements. Such arrangements highlight important aspects of Khmer cultural change in the United States, especially as regards gender ideology and individuality.

Although their memories are most certainly idealized, Khmer elders insist that before the war and the period of dislocation, parents arranged most Khmer marriages. In extreme cases, the bride and sometimes even the groom had never seen the betrothed before the engagement ceremony. More commonly, he had seen her at a temple ceremony or at the wedding of a relative or he knew of her from school and had asked his parents to make the arrangements with her family.

[Female, age 50] In Cambodia, I lived with my aunt and took care of my mother; she had a stroke and she couldn't walk or anything. My husband—the one who would be my husband—lived in the same neighborhood. He worked like a blacksmith, something with iron. He saw me at a New Year's celebration and decided to get someone to ask about marrying me. He had an older couple, his relatives I think, come to ask my aunt and my mother if he could marry me.

My mother came to me and said, "You have to marry him, because I am very old, and I am sick. If you marry him, you will have someone to take care of you when I die."

I said, "OK, if you want me to marry him, I will listen to you." I agreed even though I hated him (*khnyōm s'âb kât*). I had never talked to him, but I heard he had a lot of girlfriends—that's why I hated him. But he promised in front of my mother that if he married me, he would stop having girlfriends. He swore he was a good man.[1]

In such discussions of marriage arrangements, the theme of filial piety emerges quite strongly. To convince a child to marry, parents often remind the child that the parents are getting old and might pass away before the child has married. (Particularly during Pol Pot's era, parents justifiably feared that they would not be able to support or protect their children for long, especially daughters, and so pressured them to marry.) Women and men who agreed to an arranged marriage often say that they accepted their parents' decision because they trusted them to make the best choice and because they "owed that to them" for the sacrifices their parents had made over the years.

[Female, age 45] When my mother asked me, did I want to marry him, I said, "It's up to you, Mom. I am your daughter. I am willing to do what you say, even if you give me to a blind man." I believed totally in my parents. I trusted them completely.

For their part, parents say that "according to Buddhism," it is the parents' duty to arrange for their children's future before their own deaths. If parents see their children settle happily into a family of their own, parents say, they can die peacefully. Khmer even say that if parents die without fulfilling this duty, their souls will not find release.

> [Male, age 50] Parents want to see their children marry before they die. If the child is not married and the parent dies, their spirit will not rest peacefully. Their eyes will still be open, and the spirit will stay around the house to take care of their children. They say they can't close their eyes because they miss their children.
>
> Just like my neighbor. She lived two houses away from here. When she died, her spirit stayed around, and one family who lived nearby had a dream about that. In the dream, the soul of the mother said, "Oh, I miss my children so much. I can't go anywhere until my youngest daughter marries." [The daughter's wedding had been arranged before the mother died but had not yet taken place.]
>
> I was invited to that celebration as a good friend of the family, but the night before the wedding, I was so tired from work and I fell asleep on the couch. At 8:30 the next morning, the spirit of the mother came to wake me up: "Pho, come on, you have to go to my daughter's wedding to witness the ceremony of the ancestors (*phtõem*)." So I had to hurry and rush over to their house to see that, even though it was already 10:00 by the time I got ready.
>
> A lot of people had dreams about that woman before her daughter's wedding, but after the wedding, nobody saw the mother anymore. After the wedding, her spirit could rest peacefully.

Beneath the surface of this parental concern lies the conviction that children who are married and comfortably settled are more likely to have the stability and disposition to care for an ailing or elderly parent. Parents hope that if they provide a large and expensive wedding, their children will remember and care for them in their final years. Wedding guests act as witnesses to the union, but they are also expected to ensure that the couple stays together, offering wisdom and advice to the couple if they experience marital difficulties. The larger the wedding, the more guests invited; hence, the more community members who will shoulder this important responsibility.

Weddings, then, are a form of social security and insurance against abandonment in one's old age (see also Hanks 1963:68). Parents often link these two themes quite explicitly. If others point out this connection, however, parents deny that they see the two issues that way. (According to Buddhist doctrine, people should give or make offerings with a pure heart and without any thought of compensation; this includes giving one's children in marriage.)

The following comments, for example, came from a widow whose twenty-year-old son ran away to live with his girlfriend in another state. I asked the woman, "What would you do if your son came to ask you to put on a wedding for him?" Here is her response:

[Female, age 47] I would ask him, "Where is the money? Do you have the money?" No, I would not pay for that! It used to be that you could depend on your child to think of you, to care for you in your old age. Now they just forget about you like that [like my son did]. In the United States, it's no good. We cannot depend on our children here.

It is this functional logic of intergenerational reciprocity that is under particular strain in the Khmer American community today. Fewer and fewer Khmer marriages are arranged completely by parents; among eastern Massachusetts Khmer, the average appears to have fallen to less than one in five. In an increasingly common pattern, a young man and woman meet at school or at repeated social or religious functions. They fall in love and decide to marry. It is still critical, however, that the couple maintain the appearance of propriety and behave in a way that does not shame their families.

Within these altered circumstances, parents still make formal wedding arrangements, and young people continue to seek their elders' blessings (see also Ledgerwood 1990a:180). Few would attempt to stage a Khmer wedding without their parents' traditional knowledge and expertise—and extended social and financial support.

Considerations of filial piety, face, and status make marriage negotiations a source of significant conflict for Khmer American families. In either accepting the parents' choice of marital partner or in obtaining her parents' blessings for her own choice, the child fulfills her responsibility and indicates that she will continue to remember her parents in their old age and after death. Because unmarried young men are viewed as less responsible with regard to their filial obligations than young women, it is particularly important to ensure that sons marry "good girls," ones who will readily assume this supportive role. In the eyes of Khmer parents, however, "good girls" are in increasingly short supply in the United States. As a result, many, perhaps most, of the disputes that have arisen over marriage arrangements are ostensibly focused on the behavior of young women.

The Double Standard

A majority of Khmer parents continue to have traditional attitudes about the comportment of young women, particularly where their own sons or daughters are concerned. Because of the prevailing double standard, people commonly blame women in virtually all cases of sexual misconduct, and, in a typically market-charged idiom, say that women "lose their value" when they violate sexual norms. By contrast, Khmer men remain uncompromised in such escapades. This double standard is clear in the well-known Khmer saying *"Satrey tae thleak knong phok chroam sa'uy brachrah khâl; ae mnuh broh venh thleak knog phok chroam, dauch mea neov paa dadael"* ("A girl who falls in the filth smells against the wind; a boy who falls in the filth is like gold, its color remains.")

Many Khmer believe that because of a woman's more passionate nature, she is unable to control herself if she falls in love. One father graphically explained the dangerous potency of a young woman's sexuality by commenting, "An unmarried daughter is like spoiled meat (*sach sâvy*) in the house," attracting men as spoiled meat attracts flies.

> [Female, age 21] Cambodians think women can't control themselves when they are in love. So if they get pregnant, it isn't the man's fault. They blame only the woman, not the man.
>
> [Female, age 20] Cambodians believe that when a woman falls in love, she loves that guy 100 percent, and nothing else matters. She can't control herself. So if she falls in love, she should marry right away.

In contrast to this view of women, it is accepted that men are promiscuous by nature. A common Khmer proverb states, "Ten rivers can't equal [fill] one ocean." That is, even ten women cannot satisfy one man. Men joke about their sexual infidelities, saying, "A man can't eat *s'lah mchou* (Cambodian sour soup) everyday." Conversely, women are cautioned never to believe the words of a man: "Just as the stream never stops flowing, a man's promises should never be trusted" (see also Ledgerwood 1990a:111). Knowing of men's promiscuous nature, women who let themselves become involved with men are always considered to be at fault.

> [Female, age 50] We believe it's the girl's fault if she behaves inappropriately in front of a man. That's why the man is attracted to her and follows her. We accuse the girl, not the man. It's the girl who shows off her body. It's the girl who has to be firm, [who] has to stay away from men. It's her fault if the man is attracted.

Thus, although women are deemed the more passionate gender by nature, they are always expected to keep their passion under control and to avoid men who would compromise their virtue.

Both ethnographic reports and the memories of contemporary Khmer indicate that, to preserve this virtue, girls in Cambodia were subject to considerably more social supervision than they are in the United States (see chapter 4; see also Steinberg 1959; Ebihara 1974). Women often say of their youth, "We didn't know anything," "We were too shy," and "We didn't say anything." Unmarried women report they were barred even from seeing childbirth. Because of fears that knowledge of sex would encourage female promiscuity, most say they were told nothing about sex before marriage. One woman confided that she assumed that people married because the man needed someone to cook and keep house for him. Another thought that after marriage she would "just sleep next to her husband as she had slept next to her mother." Some said that the *achaa's* wife or an elder relative "gave them some advice" on their wedding night, but it was not necessarily helpful.

[Female, age 60] My older aunt said, "You have to respect your husband, the way he does something. You have to accept the way he does it and just keep quiet."

[Female, age 50] The old people just told me, "You have to stay in the room with him. Don't get out from that room, and don't yell or anything to shame your family."

Not all young women were so timid and ignorant, of course. Pregnant brides were not unheard of, and young women sometimes ran away with their lovers or refused to marry the man of their parents' choice. Such themes are common in Khmer folklore and literature, as well as in popular songs and movies. Nevertheless, adults use such idealized memories of life in Cambodia as a standard against which they judge the behavior of Khmer American youth. The ideals sometimes stand in painful contrast with the changing realities that adults and youths now confront.

Endnotes

1. In this and other engagement stories that older women tell, the woman often insists that she "hated" her fiancé before the wedding. Such claims seem to allow a woman to emphasize that she had an appropriate distance from the engagement process.

References

Smith-Hefner, Nancy. *Khmer American: Identity and Moral Education in a Diasporic Community.* Berkeley: University of California Press, 1999. Print.

CHAPTER 24

Out of the Killing Fields, Out of the Closet:
A Personal Narrative on Finding Identity as a Gay Cambodian American

Michael S. Sar

There is a common misconception among heterosexuals that once a homosexual comes out of the metaphorical closet all the work is done and that person can then live an openly gay life. The coming out process is not that simple. I like to equate it to the long hallway filled with locked doors in *Alice in Wonderland*. Although one may open one door, there is still a long corridor to walk before all the doors are opened. Unlike celebrities who can announce their sexuality to the world by simply holding a press conference, for most people the first announcement of one's coming out will not reach everyone at once. In my journey down that hallway of doors, I have opened several doors—some I have kicked down, pushed through, and others only cracked open. To understand my coming out process, it is important to first understand the identity that shapes who I am: Cambodian American.

The Cambodian American Dream

My family escaped Cambodia to avoid becoming casualties of a genocide that plagued the country during the reign of the Khmer

Rouge (1975–1979). I still remember my father telling me the story of how our family came to the United States. His face was expressionless, and there was sadness in his eyes. The story sounded like something that happened only in the movies and I was overcome with emotion to know that my family had experienced it firsthand. I was simultaneously coping with a sense of sadness and pride that came with learning of my parents' experience. I knew then, as I know now that it profoundly shaped my family and the person I would become.

When I was 10 years-old, I became curious about the circumstances that brought my family from Cambodia to America. My father took me to a showing of *The Killing Fields*, a film about the Cambodian genocide. The movie stuck with me and the following day I asked my father if this genocide was the reason our family came to America. He showed me a black and white photograph of his family sitting in a hut and said, "Son, you see this picture of your grandparents and your uncles and aunts?" I studied the picture and saw that it was a big family with relatives that I had never met before. I nodded my head and continued to listen. "They are victims of the Killing Fields. Your uncle and I are the only two who survived of all the people in this picture, and your uncle blames himself for that."

He continued to tell me that, because of their connections to an American group that helped refugees escape, his immediate family and my uncle's family managed to escape Cambodia to a refugee camp in Thailand. When my uncle went looking for his parents and siblings, witnesses told him that a group of Khmer Rouge soldiers had taken the family into the jungle, where they disappeared and were never again heard from. My father told me that my uncle blames himself, thinking that if he had returned sooner, they might still be alive. My family finally arrived in America in 1981, just in time for me to be born on U.S. soil weighing only 4 pounds.

With this new-found knowledge, I concluded that pleasing my parents was the least I could do in light of the trauma and terror they had endured. Because of their sacrifices, I had been born in a land of opportunity, not one of imminent death. The struggles my uncle and father had gone through to get us to America became ingrained in my mind. My awareness of the sacrifices they had made reinforced the importance of living up to the image of the "good" Cambodian man I knew they expected me to become. I grew up knowing that I was expected to be polite, respectful, and eventually become a pharmacist to support a wife and children.

Having to start from scratch in a brand new country was a challenge that my family had to face. We were out of our element and made the best of what we were forced to deal with. My family started off in Los Angeles, where we were the only Asian family in a predominantly Latino neighborhood. Later, we moved to Long Beach, home to the largest Cambodian community in the United States. Initially, we were extremely poor, always cutting corners to make ends meet. However, my father was determined to change this and build a better life for his family, despite the many obstacles and hardships we faced—poverty, divorce, and later my sexual orientation.

Recognizing I'm Different

The question of my sexuality was on my mind for most of my life, sensing I was different from other boys. I never seemed to fit in with any of my male classmates regardless of how hard I tried to be like them. The role I was expected to play in my family was that of a heterosexual Cambodian American, not a gay one. But struggling with my attraction to other guys made it difficult for me to be that person I was expected to be. Although deep down I always knew I was attracted to guys, the term "gay" invoked other feelings and I could not bring myself to say I was gay. Growing up I did not personally know any homosexuals. My brother and I used to call each other "faggot" when we fought, which in our family was considered to be the worst insult possible. My idea of what a gay man was like was from television and I associated homosexuals with being outcasts. Comedy shows such as *In Living Color* portrayed homosexuals as flamboyant, dressed in feminine clothing, and speaking with lisps. The regular occurrence of hate crimes against gays that I saw on the news shaped my idea of gay life even more. The torture and murder of Matthew Shepard in 1998 hit me particularly hard. I was in my junior year of high school at the time and became terrified of being victim to such a crime. I wanted desperately to fit in and I longed for a "normal" life—one I knew I could never have if I were gay.

Family Expectations

I vividly remember the first time my father discussed the possibility of my marrying a woman he would hand-pick from Cambodia. My brother and I had been sitting in our room when our father walked in and began talking to us about his expectations for our futures. I was thirteen years old, sitting at the desk my parents had bought especially for me because they felt it was important for their sons to have a professional work space to do their homework. "Boys, I want you to be the best that you can be in life," said my father. "I want you to be successful, go to college, and get respectable careers." My brother and I just sat there listening like good Cambodian sons. "Shane, I know you will make me proud and become a great doctor," he said to my brother. "Michael, pharmacists make really good money and I think you would be good at it. I see you doing that." Although I did not want to be a pharmacist, I figured this is what would make my parents happy so I agreed to oblige them.

My father went on to say, "You two are going to be great family men, but no dating until you finish college. When you do, your mother and I will pick good women from respectable families for you to marry. When your mother and I become old, we won't be able to take care of ourselves, and it is your duty to care for us. That is the Cambodian way. Family will always take care of each other." Admittedly, I was relieved to hear that I was not allowed to date because that gave me an excuse not to date girls. Thereafter, I used that prohibition as an excuse when my friends wondered why I wasn't dating. I was not thrilled about the part where I was expected to marry a Cambodian woman, but I figured I had time to deal with it.

Always knowing I was attracted to guys, I could not see myself marrying a woman of my parents choosing—or, any woman, really. I remember having a crush on my first grade teacher, Mr. Z, and deciding that I would forever stay single. I could not marry a woman, but I could not come out to my family because it would ruin my parents. So the reasonable plan was to just stay single forever and, to save my parents from the shame of having a gay son, make up excuses about why I could not find the "right" woman. However, not having grandchildren would be difficult for my parents as well. Although this had seemed to be a reasonable plan, I would come to realize that hiding this part of my true self would not be simple. My parents did not discuss their marriage plans for me again until I was in my early twenties, and by then they had selected a potential wife for me.

Keeping Up the Façade

My high school years were difficult on several accounts. When I was fourteen, my parents divorced because my father was having an affair with another woman. My entire concept of family was shattered and I was devastated. After discovering my father's infidelity, I viewed him as a hypocrite and stopped caring about the standards he held for me, spending most of my teen years alone in my room and growing increasingly alienated from my family. Because of my secret, I could not relate to any males my own age. I had more in common with the girls in my class, although to avoid being discovered or stereotyped as gay, I did not want to socialize with them.

Despite my attempts to fit in I found myself an outcast and a loner. The importance of gossip and image in Cambodian culture and the secret I so carefully guarded prevented me from relating to the Cambodian kids at school, fearing the gossip that would ensue should my true identity be revealed.

When my father went from being a brave hero to a villain who shattered my perception of family, I began to resent my culture. The pride I had once felt for those brave men and women who had escaped genocide to begin their lives anew was replaced by disgust for the incessant gossip and the constant emphasis on image and need to outdo one another, so prevalent in the Cambodian community.

Opening the First Door

In my last two years of high school, my two closest friends were Cambodian girls. I always made a point to keep my attraction to guys a secret. To ensure that my sexual identity was never questioned, I confided to each of them that I had romantic feelings for the other, which seemed to successfully keep my identity safe throughout my high school years. The problem, however, was that I spent those four years so focused on making it through high school undiscovered, that I overlooked considering what would happen afterwards. I needed a plan to live the rest of my life in secret, but I was aware that it was near impossible. I had survived high school, but in a state of constant depression, so guarded that I could not let anyone get to know the true me. My home life was not any better; after school, I secluded myself in my room, avoiding my mother so she could never ask if I had a girlfriend. I was so sick of my secret, yet I was deathly afraid of how my entire life would change if it was revealed. Keeping a secret for eighteen years, lying to those you love, and not being able to feel free was not bearable. For a long time I fantasized about telling someone, but reality made it impossible. One day during the summer after high school, I was so depressed that I found myself contemplating suicide. I knew I could not go on feeling utterly alone, so I finally admitted to myself and someone else that I am gay.

I sat in my room struggling to make sense of my feelings of fear, anxiety, and wanton disregard, waiting a long time before dialing my best friend, Cathleen. When I told her that I needed to meet up with her, she replied that I sounded strange. I began pacing back and forth in my room, my heart palpitating. Finally, I told her I had carried a secret for a long time that I had never told anyone. She started guessing: Did you commit a crime? Did something happen in your family? Do you have a crush on me? I replied no to all of her inquiries. "Can we just meet in person?" I asked.

Then she uttered the question I had both hoped for and dreaded, "Are you gay?"

I started shaking. I could feel my legs quivering so I sat down on the floor, blood rushed to my face, time slowed. I replied, "I like guys."

Cathleen noted that she had only been kidding, but then she said "Whatever Michael, you're still you. It's all good."

Immediately, after my world had seemed to crumble upon itself, I was overcome by a sense of relief. I had finally shared my secret with someone and she had not stopped loving me. The world, my world, had not ended. I felt empowered knowing that some day I could tell others and maybe they would continue to accept me as well. A few months later I told my other best friend, who, like Cathleen, was also Cambodian. While I received the same reaction from her, I could tell she found it hard to accept. This made me uneasy and I decided that having two people know was enough; I continued to keep up the straight ruse for everyone else.

Embracing My Two Identities

During college, I began to realize that much of my resentment toward my Cambodian culture stemmed from the Cambodian boys I had purposefully not socialized with in high school because of my sexual identity. I somehow reached an epiphany in my early twenties, realizing that I needed to stop giving those guys so much power. I could not change my ethnicity, but I could learn to take pride in it again.

Wanting to have a social life and be a part of something, I joined the Cambodian Student Society. I became very active and eventually ran and won the vice presidency of the largest Cambodian student group in the country. A whole new world opened up for me. I became involved with the Cambodian community in Long Beach, who considered me a youth leader. Throughout this time, I did not share my sexual identity with any of my peers because I knew it was still a touchy subject in our culture and I saw no compelling reason that they should know. However, during a club retreat I shared a special moment of bonding with the club president in which I decided to tell her, in strict confidence, that I was gay. Although I was tired of keeping my secret, through this confidence, I was "out-ted" accidentally.

During a club cabinet meeting, the subject turned to a male member of the Associated Students. I was speaking of him with admiration when the president suddenly blurted out, "Michael, are you attracted to him?" I was stunned at her public comment, trying to think of a way to diffuse the situation. Aware of her blunder, she began to blush. The other cabinet members began to figure out what was happening and I was forced to openly proclaim it, asking them to keep it private among cabinet members only, yet knowing they would certainly gossip. Months later, I decided to out myself fully and publicly. I used MySpace to reach the widest audience of friends that I could, simply updating the "About Me" section with the following statement:

> I guess the time has come where I'm about to burst and shout it out from roof tops . . . "I'm coming out of the closet!" I don't know if this is the perfect way to do it or whatever, but this is only one of the many steps I will be making in life. Damn, when signing onto MySpace, I never would have thought I'd be putting this on here. Anyway, where's a drag queen when you need one? Message to anyone who knows me: I'm still the same guy and I've always known about my gayness so there is no change in me. It is only ONE part of my life. So for any of you idiots who have not caught on yet, I'M GAY. AH fuck, I did it. What a release! Can someone pass me a cigarette? Was it good for you too?

I knew announcing it on MySpace would reach a large audience, but I was not fully prepared for just how big. Several people who knew me from high school commented on the announcement. One person said that I was much more fun and outgoing now. It made me realize that if I had not decided to hide my true self from the world, my teenage years would not have been so lonely. Back then, fear-ridden, I had not given anyone the chance to get to know me. I had not given myself that chance either. I was overcome with relief.

I feel no shame and will not surround myself in self pity and loneliness anymore. Word quickly spread throughout the club and the next day a steady stream of people came up to me at school to comment on it. Some just gave me a hug or a few words of encouragement, while others overcompensated, joking just a little too much. I realized that most of my fears had been unwarranted—almost all of my peers had embraced the true me. A couple of years later I became the first openly gay president of the Cambodian Student Society.

Family Backlash

While doing laundry one day, my mother discovered a flier in the pocket of my jeans, promoting a gay club with a picture of two scantily clad men embracing each other. My mother came into my room with the flier, asking why I had it. I told her it belonged to a friend, that I was keeping it for him as a joke. She just looked at me and said, "Okay." I think in that moment my mother realized what the flier really meant. However, her unwillingness to acknowledge what she knew enabled me to continue lying to her. One of the tenets of Buddhism is patience; however, the idea of patience is often misconceived and turned into passivity, particularly among Cambodian women. My mother's reaction has always been to not react at all. Years after the flier incident, when other family members acknowledged that I was gay, my mother continued to willfully deny it.

When I was 24, she called to tell me she had picked out a fourteen-year-old girl in Cambodia to be my wife. "The girl's family was willing to pay us," she said. I told her that I was Americanized and not interested in an arranged marriage with a teenager. She said, "Just think about it. One day I will be old and you and your wife will have to take care of me." I am positive that she is aware that I have come out to many others, but she continues to skirt the issue, often starting conversations with the words, "When you marry your wife...."

Outing myself publicly was a very liberating and positive experience, until I discovered it had reached my family. My older brother, who had devoted his childhood to physically tormenting me, happened to see my MySpace announcement and sent me a nasty homophobic email. My brother also told our father, who called me that night to tell me he knew my secret and said, "Think of the family name." However, I no longer cared about his disapproval. His lies and infidelity had tarnished the family name long ago. I happened to run into my father, uncle, and the rest of my paternal family at a restaurant a few months later. My brother walked out to avoid contact with me—his way of passively exhibiting his disapproval. My father, in denial and hoping I would be able to change my sexuality, acted as if our previous conversation had never occurred, asking if I was dating any woman. My coming out put tremendous strains on our family, but ours is a family that has had unspoken issues for a very long time. The happiness I have had since my coming out to my peers far surpasses the antipathy I feel from my family.

Being Gay
in the Cambodian Community

The Cambodian community has a long way to go before embracing homosexuality. Mine is a culture of old and steadfast beliefs. However, the personal acceptance I have experienced as a gay man in this community gives me hope that the following generations will be more open-minded. I have been impressed by the strides I have witnessed in just the past few years. In 2004 I was a member of a planning committee for the Cambodian New Year Parade. I remember having a discussion on which local groups we would like to invite to join us. When the Long Beach Gay and Lesbian Center was suggested, it was quickly dismissed as going against family values. I remember feeling a sense of hopelessness at the time, that Cambodians were a long way from acceptance. Four years later, however, the Lesbian, Gay, Bisexual, and Transgender (LGBT) community was invited to join in the Cambodian New Year Parade and I, an openly gay Cambodian, was asked to be one of the grand marshals. It is encouraging to see the strides being made in such a relatively short period. I am proud that I can finally live openly as a member of both communities because my association with each has made me the man I am today.

Being Cambodian
in the Gay Community

My greatest dread growing up was being the outsider of the group, and my greatest goal was to not be the outsider. I finally overcame my fear of being the outsider when I decided to come out. Now I experience the outsider position from two fronts: When I am among a group of Cambodian friends, I am the gay person in the group; when I am with a group of gay friends, I am the Cambodian.

In the heterosexual community, Asian guys are stereotyped as being more feminine. This is true in the gay community as well. Many white men exclusively date Asians, as they want to be the dominant partner in the relationship. There are even titles for pairings involving gay males. Asian men who like to date other Asians are referred to as "sticky rice"; Asians who like white men are called "potato queens"; and white men who exclusively date Asians are "rice queens."

Among my group of largely white gay friends, I often find myself being stereotyped. These friends often make joking comments about my being an "Asian driver" or joke that I am in charge of divvying-up the check when we eat out together because "Asians are good at math." These comments are made in lighthearted ways and I find myself reinforcing them by playing up my role, laughing or joking about it myself; but I am often left feeling like the *other*. Once in a gay-friendly coffee shop, a white man approached me to ask when I came to this country and where I was from. I was born here, with no trace of an accent: I was offended.

I am a minority in two ways: I am gay, and I'm a Cambodian American. Being open about it gives me an opportunity to be proud of my identities. This is the greatest gift I have given to myself.

CHAPTER 25

(Re)Imagining the Meaning of Being Cambodian and Gay

Karen Quintiliani

Introduction

I began the study of Cambodian and gay identity formation as a result of a chance meeting in the spring of 1991. While preparing to start a research project for my thesis about Cambodian childrearing beliefs, I met Savuth, a 26-year-old Cambodian man who moved to Long Beach from the Midwest to live in a place with "a lot of Cambodians" and who also happened to live nearby one of the families I had started working with. He was curious why a young white woman spent so much time in the neighborhood visiting Cambodians, so he approached me one day. I told him about my research and he expressed enthusiasm for the project since he was adopted into an American family after losing most of his family members during the Khmer Rouge reign of terror and wanted to learn more about Cambodian parenting practices in the United States. He agreed to be my research assistant and help me translate transcriptions as the research progressed.

On October 11, 1991, National Coming Out Day, Savuth told me he was gay. My response was to smile and say, "I hope you didn't think this would change anything between us." He responded by telling me he had been "testing" me and he knew that I was trustworthy. He then told something that changed both our lives: "I'm also HIV positive." We sat together crying and hugging each other. He then said, "And there's more like me. It's like living through another war." As the image of his words became clearer, he asked me to study the group of gay Cambodians he hung out with instead and "help us deal with HIV." I immediately changed the course of my study.

Savuth introduced me to the two *mae* or mothers of the group to receive their permission to conduct the study. It is critical before beginning a study to get the approval of key people or gatekeepers beforehand (DeWalt and DeWalt 2001). As an applied anthropologist, I also wanted to ensure that my research was not only theoretically based but it would also have practical benefit to the people themselves (Ervin 2004). Therefore, I met with the *mae* to discuss what they would like to accomplish as a result of the research. They decided it was critical to create HIV/AIDS education programs for Cambodians because of the lack of access and knowledge on the topic.[1]

I attended my first party with several of the Cambodian gay men and their Anglo-American friends with some apprehension. I did not know how I would be received—a heterosexual, white woman. But the *mae* ensured my warm reception by introducing me as the "real woman" of the group or simply as "one of the girls." I was quickly embraced by all the Cambodians. I was "in" the group and already had a gendered designation that both contrasted and complimented their own identities and helped to justify my presence.

By 1993 I received two HIV/AIDS grants to develop educational materials for the Cambodian population and to start a peer-based program focused on Cambodian men who have sex with other men. The funding of these programs was proof to the group members that my interest in them and their network of friends and family was far beyond answering research questions. Also, the peer-based program allowed me to delve into questions about Cambodian beliefs about same-sex relationships without appearing intrusive or inappropriate.

The study involved following the lives of thirty-nine Cambodian men with various social and cultural identities and personal circumstances. The group itself was held together by twelve gay-identified Cambodian men who organized activities that provided a social space for other Cambodians and non-Cambodians to learn about the meaning of being Cambodian and "gay," to receive social support, and to meet sexual partners as desired. For the Cambodian gay group discussed in this chapter, they constructed their gay identities based upon an image they created of the cultural gender category, *khtaay*, which is defined as a "hermaphrodite or effeminate man, mannish woman" (Headley 1977: 98) and also signifies a man who dresses as a woman or a woman who dresses as a man (Ledgerwood 1990: 39).[2] The group appropriated the English term "gay" as the closest approximation of what it means to be *khtaay* (see Jackson 1997, 2001; Murray 1995). When these men use the term gay, they are describing themselves as feminine males who have the "heart" of a woman and behave or desire to behave like a woman, while maintaining their male appearance. The group also consisted of four "real *khtaay*" or "real gay" that went all the way and lived as transvestites.[3] Finally, there are the "closet gays," which consisted of twelve married men who hung out with the group as much as possible and eleven single men who dated both men and women, but had not made the decision about marriage and family.

I conducted ethnographic research with the group up until 1996 and kept in touch with some group members over the last decade.[4] During the study period, I participated in a variety of activities including parties and informal gatherings in the private homes of group members, Cambodian families, and Anglo-Americans, and went to gay bars, restaurants, doctor visits, and Buddhist temples for ceremonies. I also went on overnight trips including going to Cambodia with five of the group members in 1995. Whenever possible, I stayed with the family members of the Cambodian men.[5] I jotted down notes of my observations and informal interviews at social and family interactions and later expanded on them. I tape recorded life history interviews and transcribed them for analysis. The main setting of the study was Long Beach, California, which became the largest Cambodian community in the 1980s as more refugees resettled there and in surrounding cities (see Needham and Quintiliani 2007; Chan and Kim 2003).

This essay traces the "tactics" or "schemata of action" the Cambodian gay group developed to express their identities in time and space (de Certeau 1984: xiv). Group values around male effeminacy are created and reinforced based upon member's memories of experiences in Cambodia. Group rituals such as drag events and parties, although in some instances modeled after the American drag queen, affirm particular Cambodian meanings, linking present with the past. These tactics give group members the ability to broaden the *khtaay* role and image, and therefore define for themselves how to be Cambodian and gay. However, a trip to Cambodia challenges the meaning of being *khtaay* and reveals how individual and group identities are fluid and can only partially be (re)imagined for immigrants and refugees in the process of rebuilding lives (Hall 1990).

The Cambodian American Gay Group

At the start of the study, the group members ranged in age from 20 to 40 years old. All the group members spoke English, but two preferred only speaking Khmer. The men in the study came from various parts of Cambodia, but most lived in or near the two largest cities in Cambodia, Phnom Penh, the capital, and Battambang. All the men came to the United States as survivors of the Pol Pot time and as refugees between 1981-1986 except one of the *mae*, Vichet, who came in 1972.

Before 1990, what became the Cambodian gay group was a loose association of men who occasionally socialized. Vichet was the catalyst for the formation of the group. He became involved with an Asian gay organization and the gay liberation movement in the 1970s, because there were not any other gay Cambodians to hang out with. As he became acquainted and reacquainted with other Cambodians sharing his same social and emotional interest in other men, he organized parties and invited these Cambodians to meet his Asian and Anglo-American gay friends. The year before I met the group, he brought together a diverse mix of acquaintances he knew to perform traditional Cambodian dances in a pageant organized by the Asian gay organization. He recruited two Cambodian men involved in the revitalization of Cambodian traditional dance in Southern California to teach the group how to perform and dress for the dances. After sharing this experience, the Cambodians started to organize their own parties. When they met other Cambodians in the community or at gay bars interested in socializing in a safe gay space, they invited them to meet the other group members.

This brief overview of the Cambodian gay group's history is important in that it established the foundation for their construction of a Cambodian and gay identity. First, one Cambodian man had already become active in the gay social activities and assisted gay-identified Cambodian men to enter the gay world soon after their arrival in Southern California. Second, the older Cambodian men in the group were active in reinvigorating Cambodian culture in Southern California through traditional dance, and they taught this knowledge to the younger Cambodian gay men whom they met, and this became the basis for drag or cross-dressing activities. The influence of the elder Cambodians strengthened and emphasized the perception of the Cambodian experience of being gay.

Remembering the Past

Memories from the gay-identified men's childhood and adolescence in Cambodia are important reference points for their feminine desires and behaviors. Many of these memories are shared regularly with each other and with non-Cambodian gay men that associate with the group to highlight the congruence between the present and the past. The practice of storytelling within the group creates the occasion for socially constructing memory, which then influences everyday practices and its meaning (de Certeau 1985: 83).

Childhood

From an early age, all the Cambodian men in the study remember being "different" or, as one respondent described it, as knowing, "I was more girl than boy." Many remember having feminine features or characteristics that made them feel like a girl: "When I was a little boy, I'm soft and walk very soft like a little girl. And so everyone think[s] because I have a baby face I was so cute." As children, they preferred to play "like a little girl," and most experienced few restrictions on their behavior:

> My mother knew too that I was different. I think she treat me extra special than the rest of my family. I can have whatever I want. Toys that most little girl and little boy want to have. But mostly I play with the little girl toy. And sometime I went to my mother's closet, dressing up in her high heels and wear her clothes. Sometime I have those sarong I wrap it like an Apsara dancer. And I was dancing in front of the mirror.

Childhood, for some of the Cambodian gay men, is remembered as a time when they expressed feminine behavior freely and felt accepted for doing so.

However, not all Cambodian parents accepted their sons' feminine behavior. One of the elders in the group with a Cambodian mother and a Chinese father describes how his father reacted when he caught him dressing up like a girl: "He beat me a lot of times when he saw me playing things like that...I know he has a nasty way to show it, his love, because he doesn't want me to be a girl." When reflecting on his father's reaction, he expressed shame for embarrassing the family and felt pain about his father's reaction. Despite these feelings, he continued to dress and act like a girl because "I know in my heart who I am." In the Cambodian gay group, this experience illustrates the courage required to defy family wishes and reinforces how following one's heart is stronger than family obligation.

Feminine boys had a special role in their play groups. They acted out the parts of "girlfriends," "wives," and "mothers" while the masculine boys played their "boyfriends" and "husbands." When playing the part of girls, one group member describes how using feminine language reinforced their roles in the play groups:

> When I was 7-8 years old, I play with my boyfriends who were a little different too. We use the language that all the girls use like called each other husband, *pdey*, and wife, *prapuen*. We attracted to the boys in the class and would call out to them, *"Pdey, pdey."* The boys didn't care, because they thought it was just playing.

The feminine acting boys served as substitute girls in these games because the "real girls" played in their own groups. As a young man explained, "Girls wouldn't allow boys to get near them," but feminine boys could get close to the girls, because "we're the same." It was in their role as intermediary between the genders that the feminine acting boys gained acceptance and recognition. For the Cambodian gay group members, remembering their advantage in socializing with the girls over other boys, whether overstated or not, is important to the group's imagining of male effeminacy as a special role or a type of intermediary.

Adolescence and Young Adulthood

These men continued to use tactics as adolescents and young adults. However, after childhood, they were expected to change and behave in concordance with their gender designation. The social pressure toward marriage and the expectation that interest in women would increase caused them to try to hide their feminine behavior from family. They played the part of a man at home, but dressed in women's style clothing when going out with their friends. One respondent explained how he obeyed his father, yet found ways around the rules: "If you have to cut your hair short you just wear a wig or put on make-up when you leave the house." Others continued to dress as a man in order to maintain friendships and to be more attractive to potential male sexual partners:

> A lot of straight men don't want to be seen with the 'real gay' who dress up like a woman and wear make-up and have long hair, because the people in the village know them and tease them and call them *khteey*. They want to be with someone that still look like a man, but deep down inside is a woman. Like myself. I never dress-up like a woman, but I always dress-up like a man, but I always love a man.

The "real gay" in Cambodia, even as this group member describes it, dresses like a woman. As long as he continued to portray himself publicly as a man, he could avoid revealing himself or his partner's intention, thus enabling him to be close to men without suspicion.

Other respondents did not hide their feminine behavior. According to these men, their parents figured they would eventually feel ashamed about acting and dressing up like a girl and stop the behavior on their own. Other parents, especially mothers, knew that their sons did not fit their gender role: "My mother she knows what I am. She see me talk to all the women, but she knew those women wouldn't want me because I was one of them."

Before leaving Cambodia, four Cambodian gay group members had at least one sexual experience with another man. Their male partners were usually single and between 16 and 23 years old. The respondents make a clear distinction between themselves and these sexual partners: "I never have a relationship with another gay man. The man I have a relationship with is a man that later on get married." Some of the sexual encounters were impersonal affairs; others were loving experiences which sometimes led to longer term relationships. These experiences serve as examples in the Cambodian gay group of the sexual role of the effeminate male in a homosexual relationship.

In these sexual relationships, the respondents make two points clear about their role in the sexual experience. First, as "women" they do not enjoy themselves; second, their sexual partner must not consider them biologically men:

> In terms of physical enjoyment for me, I don't have much of that. I'm trying to be a woman, so I don't let him touch my personal because it's not a woman. It's like I'm ashamed of that part. So he try to touch, but I wouldn't let him.

> The man have to make the first move if he want to have sex. They have to caress me and kiss me. I'm a woman; I can't do that.

The purpose of the sexual encounters described was to fulfill the sexual needs of their partners. Also, as much as possible, feminine males wanted to appear the ideal Cambodian woman: shy and inexperienced sexually.

Cambodian Gay Social Space and Performance

As a tactic in their construction of feminine personas, the Cambodian gay group organizes activities to provide the social space for being feminine and to illustrate what Barth describes as "performance in the status, the adequate acting out of the role required to realize the identity" (1969: 29). The group activities were opportunities to be "drag queens" and to act feminine through interaction with each other as well as with others who play the part of the "audience." The audience could include family members, other Cambodians and non-Cambodian gay men. These drag activities are opportunities to play and portray gender and sexuality based upon the Cambodian gay group's image of the *khtaay*, a role which had been recreated through the telling and retelling of stories of their lives prior to coming to the United States.

The most frequent group activity is for one or more of the Cambodian gay group members to give a party for a special occasion like Cambodian New Year or birthday celebration, or at other times, for an informal dinner.[6] Usually, the *mae* plan the occasion with the younger group members.

The party is either hosted by a group member or one of their Anglo-American "husbands." If the party is held at a group member's home and he lives with his family, the family assists in preparing for and giving the party. Part of expressing who they are as individuals and as a group is to be among their Cambodian families. For some of the group members, these parties are an opportunity to "come out" to their family:[7]

> Dara's brother stayed and played the Cambodian card game, *bie sii kuu*, with several group members. After about an hour of friendly gambling, Dara's brother came into the kitchen where a few of us were preparing the dessert and said, "I can't believe the way they talk." He looked flush, "It's so nasty." The other Cambodian gay men in the kitchen laughed, "You're not used to it yet."

Dara told me later that his brother accepts him and his friends, so he no longer has to hide his identity. Although Dara's experience turned out positive, other group members express discomfort about telling male family members in particular about their sexual orientation. They prefer to let their sisters or mothers gradually explain or cover for them, which is what Dara did until his brother became suspicious about his refusal to marry.

Each party or event is a personal or group expression of being Cambodian in other ways as well. At every party, Cambodian food or Chinese stir-fry is served. The tables are decorated with elaborate floral arrangements created by group members who pride themselves on developing the artistic skill for these displays. Cambodian music is played (as well as some Western selections) and a planned or impromptu traditional Cambodian dance performed or Cambodian card game played for money.

The highlight and main attraction of most parties, especially ones celebrating a special occasion, like a birthday or Cambodian New Year, is the performance of a Cambodian traditional dance. The dances are performed by one to eight of the group members, depending on the dance.

For example, more of the group members perform if they do the "Coconut Dance," a popular Cambodian folk dance requiring male and female partners. The most frequently performed dances are the "The Flower Blessing Dance" and the "Apsara Dance," which are usually performed only by women.[8] A *mae* introduces the dance by explaining its cultural meaning to the audience. This reinforces the Cambodian culture for the group members and teaches their Cambodian culture to non-Cambodians. It also gives the group members an opportunity to perform as women to an audience, which would not be available to them otherwise. When the men dress in the Cambodian traditional dress, they act like the proper Cambodian women. Although they continue to talk "nasty" while in these outfits, the group members expect this type of behavior to be tempered and to adopt the comportment of a Khmer woman characterized by walking and speaking softly and acting shy and refined (Ledgerwood 1994).

Many of these parties are planned as drag events in which the Cambodian gay group members dress in Western style cocktail dresses and transform themselves into "drag queens."[9] The older Cambodian men in the group influenced the meaning of drag based upon their memories in Cambodia and the meaning given to these memories in a new social and cultural context. Part of the reason for the popularity of these events is that it brings the Cambodian gay group members closer to each other and to their feminine personas. One of the younger men commented that "I wouldn't think to dress-up until I met this group" and "I didn't know in Cambodia you did this."

Being a drag queen is a gendered performance that both challenges the natural order of the sex and gender orders and illustrates the constructiveness of gender (Butler 2006; Newton [1972] 1979). For the Cambodian gay group, drag was also a way to temporarily enact the feminine role of the *khtaay* and blend this image with the Western drag queen (see Manalansan 2000). For the Cambodian group members, drag also allowed them to resist the stigma of the effeminate homosexual as a tactic to distinguish their Cambodian and gay identity from other gay men.

At drag events group members wear Western dresses and are organized specifically to perform as American women typified by Miss America. Dressed in their sexy evening clothes, they act wild, taking on the persona of a "slut." Often, the group members tease each other in Khmer and call each other *srey laah*, which means a woman with a shameless or bad character (Headley 1977: 1425). Other times, the group members call each other *sray samphan* which literally means "prostitute" (Huffman and Proum 1978: 453). In these clothes, the group members act the opposite of the polite Cambodian woman. Instead, they posture as Western women (as imagined by the Cambodian group) embodied in the image of Miss America with her big hair, large breasts, thick make-up, high heels, and glamorous gowns. These performances are, for the Cambodian Americans, part of an erotic aesthetic in which they display their desire to be feminine from the inside out and from the outside in.[10] Embracing, maintaining and protecting an erotic preference is a tactic in constructing identity and in struggling to be understood. The erotic feminine aesthetic performed by the Cambodian gay group is rooted in the historic setting of Southern California gay world and their Cambodian cultural imagination.

Drag Queens in Cambodia

When travel to Cambodia became safer after the United Nations elections in 1993, one of the *mae*, Kavuth, went back to Cambodia to reconnect with family. He also became reacquainted with his "*khtaay* sisters," and showed the group video and photographs of the trip. This stirred an intense desire for group members to return to Cambodia to find family members. They also imagined returning to Cambodia as drag queens and initiating their Cambodian "drag queen sisters" into how in America men can transform themselves temporarily so they maintain the "heart" of a woman. Five group members decided to go back to Cambodia in 1995 including Kavuth, the *mae*, so he could introduce us to his Cambodian *khtaay* friends in Battambang. Stuffed between the anti-malarial drugs and the Imodium, they packed their new sequin dresses, make-up, wigs and lingerie to make their debut as drag queens in Cambodia.

Once in Cambodia, however, we discover there was not a social space to be drag queens. The social category *khtaay* in Cambodia does not allow shifting between genders and sex roles, which drag challenges and requires in the performance. In Cambodia, the *khtaay* fulfill particular marginal roles. Three of the *khtaay* live at the brothel and cook and clean for the women and only occasionally have customers themselves. *Mae chaa*, which means "the old mother," is divorced and has grown children. He abandoned his family to fulfill his desire for male companionship. He is poor, homeless, and ostracized for leaving his family, but not necessarily for having sex with other men. The other two *khtaay* live in the temple compound and have taken a vow of celibacy in order to serve the monks and honor the loss of partners during the Khmer Rouge years. Sexual relationships are either arranged or random meetings between single men and *khtaay* in Battambang in which the *khtaay* provides the young men with money or food as well as sexual gratification. The Cambodian Americans played the *khtaay* role in the sexual exchange system as well, but not dressed as women as they had planned.

With no bars or local scene to be drag queens, the Cambodian Americans decided to dress their Cambodian sisters in the outfits anyway. We rented several rooms on the rooftop of the largest hotel in Battambang. In a video recorded interaction, the Cambodian Americans direct the *khtaay* on how to apply make-up, walk in high heels and to flirt with men. At one point, Kavuth tells one of the prettiest *khtaay*, Rah, to, "try on the high heels and walk downstairs for a little bit." When Rah's transformation is complete, she went downstairs and successfully brought back four Cambodian men in their early twenties. This creates a big stir with the hotel owner, who threatens to call the police and evict us for promoting prostitution. We are able to continue to entertain the young men after a couple of the Cambodian Americans calmed the owner down and pay him extra money for the rooms. However, we had already drawn too much attention and the young men soon left. As Sovann, one of the Cambodian Americans explains "When you put on stockings [pantyhose], you can't roll them up, so you have to tear them off." Since women in Cambodia roll up their *sarongs* or skirts when they go to the toilet, it is impossible to dress like Miss America. Sovann makes an implicit distinction between Cambodian and American women, and thus between being drag queens and being Cambodian *khtaay* that cannot be bridged as they had imagined. Later that night, after much laughter, the Cambodian Americans packed up their sequin gowns and accessories and gave it all to their friends, realizing that "(the cost of) one dress could feed a family for a year [in Cambodia]."

Conclusion

Until these Cambodian American gay group members could travel to their homeland, they imagined being *khtaay* through a set of social and cultural symbols available to them. When they returned to the United States they no longer held drag events as a way to portray their identities as Cambodian and gay, and this influenced the other group members.[11] Rather, being *khtaay* became a social responsibility to financially support family members they reunited with in Cambodia, to sponsor HIV/AIDS fundraisers for Cambodia, and, in some cases, to return to their homeland and to nurture relationships with Cambodian men. They gave up their "womanhood" and began to live gay transnational lives. Stuart Hall (1990) describes identity as a "production" constantly in flux as individuals and communities reinterpret experiences in diaspora and from the homeland. By understanding identity as in flux provides insight into how the meaning of being Cambodian and gay may change overtime in Cambodia and in the diaspora influenced by transnational relationships and the conditions of poverty.

Endnotes

1. Since I worked at the Southeast Asian Health Project, a joint project of United Cambodian Community and St. Mary Medical Center in Long Beach, as a program manager at the time, I could devote part of my time to ethnographic fieldwork and to analyzing findings in order to create a program linguistically and culturally relevant to Cambodians.

2. Further research needs to be conducted to determine if the social category, *khtaay*, constitutes a third gender (Herdt 1996).

3. Two of the transvestites in the group were in therapy and took hormone shots in preparation for the possibility of surgically changing their sex.

4. Over the years, some of the group members have passed away from AIDS related illnesses.

5. When I spent extended periods of time in a Cambodian home, I followed the behaviors expected of a woman in Cambodian culture. I slept next to the oldest woman in the house, usually on the living room floor. In one situation, the mother of one of the group members creatively used my employment at a local hospital as a way to introduce me to neighbors as a nurse, even though she knows I am not one. Her son was suffering from illnesses related to AIDS, and I often stayed with the family to assist them. I allowed the family to describe me and my role in their lives to ensure that I never compromised their confidentiality.

6. Although traditionally Cambodians do not celebrate birthdays, some Cambodian families in the United States are acknowledging their children's birthday, since the children learn this American custom in school. The Cambodian gay group has adopted this custom as adults and many now celebrate their birthdays. Often, these celebrations are a good rea-

son to have a party and their non-Cambodian partners and friends relate to these celebrations.

7. For a discussion about the meaning and significance of "coming out" in the gay world, see Herdt (1992). Refer also to Chauncey (1994) for a discussion of the history of the phrase and the process of "coming out."

8. In Cambodian communities in the United States, Cambodian traditional dances are "vital expressions of cultural identity" (Catlin 1987: 29).

9. Sometimes the group would wear traditional Cambodian clothing for weddings or other special occasions for these drag events. If they did wear Cambodian women's clothing, they were expected to act more refined and usually did not call each other names.

10. Joan Nestle (1987) makes an excellent point about butch-femme lesbian portrayals that apply to the Cambodian gay group members and their drag performances. Nestle writes: "Butch-femme relationships, as I experienced them, were complex erotic statements, not phony heterosexual replicas. They were filled with a deeply lesbian language of stance, dress, gesture, loving, courage, and autonomy…" (1987: 100). Although Nestle does not use the phrase "erotic aesthetic," I interpreted this passage to characterize what the Cambodian gay group members were attempting to embody through these drag events.

11. The transvestites continued to dress as women as did two of the gay identified men who occasionally went to bars that had special drag queen nights.

References

Barth, Frederik. *Ethnic groups and boundaries: The social organization of cultural difference.* Boston: Little, Brown and Company, 1969. Print.

Butler, Judith. *Gender trouble: Feminism and the subversion of identity.* New York: Routledge, 2006. Print.

Catlin, Amy. *Apsara: The feminine in Cambodian art.* Los Angeles: Woman's Building, 1987. Print.

Chan, Sucheng and Audrey U. Kim. *Not just victims: conversations with Cambodian community leaders in the United States.* Chicago: University of Illinois Press, 2003. Print.

Chauncey, George. *Gay New York: Gender, urban culture, and the making of the gay male world, 1890-1940.* New York: BasicBooks, 1994. Print.

de Certeau, Michel. *The practice of everyday life*. Berkeley: University of California Press, 1984. Print.

DeWalt, Kathleen M. and Billy R. DeWalt. *Participant observation: A guide for fieldworkers*. New York: AltaMira, 2001. Print.

Ervin, Alexander. *Applied Anthropology: Tools and Perspectives for Contemporary Practice* (2nd ed.). Boston: Allyn & Bacon, 2004. Print.

Hall, Stuart. "Cultural identity and diaspora." In *Identity: Community, culture, difference*, edited by Jonathan Rutheford. New York: New York University Press, 1990. Print.

Headley, Robert K. *Cambodian-English dictionary*. Washington DC: The Catholic University of America Press, 1977. Print.

Herdt, Gilbert, ed. *Gay culture in America: Essays from the field*. Boston: Beacon Press, 1993. Print.

Herdt, Gilbert. "Introduction: Third sexes and third genders." In *Third Sex, Third Gender: Beyond sexual dimorphism in culture and history*, edited by Gilbert Herdt. New York: Zone Books, 1996. Print.

Huffman, Franklin E. and Im Proum. *English-Khmer dictionary*. Connecticut: Yale University Press, 1978. Print.

Jackson, Peter A. "*Kathoey*<Gay><Man: The historical emergence of gay male identity in Thailand." In *Sites of desire, economies of pleasure: Sexualities in Asia and the Pacific,* edited by Lenore Manderson and Margaret Jolly. Chicago: The University of Chicago Press, 1997. Print.

Jackson, Peter A. "Pre-gay, post-queer: Thai perspectives on proliferating gender/sex diversity in Asia." In *Journal of Homosexuality* 40(3/4) (2001): 1-25. Print.

Ledgerwood, Judy. "Changing Khmer conceptions of gender: Women, stories and the social order." Unpublished manuscript. Ph.D. dissertation, Cornell University. Ann Arbor, MI: University Microfilms, 1990.

Ledgerwood, Judy. Gender symbolism and culture change: viewing the virtuous woman in the Khmer story "Mea Yoeng." In *Cambodian culture since 1975: Homeland and exile*, edited by May M. Ebihara, Carol A. Mortland and Judy Ledgerwood. Ithaca: Cornell University Press, 1994. Print.

Manalansan, Martin. "Diasporic deviants/divas: How Filipino gay transmigrants 'Play with the world.'" In *Queer diasporas*, edited by Cindy Patton and Benigno Sánchez-Eppler. Durham: Durke University Press, 2000. Print.

Murray, Stephen O. "Stigma transformation and relexification in the international diffusion of gay." In *Beyond the lavender lexicon: Authenticity, imagination and appropriation in lesbian and gay languages*, edited by

William L. Leap. The Netherlands: Gordon and Breach Publishers, 1995. Print.

Needham, Susan and Quintiliani, Karen. "Cambodians in Long Beach, California. The making of a community." In *Journal of Immigrant and Refugee Studies*, Vol. 5.1 (2007). Print.

Nestle, Joan. *A restricted country* (1st ed.). Ithaca: Firebrand, 1987. Print.

Newton, Esther. *Mother camp: Female impersonators in America*. Chicago: University of Chicago Press, 1972, 1979. Print.

CHAPTER 26

Cambodian American Women

Christine M. Su

Introduction

Following the fall of the Khmer Rouge regime in Cambodia in 1979, thousands of refugees fled the country. Approximately 145,000 refugees relocated to the United States between 1979 and 2002, with the majority arriving between 1980 and 1985. Of these refugees, a significant number of the women were widows and/or single mothers. These women began their lives as Americans with enormous complications, for in addition to surviving as individuals who had escaped a brutal regime, arriving in a country with an unfamiliar language and strange lifestyle, they also would be expected to fill both traditional Khmer (Cambodian) female roles as homemakers and caregivers, and new roles as heads of household and wage earners for their families.

The experiences of Cambodian American women reflect both setbacks and successes, struggle and resilience in the face of astonishingly difficult circumstances.

Cambodians in the United States

Fractured Lives: The Refugee Experience

More than 200,000 individuals in the United States identify as Cambodian Americans, and in their communities they confront high levels of poverty, discrimination and harassment directed toward immigrants, racial profiling by law enforcement, gang activity and violence, post-traumatic stress disorder (PTSD), and general lack of understanding of Khmer culture by the larger American society. As a result of the horrors of the Khmer Rouge regime, Cambodian Americans live with memories of extreme trauma inconceivable to many Americans. Wives were separated from husbands, and parents from children; many witnessed torture and execution of family members, and watched as others died of starvation and disease. When the Khmer Rouge fell in 1979, thousands attempted to escape into Thailand. Not welcomed by the Thais, however, Cambodians lingered in refugee camps for months or years along the Thai-Cambodia border before relocating to third countries, including the United States. The conditions in the camps were substandard, as refugees lived with primitive sanitation, limited food, and insufficient medical care, as well as the fears and anxieties resulting from their earlier trauma. Those who relocated to the United States brought those fears and anxieties with them.

Cambodian American Women: Physical and Environmental Challenges

All persons moving into new environments must make adjustments, some of which are physical, such as normalizing new time zones and overcoming related jet lag, changes in climate and weather, and differences in housing arrangements. Cambodian refugees also experienced feelings of hopelessness, guilt, fear, loneliness, and sadness as they attempted to comprehend their changed lives. The lifestyle changes and related emotional responses were intensified for Cambodian American women, for several reasons. First, Liang Tien notes that previous migrations from Asia were largely male—particularly young males who came to the United States in search of employment and economic prosperity. These men's wives or other female relatives usually arrived later, once the men were established in their new environment. Cambodian women, however, like other refugee women, generally arrived in the United States at the same time as Cambodian men, and thus did not enter "prepared" environments, such as those structured by earlier male immigrants for their wives. Second, because so many men perished during the Khmer Rouge regime, a significant percentage of the refugees were women, including widows and/or single mothers. Anthropologist Judy Ledgerwood comments that "women are better able to survive conditions of severe malnutrition, fewer [Cambodian] women were targeted for execution because of connections to the old regime, and fewer women were killed in battles." Cambodian American women thus represent resilient survivors, but also, those who grieve lost loved ones and wonder why they survived. Third, the expectations made of these women arriving in the United States involved shifting domestic power structures and related emotional, cultural, and psychological as well as physical issues.

Increasingly, Cambodian Americans are becoming more knowledgeable about their rights as legal residents of the United States. They have begun to use the American legal and justice systems to assert and protect their civil and social rights. In 1993, for example, the Washington State Supreme Court found that the People's National Bank, based in Seattle, discriminated against Phanna Xieng, a Cambodian American (who had become a U.S. citizen in 1986), by denying him promotions over a number of years because of his accented English.

Cambodian American Women: Economic, Social, and Cultural Challenges

Traditionally in Cambodia, women were in charge of child-rearing and household-related duties such as cooking, cleaning, laundering, and so forth. As in other cultures, too, women were and are believed to be the culture-bearers of Cambodian society. That is, Cambodian women carry the responsibility for transmitting Cambodian culture and traditions from one generation to the next. According to Cambodian traditional writings, the ideal Cambodian young woman is the pinnacle of virtue: innocent, modest, well-behaved (meaning shy and quiet), obedient, and deferential to men. While in reality Cambodian women have occupied various roles, have exercised considerable independence and authority (i.e., they typically managed family finances), and have been well-respected both within the family and the larger Cambodian community, much of Khmer "culture" is connected to visions and expectations of the ideal Khmer woman. Folktales, songs, proverbs, and other stories, for example, assert the merits of appropriate conduct, and the dreadful consequences of inappropriate conduct. Khmer women refer to the *chbab srey* ("rules for girls"), a traditional Cambodian text which describes appropriate female behavior, and cautions against leaving girls unsupervised or allowing them to become too independent. In particular, young, unmarried Cambodian females are not to leave the family home, lest they interact inappropriately with males. In order to sustain Cambodian identity (or "Khmerness") in the United States, Cambodian American women feel pressured to behave in accordance with different aspects of this ideal; however, the circumstances of relocation often necessitate that they behave more assertively. Family economic needs require them to obtain employment outside the home, and often as such, to interact with both males and females.

The stresses of refugee existence for both Cambodian American men and women, plus changing gender roles, can lead to marital conflict, including domestic violence. Witnessing violence or atrocities in Cambodia and consequent PTSD in refugee family members can exacerbate domestic violence, making situations even more dangerous. An Asian Task Force Against Domestic Violence study found that at least 44–47 percent of Cambodian Americans interviewed knew a woman who had experienced domestic violence, and this figure is likely low. Many Cambodians do not trust police and authority figures and are thus hesitant to report abuse. Some husbands abuse their wives because they feel threatened by women's purported "new" power, combined with their own frustration about not achieving their resettlement goals.

Female-headed households in the United States in general, however, and female-headed households among minority groups in particular, are more likely to subsist below the poverty level than other types of households. While Asian Americans have often been heralded as the most educationally and financially successful minority group, this "model minority myth" belies the fact that while there have indeed been many successes, there are many Asian Americans who have little or no education and low or negligible incomes. (While the overall Asian American average income in 1999 was $57,874, compared to the overall American average of $50,046, for example, that for Cambodian Americans was only $35,434, nearly 40 percent less than the overall Asian American and 30 percent less than the national average). In 1990, 42 percent of Cambodian families were living below the poverty level. By 1999, the percentage had fallen to 29 percent; however, today more than 25 percent of Cambodian families still live below the poverty level, and many of these are female-headed households.

Cambodian American Women: Generational Challenges and Corollaries

Younger Cambodian American women often feel particularly stressed. They play multiple roles, including caretaker both for younger children (nearly three quarters of Cambodian families in 2000 had at least one family member under 18) and non-English speaking elders (undertaking daily tasks such as shopping, bill-paying, etc); student, if attending school; and employee, as many are expected to be the family wage-earners. The pressure to function in so many ways as Cambodian Americans, as well as to continue to be cultural representatives, feeling compelled both to maintain Khmerness as well as to acculturate, causes intense stress for young Cambodian American women. Additionally, women and youth tend to have limited access to community resources, including physical and mental health care. Many young Cambodian American women join gangs, in search of support and emotional connection. While viewed by the larger community as destructive or criminal, for these women, gangs provide a sense of identity, community, and seemingly unconditional support in return for loyalty, in contrast to the alienation and hostility of their individual lives. While gang activity may not be altogether positive, however, other strategies of empowerment can provide opportunities for all Cambodian American women, and particularly the youth, to impact their communities constructively. Providing positive role models for youth encourages them to both imitate and internalize their accomplishments, and to take responsibility for their own actions (Tang 2003). Recognizing this, Cambodian American women have begun to develop indigenous leaders and community organizers

Mutual assistance associations (MAAs), grassroots, community-based organizations providing social and cultural services, began to arise soon after the peak arrivals of Cambodians in the 1980s. A significant number of these MAAs focus on issues which tend to disproportionately affect women, such as domestic violence, (lack of) sex education, health issues, and so forth (SEARC 2004). Importantly, women in these associations both celebrate Cambodian culture and discuss ways in which it might be modified (but importantly, not destroyed or replaced) to better suit life in the United States. Women can still be the culture-bearers, transmitting Cambodian ways of life from one generation to the next, incorporating new ways with old. These associations are an essential part of Cambodian American women's lives, for through them "they learn about the importance of viewing themselves as primary agents of change, as a collective who share the responsibility of both transmitting and transforming the past" (Tang 182).

References

Hardin, James. "American Women: Introduction." In *American Women: A Library of Congress Guide for the Study of Women's History and Culture in the United States* (Library of Congress, 2001), cited by the American Folklife Center at Retrieved 03 December 2004.

Hein, Jeremy. *From Vietnam, Laos, and Cambodia: A Refugee Experience in the United States.* New York: Twayne Publishers, 1995. Print.

Ledgerwood, Judy. "Women in Cambodian Society." In *Cambodian Recent History and Contemporary Society: An Introductory Course.* Department of Anthropology and Center for Southeast Asian Studies, Northern Illinois University, 2003. Web; 3 December 2004.

Niedzwiecki, Max, and Duong, T.C. *Southeast Asian American Statistical Profile.* Washington, D.C.: Southeast Asia Resource Action Center (SEARC), 2004. Web.

Niedzwiecki, Max, Pich Sophy, Yang KaYing, Tran, Thanh, and King, Barry. *Directory of Southeast Asian American Community-Based Organizations 2004: Mutual Assistance Associations (MAAs) and Religious Organizations Providing Social Services.* Washington, DC: Southeast Asia Resource Action Center (SEARAC), 2004.

Noy Thrupkaew, "The Myth of the Model Minority," In *The American Prospect.* Vol. 13 no. 7, (April 8, 2002). Print.

Sawhill, Isabel V., "Poverty in the United States." In *The Concise Encyclopedia of Economics.* Indianapolis. Liberty Fund, Inc., edited by David R. Henderson, 2002. Print.

Tang, Shirley. "Learning to Build a Healthy Community: Youth Development for Street-Involved Cambodian American Young Women." In *Asian Americans: Vulnerable Populations, Model Interventions, and Clarifying Agendas*, edited by Lin Zhan. Boston: Jones and Bartlett Publishers, 2003. Print.

Tien, Liang. "Southeast Asian American Refugee Women." In *Women of Color: Integrating Ethnic and Gender Identities in Psychotherapy.* New York: Guilford Press, 1994. Print.

Section XI

Cambodian American Religions

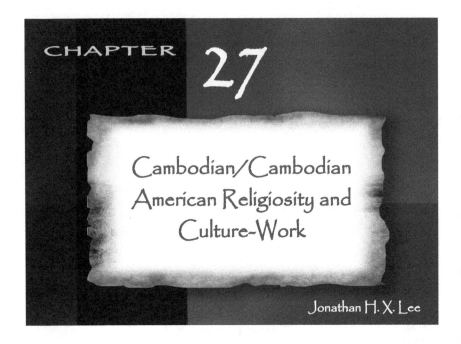

CHAPTER 27

Cambodian/Cambodian American Religiosity and Culture-Work

Jonathan H. X. Lee

"We are a country full of ghosts, trying to heal."
Ouk Bunna, Killing Field Survivor

Cambodian immigrants arrived in the United States as refugees of the "Hot Wars" in Southeast Asia. They came in the post-1965 period in several waves, after the passage of the *Refugee Act of 1980*, and again after the *Amerasian Homecoming Act of 1987*. Since 1975, nearly two million refugees from Cambodia, Vietnam, and Laos have entered the United States. Around eighty percent of the Cambodian population are Khmer, people who are ethnically "Khmer," while the remaining population consists of people mixed with Khmer, and non-ethnic Khmers (i.e., Chinese, French, and Vietnamese). All of them, wholly or mixed, are Cambodian identified. Hence, the Cambodian refugees who entered the United States during this time were a diverse assortment of Cambodians who left Cambodia to escape the horrors of Pol Pot's murderous revolution and twisted social engineering pogroms—a failed attempt to create a rural peasant society populated with only "pure" ethnic Khmers, subsisting on rice agriculture. The resettlement of Cambodian refugees in America was difficult due to this recent bloody history. Memories of violence and killing, losing family members and friends, and sustaining continued suffering, were a tremendous challenge for those wishing to rebuild life anew in America. Religion, religious beliefs, and rituals sometimes provided an avenue to channel trauma and sorrow into hope and renewal. The process of dislocation and resettlement, for many immigrants coming to America, is jarring in and of itself, and for many Cambodian refugees, the process at times seemed insurmountable, due to cultural differences, language limitations, scarcity of socio-economic resources, and unhealed individual and collective wounds. Cambodian refugees experienced a profound destabilization of self, morals, and ethics because of the sudden and traumatizing nature of their dislocation and resettlement. As a result, their adaptation and integration into American society has been uneven and unfinished—at best—which has affected the second-generation American-born children. First-generation parents, like my own mother and father, had to negotiate survivor's guilt in the face of an intense "survive or die mentality." Because my parents came to the U.S. with no English skills and no employable skills, they were often forced to work in sweatshops for outrageously low pay to provide for their families and themselves. Faced with limited financial resources, community support, and healthy social networks, some Cambodian refugees and Cambodian Americans turned to their religious beliefs and rituals to recover selfhood, regain stability, and rebuild their community. This chapter argues that the deliberate (re)creation of religious institutions, communities, and rituals among Cambodian Americans, was and is a form of Cambodian American culture-work. *Cambodian American culture-work* is the conscious efforts to remake religio-cultural forms and practices for life in America, to reflect their new identities and way of life as Cambodian *and* American.

Historical Background of Cambodian Religions

Like other Southeast Asian nations, Cambodian culture has a mixture of influences from both China and the Indian sub-continent, a mix that is reflected in the country's religious beliefs and practices—which include elements of Hinduism, Buddhism, Confucianism, Islam, and indigenous folkways. Together, these influences have forged a distinct Cambodian religiosity, that has sustained Cambodians through the war and genocide that nearly destroyed their nation in the final third part of the twentieth century, and helped anchor diasporic communities worldwide, including the largest one located in the United States.

Historically speaking, from the first century BCE to the fourteenth century CE, Hinduism (Siva and Visnu cults) and Theravada Buddhism have co-existed in Cambodia. Khmer religious expression today continues to show different influences coming from Islam and Vietnamese religions.

Cambodian Muslims in America

Very little is known about the Cambodian American Muslim communities in America. Cambodian Muslims are descendants of the Chams, who migrated from central Vietnam after the final defeat of the kingdom of Champa by the Vietnamese in 1471. Cambodian Muslims adopted a fairly orthodox version of Sunni Islam, and maintained links with other Muslim communities throughout Southeast Asia. They also incorporated various elements of Buddhist beliefs. There is also a small heterodox Muslim community, the Zahidin, who practice a form of Islam similar to the Muslim Chams of Vietnam, but who only pray once a week on Friday, and observe Ramadan only on the first, middle, and last day of the month. Khmer Muslims represent a closely-knit community, marrying only within their own faith. Their total population is more than 300,000 in Cambodia, but their numbers are much smaller in America. Like other Cambodians, Cambodian Muslims arrived to America as refugees fleeing persecution and death. According to Antonio Graceffo, when the Khmer Rouge came into power, it is estimated that 132 mosques were destroyed. Additionally, out of the 113 most prominent Cham clergy in Cambodia pre-Khmer Rouge, only 20 survived (Graceffo 2008). In the early 1980s they were resettled in Iowa and Washington states.

Marc Ramirez notes the growth of the Cambodian Cham community in Washington state:

> The mostly Cham Muslims in Lacey…illustrate how some communities grow while observing religious requirements. The Chams began with a mobile-home park, designating one trailer a mosque…. Now, prefab homes are replacing mobile ones on 10 community-owned acres in a cooperative-financing strategy that avoids mortgages…and…payment of interest, which Islam frowns upon (1999).

Besides establishing their communities, Cambodian Chams in America faced new challenges in resettlement and finding employment. Muslim women are required to wear a veil, a headscarf to protect their modesty and express their devotion to God. However, because of discrimination, Cambodian Chams had to conceal their piety by only wearing their veil around other Muslims, and not at work. As Cambodian Cham Amira Atan recalls, "I found myself getting very little work when I wore the scarf" (Ramirez 1999). Today, Cambodian Chams in America send money back to the small Cham communities in Cambodia, to assist in rebuilding mosques that were destroyed during the Khmer Rouge period.

The most outspoken Cambodian American Muslim today is Anida Yoeu Ali. Ali is a Cambodian Muslim American woman, who was born in Cambodia, but grew up in Chicago. Ali uses spoken word and performance to explore the Cambodian American refugee condition, experience, and reconciliation with history. On her personal web page, she says:

> As an artist and a Cambodian Muslim transnational, I am professionally and personally drawn to themes of recuperation and reclamation. My work synthesizes poetry, movement, video, and site-specific installations into hybrid explorations, often mapping new political and spiritual landscapes. Recalling that the oral tradition saved and preserved Cambodian art, I am inspired as an artist to seek those routes of memory. Memories surface through the body. Memories do not follow linear chronology. Artists have a power to bring out memories, stories, and moments that official history does not always account for.

Artists also have a way of disrupting meta-narratives. I perform stories in an attempt to remember my ancestry, my memories, and my relationship to the spirit world (2010).

Ali's artistic expression is as much a journey of self-discovery, as it is an act of social justice and collective healing. As such, Ali's multimedia arts and expressions is a form of Cambodian American culture-work, "rooted in autobiographical experiences," while chronicling her life, her family's experiences, and her dreams.

Khmer Folk Religion in America

Khmer folk religion conceptualizes various spirits and souls that influence peoples' lives—positively or negatively. Khmer believe that there is a guardian mother spirit, an "invisible mother" (*meba*), who protects babies during the early years of infancy, but can also be potentially dangerous. The invisible mother is a "spirit mother," akin to the Western notion of a "guardian spirit." She is understood to be the mother of each baby from a previous life, who with love and affection, watches over *her* baby in the present life. However, because she is potentially dangerous, should she happen to covet the baby, many Khmer elders will express ambivalence toward the invisible mother. This explains why Khmer mothers and elders will never leave babies unattended.

Another key element in the Khmer religious worldview, is the belief that there are many non-human life forms cohabiting with humans, some of which are benign while others are potentially dangerous and frightening. Spirits associated with specific localities (i.e., mountains and villages) are called *qnak ta* ("ancestral people"), and are thought to be relatively benign. Spirits of known or unknown deceased persons, ghosts of the dead (i.e., *khmoc lan* and *bray*), victims of murder, or babies who die at childbirth—are all potentially dangerous malevolent ghost-spirits called *phii*. Humans are believed to cohabit with the spirits and deities of the supernatural realm, which is why Khmers will rely on a shaman (*memut, rup,* or *Khmer kru*) to assist them in dealing with the supernatural. Khmer shamans employ magic rituals, traditional music (*arak* music), ancestral veneration, and the concept of folk spirits and deities, along with Buddhist rituals, in their religious work. For many Cambodian refugees, the local shaman is an important resource, not only for religious and spiritual needs, but for medical, physiological, and emotional healing (Chhean 2007).

Cambodian American culture-work, as expressed by the Khmer shaman ritual performances, meditates the tensions caused by being Cambodian and American, and the contradictions between Western and traditional healing methods. This in turn creates a space for Cambodian refugees to address real emotional, spiritual, psychological, and physical pains. An example of this occurred in Stockton, California, in 1989, after an unemployed welder named Patrick Purdy opened fire on a playground at Cleveland Elementary School, killing five children and wounding twenty-nine (Chan 2004: 88–89). Among the dead were four Cambodian Americans and one Vietnamese American. A Cambodian Buddhist monk, Dharmawara Mahathera, was called in to perform a purification and healing ritual, which made it possible for Cambodian parents to resume sending their children to school.

Theravada Buddhism

Having been the state religion since the thirteenth century, having endured French colonialism until the 1950s, and the 1970s Communist revolution under Pol Pot, Theravada Buddhism ("the Way of the Elders") remains the dominant faith in Cambodia. The Khmer Rouge ruthlessly attempted to remove religion from Cambodian life by destroying many churches, mosques, and temples. They executed many of the *sangha*, or the Buddhist community of monks and nuns. Most of the 3,600 temples that existed in Cambodia were destroyed, and fewer than 3,000 of the original 50,000 monks survived the genocide. Not until 1979, following Vietnam's occupation of the country, was religion allowed to be practiced publicly again. However, the rebuilding process relied heavily on Theravadian monks from Thailand.

Khmer religion is best characterized as a combination of Buddhist, Hindu, indigenousness folk, and Chinese beliefs and practices. However, most Khmer are Buddhist-identified, and hence share certain basic understandings and beliefs. The most central of these is the concept of *karma* (*kam*), the belief that one's actions in previous lives, and the merit (*bon*) that one has accumulated, determine one's current and future life situations. This is coupled with the notion of reincarnation, the belief that every individual will be reborn based on the accumulated *karma* or merit of the present life. Many Khmer will invoke their understanding of *karma* to make sense of their current lives. According to Theravada Buddhism, life is ultimately characterized by unease (*anicca*), obfuscated by the impermanence of all things. The principle truth of suffering (*dukkha*) is taught by the historical Buddha, in the first of the Four Noble Truths.

Theravada Buddhism also provided many rituals that Cambodian refugees relied upon to assist them in their resettlement. Venerable Master Kong Chhean notes that Khmer Buddhists will request healing and protective rituals after disasters to restore harmony to the lives of survivors and the dead (Chhean 2007). Buddhist protective chanting usually involves water, flowers, a roll of thread all neatly arranged in front of an altar. Chhean notes that,

> ...Buddhist patients believe that this ritual helps keep them happy, successful, and safe. Protective chanting is meant not only to avoid and overcome the dangers and calamities of life, but also to eradicate the corruptions that are obstructing the person from progressing on the path to Enlightenment (952).

The ability for Cambodian refugees to reproduce Buddhist rituals and communities, assisted their transition into life in America, and by extension, assisted them in reconstituting self. These rituals, beliefs, and communities are thus examples of Cambodian American culture-work that took place, and continues to take place, within Cambodian American families and communities.

Christianity among Cambodian Americans

Theravada Buddhism is the dominant religious influence in Cambodian society. The sphere of influence of Theravada Buddhism is so strong, that it has consistently been able to resist Islam and Christianity. Unlike their Vietnamese neighbors, and although Cambodia was under French control from 1863 to 1954, Khmer Buddhists were able to resist the colonial "civilizing mission," that attempted to convert them to Catholicism. This is not to say that Christianity did not penetrate Cambodian society at all. Many Cambodian refugees fleeing the Pol Pot era converted to Christianity in refugee camps. Because conversion was a means to getting social and material support from Christian aid organizations, these converts are known as "Rice Bowl Christians" (Smith-Hefner 1994). Critics have condemned various Christian aid organizations for taking advantage of the refugee plight and vulnerability to advance their own agenda—which is against United Nation policies on refugee assistance. Thus, Cambodian refugees who converted to Christianity, generally converted in refugee camps or after being sponsored to America by Christian congregations and parishes, or individual families. Once in America, some converts remained true to their new faith, while others abandoned the Christian tradition, due to secondary migration away from their sponsors, or as a result of conflicts with their sponsors. However, some remained committed to their Christian faith due to a sense of indebtedness to sponsoring churches and families that provided refuge. Still others were able to negotiate the theological differences between Khmer Buddhism and Christianity, and practice both faiths simultaneously; these constituted a new breed of Buddho-Christians in America. Thomas Douglas (2006) documents that in Long Beach, California, and Seattle and Tacoma, Washington, Christianity and Buddhism are considered to be complementary religions. Correspondingly, Carol Mortland (1994) documents Christian churches in Massachusetts that provided space for Cambodian refugees to maintain and continue Buddhist rituals and ceremonies.

The hybridity of Khmer Buddhism and Christianity is a unique form of Cambodian American culture-work, because it occurs among various Khmer American communities in America, and brings together two seemingly different religious faiths. The process of culture-work is producing a localized community and identity among a sector of Cambodian Americans who are comfortably Buddho-Christians.

Khmer Buddhism in the United States

Khmer Buddhism in the United States, as Nancy Smith-Hefner (1999) documents, plays a huge role in the socialization and moral education of younger Khmer Americans. The majority of Khmer Americans identify themselves as Buddhists, reflecting the relationship between ethnic and religious identities. In Cambodia, Buddhist temples are where young people, especially boys, learn moral lessons and proper respect towards their elders. In America, however, many Khmer elders attribute the immorality among young Khmer Americans to the scarcity of trained Khmer monks and the shortage of temples. The life and narrative of the historical Buddha is popular folklore in Khmer families. In order to adapt to American culture, Khmer American parents encourage their children to watch Bernardo Bertolucci's film *Little Buddha* (1993), starring Keanu Reeves, to learn about the life and teachings of the Buddha and, by extension, to learn what it means to be Khmer and Buddhist (Smith-Hefner 1999: 44).

Early on in the development of Khmer American communities, because of a lack of financial resources to construct a community temple, many Khmers constructed a Buddhist shrine in their private homes (Lee 2010). Temples are not only considered important sites for moral education and children's socialization, but they are equally important sites for rituals, including weddings, blessings, exorcisms, and funerals. When available, a monk is the preferred officiate for a ritual; however, a religious lay person (*achaa*) may be employed to perform rituals in lieu of a monk. The scarcity of Khmer Buddhist monks remains a big obstacle to the establishment of Khmer Buddhist temples among various communities in the diaspora (McLellan 2004: 108). However, this is not to suggest that Khmer American communities are unable to finance the construction of temples. For instance, in 1984, about eight hundred Khmers in Portland, Maine established a non-profit organization, the Watt Samaki "Unity Temple," to raise funds for the purchase and construction of a temple. Since immigrating to America, Khmer Buddhist communities have been successful in establishing and building nearly forty temples nationwide: Long Beach and Stockton, California; Seattle and Tacoma, Washington; Lowell, Massachusetts; Jacksonville, Florida; Minneapolis, Minnesota; Silver Spring, Maryland—to name a few places. Several of these temples were once home to Christian congregations, which symbolically illustrates the new religious pluralism in contemporary America.

Cambodian temple building often comes with a potential backlash from xenophobic neighbors who invoke zoning laws and regulations in attempts to stop the building of temples in their neighborhoods. This type of backlash was evidenced in Silver Spring, Maryland, where in 2008, neighbors counted cars and kept detailed records and photos of people visiting the temple during festival celebrations. The Maryland State Supreme Court denied the group, then known as the Khmer Buddhist Society, a permit to build a temple on Newtown Hilltop. Afterwards, the Newtown Zoning Board presented the Khmer Buddhist Society with a "cease all religious services and festivals permanently" order (*The Hartford Courant*). The Cambodian American community viewed this as a form of bigotry, while neighbors who did not want a vivacious Buddhist temple in their neighborhood, viewed it as enforcing current zoning laws. Cambodian Americans, as recent immigrants, did face difficulty in navigating zoning laws, which is to say, they were faced with cultural procedural challenges in their effort to build their temples.

Similar to Lao, Vietnamese, Sikh, and Chinese Americans, some Cambodian American communities faced, and continue to face, social and religious prejudice in their attempts to rebuild religious institutions in America (see Taggart Siegel 1987, *Blue Collar and Buddha* DVD; Jaideep Singh 2003; Irene Lin 1996). Rebuilding temples and other religious institutions are a fundamental aspect of Cambodian American culture-work, because this practice affirms ethnic, religious, and cultural identity among Cambodian Americans. Religious institutions, and the ritual spheres, are important social spaces in the adaptation to a completely new society.

Merit Transfers
and the Spectral Killing Fields

Many Khmers will perform merit transfer ceremonies (*thvoeu bon*) on behalf of their family members who died during the Democratic Kampuchea era, to provide the deceased with comfort, and the opportunity for a good rebirth. There are two fundamental counter-balanced principles in Theravada Buddhism: *karma* and merit. *Karma* is accumulated through actions and thoughts, especially if it is based on intentional harming. The karmic debt that one accumulates over the current lifetime determines one's future rebirth. But it is not absolute. Merit provides the counter-balance of *karma*. The most efficient way to earn merit is through supporting the community of monks and nuns. Merit is earned by distributing Buddhist doctrines, which potentially saves countless beings from a life of suffering. Merit is earned through good works (Malalasekera 1967). Charitable acts. Like *karma*, merit is also obtained through physical and mental acts. Similar to the Catholic tradition of suffrages, merit transfer is a practice and doctrine that allows the living to intervene on behalf of the dead—to ease their suffering and time in hell. The transfer of merit is also an expression of the Buddhist principle of *anatam* (no-self), because it is a selfless act, whereby the fruits of one's actions and resources are employed to profit and benefit others (Malalasekera 1967: 90).

According to Buddhist doctrine and folk belief, one becomes a hungry ghost (Pali: *petas*) if one's body is not properly cared for after death. Many Cambodians who died under Pol Pot's regime were denied a proper burial. Hence, the hungry ghost spirits of the people who suffered and were killed haunt not only Cambodians in Cambodia, but also Cambodians living in America. Those who survived thirty years of Khmer Rouge terror, those who were able to flee the Killing Fields, or left before the Khmer Rouge takeover of Phnom Penh in 1973, continue to live with the spectral Killing Fields. The phantom of violence and terror accompanies the hungry ghosts as they haunt their living kin, visiting them through dreams and visions. Survivors, whose primary religious belief is Buddhism, may intervene on behalf of their ghostly ancestors. They can make donations to Buddhist temples or charities, invite the monks to chant Buddhist *sutras*, and think good thoughts, but must do so with selfless aim: They ask that the merit from their actions be transferred to their loved ones, to offset their karmic debt, and provide them with an opportunity for another better rebirth. Once reborn, if it is a human rebirth, they can dedicate their lives to Buddhism, and enter into *nirvana* (enlightenment).

The spectral Killing Fields continue to haunt many Cambodian refugees and Cambodian Americans, at both the individual and collective levels. This is exemplified by public ceremonies held and performed to commemorate the lives lost during the Killing Fields. One such ceremony was held in 2000 by Cambodian American college students at the University of Washington. In Illinois, survivors of the Killing Fields and members of the Cambodian Association constructed a Wall of Remembrance, to, as Kompha Seth says, "find a way to deal with our pasts (sic)" (*The Asian Reporter*, 13:18 (2003): 13). Yet many other survivors and refugees perform rituals and ceremonies in the private sphere of their homes, or at local Khmer Buddhist temples. These memorials are powerful testaments to the dead, and reveal the power of rituals as a psychic defense against history, memory, and the current and future trauma of the Killing Fields.

Summary

The (re)creation of Cambodian religious beliefs and lifeways in America is a form of emerging Cambodian American culture-work. Cambodian American culture-work is an explicit creation of local, community, and cultural identities through the establishment of ethnic Cambodian institutions (such as Khmer Buddhist temples), and the performance and maintenance of religious, cultural, ritual, and folk activities. Although not the only factor in the successful and healthy resettlement of Cambodian American lives, families, and communities, it was and continues to be an immensely important variable in the process to rebuild life anew, among all generations of Cambodian Americans.

References

Ali, Anida Yoeu. Personal Web page http://atomicshogun.com/ accessed April 12, 2010. Web.

Cadge, Wendy. *Heartwood: The First Generation of Theravada Buddhism in America.* Chicago: University of Chicago Press, 2004. Print.

Cambodian Association of Illinois. Web; April 15, 2010.

Chan, Sucheng. *Survivors: Cambodian Refugees in the United States.* Urbana: University of Illinois Press, 2004. Print.

Chhean, Venerable Kong. "A Buddhist Perspective on Coping with Catastrophe." In *Southern Medical Journal* 100:9 (2007): 952-953. Print.

Douglas, Thomas J. "Changing Religious Practices among Cambodian Immigrants in Long Beach and Seattle." In *Immigrant Faiths: Transforming Religious Life in America*, edited by Karen I. Leonard, Alex Stepick, Manuel A. Vasquez, and Jennifer Holdaway, eds. Lanham: AltaMira Press, 2006. Print.

Eck, Diana L. *A New Religious American: How a "Christian Country" Has Become the World's Most Religiously Diverse Nation.* San Francisco: Harper San Francisco: 2002. Print.

Gerson, Jeffrey N. "The Battle for Control of Trairatanaram Cambodian Temple." In *Southeast Asian Refugees and Immigrants in the Mill City*, edited by Tuyet-Lan Pho, Jeffrey N. Gerson, and Sylvia R. Cowan. Hanover: University Press of New England, 2007. Print.

Graceffo, Antonio. "Cham Muslims: A Look at Cambodia's Muslim Minority." *Cambodia: Beauty and Darkness.* Site last updated May 22, 2008. Web; accessed April 23, 2010.

Hein, Jeremy. *Ethnic Origins: History, Politics, Culture, and Adaptation of Cambodian and Hmong Refugees in Four American Cities.* New York: Russell Sage Foundation, 2006. Print.

Kalab, Milada. "Cambodian Buddhist Monasteries in Paris: Continuing Tradition and Changing Patterns." In *Cambodian Culture since 1975: Homeland and Exile*, edited by May Ebihara, Carol Mortland, and Judy Ledgerwood. Ithaca: Cornell University Press, 1994. Print.

Kublicki, Mokugen, Rev. "The Transfer of Merit." In *Journal of the Order of Buddhist Contemplatives* 12:1 (1985). Print.

Lay, Sody. "Lost in the Fray: Cambodian American Youth in Providence, Rhode Island." In *Asian American Youth: Culture, Identity, and Ethnicity*, edited by Jennifer Lee and Min Zhou. New York: Routledge, 2004. Print.

Lee, Jonathan H.X. "Cambodian American Religion." In *Asian American History and Culture: An Encyclopedia*, edited by Huping Ling and Allan Austin. Armonk: Sharpe Reference, 2010. Print.

_____. "Pilgrimage of the Spirit: Connecting with My Ancestors." In *The Review of Vietnamese Studies*, 2:1 (2002). Web.

Lin, Irene. "Journey to the Far West: Chinese Buddhism in America." In *Amerasia Journal* 22:1 (1996): 107-132. Print.

Malalasekera, G.P. "'Transference of Merit' in Ceylonese Buddhism." In *Philosophy East and West* 17 (1967): 85-90. Print.

McLellan, Janet. "Cambodian Refugees in Ontario: Religious Identities, Social Cohesion and Transnational Linkages." In *Canadian Ethnic Studies*, 36:2 (2004): 101-118. Print.

Mortland, Carol A. "Khmer Buddhists in the United States: Ultimate Questions." In *Cambodian Culture since 1975: Homeland and Exile*, May Ebihara, Carol Mortland, and Judy Ledgerwood, eds. Ithaca: Cornell University Press, 1994. Print.

Nou, Leakhena. "Exploring the Psychosocial Adjustment of Khmer Refugees in Massachusetts from an Insider's Perspective." In *Southeast Asian Refugees and Immigrants in the Mill City*, Tuyet-Lan Pho, Jeffrey N. Gerson, and Sylvia R. Cowan, eds. Hanover: University Press of New England, 2007. Print.

Ong, Aihwa. *Buddha is Hiding: Refugees, Citizenship, the New America*. Berkeley: University of California Press, 2003. Print.

Puri, Rashmi. "Candlelight ceremony remembers Cambodian killings." In *The Daily of the University of Washington*, 2000. Web.

Ramirez, Marc. "Muslim in America: With some 6 million U.S. followers, Islam is one of the nation's fastest-growing faiths." In *Seattle Times* (1999).

Singh, Jaideep. "The Racialization of Minoritized Religious Identity: Constructing Sacred Sites at the Intersection of White and Christian Supremacy." In *Revealing the Sacred in Asian and Pacific America*, edited by Jane Naomi Iwamura and Pual R. Spickard. New York: Routledge, 2003. Print.

Sloan, Bronwyn. "A Country Full of Ghosts: Cambodians Honour their Dead." In *The Nation* (2008). Web.

Smith-Hefner, Nancy J. *Khmer American: Identity and Moral Education in a Diasporic Community*. Berkeley: University of California Press, 1999. Print.

_____. Smith-Hefner, Nancy J. "Ethnicity and the force of faith: Christian conversion among Khmer refugees." In *Anthropological Quarterly* 67:1 (1994): 24-37. Print.

Van Esterik, Penny. *Taking Refuge: Lao Buddhists in North America*. Arizona State University, 1992. Print.

CHAPTER

28

Cambodian American
Rice Bowl Christians

Nancy J. Smith-Hefner

In recent years studies of Southeast Asian refugees in the United States have revealed intriguing patterns of cultural accommodation and change. One of the most important, if complex, of these cultural adjustments has been conversion to Christianity. The most dramatic reports of conversion come from among Hmong (a hill-tribe minority from Laos), where Christianity appears to have made far-reaching inroads. Information is still preliminary, but several accounts indicate upwards of fifty percent of Hmong refugees have become Christian (Dunnigan 1986: 47; Scott 1987: 44; Tapp 1989: 90-91). By contrast, despite the large number of Cambodians who reportedly attended churches in border camps in Thailand and the even larger number who have been involved with churches in the United States, the total number of Khmer converts remains negligible. Within the metropolitan Boston Khmer community, the site of the research upon which the present discussion is based, there are an

Anthropological Quarterly, Vol. 67, No. 1 by Nancy J. Smith-Hefner. Copyright © 1994 by Anthropological Quarterly. Reprinted by permission.

estimated 700 Protestants in a total Khmer population of over 25,000. There are even fewer Khmer Catholics.

Students of Southeast Asia and those familiar with the diverse cultural and historical backgrounds of Southeast Asian refugee groups may not be surprised by this variation in the incidence of conversion. Unlike the Hmong, the great majority of Khmer subscribed to a world religion, Theravada Buddhism, long before their transit to North America. Furthermore, Khmer are the majority ethnic group in Cambodia and have a strong sense of national identity, an important element of which has always been Buddhism (Ebihara 1968; Keyes 1977). By contrast, Hmong are an ethnic minority in their Laotian homeland and have struggled over the years to distinguish themselves from the surrounding Buddhist majority (Keyes 1977; Tapp 1989). Christian missionaries based in mainland Southeast Asia have long been aware of these differences of religious commitment and have, as a result, typically focused their evangelizing efforts on ethnic minorities, particularly marginalized hill-tribes (Tapp 1989; Kammerer 1990). It is not surprising that cultural and historical factors like these have played a role in patterns of religious affiliation among Southeast Asian refugees in the United States.

Other features of the conversion process, however, are less easily explained in terms of these sociohistorical precedents. Among those few Khmer who do embrace Christianity, for example, it is not unusual to find a strong, self-conscious commitment to religious orthodoxy. Ethnic Khmer pastors, in particular, place great emphasis on strictly delineating belief and behavior compatible with Christianity from that which is Buddhist. Similarly, among Khmer converts themselves there is a clear tendency to affiliate with denominations that are notably less tolerant of non-Christian belief than some mainline Christian Churches. The greatest proportion of new Khmer Christians are members of evangelical Protestant churches.

Khmer conversion thus raises several intriguing questions. First, what motivates the conversion of that minority of Khmer who do convert despite the strong Khmer identification with Theravada Buddhism? Second, why is it that evangelical Protestantism tends to be so appealing among these converts? What moral and ideological concerns underlie their insistence on orthodoxy?

Rice Bowl Christians?

These examples suggest that there is within the Khmer community considerable movement back and forth between Christian church and Buddhist temple. Among the several hundred people whom I have interviewed, the number who had ever attended a Christian church was approximately twenty-five percent. It is possible, of course, that such past participation may have significant future effects, especially as Khmer assimilate to American culture, and a generation of youth who never knew Cambodia comes of age. For this younger generation, the force of identification with Khmer ethnicity and nationalism may weaken. In such circumstances a renewed interest in Christianity among Khmer would be facilitated by the fact that Khmer Buddhist themselves tend to display an open, inexclusive attitude toward other religions. Buddhist Khmer do not consider it wrong or in any way sinful to attend Christian services. Parents typically voice no objection to their younger children's involvement in church activities. Many Buddhist parents state that they would not mind if their child married a Christian, explaining that in Cambodia if interfaith marriages occurred, both traditions were commonly upheld.[1] Many Khmer readily acknowledge that they have attended a church at some time at the urging of friends or relatives, or to please their American sponsor.

As noted above, most Christian churches offer social resources and services of various types (see also Shim 1977; Palinkas 1984; Marcucci 1986). In principle, such resources are available to any Khmer who is in need, regardless of faith. Not surprisingly, however, refugees who make use of such services or who have a Christian sponsor commonly feel obligated to attend church services for a period of time to repay their sponsor for his or her kindness. Nonetheless, among Boston-area Khmer, the great majority who have attended services for these reasons alone stop doing so once they are off government assistance, have less contact with their sponsor, or less leisure time.

Most Christians, American and Khmer, are aware of this pattern. Some church leaders, moreover, accuse other Christian groups of using certain tactics such as offers of material goods and various forms of support to attract new members, luring them away from other churches. The criticisms of a Khmer Catholic lay leader against evangelicals, below, resembles accusations of a similar nature often voiced by evangelical leaders against Catholics:

> They [the evangelical churches] criticize the Catholic church. They say, you don't have to go to confession, you can go directly to God! But if they sponsor a family, they tell that family you have to go to our church and if you don't go to our church, we won't help you. We don't force the people to come to our church. We help them and then we are happy if they want to come to our church, we invited them to come and they came, but we don't force them to come, no.

Whether coercive or not, the role of the church in sponsoring resettlement, providing material and emotional support, and prose-lytizing has clearly played an important role in influencing the incidence of conversion among refugees in Boston and other parts of the country. Not surprisingly, it is in those areas of the country where refugee resettlement has been primarily sponsored by Christian churches, rather than by secular organizations or liberal denominations less concerned with promoting conversion, that the highest percentage of Khmer have converted. This pattern seems to be most strikingly apparent in Dallas, Texas, where a large number of Khmer refugees first settled. There conservative, evangelical Protestant churches played a primary role in the resettlement program, and it appears that a far larger proportion—upwards of fifteen percent—of the Khmer population has converted.[2]

Conversion Over the Long Term

Over the long term, however, one of the most important sociological features of Khmer conversion—above all for questions of Khmer assimilation to American culture—may have less to do with belief, ritual or morality than with education. As noted above, a distinguishing feature of Christian and Buddhist congregations is the degree to which young people are involved in religious activities. In Christian congregations, in contrast to Buddhist, young people typically devote several days a week to church related functions. All of the congregations offer some kind of weekly youth fellowship program which includes social activities with other Christian youth, Bible study, and worship. Some of the churches, in an effort to keep children (whose parents are often busy working) out of trouble, even offer afterschool programs which assist children with homework. Youth fellowship, Bible study, and other afterschool programs reinforce important academic and employment skills, not the least of which is English literacy.

Even more notable is the tendency for Christian Khmer parents to send their children to private, Christian institutions. A disproportionately higher number of these children then go on to four-year colleges, many on scholarship. This pattern of educational achievement is particularly striking because among Khmer youth in general there is a relatively high rate of school dropout in comparison to other Asian groups. By one local count, one out of six Khmer students does not complete high school (Lockwood 1987); teachers and community leaders argue that actual figures are considerably higher. Khmer youth who leave school typically do so in order to marry or to work to support their families or to purchase prestigious consumer goods like new cars, stereos, and jewelry. Parents who themselves lack formal education often feel financially and intellectually unqualified to suggest alternative courses for their children's development (Smith-Hefner 1993).

Many of the difficulties Khmer youth face in school are also a result, of course, of the poor quality of services in the inner-city schools they attend. On this point the institutional support provided by their American church sponsors offers Christian Khmer an important educational alternative, one that appears to provide them with a significant educational advantage over their non-Christian counterparts. Christian parents believe that religious schools offer a safer and more disciplined learning environment, and they often make great financial sacrifices to allow their children to attend.

Ironically, perhaps, this educational pattern does not seem to be the result of any specific church doctrine on social or economic mobility so much as it is a practical extension of another value complex: the church's emphasis on supporting the nuclear family. In practical terms this means, among other things, keeping youths off the streets, away from drugs, and out of gangs. It also implies encouraging parents, especially fathers, to refrain from drinking, gambling, and illicit sexual involvement. Where such efforts succeed, the result is quite real. Money previously spent on gambling, cigarettes, alcohol, and other diversions can be invested in other social projects such as school tuition or a downpayment on a house. It is this complex of social, religious, and family value, rather than an explicit concern on the part of the Church with upward social mobility, which combines to reinforce converts' educational achievement.

It is difficult to determine whether these educational and socioeconomic patterns are the result of Christian conversion or whether families already aspiring to educational and social mobility are attracted to Christianity and use it to legitimize their self-imposed estrangement from the community. The relationship is, most likely, a dialectic one, in which social ideals and the religious environment interact. Whatever the case, here in the Boston area Christian conversion appears to be having a mutually reinforcing effect on patterns of socioeconomic mobility and assimilation toward American culture. Though the Khmer example is in many ways distinctive, a similar pattern of socioeconomic mobility through assimilation was evident among earlier European immigrants to America as well (cf. Spiro 1955; Gordon 1964).

Conclusion

Educational data on Khmer Christians are still preliminary; Cambodians have been in the United States for too short a period to make any definitive assessment of their long-term accommodations. What we can say, however, is that if the educational and socioeconomic trends identified above continue, we are likely to see the reinforcement of an already existing bifurcation of Khmer population into two distinct groups. Ruben Rumbaut and Kenji Ima (1988) discuss just such a dual pattern of adaption among Khmer in a study of Southeast Asian adolescents. Among Khmer and Lao immigrants, they report, there is an emerging but striking differentiation occurring between, on one hand, a small group of "haves" and, on the other, a much larger group of "have-nots." The larger group of have-nots, they report, is overwhelmingly Buddhist. They describe its adaptive style as "more passive then reactive, less pragmatic, more fatalistic, and more oriented toward recreational values than to an ethic of personal value and hard work" (Rumbaut and Ima 1988: 77-78). By contrast, they comment that the outlook of the elite "have" group has been influenced by the values of the French middle class. They emphasize social mobility through education and hard work and, in good individualist fashion, they display fewer ethical reservations about the accumulation of personal wealth unaccountable to broader social interests. Rumbaut and Ima predict that social class and educational background (as well as the value complex that both support) will continue to be the strongest influences on the successful adaptation of Lao and Khmer refugees to American society. While a small segment of the immigrant community will thus succeed, the gap between this group and the have-nots will continue to widen (p. 78).

The present study suggests that for some Boston-area Khmer there is an alternate route—or the aspiration for such a route—into the middle class. That route involves not the acquisition of Franco-Khmer cultural values, but conversion to evangelical Christianity and, with it, participation in a new array of social institutions characterized by new social habits and American cultural values. It should be emphasized once again that, as the examples here have illustrated, the meanings and motives involved in Khmer conversion to Christianity are varied and complex. For some individuals Christianity has provided therapeutic solace, and for others access to basic social, economic, and spiritual resources. For many young Khmer Christians, however, conversion to Christianity has brought with it exposure to an array of new social institutions—Church congregations, Bible study clubs, youth groups, and Christian schools, among others. These institutions present new opportunities and socialize at least some Khmer youths into a lifeworld and value complex quite distinct from those of Khmer Buddhist.

One of the most striking aspects of this conversion is that it involves a fundamental adjustment in the terms of Khmer self-identification. In converting to Christianity, many Khmer distance themselves from the symbols and habits of Khmer ethnicity. They do not become "non-Khmer"—though some Buddhists fault them for doing just that—but they do alter the social barriers that separate them from mainstream American society. They also facilitate their involvement in religious and educational institution which seems likely to reshape the practices and commitments of their identity in the future (Gordon 1964; DeVos 1975).

One can already see the consequences of this emergent differentiation of Buddhist and Christian Khmer identity. Buddhists seem to be characterized by a stronger or more stable sense of ethnic identity, somewhat less educational achievement (if compared with people from a similar class background), and, again controlling for class, a less pronounced pattern of upward social mobility. By contrast, Christian Khmer display a somewhat more permeable sense of social community, in large part because their religious and ethnic affiliations no longer overlap. They insist that their children marry only Christians, and are tolerant of marriage to non-Khmer Christians. A growing number of Khmer Christians do in fact appear to be marrying Americans, typically met in the context of the Church. Involvement in Churches, Bible study, and religious schools provides many young converts with both the attitudes and skills required for higher education and a measure of upward mobility. With all this, converts also tend to display a more assimilationist attitude toward the values and lifestyles of American society. They are Khmer, and certainly think of themselves as such, but the way in which they conceptualize "Khmerness" is quite different from that of their Buddhist brethren.

It is not inconceivable, of course, that at some point this Christian minority within the Khmer community may experience its own neo-ethnic revival, as has recently occurred among other American minorities (Ra'anan 1980: Fishman 1989). For the time being, however, it seems equally or even more likely that large numbers of Khmer Christians may blend relatively indistinctly into the broader Asian American community. In this Khmer example, as in so many other instances of Christian conversion, then, the force of faith is and will continue to be seen not only in religious practice and belief, but in the attitudes and practice of ethnicity and community in a complex, plural society.

Endnotes

1. My Khmer associate, the daughter of the first Khmer Baptist pastor in Battambang Province, was married to a Buddhist in 1973. Her wedding involved both Christian and Buddhist ceremonies. She confirms that this pattern was quite common.

2. The figure of fifteen percent was cited in an interview with an American Protestant pastor who worked for eight years in the East Dallas Christian Khmer community. John Marcucci, who conducted ethnographic research in East Dallas, cites even higher conversion figures among the Khmer he interviewed (Marcucci 1986), but also noted the tendency for Khmer to leave the church once they are better situated and no longer need the church's support.

References

Ablin, David A. and Marlowe Hood. *The Cambodian agony*. New York: M.E. Sharpe, 1987. Print.

Barth, Fredrik. "Introduction." In *Ethnic groups and boundaries: The social organization of culture difference*. Boston MA: little Brown and Company, 1969. Print.

Coakley, Tom. "Burden of arrival felt by all." *The Boston Sunday Globe*, January 22, 1989. Print.

Costello, Nancy. "Refugee wave swells city's Asian population." *Lowell (MA) Sun*, August 14, 1989. Print.

DeVos, George. "Ethnic pluralism: Conflict and accommodation." In *Ethnic identity: Cultural continuities and change*, edited by George DeVos and Lola Rommanucci-Ross. Palo Alto: Mayfield Publishing Co, 1975. Print.

Dunnigan, Timothy. "Processes of identity maintenance in Hmong society." In *The Hmong in transition*, edited by Glenn L. Hendricks, Bruce T. Downing, and Amos S. Deinard. New York: Center for Migration Studies, 1986. Print.

Ebihara, May M. *A Khmer village in Cambodia*. Ann Arbor: University Microfilms.

Fishman, Joshua A. "The rise and fall of the 'ethnic revival' in the U.S.A." In *Language and ethnicity in minority sociolinguistic perspective*. Philadelphia PA: Multilingual Matters Ltd, 1989. Print.

Gordon, Milton M. *Assimilation in American life: The role of race, religion, and national origins.* New York: Oxford University Press, 1964. Print.

Kammerer, Cornelia A. "Customs and Christian conversion among Akha highlanders of Burma and Thailand." In *American Ethnologiest* 17.2 (1990): 277-291. Print.

Keyes, Charles F. *The golden peninsula: Culture and adaptation in mainland Southeast Asia.* New York: Macmillan Publishing Co, 1977. Print.

Lockwood, Holly. *Support services for limited English proficient Khmer and Laotian students at Lowell high school: Final report.* Chelsea: Metropolitan Indochinese Children and Adolescent Services, 1987. Print.

Marcucci, John L. "Khmer refugees in Dallas: Medical decisions in the context of pluralism." Unpublished dissertation. Southern Methodist University, 1986.

Palinkas, Lawrence A. "Social fission and cultural change in an ethnic Chinese church." In *Ethnic Groups* 5(1984): 255-277. Print.

Ra'anan, Uri, ed. *Ethnic resurgence in modern democratic states.* Elmsford: Pergamon, 1979. Print.

Rumbaut, Rubén G. and Kenji Ima. *The adaption of Southeast Asian refugee youth: A comparative study.* Final report to the Office of Refugee Resettlement. San Diego: State University Press, 1988. Print.

Scott, George M., Jr. "The Lao Hmong refugees in San Diego: Their religious transformation and its implications for Geertz's thesis." In *Ethnic Studies Report* 5(1987): 32-46. Print.

Shim, S.S. *Korean immigrant churches today in Southern California.* San Francisco: R. and E. Associates, 1977. Print.

Smith-Hefner, Nancy J. "Language and identity in the education of Boston-area Khmer." In *Anthropology and Education Quarterly* 21.3 (1990): 250-268. Print.

_____. "Education, gender, and generational conflict among Khmer refugees." In *Anthropology and Education Quarterly,* 24:2 (1993): 135-158. Print.

Spiro, Melford E. "The acculturation of American ethnic groups." In *American Anthropologist* 57.6 (1995): 1240-52. Print.

Tapp, Nicholas. "The impact of missionary Christianity upon marginalized ethnic minorities: The case of the Hmong." In *Journal of Southeast Asian Studies* 20(1989): 70-95. Web.

CHAPTER 29

Facing Death: Portraits from Cambodia's Killing Fields

Vivian-Lee Nyitray and June O'Connor[1]

> *A photograph is both a pseudo-presence and a token of absence.*
>
> Susan Sontag, *On Photography*[2]

Under the leadership of Party Secretary Saloth Sar, styled Pol Pot, the Maoist Khmer Rouge regime held power in Cambodia for three years, eight months, and twenty days between 1975 and 1979. During that time, as many as 200,000 individuals were designated enemies of the state; as traitors to the Party and counterrevolutionaries obstructing the progress of Democratic Kampuchea, they were imprisoned and tortured, or summarily executed. As "microbes" that were "infecting" society, their extermination was justified. Hundreds of thousands of other Cambodians died during the Pol Pot era from starvation, exhaustion, and disease; total estimates of the dead range up to 1.7 million people, or 21% of the country's population.[3]

As many as 20,000 men, women, and children were taken to Tuol Sleng, the former Tuol Svay Prey school complex in the Tuol Sleng district of Phnom Penh now repurposed as secret Incarceration Centre S-21 (for Security or Special Branch 21), where virtually all the prisoners were executed or died from the effects of torture and maltreatment; only seven people are known to have survived.[4] The prison administrator, Kaing Guek Eav, known as Conrade Duch or Deuch, was a man in his mid-30s.

As part of the processing of prisoners, the Khmer Rouge photographed one individual after another upon their arrival at S-21 while other prisoners, often handcuffed to those being shot by the camera, were forced to stand aside or sit on the ground, usually but not always out of camera range. The S-21 photographs were shot by a team of young recruits under the supervision of Nhem En, who joined the Khmer Rouge as a 10-year-old.[5] Sent to Mao's China for training as a photographer, filmmaker and cartographer in Shanghai, he returned in May 1976 to be named chief photographer at Tuol Sleng, in charge of several apprentices. Interviewed in 1997 in Phnom Penh by reporter Robin McDowell of the *Associated Press*, Nhem En said, "I took hundreds of photographs at a time...we did this every day."[6] He recalled seeing faces filled with fear and deep sadness: "I knew that I was taking pictures of innocent people, but I knew that if I said anything, I would be killed."[7] "One day," he recounted, "I saw the face of a close relative through my camera. I kept silent even after he was taken to be interrogated and then killed."[8] In all, Nhem En estimated that he took roughly 10,000 photographs at S-21.

Ethical questions emerge in the observers of these photos and readers of these facts. Nhem En made choices amidst the compromising circumstances in which he was embedded. Many might empathize with the terrible choice he faced, namely taking photographs routinely, knowing these camera shots preceded physical shots or other forms of cruelty leading to death. Nonetheless, many voices in the nonviolent and/or pacifist traditions emphasize the alternative option, advising that it is better to be killed than to kill. Nhem En could have chosen otherwise. His explanation for his choice (fear of death) is not in itself an ethical justification for that choice. This is not a case of self-defense but of self-surrender to intimidation.

Some prisoners were summarily executed after processing; others endured beatings, electric shocks, near-drownings, and suffocations. Written confessions were extracted under threat of additional torture. The photographs and meticulously transcribed confessions of important state enemies were sent to Pol Pot; dossiers of the less-important languished in filing cabinets until they were scattered or abandoned and left to looters when the Khmer Rouge fled in advance of the Vietnamese arrival in Phnom Penh in January 1979. With the fall of the Pol Pot regime, S-21 was again repurposed, this time as the Tuol Sleng Museum of Genocide, replete with blood-stained floors and walls, instruments of torture, and a display of some of the photographs that had been taken by Nhem En and his assistants.

The S-21 archives were opened to foreign scholars in 1980. In a back room of the museum, American photographers Doug Niven and Chris Riley discovered roughly six thousand mildewed and insect-damaged negatives and, in 1993, devised a plan to rescue, restore, and print them. They formed the non-profit Photo Archive Group and, with the assistance of Cornell University, began the work of cataloging, salvaging, and printing the negatives that now comprise the extensive and continually updated S-21 photographic database, viewable online at the Yale Cambodian Genocide Program website.[9]

It has proven extremely difficult to match photographs, lists of prisoners' names, and confessions. The numbers that often appear in the photos pinned to an individual's clothing are not unique identifiers; they referred to a batch of people being processed and were frequently recycled. Nhem En has said that the numbering system began anew every twelve hours. Number 1 was pinned on a prisoner at 1 a.m.; at 12:59 p.m., therefore, the number might be 100 or 150 or 225, indicating the total count of all those processed since 1 a.m. At 1 p.m., the count reverted to 1.[10] Early visitors to the Museum of Genocide, recognizing the face of a family member, friend, or neighbor, would sometimes write that name on the photograph; the authorities feared damage to the photos and stopped the practice. Of the nearly six thousand negatives restored by the Photo Archive Group, one hundred, chosen for their photographic quality, historical value, and the presentation of a cross-section of S-21 victims, were selected for exhibition printing and publication.[11] One edition of the collection was donated for exhibition at the Tuol Sleng

Museum, where they remain. Only a fraction of those whose faces line the walls of their final destination have been identified.

Pol Pot and his henchmen, Nhem En and the curators, are not the only ones making ethical choices that could have been otherwise. The visitor to the S-21 Museum of Genocide who knows the context of these photos must also make a decision about how to regard them, receive them, and remember them. A new field of study fosters attention to these decisions and questions. Known as "dark tourism," this phrase refers to the acts of traveling to sites and visiting exhibitions focused on atrocities involving torture, suffering, and death.[12]

> *Photographs objectify: they turn an event or a person*
> *into something that can be possessed.*
>   Susan Sontag, *Regarding the Pain of Others*[13]

The propriety of Niven and Riley's decision to select, copyright, and exhibit a hundred photos has been deeply contested. Although their rescue and restoration of the negatives was applauded, the presumption that they—and the museums hosting the exhibit—would now profit from the murder of innocents was troubling. In conjunction with a showing at the Museum of Modern Art, Guy Trebay wrote in *The Village Voice*, "The pictures from Tuol Sleng are the sole remaining evidence of 6,000 human lives. Can anyone truly own them?"[14] Peter H. Maguire subsequently refuted charges of Niven and Riley's venery, indicating that the photographers began the project at their own expense, were deeply in debt by 1994, and that, even after the publication of Facing Death in 2005, had not made money from the distribution of the photographs.[15]

One person who has profited from the notoriety of the S-21 photographs is Nhem En. He followed Pol Pot to his retreat in the northern jungle and served as the Khmer Rouge's official photographer from 1979 until 1995, when he abandoned his wife and six children to defect and serve the pro-Vietnamese regime of Hun Sen. Citing a *Wall Street Journal* report, Maguire alleges that Nhem En sold purloined film footage from S-21 to Japanese TV broadcasters and describes how the former chief prison photographer tried to pass off clever fakes of photographs and negatives to Maguire himself.[16] According to an interview sold to *Le Monde* on the occasion of the exhibition of S-21 photos at the renowned photography festival *Rencontres photographiques d'Arles* in France, Nhem En showed no remorse and, upon learning of the Arles exhibition, declared himself proud to be the "star" of a photo festival in France, "wearing a big grin on his face."[17]

> *The ethical content of photographs is fragile.*
> Susan Sontag, *On Photography*[18]

For survivors of the Pol Pot regime, viewing the photographs—whether in Phnom Penh, in any one of the international venues exhibiting Riley and Niven's prints, or online via the Yale Cambodian Genocide database—is emotionally risky. There is always the possibility of finding the face of a beloved friend or family member, provoking questions whose depths others cannot plumb. For second generation Cambodian Americans, the images may well include extended family members, but without the anchoring of personal memory or certain connection, the experience of viewing may be differently upsetting—compounding the uncertainty of diasporic identity, generational guilt, or transnational response. But for the majority of viewers, the photographs form just another exhibition. A collection—selected on what grounds?[19] An emplacement—amidst what other objects? An exhibit—for what purpose?

Without the ties of kith, kin, or country, the viewer comes to the S-21 archive as a collection of the anonymous and objectified. And yet one may wonder whether to approach and whether to appropriate Nhem En's photos. Is there something I am supposed to see? The viewer may be drawn to the beauty of a young girl, her hair neatly parted and combed, or to the lined face of an old man; one may be intrigued by the straightforward gaze of a soldier, or by the glimpses of hands holding backdrop cloths. The viewer may be shocked by the subjects' bruises or by their health; by their age or their youth; by the signs of seeming resignation; by the rare, uncomprehending, and incomprehensible smile. There are so many victims, unknown to most of those who view the photographs, that one's gaze shifts focus from the mass of faces to the identifying detail: the upturned collar on a schoolgirl's blouse, the armless sleeve tucked into a pocket, the bandage.

Am I being voyeuristic, staring at a most personal and intimate moment in life, without the subject's permission? Or am I rightly informing myself about the admittedly horrible realities of life? If it is true that all things human are the appropriate subjects of study and observation, am I essentially a student of human power and powerlessness as I examine this exhibit? Will I benefit from this horror by being more realistic about life? Or am I one who profits from this display of pain, fear, entrapment, and imminent death? Am I recognizing that profits appear in more than monetary form, as in recognition, reputation, publication, and professional peer regard?

According to the principles of Theravada Buddhism, life is characterized by unease, occasioned by the impermanence of all things. Suffering is therefore expected, yet it can be endured in the knowledge that it will end. For perhaps all but the seven who survived, the suffering of Tuol Sleng's prisoners has ended, the workings of their individual karma having now taken them on to new realms of existence. It is the viewer, the momentary possessor of their photographs, who now contemplates their past suffering.

> *The imaginary proximity to the suffering inflicted on others that is granted by images suggests a link between the far-away sufferers...and the privileged viewer that is simply untrue.... So far as we feel sympathy, we feel we are not accomplices to what caused the suffering. Our sympathy proclaims our innocence as well as our impotence.*
> Susan Sontag, *Regarding the Pain of Others*[20]

The photographs might prod the viewer to feel the questions that surely tortured the subjects as much as their physical intimidation and abuse: "Why am I here?" "What have I done wrong?" "What mistake have I made?" "Where are they taking me now?" "Am I to die here?" and "Will it be soon?" The difficulty in scanning these faces is to resist the numbness of conscience brought on by the repetition of image, to wrestle with questions of the purpose and value of the exhibit, and to wrestle with compassion for the subjects in view. Such was the challenge Thierry De Duve faced in seeing the photos at the Arles exhibit, as he tried to somehow pull individuals out from their collective anonymity:

I had to address each photo, each person in the photos, individually before I could acknowledge receipt of their gaze—which most of the time was indeed intensely addressed to the camera—as if it were addressed to me in person. Only then did the people in the photos rise from the dead, and only then did this unbearably controversial exhibition acquire its true legitimacy.[21]

No matter how intimate that gaze, however, the fact remains that the subject suffered something particular, and viewers, with but seven exceptions, have not. The subject is dead, and the viewer is alive. The viewer is not—can never be—the subject. But what they can share is a resistance to objectification.

Thus the questions for the viewer proliferate. Do I see in these photographs, myself as a victim-survivor, perpetrator, or bystander of analogous horrors, whether personal or public? Do I name this "art" and keep it at a safe distance, allowing emotions to emerge but limiting them to the exhibit, rather than the reality of genocide to which the exhibit points? Do I let that knowledge "in"? Or is the fear that knowledge implies responsibility immobilizing? Do I not feel impotent in the face of the massive, systemic evil to which the exhibit points? Do I allow this exhibit to remind me of the genocides of today? Is intervention realistic? Do I have a role in pressing for that?

Facing death is a fact of life made real to many by the observation or experience of disease and old age. We sadly acknowledge that death from old age is natural, just as we reluctantly admit that disease can also demand acceptance of death in the end. But deliberative, intentional, and torturous cruelty—as evoked in the killing of teenagers whose chief crime may have been to leave their military or factory posts in order to return to their parents, or in the slaughter of infants and children to forestall their future vengeance—bespeaks deaths we rightly refuse to accept.

The Khmer Rouge intended their meticulous record to be one of vindication of their economic and social programs. What survived the failure of the Khmer Rouge vision, however, was not the photographic justification they desired and tried to fabricate during their murderous reign but rather an unexpected remnant of what was true. The Buddha himself, the Tathagatha or "Thus-gone One," is often symbolized by a footprint left on the ground. The Tuol Sleng archives likewise comprise tangible traces of the real: each photo is a premature death mask, viewed in two dimensions. With their documentary cameras *cum* guns, the S-21 photographers have armed contemporary viewers with reality and remembrance. The faces of Tuol Sleng—posed roughly against bare wall or white cloth, forced to look directly at the camera, as down the barrel of a gun—invite meditation, moral outrage, and personal response from those who stare back.

> *Photographs that everyone recognizes are now a constituent part of what a society chooses to think about. It calls these ideas 'memories,' and that is, over the long run, a fiction. Strictly speaking, there is no such thing as collective memory.... But there is collective instruction. What is called collective memory is not a memory but a stipulating: that this is important, and **this** is the story about how it happened, with the pictures that lock the story in our minds.*
>
> —Susan Sontag, *Regarding the Pain of Others*[22]

The trial of Comrade Duch, administrator of Tuol Sleng and the first senior Khmer Rouge cadre to face prosecution by the Extraordinary Chambers in the Courts of Cambodia (jointly organized with the UN), has concluded, with a verdict expected even as this essay is written. He faces a life sentence on charges of crimes against humanity and war crimes, as well as homicide and torture. Seven years before the tribunal started, he confessed his crimes, saying, "My confession is rather like Saint Paul's. I'm the chief of sinners." In court, he repeatedly apologized for atrocities he had committed, saying that he acknowledged his crimes in both moral and legal context. He apologized to the survivors.[23] And he noted that he had feared for his own life and that he was a scapegoat for others.[24]

Endnotes

1. "Facing Death" was written originally to accompany the exhibit of one hundred photographs from S-21, titled "Facing Death: Portraits from Cambodia's Killing Fields" at the University of California, Riverside/California Museum of Photography, March 21-May 31, 1998. The essay

was published in Fototext (Spring 1998): 3, and a slightly abbreviated version is accessible online at http://www.cmp.ucr.edu. The authors wish to thank Jonathan Green, Executive Director, UCR ARTSBlock, for permission to reprint the original essay, which has been revised and expanded for this volume.

2. p. 16 (New York: Anchor Books, 1973).

3. The Cambodian Genocide Project. http://www.yale.edu/cgp; accessed February 2, 2010. Some estimates range as high as two million dead, or one in four individuals; see the PBS Frontline special *Cambodia: Shadow of Pol Pot* (episode 102, airdate: October 31, 2002); accessible online at http://www.pbs.org/wgbh/pages/frontline/video).

4. Dawne Adam, "The Tuol Sleng Archives and the Cambodian Genocide," *Archivaria* 45 (1998): 5-26, p. 11.

5. Descriptions of the equipment the S-21 photographers used are inconsistent. Nhem En recalled using "a chunky Canon" in his AP interview; other references range from a Rolleiflex 6 x 6 camera and large format 21–inch film to an inexpensive Chinese-made Seagull.

6. http://www.thefreelibrary.com/CAMBODIAN+PHOTOGRA-PHER+RECALLS+VICTIMS+OF+KHMER+ROUGE+REGIME-a083855361, accessed April 10, 2010.

7. Spring 1997 *Reportage* http://www.reportage.org/PrintEdition2/Khmer Rouge/PagesKhmerRouge/KhmerRouge08.html, accessed April 10, 2010.

8. "Khmer Rouge: 10,000 posed before killing fields," Associated Press wire story, February 16, 1997.

9. http://www.yale.edu/cgp. Photographs displayed in the Cambodian Genocide Database are accompanied by text urging viewers to suggest names and/or other biographical data for victims they may recognize; data is added to the Digital Archive of Cambodian Holocaust Survivors, which allows dispersed family members to locate each other, memorialize the dead, and preserve memories of life under the Khmer Rouge.

10. McDowell, February 16, 1997.

11. Chris Riley and Doug Niven, eds., *The Killing Fields* (Santa Fe, NM: Twin Palms, 1996).

12. The Dark Tourism Forum, an online communication for researchers, led by the University of Central Lancashire, UK, can be accessed at www.dark-tourism.org.uk.

13. Chris Riley and Doug Niven, p. 81.

14. "Killing Fields of Vision: Was Cambodia's Genocide Just a Moment of Photographic History?" *The Village Voice* (3 June 1997), quoted in Adam, 22.

15. *Facing Death in Cambodia* (New York: Columbia University Press, 2005), p. 151.

16. Maguire, pp. 150-54, citing Craig Smith, "Profiting from His Shots of Pol Pot's Terror," *Wall Street Journal*, published September 16, 1997.

17. Jean-Claude Pomonti, "Nhem Ein, photographe en chef des Khmers rouges," *Le Monde*, July 5, 1997, translated and cited in Thierry De Duve, "Art in the Face of Radical Evil," *October* 125 (Summer 2008), pp. 3-23.

18. p. 20.

19. There is a small but significant corpus of media reports and scholarly literature on the Tuol Sleng photos *qua* exhibition. Critics focus on the initial selection of one hundred images as morally problematic, on the role of the curator as "artist," and on the viewer as "artist." To enter the discussion, see Thomas Roma, "Looking Into the Face of Our Own Worst Fears Through Photographs," *The Chronicle of Higher Education,* October 31, 1997, p. B10; De Duve; and Michel Guerrin, "La photographie documentaire surexposée," *Le Monde*, July 6, 1997.

20. p. 102.

21. De Duve, p. 22.

22. p. 86.

23. http://www.nytimes.com/2010/03/18/opinion/18iht-edear.html?scp=2&sq=duch&st=cse, accessed April 4, 2010.

24. *New York Times*, April 1, 2009.

Section XII

Cambodian American
Citzenship Post 9/11

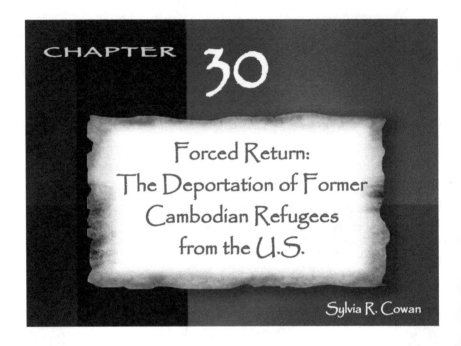

CHAPTER 30

Forced Return:
The Deportation of Former
Cambodian Refugees
from the U.S.

Sylvia R. Cowan

Cambodians who came to the U.S. as refugee children after the Khmer Rouge genocide are being sent back to the country that they barely knew. Growing up in inner city America, some of them became involved in gang activities and petty crimes; they are deported even after serving time in prison. Not allowed to return to the U.S., they are once again forced to separate from their families.

After growing up in the U.S., Karney,[1] now in his mid-thirties, is in Cambodia trying to rebuild his life and reconstitute his family. His life has been disrupted and displaced repeatedly. Fleeing Cambodia at the age of 10 after Vietnamese troops ousted the Khmer Rouge, then spending two years in Thai refugee camps, he arrived in the U.S. as one of the 145,000 Cambodian refugees who were resettled in America between 1975 and 1999 (Hing 2005). After living in the U.S. as a permanent resident for 22 years, however, Karney was forcibly "returned" to Cambodia, a country he barely knew. Most deportees, including Karney, were forced to

Courtesy of Sylvia R. Cowan. Reprinted with permission.

return to Cambodia after serving their time in prison for gang activity and other, often minor, crimes.

This wave of 'return migration' is a direct result of the changes in U.S. immigration laws in 1996. The Anti-Terrorism and Effective Death Penalty Act and the Illegal Immigration Reform and Immigrant Responsibility Act made deportation mandatory for all legal permanent residents who are sentenced to a year or more for 'aggravated felonies,' 'moral turpitude,' or use of controlled substances. Judges' discretion in individual cases was removed, so that no defendant can be exempted from deportation by considering his/her prison experience, rehabilitation, attitude, behavior, ties to family, and length of time living in the U.S. The U.S. and the Cambodian government reached an agreement in March 2002 to repatriate Cambodian citizens who had broken the law and served their terms in U.S. prisons. From June 2002 to September 2008, 192 Cambodians were 'returned,' many leaving behind families and children in the U.S. They are not allowed to return to the U.S., even to visit family members there.

Furthermore, about 1,500 more Cambodians, currently on a list 'to be deported,' are living a life of uncertain futures. Aside from the change in policies, more complex human stories lie behind the forced return.

"We're the Product of the American System"

For many refugee families from Cambodia, success in crossing mine-filled terrain to temporary camps at the end of Pol Pot's reign and reaching a new country did not put an end to the trauma. More challenges awaited them in the new territory. Confronted with a completely alien language and culture, the adults often had to work two or three jobs simultaneously in order to make ends meet. The children, often left neglected made the streets of America's inner cities their new homes. Their peers often became like family. Billy, one of the deportees, told me:

Man, our parents were traumatized, didn't know what was happening with us kids. I was a good boy at home—washed the dishes, cleaned up—so they didn't know anything about gangs. We just got into gangs to protect ourselves. We were just kids, thrown in the inner city with Mexicans and Blacks. We're the product of the American system (Personal communication, August 2008).

Similar to Billy, Karney described himself as a 'good boy,' who helped distribute water and food in the refugee camps, and has always been fair and kind. In the U.S., he tried to obey his strict uncle, who took the role of his father. But never feeling he could measure up, Karney sought comfort elsewhere:

I started going to school...and was getting harassed by everybody. The Hispanics. The Blacks and Whites. You know 'cause we stayed in a mixed community...everybody was there...all kinds of people...like the ghetto type. Then I had my bike taken. My silver necklace taken. I started meeting other Asian males around there so we started going in groups. Not just alone. That way we'd feel more protected. Which worked. At that time, yeah, they'd see us a bunch, and then they wouldn't come charge at us. They'd think twice. So that...you know, slowly but surely, it turned into more serious stuff. We started retaliating. We started fighting in school. And by the time I was 14...seventh grade...you know...I started not going to school. Then I started having problems failing. I went to different schools and after school and stuff. So that's how things got started. [It] got worse (Personal communication, August 2008).

Group solidarity was intended to protect each other, yet this also led them to more serious activities. For Karney, it was juvenile court, then later, six years in and out of prison. It was in prison that he decided to turn his life around:

My last trip [prison], you know, I started going to school and stuff. Take a trade course. A government program...anything really to help me better myself. Get my GED [General Education Development credential, equivalent of high school completion]. College courses...parenting course...you know and...and all for a guy who only went to and dropped out at seventh. When I passed my GED I was so like proud. For only two years of school (Personal communication, August 2008).

Yet when Karney completed his sentence, he was picked up by the then Immigration and Naturalization Service (INS; the agency was later merged into the Homeland Security as the Immigration and Customs Enforcement), and taken to a detention centre, where he waited for 12 months to be transported to Cambodia. His daughter, left behind in the U.S., later asked him in a telephone conversation, "When are you coming home, daddy? You said you were coming home when you got out of prison" (Personal communication, August 2006).

A New Life in Cambodia

Karney, like other 'returnees' to Cambodia, found it arduous to live in a place he had never really known. Luckier than others though, he had continued to speak Khmer in the U.S. and has some relatives still in Cambodia. Nevertheless, the process of adjustment was long and hard. The most difficult part was the forced separation from the family:

> It's the worst when they had a wife and kids in the States, and can't ever go back there. That's a punishment too harsh. They served their time…it's too hard, to keep them from their families. It's hard on them, hard on their families. The kids end up growing up with no dad. And they can't support them (Personal communication, February 2006).

Karney has made a new life. He married a Cambodian woman, and now has three children. He's found new meaning in life by helping others:

> I even help people that are the same as I was. I give 'em food, a place to stay in my house. As long as they don't mess up. Although I'm struggling with myself…it's time for me to give back and sometimes even though I get tired and wonder, why am I doing this? I'm helping a few people myself with a lot of things. I have to do it. It's a way of giving back to what I've taken from society (Personal communication, August, 2008).

But not everyone who went through these enormous upheavals is able to turn things around. Some have turned to drugs; a few ended up back in prison; one committed suicide; some are just getting by day-to-day. There was no system of assistance that was planned for these Cambodians, in anticipation of the first groups' arrival. One American who is a long term resident of Phnom Penh started the Relocation Assistance Program [RAP] with small donations to provide transitional housing, assistance with job searches and adjustment. Later, this project received U.S. AID funding and was formalized as the 'Returnee Integration Support Program.' That funding is not being renewed, and RISP may have to close down.

The deportation of the Cambodians is part of a larger programme of expulsion of the U.S. government. Annually nearly 200,000 people are forced to return to their country of citizenship. While solving complex issues of undocumented immigrants eludes politicians, they can look tough enforcing deportation on this group. The policy is justified explicitly as a necessary means for reinforcing law and order within the U.S. territory, and implicitly by the notion of 'return': is it not 'natural' for one to 'return' to where he/she was born? While return is often imagined as a warm, comforting journey home, forced return entails enormous human costs. While the deportation programme may appear to maintain social order in the U.S., it has certainly created disorder for the returnees, their families, and many in the Cambodian society. Meanwhile their children in the U.S. are growing up without fathers. The law must be changed to reflect justice and fairness, to provide judicial review in determining whether deportation is justifiable in individual cases.

Endnotes

1. This is a pseudonym. All the names in this article have been changed to protect the anonymity of respondents.

References

Hing, Bill Ong. *Deporting Cambodian Refugees: Justice Denied? Crime & Delinquency*, Vol. 51, No.2 (2005). Print.

Epilogue

Epilogue

David W. Haines

Forty years ago, in the early spring of 1970, I saw Cambodia for the first time. Driving north from Tay Ninh in Vietnam, we left the expanses of houses and fields and plunged along a narrow two-lane road through the jungle. Soon the jungle gave way to a totally different country. Here, the houses rose on stilts and the disorder of Vietnam gave way to sylvan glades of shimmering green, of tropical flowers, and a seeming feeling of peace. The people were welcoming (although not a young woman in sight). They stood along the side of the road relaying fresh pineapples to us, doing so with a welcoming slight Buddhist bow. It was beautiful.

Driving further, we turned at a crossroads and soon arrived at a large rubber plantation. The small airstrip, the parallel rows of rubber trees, and the large central plantation house presented a picture-perfect image of colonial Cambodia. Indeed, the car in the driveway was appropriately European (perhaps a Citroen?) and the man at the door was decidedly French. We wandered down into the back of the plantation to the constructed village where the plantation workers lived. This too seemed full of peace, remnant of a different age, a colonial landscape that—stripped of the ardor of exploitation—evoked a pleasing nostalgia.

But we were not tourists on a pilgrimage to a pristine land of peace. We were American soldiers, another "destabilizing encounter" of the kind that Jonathan H. X. Lee mentions in his introduction to this volume. When we left some weeks later, that narrow road through the jungle had been widened and the jungle pushed back. Countless rice bags now lay on the airstrip in Tay Ninh, carted back from Cambodia to reduce enemy supplies—bags that I methodologically counted as they piled up into a mountain of mildly moldy rice. I may actually have been the last American to leave that section of Cambodia. Having caused some damage, and perhaps run over someone's farm animal, we had agreed to pay for it with a barrel of oil. (This was one of the rules of the road during the war: run over an animal and you've bought it, usually at exorbitant prices.) So when all the rest of the Americans had crossed back from Cambodia, we made one last run to that same intersection to fulfill our promise and to say good-bye to this beautiful country whose peace we had shattered, whose balance we had tipped toward an unimaginable catastrophe.

Almost exactly five years later, the Khmer Rouge entered Phnom Penh, and the days of the killing fields began. The new Cambodia was based on a vision—much like ours when we crossed the border—of a beautiful rural Cambodia removed from the tainted influence (if not the romantic communist fantasies) of the West. That revolution was, as Sucheng Chan puts it, to "wipe the society's slate clean and start from scratch." One result was the beginning of an exodus from Cambodia, small at first, then much larger when the Khmer Rouge regime collapsed in the face of yet another invasion of Cambodia, this time by the Vietnamese in late 1978.

This wonderful volume of reprints and original contributions is both a valuable scholarly contribution and also a kind of memorial to the Cambodians who have come to the United States, to the country from which they have come, and to the people in America who reached out to them, attempting to provide for them a haven from the very damage America had set in motion. In looking back at the many contributions in this volume—including many Cambodian American voices—this epilogue reiterates some of the different contexts in which this Cambodian American experience can be seen, dealing first with how the Cambodian exodus fits within the overall refugee flow from Southeast Asia, then with some of the early attempts to understand the specific situation of Cambodian refugees in America, and finally with some of the main themes that emerge from the wide-ranging chapters in this volume.

The Southeast Asian Refugee Exodus

The roots of the Southeast Asian refugee exodus that began in 1975 stretch far back in Southeast Asian history. The three countries of Cambodia, Laos, and Vietnam had long been linked but, with

French colonialization and the succeeding American war, those links became tighter. Perhaps the crucial features of that initial Western involvement included a French administrative, educational, and cultural overlay, some significant efforts at economic development colonial style (engineering of waterways in the delta, creation of plantations, emphasis on cash crops), and a shifting alignment of majority and minority groups (military recruitment of some highland groups, greater infusion of ethnic Chinese into commercial networks). Yet the three countries (and the three different administrative divisions within Vietnam) still often went their own way. After the withdrawal of the French with the Geneva Accords of 1954, that divergence of paths continued—although now with a Vietnam in two rather than three pieces.

Compared with a French colonial presence of nearly a century, the succeeding American period was barely more than two decades, yet the social changes it unleashed were significant. Whatever the arguments about the politics of the war, South Vietnam did experience impressive economic development in some areas, significant land reform, and a surge in education, but also ultimately an enormous population displacement and a collapsing economy. Cambodia and Laos remained somewhat removed from these changes yet, whether looking at North or South Vietnam, there was indeed strong pressure to knit Cambodia and Laos into an integrated region of some kind. Constant planning for a greater Mekong River development was perhaps the emblem of that as an economic dream—and one that nicely excluded North Vietnam.

For Cambodia, the net result was being dragged into what is called, depending on one's perspective, either America's Vietnam War or Vietnam's American War. Cambodia became further synchronized with the Vietnam conflict after the 1970 coup that permitted the military incursion from Vietnam of which I was a part. Ultimately, the American-supported governments of all three countries collapsed in 1975. People from Cambodia, Laos, and Vietnam were thus joined together in a new way as refugees fleeing from communist forces that marched victoriously into the capitals of Phnom Penh and Saigon in April, and succeeded in purging the former government later that year in Laos. So many Cambodians, like the Laotians (whether lowland Lao or highland groups like the Hmong) and the Vietnamese (whether Catholic or Buddhist, native southerners or transplanted northerners), fled.

In that first flow of refugees, timing was crucial. As the certainty of defeat grew and communist armies neared Phnom Penh and Saigon, the window of opportunity for escape was narrow. People were forced to make cataclysmic personal decisions often within the space of a few days. In Vietnam, some 130,000 people escaped in that first wave (sources vary on the actual number). In Cambodia, the window was even narrower and was shut with greater ferocity as the Khmer Rouge herded people out of Phnom Penh. Only a few thousand were able to escape.

Yet after escape, the experience of these initial refugees was often quite orderly. Whether flying out in the final days, or escaping toward the sea as armies approached, the refugees were transported to temporary camps in the Pacific and then through reception camps in the United States, ultimately to be resettled out into local communities. The refugees were clearly traumatized by their experiences, and observers such as Gail Kelly (1977) warned that the U.S. efforts were unwise in trying to paper over the pain of refugee loss with an emphasis on new lives—as if the refugees were regular immigrants. Nevertheless the processing was orderly both on the government side and on that of the refugees, the welcome by local communities was impressive, and the initial status reports on how refugees were doing were positive.

This first flow of refugees, generally hailed as a great success, was but the beginning. During the late 1970s, refugees began escaping in increasing numbers from Vietnam, and across the border into Thailand from Laos. In 1978, these flows escalated. At the end of the year, the Vietnamese invasion of Cambodia opened the way west both for fleeing Khmer Rouge forces and for many other Khmer who were often fleeing from these same forces. Camp populations along the Thai border soared. The Vietnamese invasion of Cambodia was followed by a Chinese border invasion of Vietnam, which placed further pressure on ethnic Chinese in Vietnam to leave—largely toward Hong Kong. Camp populations of Lao and Hmong in northern Thailand also increased. Even more dramatic, at least in media accounts, were the surging numbers of boat escapes from Vietnam across the sea to Malaysia, Indonesia, and the Philippines.

Combined, these pressures generated a comprehensive internationalized effort to resolve the crisis. Many countries promised resettlement slots (thus easing the pressure on first asylum countries that had begun pushing refugees back to sea or back across land borders). An orderly departure program was also set up to facilitate direct movement of Vietnamese out of the country. Attempts to empty the camps, however, continued to fail in the face of renewed refugee escapes. Ultimately another round of international action was needed: a unified plan that would resolve the situation of Vietnamese refugees (including some forced repatriation) and a peace process in Cambodia that would permit a massive repatriation program from the refugee camps in Thailand. These were, respectively the Comprehensive Plan of Action (CPA) of 1989 that was largely concluded by 1996, and the Cambodian "Comprehensive Political Settlement" of 1991 that was effectively concluded when the last Cambodians left Thai refugee camps in 1999. With those steps, the numbers of refugees from Southeast Asia did indeed decline. But not before those from Cambodia, Laos, and Vietnam had become a major part of the Asian presence in America.

Cambodians in America

A decade after my first journey down that road into Cambodia, I went to work for the U.S. Office of Refugee Resettlement. That year, 1980, was a pivotal time in the relationship between America and refugees (Haines 2010). Early in the year, comprehensive legislation had finally been passed to bring the United States into conformity with international conventions on refugees, to create a more formal system of planning and approving refugee admissions, and to integrate and rationalize the very broad range of services and assistance provided to refugees. As Senator Edward Kennedy had noted in opening the hearings for that act the year before, refugees touch "our Nation's fundamental commitment to human rights and humanitarian concern" but that the system for refugee admissions and resettlement needed to be better organized and done "more humanely" (U.S. Senate 1979: 1-2).

It was also a year, however, in which refugee arrivals from Southeast Asia continued at levels that were far higher than those projected by the new Refugee Act. Those flows included a degree of economic, linguistic, cultural, and experiential diversity among refugees that was straining the resettlement system. Furthermore, it was a year in which large, unexpected arrivals from Cuba and Haiti created a public reaction against humanitarian admissions, starting a process in which the meaning of refugee—just barely ensconced in U.S. law—began to corrode. Now there was talk of people who sought refuge but were not true refugees. Their plight might be understandable, but they were "economic refugees" who, by defini-tion, were not refugees in the established legal sense. Thus began the linguistic circumlocutions: people might be fleeing something and be "refugees" in some general sense, but they weren't fleeing exactly the right thing at exactly the right time from exactly the right place to be true refugees.

It was in this period of turmoil that large numbers of Cambo-dians began to arrive in the United States. A few had managed to escape in 1975 and some 4,000 arrived in the United States that year. As with the Southeast Asia exodus generally, the numbers began to grow at the end of the 1970s, especially after refugees streamed west into Thailand with the fall of the Pol Pot government in the face of the Vietnamese invasion (in late 1978). In that first year after the fall of the government and the flow west into Thai-land, the camps grew enormously, and the flow from them to the United States began to escalate. In that first year after the Viet-namese invasion, some 6,000 refugees from Cambodia entered the United States. The numbers grew rapidly thereafter: 16,000 in 1980, 27,000 in 1981, 20,000 in 1982, then 13,000 in 1983, 20,000 in 1984, and 19,000 in 1985 (Gordon 1987).

These Cambodians arrived at a difficult time in terms of the refugee program and presented additional difficulties of their own. They brought with them not only the cultural differences with which most immigrants must contend, but also some additional eco-nomic and educational differences. Many of the Cambodian refugees, for example, were from rural areas, and sometimes with rather limited education. They also bore the marks of the ravages of their years under the Khmer Rouge, the additional hazards of flight, and the frequent dangers of refugee camps that, while providing some temporary safety, often placed them together with the very people from whom they had been fleeing. This experiential burden of refugees is perhaps where they most differ from other migrants. It is not simply that their migration is forced, but that force marks them at every stage of their movement, from before they even decide to flee, to flight itself, and to the often extended (alternatively dangerous and enervating) periods they spend in temporary refuge—usually in camps of some kind.

These arriving Cambodians thus presented a far more complex case than most Vietnamese arrivals of 1975. For those early refugees, the middle passage from the old country to the new was mercifully short. For these new Cambodian arrivals, by contrast, the middle passage from pre-Khmer Rouge Cambodia to America was long and tortuous. Some of the effects could be seen with simple numbers: for example, the large number of widows. Other effects were less obvious on the surface. What were the effects of lasting through the Khmer Rouge regime? What would these survivors see and understand in a new land with a rather different array of dangers, including a new kind of violence that appeared in the neighborhoods and schools to which many of them were sent? How could existing Cambodian communities—small as they were—provide the practical and spiritual resources that the refugees would need?

For those involved in the resettlement program—as I was at the time—it was exceedingly difficult to answer these questions. Many of us were relatively familiar with Vietnam, and there were many Vietnamese already actively engaged in the resettlement program and in community activism. Cambodia was a more difficult topic, and the existing research was quite limited. May Ebihara's work, for example, was so essential because it was virtually the only anthropological work on rural Cambodia available in English. It was immediately clear from her work, for example, how greatly different were Cambodian kinship and community structures from the Vietnamese. Indeed the Cambodians looked virtually American in their emphasis on nuclear families organized into communities around their religious institutions—although with pagodas rather than church spires at their center.

The situation improved further when several of the authors in this volume appeared on the scene, perhaps especially Carol Mortland and Judy Ledgerwood, both of whom had been students of May Ebihara. In journal articles, and perhaps especially in their breakthrough volume a decade later with her (Ebihara, Mortland, and Ledgerwood 1994), the rest of us could begin to imagine what Cambodia had been and how, often through the work of refugees in the United States, it could be imagined again. Cambodia, we began to realize, would have to be rebuilt both economically and culturally, and to a significant degree that cultural rebuilding would take place among the overseas Cambodians, often the only surviving remnants of particular cultural traditions, whether of dance, ceremony, or cultural scholarship.

That work, however, was not yet available and, even if it had been, did not fully resolve the issue of how Cambodians fit into the broader program efforts at refugee resettlement. How were they doing in economic terms, for example? The initial survey work on early Cambodian arrivals in the late 1970s had suggested a profile quite similar to the Vietnamese in terms of occupation, employment, English language competence, and use of public assistance (Aames et al 1977; OSI 1979a, 1979b). Within a few years, however, this would begin to change as employment indicators started to drop for Cambodians who now, compared to the Vietnamese, had much higher unemployment rates, more frequent low-income households (i.e., Kim 1980), and a growing number of people from rural areas who had been farmers (ORR 1981).

These data sources on Cambodian refugees were often confusing until we began to understand the wide ethnic and socioeconomic variation within the Cambodian population. There were, after all, considerable numbers of Chinese in the overall Cambodian population, just as there were for the Vietnamese. The Chinese-Cambodians tended to have a quite different profile. Furthermore, within the ethnic Khmer population, there were very sharp variations between urban (or previously urban) Khmer and those who were from rural areas. The statistical result was a bimodal pattern suggesting there were really two sets of Khmer each with quite distinctive profiles, a point particularly highlighted in the early survey data from Rubén Rumbaut and Kenji Ima—and its later updates (Rumbaut 1989; Portes and Rumbaut 2001).

The data on which we had to rely in those early days, however, still tended to lump all Cambodians together, and tended to be restricted to fairly narrow issues of economic status. The more culturally oriented accounts were helpful, but also narrow, trying to introduce the key background factors that might affect Cambodian life in America (e.g., Tepper 1980). But what was to be the longer-term Cambodian destiny in America? And how variable would that destiny be? During those early years, it was hard to assess those more difficult questions. We were too stunned, simultaneously, by the enormity of what the Khmer holocaust had been and by the unprecedented surge of arriving refugees—refugees who often challenged the very limits of diversity in the United States. Three decades later, however, as this volume illustrates so well, a much fuller understanding of Cambodians in America is possible.

A Better Understanding

The riches of this volume are manifestly clear both for the reprints that document over three decades of research and the original contributions, which include a vibrant self-reflection by a new Cambodian generation in America. Although it is impossible to recapitulate all these contributions, a brief inventory of some of their crucial themes may be of value as they appear to someone—like myself—who is not a Cambodian specialist and thus is especially concerned to identify not only the uniqueness of the Cambodian American experience but what it can contribute to a broader consideration of other refugees (and immigrants) to the United States.

Perhaps most fundamental to the Cambodian American experience, as nearly every author reiterates, is the continuing reverberation of the Cambodian holocaust. No one escapes it. It ravages even those few who did escape from Cambodia before it occurred. It ravages those who directly suffered and often died from it and those who survived it. It ravages those who remember it through their parents and those who make their first visit to Tuol Sleng and—at least metaphorically like Jonathan Lee—can take pictures of the pictures on the walls even though they cannot bring themselves to directly look at those pictures. Such acts of distancing are matched by acts of outright dismissal, of turning away from Buddhism, from traditions, and even from the Khmer language. Even for Cambodian Americans growing up in ignorance of it, the holocaust inevitably rises at some point to confront them as a central nightmare, miasma, and question: how could this have happened and how could this have been loosed upon Cambodians by Cambodians? While a few other refugee groups have this essential kind of horror at the root of their experience (Jews and Armenians, for example), even they do not have this horrible twist that the persecutors were from among the persecuted. Given this, the often horrific stories of actual escape are a paler component of this Cambodian refugee experience than is often the case for other refugees. Here is not a sudden drama of war that induces a perilous flight, but a grinding experience of physical and spiritual depredation that makes flight a seeming afterthought.

Leakhena Nou suggests in her chapter that the holocaust thus continues to be the dominant problem with which Cambodians in America struggle, that it bears on them more heavily than the daily struggles of a new life in a new land. Nevertheless, those daily struggles have been, again as virtually every author notes, difficult and unrelenting. That is perhaps especially so in the eyes of their children. The accounts of the younger Cambodian Americans in this volume portray parents working incessantly and, despite that inevitable American adage about success through effort, often with marginal results. Kuong Chhang Ly, for example, notes how her father became old before his time: "he had worked beyond his limits." That incessant daily effort with limited rewards seems often to apply to the children as well. As Cambodian parents wait for their children to find themselves, those very children are often consigned to the most difficult of American neighborhoods, the most ineffective of its schools, and the most nasty of its racial and ethnic fractures. Refugees in general often face such difficulties since, compared to other immigrants, they are relatively unprepared for life in the United States. But Cambodians seem to face such daily struggles on a far more severe and intractable basis

But there is also success. Refugee success stories are a stock in trade for those involved in refugee resettlement and for those parts of the media that value the validation of American dreams that is invoked in refugee success stories. Local newspapers are often especially supportive since refugee successes are also successes of the local community in welcoming and resettling refugees. Cambodians, too, have been the beneficiaries of such stories. Such successes are noted in this volume but are rather carefully circumscribed. There is much, most of the authors tell us, that tends to keep Cambodians at arm-length from "success" as it is normally construed in America. Cultural analysis, for example, suggests the degree to which Buddhist values—of letting children develop naturally, for example—do not work very well in America. Yes, as Kuong Chhang Ly notes, being left alone by parents did permit him to develop a solid personal core, and, yes, as Sody Lay comments, the ability of Cambodian youth to move out of gangs suggests a distinctively fluid realm of autonomous (and relatively consequence-free) exploration of alternative ways of adapting to a new society. But these still seem to be the exceptions. More generally, as Vichet Chhuon, Rebecca Kim, and Nancy Smith-Hefner note, success seems to hinge on a physical (live near the middle class) or religious (worship with the middle class) move away from the Cambodian community and into mainstream society. Cambodians thus become assimilated as individuals rather than as a group and, in Smith-Hefner's words, become so separate from the Cambodian community "that they disappear from its horizons entirely." It may well be, as Carol Mortland suggests, that there are divergent meanings of success, that there is resettlement "American style" and resettlement "Cambodian style," but the Cambodian style nevertheless seems fraught with economic cost in the American environment.

These different paths, these "astonishingly different experiences" in Mortland's words, suggest a heterogeneity within the Cambodian population that is at odds with the frequent view that they, unlike those from Laos and Vietnam, are a relatively homogenous group. To be Cambodian is to be Khmer; to be Khmer is to be

Buddhist; and to be Khmer is to speak Khmer. This formula (or at least parts of it) is invoked in many of the chapters of this book. But also invoked is the variability in Cambodian society, that this formula may work as an introductory generalization, but remains inadequate to explain the experience of individual Cambodians. Not all Cambodians, after all, are Khmer; not all Khmer are Buddhist; and certainly not all of those who identify as Cambodians in the United States speak Khmer. There is, for example, considerable ethnic variation. Many Cambodians are Sino-Khmer and, more broadly, many Cambodians simply have mixed ancestry, whether the "outside" part is Chinese, Vietnamese, or other. Such ethnic diversity plays out in sometimes predictable and sometimes unpredictable ways in the United States. Thus the Sino-Khmer (as both Smith-Hefner and Ong illustrate), have economic skills and strategies that are of clear utility in the United States. There is also religious variation, and the shifting attitudes of Christian converts seem also to lead to a better accommodation with mainstream American society. Such ethnic and religious variation is frequent among refugees in general. Perhaps more crucial in the Cambodian case is the diversity in the individual experiential background of Cambodians, especially the extent to which they were drawn from rural and urban areas, from different socio-economic backgrounds, from different experiences during the holocaust of the late 1970s, from different escape routes, and from different kinds of attachments (and visits) to Cambodia since then.

One kind of experiential diversity involves the differences between the migrating parents, the American-born children, and those who grew up partly overseas and partly in America. The difficulties that the parents have in adjusting to America and the difficulties the children have in understanding Cambodia are both very clear in this volume. The parents, after all, are Cambodians by birth and by upbringing; the children, after all, are American by birth and by upbringing at least outside their homes. Once Cambodia itself became accessible again, this fundamental divergence became even sharper: parents could and did go back and recreate their lives in Cambodia; the children—by and large—could not or would not. Despite that divergence, many of the authors in this volume also raise the possibility of durability across the generations, of something that might link parental and child experiences, a bridge between the Cambodian experience in America and the Cambodian experience in Cambodia. That bridge, of course, requires language. Sylvia Cowan notes how even a deported Cambodian American could forge a life in Cambodia given some language competence. So the bridge is open in both directions only if the people crossing it are language-enabled.

Futures

Durability (and its inevitable counterpart and companion, change) is often construed as involving the past and the present, of recognizing the past in the present and seeing at least the seeds of the present in the past. Christine Su, for example, makes a cogent argument that much of the adaptiveness needed for a new life in America is perfectly consonant with a Khmer tradition of fluidity and absorption of multiple foreign influences. But several of the authors, especially those Cambodians either born in the U.S. or born shortly before coming to the United States, shift the locus of durability into the future. For them, becoming more fully Cambodian is not simply to reflect back in time, but to act forward in time. The hip-hop lyrics of praCh, who appears in several of these chapters, provide one example. Jonathan Lee's explication of the ethics of identity provides another. For him (as for praCh perhaps) to be Cambodian is to implement the idea of being Cambodian, to do some "culture work." Furthermore, that implementation is, at core, an ethical act—although a more evangelical metaphor that to be Cambodian is to be born again Cambodian might better convey the emotional and spiritual commitment needed. Whatever the respective levels of reason and emotion, here is a vital key to understanding the migration experience, especially the very severe trauma and relocation of the Cambodian case. The point is simply that it is the creation of the future by new generations of Cambodians and Cambodian Americans that retroactively solidifies the past with the present, creating a durability of being Cambodian across time as well as across space, across the ruptures of the killing fields as well as across the ruptures of flight and relocation in an often uncomprehending new country.

There is a tremendous opportunity in America today to go beyond entrenched assumptions about immigration, and to explore more fully how migration is a continuing process with often unpredictable twists and turns, as people move back and forth and on to new destinations. Sometimes those moves are relatively permanent and sometimes temporary, sometimes episodic and sometimes part of a durable system of multiple attachments to multiple places. Sometimes those moves are more mental and emotional than physical. Inevitably these dynamics of migration continue even after death. The merit transfer ceremonies that Lee discusses are, after all, an indication that movements of bodies are also movements of spirits, and that dealing with the bodies of the past requires addressing the future of the spirits that once inhabited them.

The Cambodian experience, though also vitally important on its own terms, provides an especially valuable opportunity to rethink these longer range dynamics of people in motion, precisely because the practical, emotional, and spiritual terrain across which Cambodians continue to move is so difficult. Perhaps this volume is not, then, simply an academic memorial to Cambodia, Cambodians, and Cambodian Americans, but also an arrow into the future. If so, its value sweeps beyond its particular subject matter to a different kind of approach to migration studies, one that puts the future squarely ahead, rather than to the side, and puts it there as an issue of personal, ethical, and spiritual commitment.

References

Aames, Jacqueline, S., Ronald L. Aames, John Jung, and Edward Karabenick. *Indochinese Refugee Self-Sufficiency in California.* State of California: Department of Health, 1977. Print.

Ebihara, May. "Khmer." In *Refugees in the United States: A Reference Handbook,* edited by David W. Haines. Westport: Greenwood Press, 1985. Print.

Ebihara, May M., Carol A. Mortland, and Judy Ledgerwood, eds. *Cambodian Culture since 1975: Homeland and Exile.* Ithaca: Cornell University Press, 1994. Print.

Gordon, Linda W. "Southeast Asian Refugee Migration to the United States." In *Pacific Bridges: The New Immigration from Asia and the Pacific*

Islands, edited by James T. Fawcett and Bejamin V. Carino. Staten Island: Center for Migration Studies, 1987. Print.

Haines, David W. *Safe Haven? A History of Refugees in America*. Sterling: Kumarian Press, 2010. Print.

Kelly, Gail P. *From Vietnam to America: A Chronicle of the Vietnamese Immigration to the United States*. Boulder: Westview Press, 1977. Print.

Kim, Young Yun. *Survey of Indochinese Refugees: Introduction, Summary, and Recommendations*. Chicago: Traveler Aid Society of Metropolitan Chicago, 1980. Print.

ORR (Office of Refugee Resettlement). *Refugee Resettlement Program*. Washington, D.C.: U.S. Department of Health and Human Services, 1981. Print.

OSI (Opportunity Systems Incorporated). Sixth Wave Report: Indochinese Resettlement Operational Feedback (Vietnamese Refugee Group). Washington, D.C., 1979a. Print.

_____. Sixth Wave Report: Indochinese Resettlement Operational Feedback (Cambodian Refugee Group). Washington, D.C., 1979b. Print.

Portes, Alejandro, and Rubén Rumbaut. *Legacies: The Story of the Immigrant Second Generation*. Berkeley: University of California Press, 2001. Print.

Robinson, W. Courtland. *Terms of Refuge: The Indochinese Exodus and the International Response*. New York: Zed Books, 1998. Print.

Rumbaut, Rubén G. "Portraits, Patterns, and Predictors of the Refugee Adaptation Process. Pages 138-182." In *Refugees as Immigrants: Cambodians, Laotians, and Vietnamese in America*, edited by David W. Haines. Totowa: Rowman and Littlefield, 1989. Print.

Tepper, Eliot L. *Southeast Asian Exodus: From Tradition to Resettlement*. Ottawa, Canada: Canadian Asian Studies Association, 1980. Print.

U.S. Senate. *The Refugee Act of 1979: Hearing before the Committee on the Judiciary*. Washington, D.C.: U.S. Government Printing Office, 1979. Print.

CPSIA information can be obtained
at www.ICGtesting.com
Printed in the USA
LVHW05s0619190618
581148LV00002B/3/P